WORDS MADE FLESH

Words Made Flesh

Sylvia Wynter and Religion

JUSTINE M. BAKKER AND DAVID KLINE, EDITORS

Fordham University Press
NEW YORK 2025

Copyright © 2025 Fordham University Press

All rights reserved. No part of this publication may be reproduced, stored in a retrieval system, or transmitted in any form or by any means—electronic, mechanical, photocopy, recording, or any other—except for brief quotations in printed reviews, without the prior permission of the publisher.

Fordham University Press has no responsibility for the persistence or accuracy of URLs for external or third-party Internet websites referred to in this publication and does not guarantee that any content on such websites is, or will remain, accurate or appropriate.

Fordham University Press also publishes its books in a variety of electronic formats. Some content that appears in print may not be available in electronic books.

Visit us online at www.fordhampress.com.

For EU safety / GPSR concerns: Mare Nostrum Group B.V., Mauritskade 21D, 1091 GC Amsterdam, The Netherlands, gpsr@mare-nostrum.co.uk

Library of Congress Cataloging-in-Publication Data available online at https://catalog.loc.gov.

Printed in the United States of America

27 26 25   5 4 3 2 1

First edition

Contents

Introduction: Sylvia Wynter and Religion
Justine M. Bakker and David Kline — 1

PART ONE: The Religiosity of Being Human

1 On Self-Creation: Autopoiesis and Autoreligion
 David Kline — 21

2 Symbolic Rebirth and Ceremonies Never Lost: African Religions and the Paradoxical Progressivism of Sylvia Wynter's Work
 Oludamini Ogunnaike — 44

3 (Para)religious Traces in Sylvia Wynter's "Demonic Ground"
 Justine M. Bakker — 97

PART TWO: Science, Secularism, and Man's Political Theology of Race

4 The Wynterian Turn: Human Hybridity in the Natural and Human Sciences
 Niki Kasumi Clements — 129

5 The Ceremony beyond the Secular: Postreligious Autopoetics in Wynter's *The Hills of Hebron*
 Rafael Vizcaíno — 153

6 Sociogeny, Race, and the Theological Genealogy
    of Economy
    Tapji Garba   171

PART THREE: Counter-religiosities beyond Man

7 Interrupting the Sanctity of Man:
    Wynter, Imperial Piety, and the Unruly Sacred
    Joseph Winters   193

8 Moving to a Realm beyond Reason:
    Mapping Ontological Sovereignty
    in Counter-worlds of Liminality
    Shamara Wyllie Alhassan   211

Coda: Nuiscientia
Anthony Bayani Rodriguez   235

Acknowledgments   243
Bibliography   245
Contributors   263
Index   267

Words Made Flesh

Introduction

SYLVIA WYNTER AND RELIGION

Justine M. Bakker and David Kline

> Human beings are magical. Bios and Logos. Words made flesh, muscle and bone animated by hope and desire, belief materialized in deeds, deeds which crystallize our actualities. And the maps of spring always have to be redrawn again, in undared forms.
>
> —SYLVIA WYNTER

Sylvia Wynter has lived a decolonial life. Her writings, artistic works, and pedagogical interventions, from the very beginning, have sought a way out of the existing "coloniality of being/power/truth/freedom"[1] that has done incalculable violence to human life and the earth that holds it. Her theorization of the human as a plurality of self-inventing forms of life ("genres of being human") is a celebration of the beauty of human beings and their capacity to animate hope and desire through the always unfinished work of invention. "The rule is love," Wynter tells us in her play *Maskarade*, and it is this rule that has guided her unflinching confrontation of Western modernity's pernicious "monohumanist" story of what it means to be a human being. As Wynter has shown throughout her decades-long writing career, it is "Man," the Euro-Christian West's racialized figure of human being first grounded in the early modern rational subject of the European colonial state ("Man1"), and later the "biocentric" subject of the natural and social sciences ("Man2"), that has defined our shared global existence in the contemporary world around the lie that its particular form of life represents the normative metric for all humanity. As Wynter continuously exposes in drawing from the deep well of Caribbean and global anticolonial thought and praxis that is the foundation of her intellectual and political formation, Man's lie has been unable to contain the spirit of resistance and invention that manifests in human solidarity across the earth. It is from the examples of anticolonial movements in global modernity—ranging from slave revolts to pan-Africanism to the American Indian Movement and beyond, as well as the Fanonian imperative to "take the leap" out of Man's order of knowledge—that a global human future remains open to new possibilities. In her unique ability to see this opening, as humanity writ large now struggles to conceive a future beyond the devastating effects of climate instability, economic inequality, and political stalemates that mark the exhaustion of Man's overdetermination in the twenty-first century, Wynter has given us an invaluable gift.

In this introduction, we aim to acquaint readers with Wynter as a key thinker for the current generation of global Black and transcultural studies, as well as position her as a thinker with much to offer religious studies and other academic perspectives interested in the intersections of religion, culture, epistemology, and race.[2] While Wynter has long been a fixture of the Caribbean literary and theoretical scene and Black studies in the United States, we are currently in the middle of what we might call a "Wynter boom" across the broader humanities and (some) social sciences.[3] Since the publication of Katherine McKittrick's groundbreaking edited collection *Sylvia Wynter: On Being Human as Praxis* (2015), we have witnessed a quick and remarkable uptick in publications that set out to explore some of the manifold ways that religion and religiosity show up in Wynter's work. This new wave of scholarship includes essays by Ariella Aïsha Azoulay, Justine Bakker, J. Kameron Carter, M. Shawn Copeland, Tapji Garba and Sara-Maria Sorentino, David Kline, Mayra Rivera, Benjamin Robinson, Rafael Vizcaíno, and a number of contributions to the series on decolonial thought and the study of religion on the blog *Contending Modernities*.[4] Further, two recent edited volumes—*Beyond the Doctrine of Man: Decolonial Visions of the Human* (2020; based on a 2016 colloquium held at KU Leuven) and *Beyond Man: Race, Coloniality, and Philosophy of Religion* (2021)[5]—take Wynter's work as a starting point to rethink the production of knowledge in theology and in philosophy of religion, respectively. These are important, necessary books. Yet, we remain convinced of the need for a volume that stays with Wynter and religion all the way through, with chapters that help us understand, nuance, or critique how religion and religiosity operate in Wynter's oeuvre, and chapters that use Wynter's work to better understand, nuance, or critique concerns, themes, and questions in the study of religion. A volume, in short, that explores at once what Wynter's oeuvre could mean for the study of religion and what the study of religion could contribute to the seemingly ever-growing interest in Wynter's scholarship.

A Brief Biography

One crucial aspect of reading Wynter is to understand the Caribbean context in which she is deeply grounded.[6] Born in 1928 on the island of Cuba to Jamaican parents who had emigrated to work in the booming Cuban sugar industry being fueled by rising sugar consumption in the United States, Wynter has been shaped throughout her life by the complex realities of a world made by colonialism. When she was two years old, her parents returned with their family to Kingston, Jamaica, where she would spend the remainder of her childhood. Here, the family was active in a Seventh-day Adventist church, which provided a social center for the family. She would also frequently visit her grandparents in the countryside, where she became acquainted with the "peasant world" and its "infinite charity of the poor."[7] When she was enrolled in the British colonial education system, despite the conditions of poverty that came along with being a Black colonized subject in Jamaica, Wynter excelled in her studies and eventually won a scholarship to attend St Andrew High School, a prestigious all-girls school founded by Methodists and Presbyterians in 1925. It was here that Wynter, recognizing the privilege of studying at a school whose resources marked such a sharp contrast with the schools she had attended previously, became fully aware of the stark difference in opportunities available to the poor and the wealthy within the Jamaican colonial system. At St Andrew, Wynter made top marks in her exams and was awarded the Centenary Scholarship, instituted in 1938 to commemorate the hundred-year anniversary of the abolition of slavery in Jamaica. The bursary allowed her to leave Jamaica to study Romance languages and Spanish "Golden Age" literature at King's College London. There, she completed the BA Honors Program in 1951 and a Masters research thesis in 1953. In 2018, King's College honored Wynter as "one of the most important and influential thinkers and public intellectuals of our time," a case of "better late than never," as the Jamaican newspaper *The Gleaner* noted.[8]

During her university years, Wynter was also a member of Boscoe Holder's London-based dance troupe and aspired to a professional dancing and acting career. However, she became frustrated with the lack of opportunities for Black performers in the European arts scenes and turned to writing, initially as a playwright and later as a novelist. Her 1962 novel, *The Hills of Hebron*, based on an earlier play, tells the story of a Black millenarian religious community (modeled after the early twentieth-century Bedwardism movement) trying to live an alternative life in the Jamaican hillside outside the normative colonial order. Much of the material of *The*

Hills of Hebron is inspired by Wynter's childhood experience in the Seventh-day Adventist Church as well as the kinds of poor religious communities she was around in her grandparents' countryside. As Shamara Alhassan shows in this volume, the novel also takes inspiration from Rastafari communities in Jamaica.

Wynter's early formative years coincided with a time when Jamaica and the broader Caribbean region were undergoing significant transformation. Beginning when she was still a child, a series of labor strikes and other forms of political resistance against the colonial plantation economy would ultimately provide the foundation for the anticolonial movements through which Jamaica would achieve national independence in 1962. It was this environment and Wynter's experience as a colonial subject that led her to the Caribbean intellectual tradition of decolonial thought represented by thinkers such as Frantz Fanon, Aimé Césaire, George Lamming, C. L. R. James, and Édouard Glissant, to name but a few. This is the tradition in which Wynter has remained grounded for the entirety of her career.

After publishing *The Hills of Hebron*, Wynter returned to Jamaica in 1963 and began her academic career in the Department of Spanish and Portuguese at the Mona campus of the University of the West Indies in Kingston. In the 1960s and early 1970s, she gained a reputation as a leading anticolonial cultural theorist and critic of the postcolonial government in Jamaica, where the legacy of colonialism remained a painful reality for the impoverished masses. After two visiting professorships in the United States, where she encountered various communities of scholars, activists, and university students who were at the forefront of transforming the academic humanities and social sciences through the establishment of Black, Chicano, and Third World studies, Wynter began to develop the kind of transcultural perspective that would be a cornerstone of her long intellectual project. In 1974, she permanently moved to the United States after accepting a teaching job at the University of San Diego, and four years later took up a joint appointment in the African and Afro-American Studies Program and Department of Spanish and Portuguese at Stanford University, a position she would hold until her retirement from teaching in 1994. Since her retirement as a professor, Wynter has continued to write and give interviews, publishing some of her best-known essays, including "Towards the Sociogenic Principle: Fanon, Identity, the Puzzle of Conscious Experience, and What It Is Like to Be 'Black'" and "Unsettling the Coloniality of Being/Power/Truth/Freedom: Towards the Human, after Man, Its Overrepresentation—an Argument."

Wynter's Intellectual Trajectory

We may discern two primary phases of Wynter's writing career, a division that is somewhat superficial, as the questions and concerns that drive her earlier work remain central to her later period. The first phase includes roughly the years 1967 to 1984, when Wynter focuses on questions of literary and cultural theory, Caribbean/Jamaican history, and anticolonial resistance in the Americas.[9] This phase culminates with "Black Metamorphosis: New Natives in a New World," a massive 900-page unpublished study on the retention and reinvention of African culture in the colonial Americas and its slavery regimes. This study can be read as a kind of conceptual bridge to the epoch-spanning thinking that would propel Wynter into her later project of rethinking human being beyond the colonial order of Man. It also provides a powerful theoretical supplement to her novel *The Hills of Hebron*, as examples of Afro-Caribbean religions feature prominently as sites of "transplantation" (Wynter's term for how Africans reinvented themselves as "new natives" in a new world) and resistance to the dehumanizing forces of slavery and colonialism.

In the second phase, which begins with the 1984 essay "The Ceremony Must Be Found: After Humanism," Wynter turns her intellectual energy to addressing the "overrepresentation" of "Man," the Christian West's figure of the human that has determined the modern epistemological, political, and economic global order. It is here that Wynter also initiates what she will later call, drawing from Chilean biological systems theorists Humberto Maturana and Francisco Varela's concept of "autopoiesis," the "autopoetic turn." This turn, which is marked by a vast synthesis of Black studies, natural sciences, philosophy, history, literary studies, evolutionary biology, and systems theory, is aimed at founding a "new science of the word" that is grounded in the idea that all living beings are self-generating (autopoietic) entities that organize and reproduce themselves. Wynter creatively reads the theory of autopoiesis through Frantz Fanon's notion of "sociogenesis" and Aimé Césaire's understanding of poetic knowledge as she constructs a theory of the "hybrid" human being of "*bios/logos*": human beings create themselves not only through their biological processes but also through the open-ended *techné* of language and storytelling. Together, the theoretical frameworks of Fanon, Césaire, and Maturana and Varela provide Wynter a kind of poetic-scientific *avant-garde* capable of generating a revolutionary new understanding of the human that is both adequate to the global diversity of "genres of being human" and capable of overturning the current epistemic hegemony of Man. While religion remains an important category during this phase, there is a noticeable shift away from the kinds of local religious examples she engaged in her work on "transplantation." In her post-1984 work—which culminates in 2015 with "The Ceremony Found: Towards the Autopoetic Turn/Overturn, Its Autonomy of Human Agency and Extraterritoriality of (Self-)Cognition" (an explicit answer to the 1984 essay)—she takes a more removed perspective and begins to theorize religion more abstractly as a universal function of human meaning-making that is a key aspect of the origins of human social production.

Wynter and the Study of Religion

Wynter is not a religious studies scholar. Although religion plays a significant role in her thinking, it is important to understand that it is not the primary object of her study. However, as she approaches the category of religion through her intensely interdisciplinary set of intellectual resources, some very interesting insights emerge. Many of these will be explored in this volume; here at the outset, we would like to briefly highlight three.

First, Wynter's essays underscore the intimate relationship between race and religion. Her expansive take on the origin of the Du Boisian "color line"—which takes us back to medieval Europe and the modes of categorization and distinction that were central to Christian scholasticism—contributes important insights to the growing body of scholarship that demonstrates the extent to which modern racial categories are grounded in, or shaped by, Christian theological thinking.[10] In "Unsettling the Coloniality of Being/Power/Truth/Freedom"—which, published in 2003, remains her best-known and most often cited essay—she writes,

> "Race" was therefore to be, in effect, the nonsupernatural but no less extrahuman ground (in the reoccupied place of the traditional ancestors/gods, God, ground) of the answer that the secularizing West would now give to the Heideggerian question as to the who, and the what we are.[11]

With her notion of "extrahuman," Wynter helps us understand that even if race is a cultural construct, a human invention, and an ideology, it works like a religious/theological discourse in that it claims authority outside of the human. She observes, in other words, the persistence of a particular structure of thinking. In this volume, we aim to further investigate this structure. Essays by Justine Bakker and David Kline home in on Wynter's theory of religion, while Tapji Garba and Joseph Winters demonstrate the entangled relationship between coloniality and theological thinking.

Second, Wynter's consistent problematizing of knowledge production and disciplinary formation (a point to which we briefly return below) offers new ways to study how colonialism and coloniality shape(d) the study of religion. Such work finds an important foundation in Charles Long's 1986 groundbreaking decolonial essay collection *Significations: Signs, Symbols, and Images in the Interpretation of Religion*.[12] *Significations* demonstrated that the modern academic study of religion finds its origin in colonialism, whose many afterlives still reverberate in the concepts we use, frameworks we develop, and methods we embrace. More recent studies have confirmed and deepened Long's intervention.[13] These works often emphasize the conceptual entanglement of race and religion—"conjoined twins," in Theodore Vial's quip[14]—and pay increasingly more attention to the role and importance of whiteness in establishing and maintaining hegemonic thought and funding patterns.[15] As Shamara Alhassan's essay shows, Wynter's deep analysis of Man as the central locus of dominant epistemology helps us understand why this is the case—and offers, with her push toward Wynter's new "science of the word," a glimpse of a wor(l)d beyond.

Third, Wynter helps us place the category of the human at the forefront of our inquiry. Of course, many in the study of religion work with the assumption that religion is, as Jonathan Z. Smith would have it, an "inextricably human phenomenon."[16] Smith's phrasing here seems to suggest that "human" in this phrase is self-explanatory and self-evident. Yet, Wynter's writings on the universalization of Man help us understand that although the "human" is often mobilized as a universal and general category, such unifying tendencies are constituted by a hierarchy of humanness. Race, gender, and other markers of difference overdetermined some people as "fully" human and others as "not-quite-human" or even "non-human." The study of religion has often obscured these histories of violence, which is remarkable when we consider that "religion" was a category that was often used as a kind of "test for humanness," to use Paul Christopher Johnson's apt description.[17] In the colonial context, whether one had an authentic religion (and if so, what kind) was a question that played an integral role in determining the (not-quite-)human nature of the colonized. Both "human" and "religion" have worked as exclusionary categories, that, often in tandem, were used to exclude or selectively include groups of people. In the history of the study of religion, then, perceptions of the human did not begin as the ostensibly universal category that scholars in the field often seem to assume it is. This is precisely the problem Wynter helps the field address, if in a much broader sense: the study of the nature and origins of the "color line" exposes how received notions of the human, grounded in

Western conceptions of religion, are essential to the production and reproduction of the racial order of colonial modernity.

Yet, there are also elements in Wynter's work that make it less immediately available to scholars of religion. For instance, although religion shows up consistently throughout Wynter's oeuvre, it is also an understated and somewhat undertheorized category of analysis. As the chapters by Bakker and Kline demonstrate, religion in Wynter's writing is difficult to pin down with any precision. At moments, she seems to use "religion" to name and identify a universal human social function that revolves around the production of "extrahuman agents of determination." A superficial or cursory reading of this argument may lead scholars of religion to conclude that Wynter seems to fall into the trap of universalization that scholars in the field of religious studies have tried to get away from since the 1990s (if not earlier). As we understand the danger and risk of such universalizing narratives, we hope that this book complicates, nuances, and problematizes this conclusion. At other times, Wynter seems to equate "religion" with culture more generally, or with mythmaking. Given that "mythos" is such a central term in her oeuvre, this may have led scholars to think that the category carries less importance. And yet, at other times, it seems that her main concern is not with religion as such but with Christianity and its later secularized formations in the so-called West, a concern that in many ways mirrors the claims of those who maintain that "religion" is a category tainted by its Christian bias. The chapters in this volume will demonstrate that these different usages and readings of religion can exist next to one another, thereby complicating existing theories and offering "epistemic alternatives" to engaging the complex relationship between religion, race, and coloniality.[18]

If the category of religion itself is hard to pin down in Wynter's writing, then so are her scattered reflections about the potential for liberation through forms of religiosity. In some of her essays, she celebrates the survival and transformation of African forms of religiosity in the Americas,[19] and, as Alhassan shows in her chapter, the liberative possibilities of Rastafari thought. Other essays, as discussed in Winters's chapter, gesture toward a "demonic piety," a wild and heretical notion of the sacred that exceeds Man's epistemic grasp. Yet, despite these positive references to religion, as Rafael Vizcaíno's reading of *The Hills of Hebron* argues, we might say that to the extent that the secular and religious are co-constitutive, Wynter ultimately seeks to move beyond both. Moreover, in her writings on the "science of the new word," as Bakker and Kline argue in their chapters, she seems to critique "religion" (or, in Kline's terms, "autoreligion") while seeking a way beyond any overt reliance on the supernatural and other, more secular "extrahuman agents of determination." Oludamini Ogunnaike's chapter provides a powerful intervention here by showing that we find precisely the kind of liberative potential that Wynter seeks to unlock through the science of the word already in certain Islamic traditions and forms of indigenous African religions.

Finally, one more reason why religion is difficult to parse out in Wynter's writing is simply the sprawling transdisciplinary nature of her work. In order to break and transcend disciplinary boundaries and, as Clements emphasizes and theorizes in her chapter, the divide between the natural and the human sciences, Wynter draws from and builds on a select if ever-expanding group of scholars from a wide variety of disciplines and fields whom she puts in generative conversation with each other: Aimé Césaire, W. E. B. Du Bois, Edouard Glissant, and Frantz Fanon return frequently, as do Michel Foucault, Hans Blumenberg, V. Y. Mudimbe, Aníbal Quijano, Anthony Pagden, Jacques Le Goff, Bruno Latour, and Humberto Maturana and Francisco Varela. Wynter's writings, as Walter Mignolo writes, exist in "a network, wherein her ideas and writings are in conversation with and refer back (and forth) to one another."[20] Part of understanding how this network emerges and works is tracing how the same scholars show up again and again. When it comes to religion, she often draws from N. J. Girardot, Alex Comfort, Antonio T. de Nicolás, and Maurice Godelier. That these are not scholars frequently cited in contemporary scholarship may have also contributed to the somewhat delayed engagement with Wynter in religious studies. What's more, even if the field of religious studies typically welcomes and engages a range of approaches and methodologies, it has been slow to pick up scholarship in Black studies more generally (which relates back to the more general historical lack of interest in exploring race), even if that is currently, and fortunately, rapidly changing. This is all to say that Wynter's engagement with religion and religiosity is ambiguous, generative, and perhaps even unruly. This is part of the reason why her thinking on religion is so interesting, and why this volume is a necessary part of the burgeoning field of Wynter studies.

From and beyond the Field of Religious Studies

With this volume, we intend to place Wynter on the map as an important—indeed, necessary—thinker for scholars of religion and the sprawling, expansive field of religious studies. In doing so, however, we risk reifying the disciplinary binaries and boundaries that her "science of the word"— and, indeed, Black *study* more generally—seeks to problematize.[21] As Anthony Bayani Rodriguez beautifully illustrates in the coda of this volume, one of the things that is so powerful about Wynter's thinking is the way disciplinary boundaries are cracked open and ultimately dissolved as she exposes the very notion of academic disciplinarity as a boundary-enforcing mark of Man's bourgeois order of knowledge, an order that thrives on the illusion of disciplinary objectivity. To follow Wynter is to enter the "heretical" territory of interhuman knowledge that exceeds any disciplinary claim of capturing the truth of our existence. She invites us to look beyond our narrow categories, classification systems, and ingrained habits of thinking, and out toward a new horizon of knowledge where the scientist and the poet, the organizer and the artist, the philosopher and the priest all come together to study what it would mean to create a new mode of human existence that serves not just a single vision of human life, but the totality of life found across our shared existence. Of course, following Wynter, the first task of moving beyond the stifling boundaries of disciplinarity is to recognize just how much we (professional scholars) are stuck in its protocols. While the present volume does not pretend to have transcended the academic discipline of "religious studies," we hope that it represents, in its own small way, a movement toward the dismantling of some of the field's conceptual borders that keep it safely within the confines of Man's order of knowledge. If there is a future for religious studies that does not succumb to the suffocating fear and despair of Man$_2$'s biocentric trajectory of neoliberal austerity, knowledge commodification, and antihumanity, it will be one that has dared to join the ranks of those who have long known that "there still remains one sea to cross / oh still one sea to cross / that I may invent my lungs."[22]

Chapters

We suggest readers approach this book with Mignolo's sense of a "network" in mind. Although our contributors did not read one another's essays and therefore do not consciously refer "back and forth," readers will find that they engage overlapping issues, themes, and questions—often with different outcomes and sometimes in disagreement. This is why many of the essays, to give just one example, will rehearse an overview of Wynter's best-known and most often cited argument: the emergence and "overrepresentation" of Man in the modern period. While some of this overlap inevitably leads to repetition, the contributors enter and engage Wynter's account of Man with different methodologies, frameworks, questions, and concerns, highlighting and zooming in on different parts, leading to a tapestry of different engagements with Wynter's capacious project.

Words Made Flesh is organized across three sections. Part 1, "The Religiosity of Being Human," includes three chapters that directly address the category of religion in Wynter's thinking. In chapter 1, "On Self-Creation: Autopoiesis and Autoreligion," David Kline does a deep dive into Wynter's understanding of religion by reading it through one of her most important analytical sources: Humberto Maturana and Francisco Varela's concept of "autopoiesis" (self-creation). This chapter provides an overview of Maturana and Varela's theory and shows how the emergence of the human species as a self-generating entity dependent on complex processes of environmental adaption in relation to both the biosphere and the development of sociocultural systems of communication and meaning provides the foundation for Wynter's new science of the word. Within this framework, Wynter situates the emergence of human forms of life within a metahistorical account of self-generating living systems operating around specific processes of neurobiological and linguistic production and reproduction. It is within this metahistorical framework of autopoiesis that the category of religion in Wynter should be understood. Kline coins the term "autoreligion" to account for its specific autopoietic grounding, and defines it as the human techno-rhetorical social function that produces transcendent narratives of group homogenization and behavior regulation. After tracing this account of religion in Wynter's later writings, he concludes with a set of questions about the possibility of fully moving beyond autoreligion and achieving a truly objective and trans-genre "outside" perspective free of autoreligious "illusions."

Chapter 2 turns to an encounter between Wynter's project and the study of African religions with Oludamini Ogunnaike's "Symbolic Rebirth and Ceremonies Never Lost: African Religions and the Paradoxical Progressivism of Sylvia Wynter's Work." What makes Wynter's work particularly valuable for the study of Africana religiosity, Ogunnaike argues, is that she shows the extent to which "inequities and structures of domination shape knowledge production and academic disciplines." Typical approaches to African religions have privileged Western frameworks, methods, and theories, which in turn have prevented them from approaching these forms of religiosity "on their own terms" and as equal. While Wynter powerfully identifies the problematic nature of such study, Ogunnaike suggests that she is not entirely above it. Her writings on African culture and religiosity suffer from many of the same problems that have shaped the field: she is adamant about the historical necessity of Africana traditions, yet sees their current iterations as "naïve, limited humanisms of the past, of the sunset, to be transcended in the dawn of the Second Emergence." Ogunnaike contests this view as he argues that the self-consciously autopoietic Second Emergence for which Wynter calls is, in some ways, already present in certain African religious traditions like Ifá and certain forms of Sufism. As these traditions continue to function from epistemological grounds "outside" the Western order of knowledge, they complement, Ogunnaike concludes, Wynter's immanent critique, which works from the "inside-out."

In chapter 3, "(Para)religious Traces in Sylvia Wynter's 'Demonic Ground,'" Justine M. Bakker engages Wynter's theory of religion and her relentless and hopeful push to move beyond religion's seemingly persistent grasp on human nature, experience, and reality. Tracking the origins of Wynter's frequently used concept "demonic ground" to the work of idiosyncratic intellectual Alex Comfort—best known for writing the manual *The Joy of Sex* but also a well-known pacifist and conscientious objector interested in quantum mechanics and Hindu and Buddhist ontology—Bakker observes that even though Wynter privileges scientific over theological approaches to the "demonic," the term nevertheless carries implicit religious traces. After identifying these traces, Bakker follows their winding path to look anew at Wynter's engagement with religion. The chapter demonstrates that religion, for Wynter, is marked and characterized by a twofold mechanism of, firstly, producing categorical distinctions and, secondly, displacing these onto "extrahuman agents of determination." Where Kline grounds Wynter's theory of religion in the work of Maturana and Varela, Bakker emphasizes and studies a different source: the "biological study of religion." This term comes from Antonio de Nicolás, whose engagement with Comfort's work formed, Bakker argues, another important impetus for Wynter's ideas on religion and human nature. In the third and final part of the chapter, Bakker builds on Wynter's critique of the two mechanisms of religion to name and theorize the work of contemporary visual artist Ellen Gallagher as a form of parareligion that emerges from a "demonic ocean."

Part 2, "Science, Secularism, and Man's Political Theology of Race," includes three chapters that focus on the questions of science and secularism in Wynter's writing. In chapter 4, "The Wynterian Turn: Human Hybridity in the Natural and Human Sciences," Niki Kasumi Clements offers a deep and thorough analysis of Wynter's genealogy of Man, her critique of dominant epistemes (with a specific eye toward the intertwined histories of religion and science), and her wide-ranging, groundbreaking transdisciplinary epistemological intervention. Clements frames her engagement with Wynter by opening with C. P. Snow and E. O. Wilson's critique of the split between "two cultures," the humanists and the scientists. Wynter's attempt to bridge this impasse, Clements argues, at once challenges Wilson's scientific hierarchy of vertical integration and reckons with the histories of racism, eugenics, and violence against Black and indigenous peoples in the natural sciences, while simultaneously embracing their prescriptive and descriptive power. Wynter does so through taking up Aimé Césaire's 1945 "science of the Word" and Frantz Fanon's 1952 "meta-Darwinian terms," which allows her to forge a new, hybrid science. In so doing, Wynter's constructive project develops a praxis for understanding the hybridity of being human. Although incorporating the human and the natural sciences, Wynter's Autopoetic Turn—the Wynterian Turn of the chapter title—goes beyond Snow's and Wilson's solutions to the problem of "two cultures," Clements concludes, because it draws attention to "local and distributed ways of understanding human praxis as a way of life." Clements's chapter thus offers an engaging, thorough analysis of where and how Wynter's central arguments intervene in extant debates about science, the "two cultures," and interdisciplinarity.

In chapter 5, "The Ceremony beyond the Secular: Postreligious Autopoetics in Wynter's *The Hills of Hebron*," Rafael Vizcaíno turns to Wynter's only novel. He builds on scholars who have understood her early literary exploration as both foreshadowing and putting into practice many of the elements that her later works would seek to expound in critical-theoretical fashion. In conversation with such critical commentary, Vizcaíno articulates how *The Hills of Hebron* is an attempt to find the "ceremony," as the later Wynter would put it, that can unite the cognitive emancipation initiated by the modern secularizing epistemologies of Man, on the one hand, and the "demonic" perspectives of those subjects upon whom such secular order has been built in the first place, on the other. The novel is in this sense a meditation on a certain *postsecular* (and, because the religious is co-constitutive of the secular, always already *postreligious*) praxis needed to overcome the modern/colonial wor(l)d of Man. Vizcaíno further argues that the ceremony found in this literary exploration could rewrite a revolutionary relationship with two essential sources of the modern Western revolutionary imagination: Marxism and the Bible. By rereading these sources through Wynter's decolonial lens, Vizcaíno suggests that we now have the resources to generate nothing less than the symbolic rebirth of humanity, this being a kind of "reincarnation" beyond the Christian politico-theological matrix that defines Western modernity as a secular-religious complex. Moreover, if taken to its ultimate conclusion, such postsecular and always already postreligious ceremony of rebirth/reincarnation can be encapsuled by what, in terms of Wynter's later theoretical work, we can call the praxis of an autopoiesis/autopoetics of the flesh.

In chapter 6, "Sociogeny, Race, and the Theological Genealogy of Economy," Tapji Garba engages Wynter's notion of sociogeny through recent writings on the theological genealogy of economy as a way to identify the ethical and methodological stakes of Wynter's critical theory of contemporary society. Garba argues that Wynter's sociogenetic method offers a protocol for approaching theological problems as matters of social reproduction and elaborating the fundamental role of racial slavery in the genesis of the modern world. By tracing the ways that racial slavery comes to mediate the shifting relationship between theology and politics in the modern West, Garba shows that slavery functions as the hermeneutical key for understanding how race comes to reoccupy the waning legitimacy of theological structures of authority by providing new answers to pressing questions regarding the origins and intelligibility of the world as well as the telos and possibility of self-determination.

Part 3, "Counter-religiosities beyond Man," provides two chapters that engage Wynter as a resource for thinking beyond the violent discourse of Man through alternative modes of religiosity. In chapter 7, "Interrupting the Sanctity of Man: Wynter, Imperial Piety, and the Unruly Sacred," Joseph Winters interrogates the category of the sacred by reading Wynter's work in conversation with Émile Durkheim, Robert Bellah, and W. E. B. Du Bois. On the one hand, Wynter's expansive analysis of the emergence of Man provides us with the means to study the religiosity of coloniality and its afterlives as it demonstrates how certain "theological divisions and demarcations" get reinvented in modern iterations of what it means to be human. Wynter thus exposes, Winters argues, that a certain grammar of sacrality—with order, purity, and stability as central qualities—propels the project of Man, a grammar that Winters sees taken up by US president Donald Trump and his former defense secretary James Mattis. On the other hand, Wynter's writing also points to an alternative and heretical sacred, which Winters characterizes as an unruly and demonic piety that "frustrates the desire for wholeness, possession, and order." In articulating this double quality of the sacred in Wynter's work, Winters is careful not to simply reinscribe Blackness and indigeneity in terms of disorder or chaos: the demonic sacred, he writes, "would not only have to depart from a conception of sacrality that safeguards order and property; it would have to depart from the kinds of unyielding oppositions that Man's call to order relies on and replicates."

In chapter 8, "Moving to a Realm beyond Reason: Mapping Ontological Sovereignty in Counter-worlds of Liminality," Shamara Wyllie Alhassan returns us to *The Hills of Hebron*, demonstrating that it provides unique insight into some of Wynter's key concepts and interventions into the problem of Man's epistemological violence. Alhassan engages Wynter's account of "ontological sovereignty" and the possibility of moving beyond

Man's order of knowledge. She looks to Rastafari, a significant source of inspiration for *The Hills of Hebron*, as a model for thinking the counter-symbolic "worlds of liminality" that are key for Wynter's understanding of alternative epistemologies against Man. Alhassan reads *The Hills of Hebron* as a map of the counter-worlds of Caribbean liminality that Wynter understands as crucial to the possibility of an interhuman future beyond the reason of Man. Rather than dismissing the book's protagonists such as Prophet Moses and his followers as mad, she centers them as political and social theorists who are fleshing out the contours of a realm beyond reason and thereby making way for the "communitarian viability" of our species.

Finally, the coda to the volume by Anthony Bayani Rodriguez, "Nuiscientia," reflects on physicist Ronald Mallett's work on the possibility of time travel and Wynter's own decolonial journey to a new *scientia*. Rodriguez thus returns us to the imperative of breaking open academic disciplines in search of a new form of humanistic knowledge "made to the measure of the world." For religious studies, as for all academic disciplines that would choose the "safety" of remaining enclosed in their proper protocols and boundaries, Rodriguez writes that it is "not only permissible, but urgently necessary, to subject all forms of knowledge to critical inquiry." As Wynter's writings and her writing life witness, the imperative of real human knowledge beyond the disciplinary boundaries of biocentric Man is only realized in the active struggle (*praxis*) of invention.

Notes

1. Sylvia Wynter, "Unsettling the Coloniality of Being/Power/Truth/Freedom: Towards the Human, after Man, Its Overrepresentation—an Argument," *CR: The New Centennial Review* 3, no. 3 (Fall 2003): 257–337.

2. A good place to start engaging with Wynter's work are her interviews and conversations. See David Scott, "The Re-enchantment of Humanism: An Interview with Sylvia Wynter," *Small Axe: A Caribbean Journal of Criticism* 8 (September 2000): 119–207; Sylvia Wynter and Katherine McKittrick, "Unparalleled Catastrophe for Our Species? Or, to Give Humanness a Different Future: Conversations," in *Sylvia Wynter: On Being Human as Praxis*, ed. Katherine McKittrick (Durham, NC: Duke University Press, 2015), 9–89; Sylvia Wynter and Greg Thomas, "ProudFlesh Inter/Views: Sylvia Wynter," *ProudFlesh: New Afrikan Journal of Culture, Politics and Consciousness* 4 (2006): 29; Sylvia Wynter, Joshua Bennett, and Jarvis R. Givens, "'A Greater Truth than Any Other Truth You Know': A Conversation with Professor Sylvia Wynter on Origin Stories," *Souls* 22, no. 1 (2021): 123–37; Bedour Alagraa, "What Will Be the Cure? A Conversation with Sylvia Wynter," *Offshoot*, January 7, 2021, https://offshootjournal.org/what-will-be-the-cure-a-conversation-with-sylvia-wynter/.

3. Wynter's work has been subject to two edited volumes, *After Man, towards the Human: Critical Essays on Sylvia Wynter* (2006) and *Sylvia Wynter: On Being Human as Praxis* (2015); her early essays have been collected in one volume, titled after one of

her essays, *We Must Learn to Sit Down Together and Talk about a Little Culture: Decolonising Essays, 1967–1984* (2022); and the past decade witnessed the publication of special issues on Wynter's scholarship in a wide variety of journals, from *Small Axe: A Caribbean Journal of Criticism* (2016), to *American Quarterly* (2018), to *Curriculum Inquiry* (2019).

4. Ariella Aïsha Azoulay, "Letter to Sylvia Wynter," *The Funambulist* 30 (2020), https://thefunambulist.net/magazine/reparations/open-letter-to-sylvia-wynter-unlearning-the-disappearance-of-jews-from-africa-by-ariella-aisha-azoulay; Justine M. Bakker, "Locating the Oceanic in Sylvia Wynter's 'Demonic Ground,'" *Journal for Cultural and Religious Theory* 21, no. 1 (2022): 1–22; J. Kameron Carter, "Black Malpractice (A Poetics of the Sacred)," *Social Text* 37, no. 2 (2019): 67–107; M. Shawn Copeland, "Blackness Past, Blackness Future—and Theology," *South Atlantic Quarterly* 112, no. 4 (2013): 625–40; Tapji Paul Garba and Sara-Maria Sorentino, "Blackness before Race and Race as Reoccupation: Reading Sylvia Wynter with Hans Blumenberg," *Political Theology* (2022), https://doi.org/10.1080/1462317X.2022.2079216; David Kline, *Racism and the Weakness of Christian Identity: Religious Autoimmunity* (London: Routledge, 2020); Mayra Rivera, "Poetics Ashore," *Literature and Theology* 33, no. 3 (2019): 241–47; Benjamin Robinson, "Racialization and Modern Religion: Sylvia Wynter, Black Feminist Theory, and Critical Genealogies of Religion," *Critical Research on Religion* 7, no. 3 (2019): 257–74; Rafael Vizcaíno, "Sylvia Wynter's New Science of the Word and the Autopoetics of the Flesh," *Comparative and Continental Philosophy* 14, no. 1 (2022), https://doi.org/10.1080/17570638.2022.2037189.

5. Joseph Drexler-Dreis and Kristien Justaert, eds., *Beyond the Doctrine of Man: Decolonial Visions of the Human* (New York: Fordham University Press, 2020); An Yountae and Eleanor Craig, eds., *Beyond Man: Race, Coloniality, and Philosophy of Religion* (Durham, NC: Duke University Press, 2021).

6. For this brief biographical sketch, we draw primarily from Scott, "Re-enchantment of Humanism"; Demetrius L. Eudell, "Afterword: Toward Aimé Césaire's 'Humanism Made to the Measure of the World': Reading *The Hills of Hebron* in the Context of Sylvia Wynter's Later Work," in *The Hills of Hebron*, by Sylvia Wynter (Kingston: Ian Randle, 2010), 311–40; Anthony Bayani Rodriguez, "Introduction: On Sylvia Wynter and the Urgency of a New Humanist Revolution in the Twenty-First Century," *American Quarterly* 70, no. 4 (2018): 831–36; and private correspondence with Anthony Bayani Rodriguez, who is currently working on a biography of Wynter.

7. Scott, "Re-enchantment of Humanism," 125.

8. Michael Reckord, "For the Reckord: J'can Sylvia Wynter to Be Honoured by King's College," *The Gleaner*, August 20, 2018, https://jamaica-gleaner.com/article/entertainment/20180824/reckord-jcan-sylvia-wynter-be-honoured-kings-college-part-i.

9. See Sylvia Wynter, *We Must Learn to Sit Down Together and Talk about a Little Culture: Decolonising Essays, 1967–1894*, ed. Demetrius L. Eudell (Leeds, UK: Peepal Tree, 2012).

10. See here, in particular, J. Kameron Carter, *Race: A Theological Account* (New York: Oxford University Press, 2008); Willie Jennings, *The Christian Imagination: Theology and the Origins of Race* (New Haven, CT: Yale University Press, 2011); Terence Keel, *Divine Variations: How Christian Thought Became Racial Science* (Stanford, CA: Stanford University Press, 2018); Kathryn Gin Lum, *Heathen: Religion*

and Race in American History (Cambridge, MA: Harvard University Press, 2022); Nelson Maldonado-Torres, "Religion, Conquest, and Race in the Foundations of the Modern/Colonial World," *Journal of the American Academy of Religion* 82, no. 3 (2014): 636–65; Oludamini Ogunnaike, "From Heathen to Sub-human: A Genealogy of the Influence of the Decline of Religion on the Rise of Modern Racism," *Open Theology* 2, no. 1 (2016): 785–803; Anya Topolski, "The Race-Religion Constellation: A European Contribution to the Critical Philosophy of Race," *Critical Philosophy of Race* 6, no. 1 (2018): 58–81.

11. Wynter, "Unsettling the Coloniality of Being/Power/Truth/Freedom," 264.

12. Charles H. Long, *Significations: Signs, Symbols, and Images in the Interpretation of Religion*, 2nd ed. (Aurora, CO: Davies Group, 1999).

13. The literature here is vast and expanding. See, in chronological order, Talal Asad, *Genealogies of Religion: Discipline and Reasons of Power in Christianity and Islam* (Baltimore: Johns Hopkins University Press, 1993); David Chidester, *Savage Systems: Colonialism and Comparative Religion in Southern Africa* (Charlottesville: University of Virginia Press, 1996); Richard King, *Orientalism and Religion: Postcolonial Theory, India, and the "Mystic East"* (New York: Routledge, 1999); Peter van der Veer, *Imperial Encounters: Religion and Modernity in India and Britain* (Princeton, NJ: Princeton University Press, 2001); Daniel Dubuisson, *The Western Construction of Religion: Myths, Knowledge, and Ideology* (Baltimore: Johns Hopkins University Press, 2003); Tomoko Masuzawa, *The Invention of World Religions, or, How European Universalism Was Preserved in the Language of Pluralism* (Chicago: University of Chicago Press, 2005); Timothy Fitzgerald, *Discourse on Civility and Barbarity* (New York: Oxford University Press, 2007); Brent Nongbri, *Before Religion: A History of a Modern Concept* (New Haven, CT: Yale University Press, 2013); David Chidester, *Empire of Religion: Imperialism and Comparative Religion* (Chicago: University of Chicago Press, 2014); Sylvester Johnson, *African American Religions, 1500–2000* (Cambridge: Cambridge University Press, 2015); Theodore Vial, *Modern Religion, Modern Race* (New York: Oxford University Press, 2016); Lucia Hulsether, "The Grammar of Racism: Religious Pluralism and the Birth of Disciplines," *Journal of the American Academy of Religion* 86, no. 1 (2018): 1–41; Christopher Driscoll and Monica Miller, *Method as Identity: Manufacturing Distance in the Academic Study of Religion* (London: Rowman and Littlefield, 2018); Malory Nye, "Decolonizing the Study of Religion," *Open Library of Humanities* 5, no. 1 (2019), https://olh.openlibhums.org/article/id/4580/; Rachel Schneider and Sophie Bjork-James, "Whither Whiteness and Religion? Implications for Theology and the Study of Religion," *Journal of the American Academy of Religion* 88, no. 1 (2020): 175–99; An Yountae, "A Decolonial Theory of Religion: Race, Coloniality, and Secularity in the Americas," *Journal of the American Academy of Religion* 88, no. 4 (2020): 947–80. See also the contributions to the series "Decolonizing Continental Philosophy of Religion" and "Decoloniality and the Study of Religion" on *Contending Modernities* blog.

14. Vial, *Modern Religion, Modern Race*, 1.

15. Schneider and Bjork-James, "Whither Whiteness and Religion."

16. Jonathan Z. Smith, *Map Is Not Territory* (Chicago: University of Chicago Press, 1993), 290.

17. Paul Christopher Johnson, *Automatic Religion: Nearhuman Agents of Brazil and France* (Chicago: University of Chicago Press, 2020), 28.

18. "Epistemic alternatives" is Eleanor Craig and An Yountae's phrase. See their introduction to *Beyond Man: Race, Coloniality, and Philosophy of Religion*, ed. An Yountae and Eleanor Craig (Durham, NC: Duke University Press, 2021), 5.

19. See Rivera, "Poetics Ashore," 241–47.

20. Walter D. Mignolo, "Sylvia Wynter: What Does It Mean to Be Human?," in *Sylvia Wynter: On Being Human as Praxis*, ed. Katherine McKittrick (Durham, NC: Duke University Press, 2015), 111.

21. We would like to thank one of our reviewers for encouraging us to address this discrepancy head on and would like to point readers to a work and quotation cited in the review: Josh Myers claims, in *Of Black Study* (right before he delves into Wynter's scholarship): "It is that *disciplines* conserve the present order of knowledge. And that is the crisis." Joshua Myers, *Of Black Study* (London: Pluto, 2023), 67 (emphasis original).

22. Aimé Césaire, *Notebook of a Return to the Native Land,* trans. Clayton Eshleman and Annette Smith (Middletown, CT: Wesleyan University Press, 2001), 49.

Part One: The Religiosity of Being Human

1 / On Self-Creation: Autopoiesis and Autoreligion
David Kline

> We human beings are human beings only in language. Because we have language, there is no limit to what we can describe, imagine, and relate. It thus permeates our whole ontogeny as individuals.
> —HUMBERTO MATURANA AND FRANCISCO VARELA

> The business of living keeps no records concerning origins.
> —HUMBERTO MATURANA AND FRANCISCO VARELA

Sylvia Wynter's story of human life is told on an enormous temporal scale. Her interest in the conditions and possibilities of the natural and cultural history of human beings finds much common ground with what the historian David Christian calls "big history," a metahistorical approach that takes the entire 13 billion years of the known universe as its historical object. In *Maps of Time: An Introduction to Big History,* Christian notes that the aim of big history is to "see if it [is] possible . . . to tell a coherent story about the past on many different scales, beginning, literally, with the origins of the universe and ending in the present day."[1] With echoes of historian of religion Charles Long's definition of religion as "orientation in the ultimate sense,"[2] Christian also refers to big history as a "modern creation myth [providing] universal coordinates within which people can imagine their own existence and find a role in the larger scheme of things. . . . [It] provides a fundamental sense of orientation."[3] This chapter situates Wynter's post-1984 work, beginning with "The Ceremony Must Be Found: After Humanism,"[4] as a distinct form of "big history" centered around her own creation myth of human self-inscription and her constructive project of an ultimate decolonial orientation pointed toward the autonomy of human cognitive agency. I read both Wynter's creation myth and decolonial project as formally constructed around Chilean systems biologists Humberto Maturana and Francisco Varela's category of autopoiesis ("self-creation"). Wynter's turn to autopoiesis provides her a phenomenological and ecological framework for understanding the emergence of the human species as a self-generating entity dependent on complex processes of environmental adaptation in relation to both the biosphere and the development of sociocultural systems of communication and meaning. Within this framework, Wynter situates the emergence of human forms of life within a "big history" of self-generating living systems operating around specific processes of neurobiological and linguistic production and reproduction.

In Wynter's writing, one of the key autopoietic operations she identifies in the emergence of human sociocultural formations is the system of religion, which enables human beings to experience their own auto-instituted social reality as if it were the product of an outside "extrahuman" agent of determination. I refer to this account of religion in Wynter's writing as "autoreligion," which names a human techno-rhetorical social function that produces transcendent narratives of group homogenization and behavior regulation. Autoreligion is foundational for the process of sociogenesis and, as I will show, despite Wynter's tendency toward the language of Man2's "purely secular" mode of knowledge, the "overdetermination" of Man in the modern period. Against Man and its autoreligious fantasy of universality presented under the guises of Christian-, rational-, and bio-economic taxonomies of human authenticity, Wynter's "autopoetic turn/overturn" and "new science" aim to get beyond the autoreligious production of extrahuman agents of determination and move toward a "trans-genres-of-being-human" "autopoetics" grounded in the realization of a new collective human creation myth no longer blind to its own autopoietic self-creation. After tracing this turn in Wynter's later writings, I conclude with a set of questions about the possibility of fully moving beyond autoreligion and achieving a truly objective and trans-genre "outside" perspective.

The Three Events:
The Big Bang, Truth-For/Autopoiesis, and Language

Wynter's constructive human project is centered on the urgent necessity of a new story of human life beyond the state- and biocentric-creation myths of Man. She is interested in the potential of a new creation myth or "counter-cosmogony"[5] centered on the self-inscripting, hybrid human being of *bios-logos* that is linked to three events of cosmological and evolutionary scale. In her dialogue with Katherine McKittrick, "Unparalleled Catastrophe for Our Species?," she describes the three events:

> The First and Second Events are the origin of the universe and the explosion of all forms of biological life, respectively. I identify the Third Event in Fanonian-adapted terms as the origin of the human as a hybrid-auto-instituting-languaging-storytelling species: *bios/mythoi*. The Third Event is defined by the singularity of the *co-evolution* of the human brain *with*—and, unlike those of all the other primates, *with it alone*—the emergent faculties of language, storytelling. This co-evolution must be understood concomitantly with the uniquely *mythmaking* region of the human brain.[6]

The first two events in this story set up Wynter's deep excavation of the third and her project of reimagining human being through a recognition of its own agency of self-creation. Wynter does not give much attention to the first event, which frames the basic fact of the physical universe and its creation around 13 billion years ago in what physicists refer to as the "big bang." The second event, which will be necessary to unpack in depth before we arrive at the third event, is the more specific emergence and exponential expansion of sentient life on earth that began with the emergence of life around 3.5 billion years ago and eventually introduced into existence the experience of subjective cognition across myriad forms of eukaryotic and multicellular life.[7] Wynter describes the second event in terms of the entry of "truth" into the world. This is not (yet) truth in any kind of religious or philosophical sense, but truth in terms of the general functional cognition of living beings. In the second event, Wynter notes, "every living species would now be able to know its reality only in terms of its specific *truth-for,* that is, in terms that were/are of adaptive advantage to its realization, survival and reproduction as such a form of life—to know its reality only adaptively."[8] By locating the advent of truth in the emergence of sentient life and its varying modes of functional cognition, Wynter establishes her epistemological approach by, first, foregrounding the production of cognition and/or knowledge across a multiplicity of forms of life and, second, rejecting representationalist schemas of cognition that posit an objective correlation between thought and its external environment, or what the philosopher Richard Rorty describes as epistemologies that assume thought as the "mirror of nature."[9] This epistemological approach will be foundational both in terms of her understanding of the production of truth and knowledge and her critique of Man as an overdetermined cognitive-epistemological form of life that falsely projects its own *truth-for* as universal.

It is within the story of the emergence of a general ecology of adaptive *truth-fors* that Wynter will adopt Maturana and Varela's term *autopoiesis* and use it prominently in almost all of her writing beginning with 1984's "The Ceremony Must Be Found: After Humanism." The development of the term *autopoiesis* is an interesting story in itself that links it to exactly the kind of "liminal" social struggles that Wynter associates with the "cognitive breakthroughs" that have historically ushered in new descriptions of the human. As Maturana tells the story of the term's coinage, in May 1968 he was one of the faculty supporting a student group at the University of Chile that had taken over the university in protest of its policies with the aim of reformulating its organizational philosophy. As they tried to say something new that might realize their revolutionary goals, the students and supportive faculty found that "language was a trap." It was nearly inconceivable that anything truly new might be said, and in their struggle against the university administration they discovered just how limited they were with the available vocabulary. However, as Maturana puts it, "if one succeeded in attaining at least some degree of freedom from [one's ego], one began to listen and one's language began to change; and then, but only then, new things could be said." A few months later when he accepted an invitation to speak on the "neurophysiology of cognition" at the University of Illinois at Urbana in the lab of cyberneticist Heinz von Foerster, Maturana decided to deviate from the standard approaches to cognition—"neuronal circuits, nerve impulses or synapses"—and "consider what should take place in the organism during cognition by considering cognition as a biological phenomenon." It was here that he realized both his talk and his participation in the student protests (and, in subsequent years, the Chilean struggle against Pinochet and fascism) were addressing the same phenomenon: "cognition and the operation of the living system . . . were the same thing." Just as the students had created a new vocabulary out of organizing their protest against university conditions, so living systems create themselves and their *truth-for* in their action (*praxis*). In this realization, and through further work with Varela, who was also supportive of the Chilean struggle against fascism and the search for new descriptions of cognition, the term *autopoiesis* was introduced as designating something new in the knowledge of "the organization of living systems."[10]

Autopoiesis can be a difficult concept to grasp. Its description is often weighed down by paradox and tautology. Literally translated as "self-creation," it generally describes a living thing that generates and reproduces itself through itself. In 1972's *Autopoiesis and Cognition: The Realization of the Living*, Maturana and Varela offer a more filled-in definition, which I'll paraphrase here for brevity: an autopoietic system is a unified network of relational processes and components that, through their interactions and in a recursive feedback loop, continuously realize and regenerate the network of relational processes and components.[11] In contrast to an allopoietic system that produces something other than itself (for example, a mechanical assembly line), an autopoietic system produces nothing but itself. For Maturana and Varela this amounts to a definition of living systems: a thing is living as long as it "continuously generates and specifies its own organization through its operation as a system of production of its own components and does this in an endless turnover of components under conditions of continuous perturbations and compensation of perturbations."[12] "Perturbations" refer to the system's encounter with an outside environment, which is anything that is not the system. The distinction from the environment can be confusing because the system is not just the system, but the *unity* of its distinction between itself and its environment. Just as there is no life without its distinction from death, there is no system without an environment against which it defines itself. This means that for the autopoietic system, the outside is always an operation of the inside. Each system's specific environment is a "virtual" product of the system's own self-referentiality and is encountered only as an operation of the system. In this sense, Wynter's *truth-for* implies a virtual ecology of forms of life, not in the sense that it has no material reference but rather that it is made up of infinitely heterogeneous forms of life that each have their own world, or "truth." For Maturana, such a virtual framework is the only truly "realist" account of lifworlds. As he puts it, "I sometimes call myself . . . a 'super-realist' who believes in the existence of innumerable equally valid realities. Moreover, all these realities are not relative realities because asserting their relativity would entail the assumption of an absolute reality as the reference point against which their relativity would be measured."[13] In this ecology of living systems there is no accessible point of reference that would bind any two worlds to a single absolute and shared experience of reality, and this is precisely what makes each system "real."

The phrase Maturana and Varela use to describe the self-referential and autonomous organization of the system/environment distinction is "operational closure."[14] The principle of operational closure marks a key difference between an understanding of system cognition through the representationalist idea that the system acquires and then "re-presents" information from an outside environment versus an understanding of cognition as a self-referential function of the system's autopoiesis. "It would . . . be a mistake," Maturana and Varela write, "to define the [organism] as having inputs and outputs in the traditional sense. . . . The [organism] does not 'pick up information' from the environment, as we often hear. On the contrary, it *brings forth a world* by specifying what patterns of the environment are perturbations and what changes trigger them in the organization."[15] Though operational closure means that the system only produces environmental information as its own internal operation, it does not imply "solipsism" or a lack of relation with others. To the contrary, as Cary Wolfe phrases it, autopoietic systems function on a principle of "openness from closure": it is precisely in their operational closure that systems are able to respond and adapt to changes in the environment, where, as Niklas Luhmann notes, "closure is a form of broadening possible environmental contexts; closure increases, by constituting elements more capable of being determined, the complexity of the environment that is possible for the system."[16] For Maturana and Varela, the principle of openness from closure is made possible through the distinction between what they call the system's organization and its structure. As they describe, "*organization* denotes those relations that must exist among the components of a system for it to be a member of a specific class. *Structure* denotes the components and relations that actually constitute a particular unity and make its organization real."[17] Structural adjustment or adaptation in the cognitive experience of environmental perturbation marks a system response that changes the physical or noetic makeup of the system but does not change its organization or its basic operation. In this way, environmental "perturbations" are events for the system that take place on the level of structure but are recognized by the system on the level of its organization.[18] It is this relation between system organization and structure that determines what is referred to as "ontogeny," which is "the history of structural change in a unity without loss of organization in that unity."[19]

While there is much more to say about the concept of autopoiesis and its implications for understanding neurophysiological systems, the three characteristics of the unity of distinction between system and environment, operational closure, and the distinction between organization and structure are key for the broader aim of Maturana and Varela's cognitive-epistemological project. As they put it in *The Tree of Knowledge,* the aim of this project is to "negotiate a middle path between the Scylla of cognition as the recovery of a pregiven outer world (realism) and the Charybdis of cognition as the projection of a pregiven inner world (idealism)." The issue with both accounts of cognition, they contend, is that neither can escape the snare of representation, which according to them "contradicts everything we know about living beings."[20] Realism assumes an objective world of objects for all forms of cognition in which "representation is used to recover what is outer"; idealism uses representation "to project what is inner" onto an objective outside. In contrast, as Varela, Evan Thompson, and Eleanor Rosch put it, "our intention is to bypass entirely this logical geography of inner versus outer by studying cognition not as recovery or projection but as embodied action."[21] What is so valuable about the concept of autopoiesis for Maturana and Varela (and Wynter) is that it allows them to "walk the razor's edge" between representationalism and solipsism and thereby avoid an epistemology that contradicts the *self-positing* production of knowledge by living systems—their *"truth-fors"*—without falling into the problem of relativism:

> on the one hand there is the trap of assuming that the nervous system operates with representations of the world. And it *is* a trap, because it blinds us to the possibility of realizing how the nervous system functions from moment to moment as a definite system with operational closure. . . . On the other hand, there is the other trap: denying the surrounding environment on the assumption that the nervous system functions completely in a vacuum, where everything is valid and everything is possible. . . . We wish to propose now a way to cut this apparent Gordian knot and find a natural way to avoid the two abysses of the razor's edge. . . . The solution is to maintain a clear *logical accounting*. It means never losing sight of what we stated at the beginning: everything said is said by someone.[22]

This insight regarding cognition's embodied and subjective nature is key for Wynter's understanding of the second event and the introduction of truth into the world. It is important to keep in mind that Wynter's understanding of the second event is still framed around "purely biological forms of life," where the fact of embodiment is also the fact of subjective autopoietic "worlds" that make up a virtual ecology of living systems. While Wynter's exploration of human life (and its relation to religion) will reference the third event in her creation story, it is the second event as the autopoietic emergence of living systems that provides the foundation for her approach to cognition.

The third event is, so to speak, the crown jewel of Wynter's big history. On the foundation of the biological autopoiesis of living systems, which she often refers to as "the second level" of our existence (behind the "first level" of the basic fact of the universe), Wynter reads into her creation story a "third level" evolutionary event of massive planetary effect: human language. In "The Ceremony Found: Towards the Autopoetic Turn/Overturn, Its Autonomy of Human Agency and the Extraterritoriality of (Self-)Cognition," she notes that the third event is "the [origin] of the co-mutational emergent properties of language and narrative with the brain, themselves as the indispensable conditions of being the uniquely auto-instituting mode of living being that we are."²³ Wynter dates the third event as occurring around 200,000 years ago in the southwest corner of the African continent.²⁴ It marks the broad historical period in which human beings emerged as a "hybrid-auto-instituting-languaging-storytelling species"²⁵ (*homo narrans*) and began to spread across and eventually out of the African continent. As the species expanded geographically it developed widely varying social systems differentiated through various languages and cultural narratives. Wynter calls these diverse social systems "genres of being human."

The question of language being the criterion of what distinguishes human beings from all other nonhuman animals is a topic of much debate between anthropologists, evolutionary biologists, linguists, and philosophers. Language itself is not the sole defining factor of the third event for Wynter, but it does provide the basic condition upon which genres of being human emerge as a unique species of living beings. The question of where human language comes from and how it relates to autopoiesis is complex. Maturana and Varela speak of "linguistic domains" that arise in ontogenic structural coupling between organisms where communicative actions (movements, gestures, sounds, etc.) constitute a structural "co-ontogeny" between them. Such spontaneously produced co-ontogenies establish the rudimentary conditions of "social systems [as] third-order unities that are thus constituted."²⁶ This is also where Maturana and Varela speak of "cultural behavior" as the recursive stabilization of co-ontogenic behaviors established in the communicative actions of a social system.²⁷ In this way, social systems and cultural behavior are autopoietic phenomena that arise and recursively reproduce themselves in a specific linguistic domain. Such linguistic domains, which are found across a multitude of species, "constitute the basis for language, but they are not yet identical with it."²⁸

Where human language comes into the picture as a unique entry into (and departure from) the neurobiological ecology of second-event living systems is when "the operations in a linguistic domain result in coordinations of actions about actions that pertain to the linguistic domain *itself*."²⁹ Language is an ongoing process of linguistic "doubling" that produces distinctions that stand in for or "obscure the actions they coordinate." As Maturana and Varela put it, "we are in language or, better, we 'language' only when through a reflexive action we make a linguistic distinction of a linguistic distinction."³⁰ What is important about this operation in which the linguistic domain itself becomes an object of observation is the possibility of *self-description*, which, and this is key, is itself an act of *self-creation*. Human beings are a specific kind of linguistic observer that produces itself precisely "as a languaging entity" which "by operating in language with other observers . . . generates the self and its circumstances as linguistic distinctions of its participation in a linguistic domain."[31]

Maturana and Varela's natural history of language in *The Tree of Knowledge* gives much attention to the evolutionary progression of primates and their linguistic capacities that, at the very least, blurs the species line in terms of being an ontological threshold for language. What is clear, however, is that modern human beings emerged through highly specific behavioral preferences that allowed their linguistic domains and languaging practices to expand and complexify in unique ways compared to other hominids. Looking to the fossil record, the evolutionary development that leads to *homo sapiens'* bipedalism, cranial capacity, anatomical features, and sexual practices all played a strong factor in how particular styles of social bonding were developed and conserved through linguistic interactions. For example, because of the anatomy of these bipedal hominids, "their sexual life must have engaged their linguistic interactions through facial expressions and frontal coitus. At the same, females shifted from estral cycles to regular (non-seasonal) sexuality—a strong factor in social bonding."[32] While such factors played important roles in forming proto-human social systems and cultural behavior, the real human difference for Maturana and Varela is that in these specific domains and acts "language arose as a result of loving cooperation":

> We can picture these early hominids as beings who lived in small groups, extended families in constant movement through the savanna. . . . Since they walked on two feet, their hands were free to carry food back and forth among the members of their group; they did not have to do so in their digestive system, as in the case of other social animals that share food. This resulted in the integration of social life [and] led to a biology of cooperation and linguistic coordination of actions.[33]

It is here in these particular modes of cooperation and coordination that the third event happens as a new development out of the neurobiological ecology of living beings. In the intimacy of shared space and communal necessity, linguistic distinctions developed and complexified in novel ways. Languaging acts such as personalization through names and other distinctions of identity made possible "the appearance of a self as a distinction in a linguistic domain."[34] The appearance of a "self" through the event of language applies both to the individual and to the collective level. For the former, which does not precede the latter but only happens in isomorphic emergence with it, language places the individual within a broader system of linguistic meaning that enables one to use that system as a basis of self-identification and belonging within a larger group. For the latter, languaging practices make possible a form of group cohesion and identification that is reproduced and expanded through the language system's unprecedented capacity to transmit and store information that goes well beyond individual brains. As David Christian describes,

> Human language ... allows more precise and efficient transmission of knowledge from brain to brain. That means that humans can share information with great precision, creating a common pool of ecological and technical knowledge, which in turn means that for humans, the benefits of cooperation increasingly tend to outweigh the benefits of competition.... Furthermore, the ecological knowledge contributed to that pool by which each individual has access to the stored knowledge of many previous generations. Thus what is distinctive about humans is that they can learn *collectively*.[35]

The ability to learn and transmit knowledge collectively through language introduced a new kind of relationship to the social system's sense of temporality and its environment. The observational system of language, which is a communicative system (a *techné*) that can both outlast and sustain meaning outside of individual human beings, enables a reflective sense of past and future and a descriptive relationship with the (self-referential) environment in which it lives. For emergent human communities, cultivating and complexifying both senses were integral elements of group preservation and reproduction as they spread out across the earth and adapted to their particular environments.

The Third Event and Autoreligion

In its capacity to produce the experience of a self, human language is also much more elastic and "open" than other forms of linguistic communication. Its grammatical organization enables a virtually infinite range of structural invention and meaning. Language, moreover, provides the semantic possibility of reference "not just to what is in front of us but also to entities that are not present, and even to entities that could never be present."[36] The open-ended nature of linguistic invention and meaning makes possible a wholly new technology in the natural history of living systems: storytelling. In Wynter's terms, this is where the "magic" happens. Like Maturana and Varela's insistence that the neurobiological cognition of living systems brings forth a "real" world, the stories that human beings tell about themselves and their environments are also essential acts of creation in which "words [are] made flesh, muscle and bone animated by hope and desire, belief materialized in deeds, deeds which crystallize our actualities."[37] More than any other social mechanism, stories of origin and environment—performed through oral (and later written) narrative, ritual, music, visual art, and dance—enable both the invention and the codification of a world.

Notably, Wynter's descriptions about the third event and the making of human worlds through storytelling are almost always accompanied by the term "religion." For example, in her dialogue with McKittrick, she explains that with the third event of language is the "already presupposed . . . behavior-regulatory phenomenon of religion, together with its vast range of Holy Kosmoi."[38] This is an interesting assertion, as Wynter never really defines what exactly she means by religion (specifically as that which is "already presupposed" in the third event) except in terms of somewhat vague references to "storytelling," "myth," "cosmogony," and "extrahuman" agents of determination. Sticking with the autopoietic framework of cognition and human language helps clarify Wynter's thinking and fill in a working definition of religion in the third event.

As we have already established, the human difference as a hybrid species of *bios/logos* is language's capacity to create out of a linguistic domain an observational perspective of a "self" that is sustained through stories and narratives that situate it in a specific temporal and environmental frame of reference. Wynter stresses that this "sociogenic" mode of creation is subject to the same autopoietic cognitive laws of all biological organisms, meaning that all human groups "must know the world, too, in response to the *telos* of securing the conditions of the subject's realizing its system-specific mode of being, as imagined in its governing template of identity."[39] In the third event, there is continuity with the second event biology of autopoietic cognition in the "genetic" basis of group bonding (which includes the production of "linguistic domains"), while at the same time a discontinuity in the emergent operation of language that sets loose the form of life to produce its own narrative schema of existence. For Wynter, it seems that "religion" enters the picture as the primary languaging act that makes the narrative framing of human life possible. Its function appears to be that which bridges the difference between the ontogenic basis of social bonding and the introduction of narrative as a new basis of group cohesion. Where the ontogeny of living systems operates around a "biochemical system of reward and punishment"[40] that structurally regulates the system's bio-neuro-chemical response to physical environmental perturbations, the sociogeny of human groups takes on this rewards/punishment schema and "transposes" it onto *symbolic* sanctions through language. For Wynter, this transposition seems to be the key operation of religion. As she describes in "The Ceremony Must Be Found,"

> the link of continuity/discontinuity [between pre-linguistic biological processes and human language] is the shift from genetic to rhetorical-figurative systems of group bonding, with the latter carrying affective loadings from the former and the inheritable programs which determined cognition/behaviors being transferred to the governing systems of figuration called religion. For it was this system of figuration which now took the place of the environment of its rewards/punishment sanction systems, replacing it with the sanction systems of the gods and then of the Single God.[41]

In this formulation, religion emerges precisely as a social mechanism of "affective load bearing" for complex human language systems. It enables what was once limited to the pre-language function of cognitive responses to environmental perturbations to be rhetorically and narratively offloaded as a languaging operation of the collective self's social preservation and reproduction. In this way, religion in Wynter's third event should be understood as a specific kind of autopoietic operation of the *hybrid* human being that is crucial to its emergence and flourishing. So crucial, in fact, that

> religion had . . . been isomorphic with the hominization process of the human itself. It enabled this new mode of being, the bearer of self-consciousness, to win its way from more closed to more open programs of co-identification and of cognition, handing down what it had won . . . as a human cultural heritage in the long perspective of the processes . . . of the human's collective self-making.[42]

The "new mode of being" that religion enables is the key difference between the second and third events in Wynter's thinking. When human culture emerged as a program of collective self-identification through language, religion was there from the beginning as that mechanism which provided the stories codifying the communal self. This much is clear in Wynter's thinking. Because of this important role in human self-creation, I propose the term "autoreligion" as a reference to this specific autopoietic operation in Wynter's understanding of the third event.

The Autoreligious Code

If "autoreligion" was there from the beginning and plays the role of transposing the genetic rewards/punishment schema of biological autopoiesis onto symbolic language, there still remains the question of what exactly makes up the specific content of religion that would differentiate its mode of cultural production from other sociocultural systems or mechanisms. The primary theme that tends to show up whenever Wynter discusses the autoreligious origins of human storytelling is the narrative production of transcendent forces of determination. One of the names she gives to these forces is the "Sacred Logos," which, "by ritually prescribing what *had* to be said, and what *had* to be done," predetermines the form and proper mode of being for each human genre. Wynter emphasizes that this Sacred Logos and its directives are no less powerful in their behavior compulsion than the genetic autopoietic operations of "purely organic forms of life."[43] The experience of this compulsion as "lawlike" happens as autoreligion functions to conceal the auto-instituted nature of the Sacred Logos by connecting it to a story of transcendent order given from beyond. Following the work of anthropologist Maurice Godelier, autoreligion and the Sacred Logos are linked to the production of an "extrahuman agency of supernatural Imaginary Beings . . . [which] has been total in the case of all human orders."[44] Godelier calls this production the "disappearance" of "real humans" through the sociogenic appearance of transcendent or "imaginary" "superhuman beings" which symbolically take their place and "[obliterates] from the conscious mind the *active presence* of man [sic] at his own origin."[45] In this "*occultation* of reality" there is an "*inversion* of the relationship between cause and effect."[46] In Wynter's autoreligious frame, this means human beings experience themselves as the effect of an "extrahuman" cause, which allows them "to repress the recognition of [their] collective production of [their] modes of social reality."[47] In other words, as the affective bridge between the genetic and the rhetorical-figurative, stories of supernatural agents and their determinations of origin and environment enable human beings to "offload" a recognition of their own genetically auto-instituted modes of cognition onto a belief in a reality given in advance and from a point of transcendence. The range of possible "realities" in this operation is virtually infinite. Autoreligion is the vehicle through which it is possible for "each mode of sociogeny and its artificially imprinted *sense of self* to be created as one able to override, where necessary, the genetic-instinctual sense of self, at the same time as it itself comes to be subjectively *experienced as if it were instinctual.*"[48]

The autoreligious production of transcendent "extrahuman" agents of determination is essential for genres of being human to develop their respective governing systems of figuration that mark a particular sense of self. In this operation, each genre of being human invents its own Sacred Logos and accompanying cosmogonic reality. Wynter, drawing from Gregory Bateson and James Danielli, refers to this as the "descriptive statement" which sets the specific "mode of the 'I' and correlated symbolically/

altruistically bonded mode of the eusocial 'we.'"[49] One of the implications of this, and one that Wynter attempts to think beyond in her constructive "autopoetic turn/overturn," is that in the third event there is no imperative of social solidarity across differing human cultures. As autopoietic social systems, genres of being human are conditioned by a *lawlike* operational closure where "there is . . . *no such altruism towards, or genuine co-identification with* those whom our founding origin narratives have defined by the oppositionally meaningful marker of Otherness to the 'us.'"[50] The integration of outsiders may occur, but only through a structural process of filtering them as environmental "perturbations" that are then operationally subordinated to the proper "we" of the particular genre of being human.

The distinction between the social inside and the outside (system and environment) enables a range of other distinctions that serve the purpose of fortifying and reproducing a "mode of desire" in which a series of oppositional codes set the specific parameters of proper behavior and expectations of the social order.[51] The production and repetition of these codes are the "ceremony" that legitimates and grounds each genre of being human's sociogeny. Wynter often frames this around the "master code of symbolic life (the name of what is good) and death (the name of what is evil)" that she links to religious schemas of inclusion and exclusion.[52] It is through this master code (and its twin "order/chaos") that the binary between the proper community and its existentially threatening others is narrativized and made "real" through praxis. This has been the case for all human social orders. For example, Wynter points to the organization of the royal dynasty of the Bakama cult of Iron Age East Africa, which defined itself in part through the marginalization of the spirit-medium cults of the Bacwezi.[53] The royal dynasty was able to ascend only when "it had managed to transform the conceptions of Life/Death, Order/Chaos, with its newly created Bakama cult coming to signify Culture/Safety and the Bacwezi coming to be figured as a 'dangerous uncivilized force' against which the royal order needs to confirm its legitimacy as the bearer of 'Life' to the Bacwezi 'death.'"[54] As Wynter traces, the same kind of binary coding and resulting practices of exclusion show up in the Medieval European scapegoating of Jews and Muslims as the contaminating threat to the "true Christian subject," the European colonial enslavement and segregation of "Indians" and "Negroes" in the New World separating the "irrational" from the "rational," and the Darwinian marking of Africans as evolutionarily "dysselected" against the "selected" white Europeans. In each case, the former functions as the "name of what is evil" to the latter's "name of what is good," marking the autoreligious coding of Man's social self and its imperative of maintaining its descriptive statement and accompanying "ceremony."

Autoreligion, Christianity, and Secular Man

For Wynter, autoreligion is a general function of the third event and the emergence of human language and storytelling. While it is difficult to parse where autoreligion ends and other social systems of cultural production begin, historically autoreligion manifests most clearly in particular religious-cultural forms that have produced specific Gods or other extra-human agents of supernatural determination. In her earlier work, Wynter gives much attention to a range of particular religious forms, most notably those Afro-Caribbean traditions which were forged in the fires of European colonialism and slavery and represent counter-cosmogonies to the dominant religion and culture.[55] Across her post-1984 academic work, Medieval European Christianity is the only particular religious form that Wynter consistently engages in depth. In her focus on the modern Christian West's genre of being human, "Man," the Medieval European proto-racial distinction between "True Christian" and its "untrue other" provides the foundation for Man's ascendence as the "overdetermined" global model of a universal human form. While Christianity still held an explicit influence on the conceptual and political order of early modern Man ("Man1"), Wynter describes later Man ("Man2") as having moved beyond the particular religion of Christianity as its conceptual ground while still holding on to the racial, sexual, and colonial distinctions it had set in place. For Wynter, Man2 in its nineteenth- and twentieth-century context marks the culmination of an "exit from religion" which had first been set in motion by the "heresy" of the *Studio Humanitas* and its humanist overturning of the Medieval scholastic order of theological knowledge in the fourteenth century.[56] What this "exit" opened up, first by way of the Cartesian rational subject and the advent of the modern secular state, and later through Darwinian concepts of a purely biocentric human essence, was the idea that human life is determined by laws of nature and (secular) politics as opposed to theological laws.[57] The displacement of the Church and theology by the secular state and the natural sciences marks the disenchantment or, as Wynter describes it, "degodding" of the world. Man's ascent seems to coincide precisely with religion's decline as the primary ground of knowledge and truth.

It is important to keep in mind that when Wynter describes this transition into the secular era, she is referring primarily to the West's shift away from the explicitly Christian-scholastic *episteme* of the Medieval period.

At times, however, Wynter appears to suggest that what is happening in this shift is the epistemic disappearance of religion as such—"autoreligion"— as if this were a social function exclusive to those that either preceded or now exist as Man(2)'s others and which has completely fallen away as a mechanism through which human being is understood in the era of Western scientific rationality and biocentricity. For example, in "The Ceremony Found," citing anthropologists Sylvia Yaganisako and Carol Delaney, she notes that whereas myth and religion have been key factors in the evolutionary development of human cultures, "both have now been 'relegated to a dim past,' as stages that *we* have outgrown and replaced with *science*."[58] This claim is further reinforced with Wynter's frequent use of the term "secular" as a description of Man2's current epistemic hegemony on a global scale. Yet alongside these claims Wynter continues to describe Man2 as an *episteme* driven by stories of "extrahuman" agents of determination, the very function of autoreligion. While the language of "supernatural" determination is no longer employed by Man, if held against the specific way in which Wynter understands autoreligion in the third event, Man is still every bit as religious as the Medieval Christian subject, or, for that matter, the East African Bakama cult of the Iron Age. This is clear when considering that the "natural" determination referred to under the biocentric names "evolution" and "natural selection," with their "imagined entity of 'Race,'" is just as much of a *story* as was that of the divine creation in the Abrahamic traditions or the demiurge in Greek mythology.[59] In Man2's *episteme*, theories of evolution and race clearly function as narratives of an extrahuman objective order that has determined a "natural" hierarchical division of the species. The story of evolution, just like that of the Medieval "true Christian" or Man1's "rational subject," is projected *as if* the species were naturally divided into a hierarchy of "races" and all human beings were "selected" by evolution to behave in particular ways that are predetermined and unchangeable. If such a projection goes by the name "secular," then secularism is still very much an autoreligious story.

The Critique of Man and the Autopoetic Turn/Overturn

There are two main avenues of Wynter's critique of Man. On the one hand, the *episteme* of Man is a scourge of the earth. Its overdetermined conception of the human is responsible for the global colonial order, racism(s) and the color line, and the out-of-control spiral of imperial-capitalist-driven climate change that threatens the very habitability of the Earth. On the other hand, as Wynter consistently points out, the cognitive "breakthroughs" that have accompanied Man's overdetermination have given human beings an unprecedented potential to know the world in more and more precise ways. While this knowledge has produced various "dazzling triumphs" of techno-scientific knowledge, the problem is that they are "half-starved," meaning for Wynter that "they remain incapable of giving us any knowledge of our uniquely human domain, and have nothing to say to the urgent problems that beleaguer humankind."[60] This is not simply because of Man's relation to the violence and incoherency of settler-colonialism and fantasies of universality—although these are not insignificant aspects of its starvation—but also because Man, just like all other genres of being human before it, still operates within two overarching "prices" paid by human beings in their third event, autoreligious emergence. First, because the particular "life/death" and "good/evil" codes of each genre of being human are linked to the "opiate reward and punishment biochemical implementing mechanisms of the brain," each genre (Man included) remains *"non-consciously* subordinated" to the symbolic codes governing their production of reality. Second, the stories that have enabled and differentiated each genre of being human must function "lawlikely" as "the imperative boundary of *psycho-affective closure*" that prevents the possibility of inter-genre altruism and solidarity.[61] For Wynter, both "prices" were effects of the third event rupture with the genetically determined limits of purely biological life forms. In other words, for the duration of human history, these unconscious subordinations to closed symbolic codes and stories—to autoreligion—have been the condition of being human.[62]

What Wynter wagers, however, is that we are now at a historical moment in which a new "breakthrough" is possible that would undo our subordination to the subjective codes and narratives that close one genre of being human off from another. In the twentieth century, the first glimmers of this breakthrough became visible in various formal scientific disciplines (most notably cognitive science and the category of autopoiesis) and the sociological and poetic interventions of Black intellectuals such as W. E. B. Du Bois, Frantz Fanon, C. L. R. James, and Aimé Césaire. Wynter argues that a new mode of consciousness has become possible through interventions such as Fanon's "sociogenic principle" and Thomas Nagel's "objective phenomenology," both premised on the recognition of the sociogenically produced "particularity of the point of view" of each specific form of life while postulating a "'common reality' outside the terms of that point of view."[63] The "common reality" outside each genre names the "transcultural constant" of each culturally programmed sense of self that is *not* tied to any genetically programmed ontogeny.[64] The study of genres of being human in relative relation to this common outside reality would be the basis of an "autopoetic turn/overturn" or "new science of the word" that would be grounded in the *hybrid* nature of human *bios-logos,* as opposed to the biocentric framework of the modern natural sciences. Elsewhere I have referred to this two-level, hybrid perspective as Wynter's "human real," or the unity of distinction between each genre's own autopoietic and therefore virtual "reality" and the "common" trans-genre reality that exists outside it.[65] It is the discovery of this unity that is the basis of the new science in which an "external observer" is established that "[brings] together... that which is observed from many different observer positions, enabling each to extend and to cancel out elements of the other."[66] In this collective observation of the universal fact of hybrid human autopoiesis, humanity collectively reorients itself to be set free from Man's biocentric reduction and be able to consciously live into its shared horizon of an indeterminate humanity.

As Wynter argues, it is Frantz Fanon who first discovers such an outside perspective in his realization that the "self-evident consciousness" of the Euro-colonial world is, in fact, a very particular form of socially conditioned consciousness premised on the "lawlike" structure of anti-Blackness that permeates all experience within its boundaries. "It is precisely this self-evident consciousness," Wynter writes, "that Fanon has found himself not only compelled to call into question, but also to indict, as it itself is the cause of the Black's autophobia as well as the white's anti-Black 'aberration of affect.'"[67] In *Black Skin, White Masks,* when Fanon finds himself under the white gaze "an object among other objects," he realizes that the sense of self he has been given as a colonized subject, as the product of an autopoietic (and in my terms *autoreligious*) production of the colonizer's own virtual-subjective reality, is one that "compels him to know his body *through* the terms of an always already imposed 'historico-racial schema'; a schema that predefines his body as an impurity to be cured... to be amended into the 'true' being of whiteness."[68] It is this realization that leads Fanon to take the "leap" of invention outside the anti-Black terms of order and set out anew in conscious self-creation. While in *Black Skin, White Masks* Fanon leaves this invention as an ellipsis, Wynter looks to the poetic praxis of Black intellectuals and artists as a concrete way forward for the new science. In her *ProudFlesh* interview with Greg Thomas, for example, she notes that Black popular music and other forms of Black artistic expression are so important because "essentially, they're part of the process by which we are transforming the *poiesis* of being.... You could call it *the new autopoetics of cognition.*"[69] What Black music and other forms of cultural production in resistance and refusal of Man's overdetermination show is that it is precisely in the conscious and creative praxis of human beings that new worlds and futures become possible.

There is an interesting tension in reference to autoreligion in Wynter's gestures toward the new "autopoetic" modes of these artistic examples, which she sometimes describes through terms such as "spiritual," "soul," and even "religious."[70] That is, the "autopoetic turn/overturn" seems to necessitate the rejection of and movement beyond the *autoreligious* function of storytelling while moving toward a new mode of collective storytelling grounded in self-conscious invention. The achieved knowledge of the hybrid and autopoietic nature of human worlds not only has made autoreligious "illusions" of extrahuman agents of determination unnecessary for human existence but also has completely exposed the now global existential threat of Man's fantasies of anthropological universality.[71] For Wynter, this means it is now imperative for the collective future of human beings and their earthly environments that they move beyond the illusions of autoreligion and fully recognize their own particular autopoietic creations through the new scientific objectivity and poetics of the trans-genre common outside.

However, while Wynter's reference to the illusions of autoreligion are rightfully aimed at Man2's "substitute religion 'evolution'" and any other "extrahuman" fantasy that would repress the fact of its human auto-institution and keep the violent story of Man going,[72] there are questions regarding what this means for other genres of being human, including the "counter-cosmogonies" and other ostensibly autoreligious productions of otherwise worlds against Man. If autoreligion is something to be consciously done away with in the autopoetic turn/overturn, what exactly is the status of particular contemporary religions in Wynter's vision of the liberated human future? While affirmative explorations of the religious sensibilities of Afro-Caribbean traditions abound in her early work, and while there are some references to counter-religious traditions such as Rastafarianism in her post-1984 work, it seems that her critique of Man and the implementation of the autopoetic turn/overturn is premised on the necessity of rejecting the specifically *religious* nature of those examples, at least to the extent that they are premised on a belief in or adherence to transcendent, extrahuman forces of determination. While this seems necessary in terms of exposing Man's autoreligious fantasies of universality, would these religious and/or cultural traditions also be called to transcend their own claims to cosmic truth and determination via the universality of sociogeny and an objective phenomenology? Is the valorization of the new science and the need to objectively separate it from one's own particular perception of reality the *only* way to get beyond the overdetermination of Man? Would this imperative be plausible for all human communities living in resistance to Man, including those invested in religious and theological descriptions of reality?

Furthermore, if autoreligion is an essential function of the third event and therefore human being's *logos*, how exactly would one know that there has been a breakthrough to a truly objective common outside of the autoreligious production? Wynter's sociogenic principle posits that a true objectivity of human social production via the collective observation of human being's virtual worlds of perception is possible—that the "new science" can somehow itself avoid the third event "price" of psycho-affective closure and the "blind spots" of subjective observation.[73] It is interesting that Wynter still employs the language of "transcendence" when she describes the achievement of the new science, as if this term most often associated with religion remains a necessary device for writing a new story of our shared human existence. As she writes in "Towards the Sociogenic Principle," the new science would be "able to harness the findings of the natural sciences (including the neurosciences) to its purposes, yet able to *transcend* them in the terms of a new synthesis able to make our uniquely hybrid nature/culture modes of being human, of human identity, subject to 'scientific description in a new way.'"[74] If the new science has enabled human beings to achieve a transcultural perspective of objectivity in which they, from the transcendence of an outside "trans-genre-of-the-human perspective,"[75] can now describe their own immanent productions of reality as *human* productions, how would one know if this is not still an autoreligious story of transcendence that conceptually elevates "the self-inscripting human" precisely as an "extrahuman" agent able to produce a desirable future for all particular human groups?

Wynter's new science provides invaluable resources for moving beyond the biocentric story of Man and thinking an ecumenical human future in which investigations of human being's hybrid existence open up new pathways for the production of knowledge beyond Man's epistemological regime and its systems of racial violence. One of the most powerful pathways Wynter forges is the reorientation of human being not as essence, but as praxis—as the auto-institution of worlds through the poetically embodied animation of hope and desire. In this reorientation, the knowledge and conscious harnessing of this auto-institution marks a potentially revolutionary mode of forging new worlds and interhuman alliances. Yet, with a scruple of hesitation that, perhaps as the last vestige of autoreligion and the third event, pulls us back from the assurance of collective self-determination at the very instant of scientific knowledge, maybe we, which would appear to still remain a particular "we" even in its observational transcendence, have yet to truly see behind the curtain.[76] Maybe the inability to see behind it is precisely what keeps us open to whatever possibilities might exist beyond it.

Notes

1. David Christian, *Maps of Time: An Introduction to Big History* (Berkeley: University of California Press, 2004), 2.

2. See Charles H. Long, *Significations: Signs, Symbols, and Images in the Interpretation of Religion*, 2nd ed. (Aurora, CO: Davies Group, 1999).

3. Christian, *Maps of Time*, 2.

4. Sylvia Wynter, "The Ceremony Must Be Found: After Humanism," in *"On Humanism and the University I: The Discourse of Humanism"*, ed. William Spanos, special issue, *boundary 2* 12, no. 3/13, no. 1 (1984): 19–70.

5. Sylvia Wynter, "The Ceremony Found: Towards the Autopoetic Turn/Overturn, Its Autonomy of Human Agency and Extraterritoriality of (Self-)Cognition," in *Black Knowledges/Black Struggles: Essays in Critical Epistemology*, ed. Jason R. Ambroise and Sabine Broeck (Liverpool: Liverpool University Press, 2015), 207.

6. Sylvia Wynter and Katherine McKittrick, "Unparalleled Catastrophe for Our Species? Or, to Give Humanness a Different Future: Conversations," in *Sylvia Wynter: On Being Human as Praxis*, ed. Katherine McKittrick (Durham, NC: Duke University Press, 2015), 25.

7. See Christian, *Maps of Time*, 16.

8. David Scott, "The Re-enchantment of Humanism: An Interview with Sylvia Wynter," *Small Axe: A Caribbean Journal of Criticism* 8 (September 2000): 196.

9. Richard Rorty, *Philosophy and the Mirror of Nature* (Princeton, NJ: Princeton University Press, 1979).

10. Humberto R. Maturana and Francisco J. Varela, *Autopoiesis and Cognition: The Realization of the Living*, 2nd ed. (Dordrecht: D. Reidel, 1980), xvi–xvii. Also see Varela's account of the development of the term in Francisco J. Varela, "The Early Days of Autopoiesis: Heinz and Chile," *Systems Research* 13, no. 3 (1996): 407–16.

11. The full definition states: "*An autopoietic machine is a machine organized (defined as a unity) as a network of processes of production (transformation and destruction) of components that produces the components which: (i) through their interactions and transformations continuously regenerate and realize the network of processes (relations) that produced them; and (ii) constitute it (the machine) as a concrete unity in the space in which they (the components) exist by specifying the topological domain of its realization as such a network*" (italics in original). Maturana and Varela, *Autopoiesis and Cognition*, 78–79.

12. Maturana and Varela, *Autopoiesis and Cognition*, 78–79.

13. Humberto R. Maturana and Bernhard Poerksen, *From Being to Doing: The Origins of the Biology of Cognition* (Heidelberg: Carl Auer International, 2004), 34.

14. Humberto R. Maturana and Francisco J. Varela, *The Tree of Knowledge: The Biological Roots of Human Understanding*, rev. ed. (Boston: Shambhala, 1987), 89.

15. Maturana and Varela, 169. Emphasis mine.

16. Cary Wolfe, *What Is Posthumanism?* (Minneapolis: University of Minnesota Press, 2010), 15; Niklas Luhmann, *Social Systems*, trans. John Bednarz Jr. with Dirk Baecker (Stanford, CA: Stanford University Press, 1995).

17. Maturana and Varela, *Tree of Knowledge*, 47. Luhmann, *Social Systems*, 37.

18. Cary Wolfe, *Critical Environments: Postmodern Theory and the Pragmatics of the "Outside"* (Minneapolis: University of Minnesota Press, 1998), 60.

19. Maturana and Varela, *Tree of Knowledge*, 74.

20. Maturana and Varela, 133.

21. Francisco J. Varela, Evan Thompson, and Eleanor Rosch, *The Embodied Mind: Cognitive Science and Human Experience*, rev. ed. (Cambridge, MA: MIT Press, 2016), 172.

22. Maturana and Varela, *Tree of Knowledge*, 133–35.

23. Wynter, "Ceremony Found," 215.

24. Wynter, 217.

25. Wynter and McKittrick, "Unparalleled Catastrophe for Our Species?," 25.

26. Maturana and Varela, *Tree of Knowledge*, 193. For Maturana and Varela, individual cells are understood as "first order" unities, and multicellular organisms are understood as "second order" unities.

27. "By *cultural behavior* we mean the transgenerational stability of behavioral patterns ontogenically acquired in the communicative dynamics of a social environment." Maturana and Varela, *Tree of Knowledge*, 201.

28. Maturana and Varela, 207.

29. Maturana and Varela, 210.

30. Maturana and Varela, 210.

31. Maturana and Varela, 211.

32. Maturana and Varela, 220.

33. Maturana and Varela, 222.

34. Maturana and Varela, 222.

35. Christian, *Maps of Time*, 146.

36. Christian, 147.

37. Sylvia Wynter, "The Pope Must Have Been Drunk, the King of Castile a Madman: Culture as Actuality, and the Caribbean Rethinking Modernity," in *The Reordering of Culture: Latin America, the Caribbean, and Canada in the Hood*, ed. Alvina Ruprecht and Cecilia Taiana (Ottawa: Carleton University Press, 1995), 35.

38. Wynter and McKittrick, "Unparalleled Catastrophe for Our Species?," 25–26.

39. Wynter, "Ceremony Must Be Found," 24.

40. Wynter, "Ceremony Found," 211.

41. Wynter, "Ceremony Must Be Found," 24.

42. Wynter, 25. Here, Wynter is drawing from John Gowlett, *Ascent to Civilization: The Archaeology of Early Man* (New York: Alfred A. Knopf, 1984).

43. Sylvia Wynter, "Towards the Sociogenic Principle: Fanon, Identity, the Puzzle of Conscious Experience, and What It Is Like to Be 'Black,'" in *National Identities and Sociopolitical Changes in Latin America*, ed. Mercedes F. Durán-Cogan and Antonio Gómez-Moriana (New York: Routledge, 2001), 46.

44. Sylvia Wynter, "Unsettling the Coloniality of Being/Power/Truth/Freedom: Towards the Human, after Man, Its Overrepresentation—an Argument," *CR: The New Centennial Review* 3, no. 3 (2003): 273. Also see Maurice Godelier, *The Enigma of the Gift*, trans. Nora Scott (Chicago: University of Chicago Press, 1999), 171–75.

45. Godelier, *Enigma of the Gift*, 171.

46. Godelier, 171.
47. Wynter, "Unsettling the Coloniality of Being/Power/Truth/Freedom," 273.
48. Wynter, "Towards the Sociogenic Principle," 48.
49. Wynter, "Unsettling the Coloniality of Being/Power/Truth/Freedom," 274.
50. Sylvia Wynter, "Columbus and the Poetics of the *Propter Nos*," *Annals of Scholarship* 8, no. 2 (1991): 263.
51. Wynter, "Ceremony Must Be Found," 27.
52. Scott and Wynter, "Re-enchantment of Humanism," 179.
53. See Peter R. Schmidt, *Historical Archaeology: A Structural Approach in an African Culture*, rev. ed. (Westport, CT: Praeger, 1978).
54. Wynter, "Ceremony Must Be Found," 27.
55. See especially Sylvia Wynter, "*Black Metamorphosis: New Natives in a New World*," unpublished manuscript, IBW Papers, Schomburg Center for Research in Black Culture, New York, Box (Sylvia Wynter), and *The Hills of Hebron* (Kingston: Ian Randle, 2010).
56. Wynter and McKittrick, "Unparalleled Catastrophe for Our Species?," 26. Also see Wynter, "Ceremony Must Be Found."
57. Wynter, "Towards the Sociogenic Principle," 55: "the postulate of the non-arbitrarily and autonomously functioning (rather than divinely and arbitrarily regulated) laws of nature . . . indispensable to the emergence of the natural sciences."
58. Wynter, "Ceremony Found," 215.
59. Wynter, "Unsettling the Coloniality of Being/Power/Truth/Freedom," 273.
60. Wynter, 328.
61. Wynter, "Ceremony Found," 218.
62. Oludamini Ogunnaike's chapter in this volume provides a convincing and compelling critique that unconscious subordination to closed codes and stories is *not* a universal human experience, and that many indigenous African genres of being human have historically developed consciously open inter-altruistic forms of life.
63. Wynter, "Towards the Sociogenic Principle," 55.
64. Wynter, 59.
65. David Kline, *Racism and the Weakness of Christian Identity: Religious Autoimmunity* (London: Routledge, 2020), 36.
66. Wynter, "Ceremony Must Be Found," 48.
67. Wynter, "Towards the Sociogenic Principle," 56.
68. Wynter, 41.
69. Sylvia Wynter and Greg Thomas, "ProudFlesh Inter/Views: Sylvia Wynter," *ProudFlesh: New Afrikan Journal of Culture, Politics and Consciousness* 4 (2006): 33.
70. See, for example, the *ProudFlesh* interview where she discusses Black popular music as "bringing the spiritual into the secular" and also finding analogy with the Islamic *umma* ("ProudFlesh," 33); or her references to Jamaican Rastafarian "politico-religious" counter-cosmogonies in "Ceremony Found" (207).
71. Wynter, "Ceremony Found," 245.
72. Wynter and Thomas, "ProudFlesh," 31–32.
73. On the unavoidable blind spot of all autopoietic observation, see the work of Niklas Luhmann.
74. Wynter, "Sociogenic Principle," 60 (emphasis mine).
75. Scott and Wynter, "Re-enchantment of Humanism," 206.
76. On religion as "scruple," see Émile Benveniste, *Indo-European Language and Society*, trans. Elizabeth Palmer (Miami, FL: University of Miami, 1973), 519–52.

2 / Symbolic Rebirth and Ceremonies Never Lost: African Religions and the Paradoxical Progressivism of Sylvia Wynter's Work

Oludamini Ogunnaike

Let humanity consider from what it was created.
—QUR'AN 86:5

. . . *a wa gẹgẹbi ènìyàn,*	We as human beings,
a wa ni Olódùmarè yàn	We are those whom God has chosen,
láti ló tún ilé ayé ṣe,	to renew the world,
Ẹni-a yàn ni wa . . .	We are the chosen ones.

—ODÙ ÌROSÙN-ÌWÒRÌ

For He permeates existence, so none denies Him but someone who is delimited. But the Folk of Allah follow Him whose folk they are, so His property flows over them and His property is the lack of delimitation, for He possesses all-pervading Being; so His folk possess all-pervading vision. When someone delimits His Being, he delimits his own vision of Him; such a one is not of the Folk of Allah.

—IBN AL-ʿARABĪ

Since the 15th century, the idea of Africa has mingled together new scientific and ideological interpretations with the semantic fields and concepts such as primitivism and savagery. The geographic expansion of Europe and its civilization was then a holy saga of mythic proportions. The only problem—and it is a big one—is that, as this civilization developed, it submitted the world to its memory.

—V. Y. MUDIMBE

I was first introduced to the work of Sylvia Wynter in 2018, when a colleague read an article based on a graduate seminar paper of mine, remarking that my thesis was very similar to that developed by Wynter.[1] The next year, I attended a panel at the American Academy of Religion on the significance of Sylvia Wynter's work for the philosophy of religion, whose participants introduced me to more of Wynter's oeuvre and the burgeoning literature on and inspired by it.[2] For me, it was love at first read. I felt as if I had found an "intellectual auntie" (in the African sense of a relationship of deep affinity and respect). In many of the areas I had tried to explore in my own work (neuroscience, African religions, art, poetry, education as initiation, decoloniality), I found that the brilliant, dancing flame of Sylvia Wynter's intellect had already preceded me.[3] I am only disappointed that I had not begun to read her work earlier, as I believe it would have significantly improved my educational formation and work, giving voice and structure and argument to many of the intuitions and misgivings I had, but struggled to write—but better late than never, I suppose.

However, my late introduction to Wynter's work meant that in addition to operating from a distinct problem space,[4] background, and institutional and extra-academic training (for me, the disciplines of African and Religious Studies and the "extracurricular" traditions of West African Sufism, Ifá and Òrìṣà worship, and Islamic philosophy), led me to distinct approaches to some of the same topics and themes. It is these distinctions and similarities that I wish to explore in this essay, after first giving a brief summary of Wynter's later work and its significance for the study of African and Afro-diasporic religions. Specifically, I will explore how the study of African religions, including Islam,[5] can complicate some of Wynter's arguments (particularly in relation to cosmology, transcendence/transculture, and teleology) and suggest that the self-consciously autopoietic Second Emergence for which Wynter calls is, in a sense, already present in traditions such as Ifá and certain forms of Sufism (not to mention other religious traditions). In particular I will examine how the different formations of "transcendence" in traditional African religions and "transculture" in Wynter's constructive project lead to different orders of inclusion and exclusion, and different visions of change. Finally, I will conclude by arguing that Wynter's work functions as a kind of *upāya* (liberating ruse) that works within the present, biocentric Western order of knowledge to liberate us from it (from the "inside-out"), while traditions such as Ifá and Sufism continue to function from epistemological grounds "outside" this order, complementing Wynterian and other decolonial approaches by working from the "outside-in."

Wynter's Work and Its Significance for the Study of African Religions

> At the very time when it often mouths the word, the West has never been further from being able to live a true humanism—a humanism made to the measure of the world.
>
> —AIMÉ CÉSAIRE

> Human beings are magical. Bios and Logos. Words made flesh, muscle and bone animated by hope and desire, belief materialized in deeds, deeds which crystallize our realities.
>
> —SYLVIA WYNTER

Wynter's Theory of the Human

Summarizing Wynter's multifaceted oeuvre is not an easy task, particularly because her wide-ranging and erudite work is always evolving,[6] but it all seems to revolve around a few key arguments and themes grounded in her theory of the Human.[7] In various ways, Wynter identifies the root of our current problems as resulting from the overrepresentation of a particular, limited, normative conception of Man (rooted in the colonial, humanist, bioscientific, and economic projects of Western modernity) as if it were humanity as such, and the resulting denial or marginalization of other modes of being human that undergird our current order of knowledge and sociopolitical hierarchies.[8] Drawing on Thomas Kuhn's work on scientific paradigms, Michel Foucault's work on epistemes (orders of knowledge), Clifford Geertz, Jacob Pandian, and Asmaron Legesse's work in anthropology and much, much more, Wynter traces the genealogy of this current overrepresented conception of Man from the origins of humanity to the early twenty-first century, arguing against the Marxist conception that infrastructure or economic production determines and is separable from superstructure or culture, but instead that "the phenomenon of culture rather than 'nature' or 'history' . . . provides the ground of all human existential reality or actuality."[9] She further explains: "No order can exist except as it exists within the logic of a formulation of a general order of existence; and this is elaborated by intellectuals, whether theologians or shamans or ourselves. . . . The heresy I'm putting forward is that capitalism is itself a function of the reproduction of 'Man,' that 'Man' whose conception we institute in our disciplines."[10]

Specifically, she argues that "*we humans cannot pre-exist our cosmogonies or origin myths/stories/narratives* any more than a bee, at the purely biological level of life, can pre-exist its beehive."[11]

In various essays, Wynter traces the development and "mutations" of the "genres" or various practices of being human, beginning from the "First Emergence" when human beings in Africa first self-consciously designated themselves as separate from their environments through the creation of origin myths and rituals that defined themselves, their society, and their boundaries. Wynter identifies this act of self-definition or "auto-inscription" with Fanon's "sociogeny" (society/culture being both "what a human being creates and *what creates a human being*"[12]) and the biological term "autopoiesis,"[13] explaining that humans create these origin myths and rituals which they use to define and shape their own humanity, but then occlude this act of self-creation by projecting them as extrahumanly and aculturally—that is, supernaturally or naturally—ordained.[14] To give a more everyday analogy, people created the Captcha codes that we all have to click through to access certain websites. We may think that these codes, which are supposed to sort out human from nonhuman online visitors, are regulated and controlled by algorithms, but it is people who made these algorithms "in their own image" of what a human can do and is and what a "bot" cannot do and is not. Even more apropos, the so-called artificial intelligence programs used in everything from facial recognition to legal proceedings and the evaluation of job and university applications are often naïvely touted as being "objective" and "free of human bias," but have been repeatedly shown to merely amplify the biases of the creators of their algorithms and the data sets on which they are trained, typically centered around a wealthy, "pale, male" norm overrepresented as if it were all—or the ideal form—of humanity.[15] These algorithmic codes are created by particular people, in a particular way, representing their particular ideals, but this act of creation is occluded and these codes are held up as being trans- or suprahuman, and thus silently structure the lives of the people over which they have been given dominion.

Likewise, the "codes" defining "Man and its human Others" are not only the means through which members of these cultures define and judge what a human is, but the means through which they experience being.[16] Wynter writes, "What is normally imperative to each culture-as-a-living system is that it know its reality adaptively, *i.e.*, in ways that can best orient the collective behaviors of its subjects, together with its mode of subjectivity (the I) and of conspecificity (the We)."[17] That each culture has limitations means that each judges others according to its own local ideal (imagined as acultural), rendering difference as deviance and privation from its specific ideal conception of the human subject, and moreover that members of the culture who deviate from its ideal self are also deemed inferior.[18]

Wynter argues that the theocentric European medieval dichotomy between Heaven/earth, supernatural/natural, spirit/flesh grounded the medieval Christian, supernatural "theological code" characterized by the social dichotomy between redeemed/fallen, priest/laity, and Christian/heathen. Through the processes of early modern imperial expeditions and the "degodding" of the Renaissance humanism, this code mutated to create what Wynter terms Man1, a rational and political subject, defined against its human Others, Indian serfs and Negro slaves, grounded in the dichotomy of rational man/irrational animal and natural law. The nineteenth-century "half-mythic, Darwinian origin narrative" biologized this narrative, giving rise to the next mutation of Man2—a bioeconomic conception of Man governed by physical laws and a racial code characterized by the dichotomy between the eugenic evolved / naturally selected and the dysgenic non-evolved, and the related Western bourgeoisie and its working-class, colonized, and native others.[19] This local ideal was globalized through colonialism, "neocolonialism," and education, becoming a global, hegemonic norm by which nearly all people are judged. Wynter argues that the competitive view of nature and human evolution that governs this order of knowledge is also reflected in Malthus's theory of natural scarcity, which then informs the metaphysical and even theological foundations of modern economics. Whereas in the theocentric medieval formulation, original sin was the illness and salvation mediated by the Church was the cure; in the ratio-centric early modern formation, madness/irrationality was the illness and reason mediated by the rational rule of the State was the cure; and in our current biocentric formation, scarcity and dysgenesis is the illness and health/wealth mediated by the invisible hand of natural selection and the free market is envisioned as the cure.[20] Wynter says,

> It is only the capitalist mode of production that can produce and reproduce our current biocentric, and therefore *economic*, integrating conception of being human. That conception is *the* imperative. This is why, however much abundance we can produce, we cannot solve the problem of poverty and hunger.... The goal of our mode of production is *not* to produce for human beings in general, it's to provide the material conditions of existence for the production and reproduction of our present conception of being human: to secure the well-being, therefore, of those of us, the global middle classes, who have managed to attain to its ethno-class criterion.[21]

Given the obvious obscene distributions of wealth, health, and violence in the current social order, which we can see in "the degradation of the jobless, of the incarcerated, the homeless, the archipelago of the underdeveloped / the expendable throwaways,"[22] Wynter argues that "the only cure will be a transformation of the whole society, and an entirely new knowledge order altogether—otherwise we will remain trapped in this."[23] This is because the current order of knowledge is so rooted in the overrepresentation of the racialized, biocentric Man2 as if it were the human itself that its disciplines continue to unconsciously reproduce the current hierarchies of humanity just as the "degodded" rational Renaissance/Enlightenment classical episteme reproduced and justified the emerging modern world order of Man1, and the theocentric episteme of medieval European Christendom reproduced and justified its own clerical-feudal order. This is due to the fact that

> as academics/intellectuals of our contemporary Western worldsystem, who are also its normative middle-class (i.e. bourgeois) subjects, we must necessarily function to elaborate the mode of knowledge production that is epistemologically indispensable to its replication as such a system. . . . In consequence—and as the indispensable condition of the formation and stable replication of each respective societal order, together with each order's answer given to the question of who-we-are by its cosmogonically chartered sociogenic replicator codes—*no ceremony could have been found* that would normally have freed human knowledge of the physical and purely biological levels of reality from the order-stabilizing, order-legitimating codes of symbolic life/death about which these realities had autopoetically instituted themselves as *genre*-specific living systems.[24]

That is, in spite of their/our rhetoric and radical posturing, the function of intellectuals and scholars of the present Western and Westernized academies is to legitimate and reproduce the epistemic and socio-politico-economic order of Man2, just as previous generations of scholars did for their conception of Man in Christendom and early modern Imperial Europe.

Wynter's Science of the Word and New Humanism

Thus, for Wynter, the only way out, the implementation of a "humanism made to the measure of the world," is through a new order of knowledge based on a new, transcultural, "science of the Word" (in Césaire's formulation)[25] that erases the division between the humanities and the sciences, culture and nature, language and matter, *mythos* and *bios*, to understand

and consciously operate on both the autopoietic, sociogenic and biological, material dimensions of being human, and their interactions.[26] Wynter says,

> Why could we not have continued to have our behaviours, necessitated entirely by our genetic programmes, as in the case of all other species? Why did our social behaviours have to be necessitated both by our genes and by our culture-specific codes? I am going to propose that the emergence of language should be seen in a somewhat different manner from which we now see it. That we see it instead as part of an entire ensemble of mutations by means of which we were bioevolutionarily pre-prepared both to artificially reprogramme our behaviours, by means of narratively encoded behaviour-motivating programmes . . . and at the same time artificially individuate/speciate the modes of the I and the we, for whom the behaviours motivated by the narrative schemas will be of adaptive advantage. This would therefore mean that the always already socialized, and therefore symbolically coded, orders of consciousness through which we experience ourselves as this or that mode of the human have to be seen as the expression of a mutation in the processes of evolution, one by means of which a new level of existence, discontinuous with evolution, is brought into existence or, rather, brings itself into existence. Therefore, you see, as a level whose self-instituting modes of being will respond to and know its order of reality, not in the species-specific terms of its genome, of its genomic principle, but in the genre-specific terms of its narratively prescribed master code or sociogenic principle.[27]

Elsewhere Wynter equates this "sociogenic principle" with "culture," commenting on Mikhail Epstein's maxim, "culture frees us from nature; transculture frees us from culture, any one culture":

> The problem here, nevertheless, is that while culture freed us from nature it was able to do so only on the condition of subordinating us to its own categories, since it is through all such culture specific categories that we can alone realize ourselves, as in Fanonian terms, always already socialized beings. Epstein's proposal here is therefore, that it is only transculture, the transcultural space opened between different cultures, that can in turn free us from our subordination to the categories of the single culture through the mediation of which we come to realize/experience ourselves as human beings.[28]

That is, in contrast to the naïve acultural framing of our present orders of knowledge, the opening of a transcultural space between or beyond such framings would allow us to understand these cultures and orders of knowledge from an "outside" vantage point that can include and understand all these cultural conditionings and limited genres of humanity. Wynter calls this creation of a new order of knowledge, or a new humanism, the "Second Emergence" (the "First Emergence" being the emergence of humans as a distinct, self-narrating species in Africa). She terms this First Emergence the "Third Event" (the first event being the emergence of the universe and the second event being the emergence of biological life), and argues that we need a new understanding of this Third Event, of how our ancestors first created themselves, in order to re-create ourselves beyond the present limited and exclusionary terms of being human. For Wynter (echoing Marx), such a transformation can only come "from below" or "from the margins" of the current order of knowledge (for her, particularly from disciplines such as Black studies):

> *The liminal categories* ... experience a structural contradiction between their lived experience and the grammar of representations which generate the mode of reality by prescribing the parameters of collective behaviors that dynamically bring that "reality" into being. The liminal frame of reference can provide ... "the outer view," from which perspective of the grammars of regularities of boundary and structure maintaining discourses are perceivable.[29]

Thus, Wynter characterizes her project as moving beyond the old partial humanisms (such as Man1 and Man 2) characterized by the schema of inclusion/exclusion whose truths were only *truths-for* a particular ethnoclass, a particular, limited genre of being human, toward a new universalism "whose *truth-for* will coincide with the empirical reality in which we now find ourselves, the single integrated history we now live."[30] She concludes,

> The problems we confront—that of the scandalous inequalities between rich and poor countries, of global warming and the disastrous effects of climate change, of large-scale epidemics such as AIDS—can be solved only if we can, for the first time, *experience* ourselves, not only as we do now, as this or that *genre* of the human, but also *as* human. A new mode of experiencing ourselves in which every mode of being human, every form of life that has ever been enacted, is a part of us. We, a part of them.[31]

Wynter on the Study of African Religions

> You see, part of what we need to do is to grapple with Africa itself. Because we all originated from Africa.... Where Africa as our "origin" becomes

important is in recognizing that if we are going to tell a different story of ourselves, we must grapple with the beginnings, in which Africa is not only important for Blacks but the *key*. They want us to think about Africa as a way to think about *affliction* but it is Africa that gives us so much of our language world, and gave us much of what has been transformed over time, and continues of course into the present. And so you see, we cannot have the Third Event without Africa right at the middle—because how do you tell the story differently if the *beginning* hasn't been grappled with? How can you have a Third Event, without Africa, which has given the world its character, playing a central role in claiming our *past, present and future* selves?

—SYLVIA WYNTER

Wynter's early work in her unpublished monograph, "*Black Metamorphosis*," and the essays collected in *We Must Learn to Sit Down Together and Talk about a Little Culture* anticipates—by decades—much of the best scholarship on the political, theological, cosmological, social, embodied, and performative dimensions of rituals, rebellions, sovereignty, festivals, masquerades, music, and dance in African and African-derived religious traditions. But in her later essays, the focus of the present chapter, which take up African religions in two ways: (1) as a mirror to relativize and reveal the similarly provincial, culturally specific, and auto-inscripted nature of the modern, Western order of knowledge and world system; and (2) as the site of her own origin myth of the "First Emergence," Africa and its "primitive" cultures and religious traditions are an important resource for understanding and constructing the "Second Emergence." Wynter's early work is significant in recognizing and underscoring the profound work that Africana religio-cultural traditions accomplished in "humanizing" the inhuman colonial landscape of the so-called New World and later, the colonized continent, particularly the role played by the radically different genres of humanity and orders of knowledge, society, geography, and cosmology that these traditions constructed in creating spaces in which Black people could survive and even thrive. Wynter's later work builds on these insights, underscoring for contemporary scholars of African traditions the importance of the "gaze from below, religio-political . . . counter cosmogon[ies]" that stand against current hegemonic orders of justice, knowledge, and Man.[32] Wynter's later essays also anticipate the provincialization of the modern "religion-secular" formation, and the role played by race therein,[33] while her early work vividly illustrates how Africana traditions exceed these and many other boundaries and dichotomies rooted in modern orders of knowledge and divisions of academic disciplines.

But perhaps the most important lesson Wynter's work has for the academic study of Africana religions is the way it reveals the (racial, colonial, gendered, and other) inequalities and structures of domination and degradation animating its various disciplinary formations that prevent scholars from engaging with these traditions "on their own terms," or as being equal to their own. Nobel Laureate Wọle Ṣoyinka once commented on this peculiar difficulty affecting scholars of Africa, noting that "they lack the comparative sense of being able to see Yoruba religion as just another system—whether you want to call it superstition, belief, world view, cosmogony or whatever—you have to do it on the same level with any other system."[34] Wynter's work gives a compelling account as to why this is the case. In a particularly pertinent passage of "Africa, the West, and the Analogy of Culture," Wynter writes,

> In addition, the further proposal here is that if it is the rules generated by this code that govern the representations of Africa and peoples of African descent as well as of all other "native" non-white peoples, doing so *outside* the conscious awareness of their Western and Westernised filmmakers, these are the same rules that have led Western as well as African and other non-Western scholars trained in the methodologies of the social sciences and the related disciplines of our present order of knowledge (or Foucauldian episteme) to systematically know and "represent" Africa by means of parallel symbolically coded discourses that were first identified by Aimé Césaire in his *Discourse on Colonialism* and Edward Said in his book *Orientalism*. To thereby know and "represent" Africa through what is ... "an immense gallery of mirrors which only reflect the image of our (Western and Westernised) selves, our desires or our passions ... [through] mirrors which deform." ... It would suggest that not even we ourselves, as African and Black diaspora critics and filmmakers can, in the normal course of things, be entirely freed from the functioning of these rules; and therefore, from knowing and representing the "cultural universe of Africa" through the same Western "gallery of mirrors" which deform—even where this deformation is effected in the most radically oppositional terms which seek to challenge rather than to reinforce deformation.[35]

In "The Ceremony Found," citing Sylvia Yanagisako and Carol Delaney's essay "Naturalizing Power," Wynter develops this critique in a more general sense:

> This dilemma Yanagisako and Delaney have identified with specific reference to the community of (Western) anthropologists, yet is one necessarily generalizable in our contemporary purely secular context,

to all Western and westernized academics/intellectuals. . . . Yet although this identification then led anthropologists to "include in their [scholarly] accounts origin stories of the people they study," these same anthropologists nevertheless "hesitate at the threshold of their own [social organization], reluctant to explore their own origin myths whether religious or secular." This reluctance on the part of anthropologists is a lawlike one, hence one that they share with the peoples they study and who are classified generically as their "*native informants.*" In turn, the authors continue, anthropologists are akin to the groups they study in that these Western academics/intellectuals also "treat their own stories of origin" as "taboo," "set apart," and "sacred," whether it be their treatment of the (Judeo-Christian) religious story of *Creation* and/or the non-religious, ostensibly purely objective Darwinian story of *Evolution*.[36]

In the same essay, Wynter concludes:

This *genre*-specific, Western-bourgeois representation of origins or ethno-class "legend of descent" [from myths, to religion, to science] thereby makes it normally impossible for anthropologists and Western academics/intellectuals in general to see themselves/ourselves as in any way *coeval*, as Johannes Fabian was seminally to observe (Fabian, 1983), with the other human groups who are their/our objects of study. Indeed, this representation makes it normally impossible for them/us normally to see other human groups as fully—if differently—*co-human*. To breach this projected *Line/Divide* of co-humanity would necessarily call for Western and westernized academics/intellectuals to effect their/our own Autopoetic Turn/Overturn. For such a *turn* would force them/us to accept the *relativization* of their/our own "part science, part myth" origin-story—together with its autopoetically instituted *genre* of being hybridly human and Western civilizational *cum* nation state fictive mode of kind—by correctly identifying this narration as that empirically of *mankind rhetorically overrepresented as if it were that of humankind*.[37]

These caveats and critiques cut to the foundations of the modern, Western academic study of Africa, and no serious scholar of Africana religions can afford to ignore them. That is, the theories and methods and assumptions of Western and Western-trained academics necessarily distort African traditions as they attempt to study and represent them from their own, particular, Western epistemological locus, whose particularity is erased or ignored as it is projected as "objective," "scientific," "evolved," "rigorous," or "disciplined," over and against the African traditions it interrogates. African traditions cannot be taken seriously on their own terms, because to do so would require the relativization of the entire order of knowledge and related conception of humanity, what Fanon called, "becoming an enemy to one's consciousness."[38]

However, in the remaining half of this chapter, I will argue that aspects of Wynter's own project actually suffer from the same problems she incisively diagnoses here. That is, her own writing on Africana traditions is not yet "entirely freed from the functioning of these rules" of the current episteme, making aspects of it another hall in the Western "gallery of mirrors," which "deform—even where this deformation is effected in the most radically oppositional terms which seek to challenge rather than to reinforce deformation." Among other things, Wynter treats her own African autopoietic, bioevolutionary origin story as "taboo" and "set apart" from the particularizing and historicizing processes she deploys to relativize other origin myths, and her later work, to my knowledge, does not recognize African traditions as *coeval* with the Second Emergence humanism of the horizon—they are characterized as having once had important adaptive functions, but are ultimately described as naïve, limited humanisms of the past, of the sunset, to be transcended in the dawn of the Second Emergence.

The Role of African Religions in Wynter's Work

The two functions of Africana religious traditions (as a relativizing and provincializing counterpart to Western orders, and as the primordial site of the "First Emergence") in Wynter's work are probably most evident in her brilliant essay, "'Genital Mutilation' or 'Symbolic Birth'? Female Circumcision, Lost Origins, and the Aculturalism of Feminist/Western Thought," which is a kind of commentary on L. Amede Obiora's 1996 article, "Bridges and Barricades: Rethinking Polemics and Intransigence in the Campaign against Female Circumcision," situating Obiora's transcultural analysis of the dynamics of Western feminist cultural chauvinism and violence vis-à-vis the staunch defense of rituals of female circumcision in African societies within Wynter's own theory of the human. She writes,

> I shall propose that we use this antagonism as the point of departure for the elaboration of a "trans-cultural critique" of *both positions*— one able to reveal the respective cultural *relativity* of each of their conceptions of the human; to reveal thereby the relativity of the purely biologized conception of the human on whose basis alone feminism is enabled to posit the existence of an acultural category,

woman, and thereby to propose an emancipatory project ostensibly encompassing of all women—rather than as one that is veridically merely unifying of Western middle class women with their Westernized middle class and essentially urban professional *native* peers.[39]

Wynter maps these positions in the debate on female circumcision onto different places on a single evolutionary timeline:

> Given the confrontation of two indigenous hermeneutics, two frameworks of rationality, and two modes of reflective thought and motivation—*one belonging to the Neolithic Agrarian order of things, the other to our contemporary techno-industrial order*, yet with each as cognitively closed in the last instance as the other—it will be only on the basis of an entirely new conception outside the limits of their respective criteria and conception of what it is to be a "good man or woman of their kind," outside the terms, therefore, of their cultural ontologies, and their respective indigenous behavioral repertoires and hermeneutics, that Professor Obiora's proposed middle course will be hearable.[40]

This allochronism, the "persistent and systematic tendency to place the referent(s) of anthropology in a Time other than the present of the producer of the anthropological discourse,"[41] runs throughout several of Wynter's later essays and interviews. For example, in a 2005 interview, she states:

> Rather, it is the way in which in Africa we can say an "other" exists to what the West calls human. When you are looking at Voudun, we are seeing an "other" to what the monotheistic religions have called "human." *We are going back to our very origin as humans and the processes of hominization and that is to me what Africa has to offer, when we look at it this way.*
>
> By the way, taking this magnificent body of knowledge that has been built up by the West, but seeing it differently from them because they could not see these ("others") as alternative forms of life. So when Evans-Pritchard says so brilliantly about the Azande and their belief in "witchcraft": "It is the very texture of their thought and they couldn't think that their thought was wrong, not as long as they were Azande," so it is with us as the embodiment of ethno-class "Man" in the mode of the Western bourgeoisie. All of our beliefs about IQ, about the Bell Curve, these are the very texture of our thought and we can not normally think that our thought is wrong.[42] So that is what Africa will give us: the fundamental rules.[43]

That is, African religious traditions function as a mirror in which to contemplate the limits of "our" current order of knowledge, and as the "common origin of humankind," Africa and her traditions are a vital source for the new "science of being human." But these African traditions and their genres of humanity are always linked and limited to the past and characterized as being just as incomplete, *if not more incomplete*, than the genres of Man1 and Man2. The persistence of this Hegelian/Marxist teleology of progress in Wynter's thought is made explicit in several passages where Wynter identifies all such African and "religious" traditions with early so-called Judeo-Christian or pre-Christian "pagan," naïvely supernatural codes.[44] While decrying the imperial and genocidal violence and degradation occasioned by the emergence of the genres of Man1 and Man2, Wynter still regards them as "partial emancipatory breakthroughs," "incomplete victories,"[45] "advances" or "achievements" in contrast to Foucault's more agnostic characterization of such changes as "breaks" and "mutations."[46]

The "danger of this single story"[47] is that it distorts African traditions, "submitting them to the memory" of the modern West (in Mudimbe's formulation[48]), subjugating them to an exogenous cosmology, temporality, and teleology (ironically overrepresented here as acultural).[49] That is, in Wynter's formulation, it appears that traditional African and "religious" humanisms and orders of knowledge must first pass through the brutal and narrow gauntlets of Man1 and Man2[50] in order to achieve the utopian Second Emergence. This is indeed a strange theodicy of coloniality. Wynter actually advocates the development of "new cognitive terms . . . that would therefore call for the disenchanting of all belief—from Vodoun, the 'root of all belief,' to our contemporary Westernized own."[51] Moreover, this supersessionist teleology renders African religious traditions illegible as anything other than local, limited codes to be transcended, whereas, as we will argue, Africans have and continue to use them to self-consciously and nonlocally "auto-inscript" themselves in terms very similar to those towards which Wynter gestures.

That is, these "ceremonies" were never lost, but Wynter's epistemological locus in Europhone academic traditions, even those of the Black radical tradition, has rendered them opaque. Thus, paradoxically, Wynter's move to include the much-maligned traditional African modes of being human in the "truly universal" "new humanism" requires that they first be excluded and transcended as partial humanisms that have not yet attained "the measure of the world." For example, Wynter remarks:

> Do you see? Because we have been doing it. *We have been putting it in place but we have been doing this nonconsciously, as a spider spins its*

elegant web. But the fact is that we have also been changing these conceptions (of the human). All the great movements of history have actually been changes and struggles against (the prevailing) conception. *Now, for the first time, we would literally come into full consciousness of the fact that it is we who are the agents and authors of ourselves and that we do it according to rules. And these rules function in the same way for the first human cultures.* When we look at circumcision—a biocentric perspective—we see genital mutilation, because we can't afford to see what we are seeing. We see the first "writing" on the flesh, as Nietzsche says: "That tremendous labor of the human upon itself by means of which it was to make itself calculable." So in instituting ourselves, we institute our order of consciousness. As Fanon would say, "We are going to have to become enemies to our own consciousness!"[52]

In the next section of this essay, I will argue that this auto-inscription has been done consciously in certain African (and non-African) traditions, and thus is not novel; and therefore, the opposition to our/their consciousness may be more radical than either Fanon or Wynter imagines, necessitating the migration to very different epistemological grounds.

Humanity Unbound and Ceremonies Found in African Traditions

> There are two paths to doom: by segregation, by walling yourself up in a particular or by dilution, by thinning off into the emptiness of the "universal." I have a different idea of a universal. It is of a universal rich with all that is particular, rich with all the particulars there are, the deepening of each particular, the coexistence of them all.
>
> —AIMÉ CÉSAIRE

> If I am created,
> I will re-create myself
> I will observe all the taboos
> Having been created,
> I shall now re-create myself.
>
> —ODÙ OGBÈ-ATẸ

> Your remedy is within you, but you do not see it
> Your malady is from you, but you do not sense it
> You claim that you are a small body,
> but within you is enfolded the greater world
>
> —ʿALĪ IBN ABĪ ṬĀLIB

> Man is a small world, everything in the world, all the powers of the world exist inside him
>
> —AWO FANIYI

> But the Adamic personhood encompasses the entirety of existent beings. So in reality, each gnostic [*ʿārif*] contains all of the angels and all of the existent beings, from the heavenly throne to the earthly canopy. He sees all of them in himself, each one individually.
>
> —SHAYKH AḤMAD AL-TIJĀNĪ

> Within us, all the ages of mankind. Within us, all humankind. Within us, animal, vegetable, mineral. Mankind is not only mankind. It is *universe*.
>
> —AIMÉ CÉSAIRE

In her other essay that deals extensively with African religions, "Africa, the West, and the Analogy of Culture," Wynter concludes with a meditation on Amadou Seck's 1988 film, *Saaraba*:

> The hero is shown as having to recognize that his "roots" are not the answer, that the "remedy" cannot be found there either. For the traditional answers of Islamic theology cannot tell him how to deal with an increasingly degodded world,[53] nor how to escape the pervasive technological tentacles of the West, together with its remorseless displacement of all other "forms of life," its ongoing homogenization of belief, desire, consciousness. Nor, however, can the secular creed of the West, with its reasons-of-the-economy ethic, any more solve the problems of Senegal's swarms of beggars . . . than can the religious belief cum ethical systems of traditional Africa or of Islam.[54]

My proposal here will be nearly the exact opposite, that the religious traditions of Africa, including Islam,[55] can provide a remedy beyond that of the "secular creeds" of the modern West. Wynter's fundamental mistake here, I believe, is in conceptualizing these African traditions to be static and as "cognitively closed" as their secular Western counterparts.[56] In the same essay she writes, "what Evans-Pritchard says of the Azande and of the cognitively closed nature of their culture-systemic memory and order of consciousness, can therefore be seen to apply, if in different terms, to the culture-specific memory and order of consciousness of *Man*."[57] While I cannot speak with knowledge about the Zande case, it is abundantly clear that the Afro-Atlantic traditions of Ifá, Òrìṣà devotion, and Vodou (among many others, not to mention African Islamic traditions) are exceptionally dynamic and very much not "cognitively closed" in that they are aware of, and even celebrate and integrate, alternative traditions and "orders of consciousness," that is, other "modes of being human."[58] Whereas Evans-Pritchard writes that "an Azande cannot get out of the meshes because it is the only world he knows. This web is not an external structure in which he is enclosed: it is the very texture of his thought, and he cannot think his thought is wrong,"[59] the vast diversity both between and within Òrìṣà traditions[60] and the pragmatic and even skeptical-empirical nature of these traditions[61] have given rise to the proverb "The òrìṣà that doesn't hear you when you cry, or doesn't help you when you worship it, get rid of it!"[62] As early missionary accounts reveal, this attitude was responsible for many "conversions" back and forth between various Òrìṣà traditions, Christianity, and Islam and the (in)famous religious creativity, nomadism, and "promiscuity" of Yorùbá and other West African peoples well into the twenty-first century.

While often tied to particular sites of sacred geography (such as rivers, rocks, and places in Ilé-Ifẹ̀), many traditions of Òrìṣà worship were not limited to particular lineages, ethnolinguistic groups, or polities, with traditions such as Ifá traveling to Fon-Ewe-speaking communities and the royal court of Dahomey, and others being adopted from "outside" (for example, several òrìṣà worshipped by Yorùbá-speaking people are said to be from the Tapa (the Nupe—a neighboring ethnolinguistic group) and even speak their language ritually, and the Prophet Muhammad and Jesus are considered òrìṣà in some Ifá myths) even before the transatlantic slave trade spread them beyond West Africa, spurring other dimensions of dynamic evolution in response to the radically different and difficult circumstances of the Americas (which then in turn influenced traditions on the West African coast, these Afro-Atlantic traditions evolving in conversation and competition with each other at various and increasingly widespread sites).[63]

Traditional Auto-Inscription

This awareness and openness to alternatives is not unconnected with the fact that devotees of many Afro-Atlantic traditions self-consciously "make" the "gods" that they worship. As summarized in the Yorùbá proverb, "if not for people, the gods would not be," the existence of òrìṣà is understood to depend on human veneration and ritual activity, even as these òrìṣà shape the lives of their human devotees. In fact, in some circumstances, òrìṣà devotees actually threaten that if their prayers go unanswered, they will turn to another form of worship and leave the òrìṣà starving without devotees.[64] Karin Barber explains, "The Yoruba conviction that the *òrìṣà* need human attention [for their continued existence] in no way questions the existence of spiritual beings as a category.... It is rather that, because of the element of choice in the system, the survival in the human community of any particular òrìṣà depends on human collaboration."[65] These are clear cases of self-conscious "auto-inscription" (or ìtúnra'nìtè, in Yorùbá, self-reflection and self-re-creation), as Matory explains, defining his use of the term "fetish":

> By "fetish," I mean to say that they are beings constructed and materially activated by humans, as all gods and spirited things are, that their value and agency result from a displacement of value and agency from other things or people, and that their legitimacy as concentrated repositories of value and agency is contested by the partisans of rival fetishes. In this sense, Afro-Atlantic gods and spirited things resemble multinational corporations, universities, nation-states, homelands, homes, and social theories. All of these institutions are networks of material things, plants, animals, and people animated by ideas asserted in the context of rival ideas about the value of and relationships among beings and things.[66]

The difference being that in the case of Afro-Atlantic traditions (perhaps due, in part, to their long-standing transculturalism) there seems to be a greater awareness, recognition, and intentional use of these processes of "auto-institution" or "auto-inscription" (and their locality and relativity), in Wynter's terms, than among their "degodded" counterparts. Moreover, this dynamic is not limited to so-called indigenous African traditions, but can also be found in many Dharmic traditions and "mystical" Abrahamic traditions such as Sufism.[67] For example, the incredibly influential Andalusian Sufi, Ibn al-'Arabī, explains that there can be no lord (rabb) without a vassal, or one who is lorded over (marbūb), and that there can be no divinity (ilāh) without something for whom it is a divinity (ma'lūh), so that without the creation over which He is lord, God could not be God. Ibn al-'Arabī further argues that all objects of worship are actually "gods created in belief," writing, "no individual can escape having a belief concerning his Lord. Through it he resorts to Him and seeks Him.... No believer believes in any God other than what he has made in himself, for the God of beliefs is made. The believers see nothing but themselves and what they have made within themselves."[68] Elsewhere in his oeuvre, the Andalusian visionary calls these "gods created in beliefs," "knottings" (signifying on the etymological derivation of the Arabic 'aqīda [creed] from 'aqd [knot]) and encouraging his readers to consciously undergo a process of spiritual transformation to "untie all knottings." He writes,

Beware of becoming delimited by a specific knotting and disbelieving in everything else, lest great good escape you. Or rather, knowledge of the situation as it actually is in itself will escape you. Be in yourself a *hyle* (prime matter) for the forms of all beliefs, for God is wider and more tremendous than that He should be constricted by one knotting rather than another. For He says, "Wheresoever you turn, there is the Face of God" (Qur'an 2:115). He did not mention one place rather than another; and He said that the "face" of God is there, and the face of a thing is its reality.[69]

No less a figure than Emir ʿAbd al-Qādir, the leader of the Algerian resistance to French colonial occupation and an ardent follower of Ibn al-ʿArabī, explains,

> Each of His creatures worships Him and knows Him in a certain respect and is ignorant of Him in another respect.... Therefore, everyone necessarily knows Him in a certain respect and worships Him in this same respect. Because of that error does not exist in this world except in a relative manner.... And He has manifested Himself to each person who worships Him in some particular thing—rock, tree, or animal—in the form of that thing, for no one who worships a finite thing worships it for the thing itself.... But He whom all these worshippers worship is One, and their fault consists only in the fact that they restrict themselves in a limiting way.... Thus the religions are unanimous regarding the object of worship—this worship being co-natural to all creatures, even if few of them are conscious of it—at least insofar as it is unconditioned, but not when considered in relation to the diversity of its determinations.... There is not a single being in the world—be he one of those who are called "naturalists," "materialists" or otherwise—who is truly an atheist. If his words make you think to the contrary, it is your way of interpreting them which is flawed. Infidelity (*kufr*) does not exist in the universe, except in a relative way.[70]

That is, we all delimit the Real through our limited conceptions of reality, and even though these limited conceptions are not other than the Real, these "self-imposed" limits condition our "worship" of the Real, our praxis, and therefore ourselves. Thus, we create or shape the limited and limiting "gods of belief" that "create" and shape us.

While there is not space here for a more complete exposition of these consciously auto-inscripting features of these traditions, my point is simply that self-conscious autopoiesis is nothing new. In fact, prefiguring Wynter's metaphors of the bee and the beehive and the spider and its web, the Andalusian/North African Sufi poet al-Shushtarī writes in his famous philosophical poem *al-Nūniyya*:

> For we are like a silkworm, enveloped by what we fashion
> In pushing back the bounds, we are imprisoned within them
> How often it [reason] destroys the bystander, and how often it
>   rightly guides the traveler

The eighteenth/thirteenth-century Moroccan Sufi Ibn ʿAjība comments upon these verses, explaining that just as silkworms are born bare to the world (open to reality), but weave around themselves a cocoon of valuable silk, so too do people, individually and collectively, through their reason/intellect (*ʿaql*), weave around themselves cocoons that separate them from and condition their experience of and interactions with reality. The goal is to get back to the direct knowledge and experience of reality, beyond any such constructed limitations.[71] So when Wynter writes of one of Ousmane Sembène's films that "Sembène's point here is that the Spirits only exist because of the chief's and the Diola villagers' collective belief in them, in the same way as, in my own terms, 'Man' (and its purely biologized self-conception) exists because of ours,"[72] this equation may not be entirely correct because the African "chiefs and villagers" and devotees of Afro-Atlantic traditions may have been more aware of these auto-inscripting dynamics, and thus of other possibilities of cultivating humanity. This recognition has significant consequences, as Matory explains:

> The real-world Brazilian, Cuban, Haitian, and Nigerian worshippers of the Afro-Atlantic gods are as complex and ambivalent as any European social theorist. The difference is that few of the priests will construct the foreign Other as the antithesis of their ideal selves. Rather, it is the interaction with the Other that, quite normatively, makes them who they are. Just as the Abrahamic religions profess the exclusion of other religions, the Enlightenment and its scions have professed a relationship of oppositeness and antagonism to the Afro-Atlantic religions.[73]

As we will explore later, the "non-oppositional" nature of these traditions and the recognition of their own relativity and autopoietic "construction" is due to their recognition of a transcendent reality beyond and yet immanent in all conceptual constructions. The Yorùbá proverb "no one head contains all knowledge" and the description of the òrìṣà Ọrúnmìlà (the founder of the Ifá tradition) as *àmọ̀ìmọ̀tán*, "one whose knowledge can never be known completely" allude to this fact, which is the foundation of the flexibile and capacious—if not limitless—conceptions these traditions have of the potentialities of being human.

Humanity Unbound and Ceremonies Found

> No attempt must be made to encase man, for it is his destiny to be set free.
> —FRANTZ FANON

One of the most profound reasons for this difference between European social theorists and priests of Afro-Atlantic traditions is their radically different conceptions of humanity and being. From the perspective of traditions such as Ifá and Sufism, Man1 and Man2 and his rational-cum-scientific worlds appear very limited and limiting—"half-starved," as Césaire says, or in the words of the Seneglaese novelist Cheikh Hamidou Kane, "it [modern science] makes you the masters of the external, but at the same time it exiles you there, more and more."[74] In the case of Ifá, and many other Afro-Atlantic traditions, the cosmos is governed by a logic of complementarity, not competitive, eliminative opposition: the outer, apparent, or "physical" (*òde*) cannot exist without the inner, hidden, or "spiritual" (*inú*) any more than there can be a left without a right or a front without a back. Things which are separated by time and space (*ayé*) in the outer world are unified or identical in the inner world or heaven (*ọ̀run*), as represented in the tropes of descent, division, and scattering from *ọ̀run* to *ayé* (the world) in numerous myths of Ifá, particularly those surrounding the *Orí-inú*—"inner head," which refers to a reality that is at once one's destiny, personal divinity, guardian angel, and even creator (*ẹlẹ́dà mi*)[75]— and the conical shape of the *Ìborí*—the symbol, icon, or idol which externalizes the *Orí-inú* and where it is worshipped) and its container (*Ilé-orí* ("house of the head")—as well as Yorùbá crowns and *ìròkẹ̀* (divination tappers used by babaláwo, priests of Ifá).[76] As Abiọdun explains,

> Orí-Ìṣèṣe (Orí, the Originator) . . . the first and the most important *òrìṣà* in *ọ̀run*, the otherworld. Because of its primal place, Orí-Ìṣèṣe has jurisdiction over all other Orí-Inú (the spiritual and personal head or divinity possessed by each and every being and *òrìṣà*). . . . In other words, while the Orí-Inú of each being, thing, or *òrìṣà* determines the allotment of their owner, Orí-Ìṣèṣe rules supremely over all of them from *ọ̀run*, the otherworld. . . . For the religious devotee it is the tangible focus of address for all supplications, the point of contact with the spiritual self. In Yoruba thought, Orí is the source, as well as the most active component, of the psychological identity of humans. The graphic reduction of Orí-Inú to the cone is not just symbolically

appropriate but evokes perfectly the mythical allusions characterizing the whole concept of the spiritual Orí.[77]

Paradoxically, this kind of "vertical" cosmological hierarchy is what allows for the wide array of "horizontal" or nonhierarchical difference that is celebrated in Yorùbá and other Afro-Atlantic religious traditions (even as the priesthoods themselves are governed by initiatic hierarchies of knowledge and seniority). Instead of a temporo-spatially (ayé) immanent ideal against which everyone and all practices are measured, Yorùbá traditions, particularly Ifá, emphasize the fulfilment or living in accordance with one's individual orí-inú ("destiny") as the ideal, which is necessarily different for each person and being in the cosmos. While there are certain general cultural ideals such as ìwà-pẹlẹ ("gentle character") and ọmọlúwàbí ("well-mannered child"),[78] the emphasis on one's own individual orí, particular òrìṣà (and Odù for babaláwo) means that a devotee of the fiery òrìṣà, Ṣàngó, is not expected to have the same character (ìwà) as that of a devotee of Òbatálá or Ọ̀ṣun, nor are all devotees of a particular òrìṣà supposed to have the same kind of character. Even the personal taboos, rites of initiation, and other rituals of òrìṣà devotees are determined by the highly individualized process of divination—communication with òrìṣà, ancestors, and/or one's orí—so an overrepresented universal, one-size-fits-all approach is quite foreign to these traditions.

It is this cosmology that allowed for the recognition and integration of Catholic saints as local manifestations of the òrìṣà in the Caribbean and Americas, and of Islam and Christianity as òrìṣà traditions by Ifá in West Africa, and has contributed to the remarkable dynamism and resilience of these traditions across diverse contexts.[79] A transcendent ideal allows for equal participation by multiple distinct, different, and even opposing manifestations, whereas an immanent ideal necessitates unequal participation and exclusion (all points on the surface of a sphere are equidistant from its center, but not from each other). In the visual symbolism of Orí shrines and mythology, it is the àṣẹ (authority, power to make something happen) at the cone's singular peak that permits the equality and diversity of the circular base. In fact, it is the comprehensiveness or inclusiveness of one's perspective that typically mark seniority in these traditions—many òrìṣà priests in Nigeria have explained to me that they see themselves and their traditions as "the elder siblings" or "parents" of Christians and Muslims, because they recognize these newcomers who do not recognize them.

That is, the complementary or hierarchical structure of the Yorùbá cosmos allows it to be governed by a logic of similarity (things derive their identity from both "vertical," inner and "horizontal," outer relationships) that structures ritual activity, whereas the flattened or "degodded" *cosmoi* of Man1 and Man2 are governed by logics of difference (where "horizontal," outer relationships of difference are considered more real than "vertical," inner relationships of identity), and this can even be seen in the different theories of language and meaning (the Yorùbá ritual emphasis on puns, etymology, and the identification of the name with the named vs. Saussurean, Lacanian, or Derridean semiotics). Paradoxically again, Yorùbá traditions' logic of transcendent similarity or identity favors immanent, inclusive, complementary or comprehensive heterogeneity, whereas—as Wynter's work elegantly demonstrates—modern, Western traditions' logic of immanent difference favors competitive and even eliminative, hierarchical heterogeneity leading to a kind of repressive homogeneity. Instead of Man being defined against its human Others, in Òrìṣà and other Afro-Atlantic traditions, human beings are defined by their inner and outer relationships to suprahuman, nonhuman, as well as other human beings. This does not mean that precolonial Yorùbá societies or Afro-Atlantic religious communities were/are egalitarian or utopic by any means, but rather that the project of a "humanism made to the measure of the world" is more congruent with, and could be better established upon, the epistemological grounds of these traditions than those of a modified Man2.

In further illustration of this point, in the Islamic cosmology of some schools of philosophical Sufism, the radical emphasis on *tawḥīd* (Divine unity) unsettles and even erases the dividing line between the codes of Muslim/non-Muslim, *Īmān* (faith)/*Kufr* (infidelity), *al-Ḥaqq* (the Real, God)/*khalq* (creation), transcendence/immanence, Being/nonbeing, perfection/imperfection, etc. The basic logic is that if God, the Real, is truly transcendent, then He must transcend His transcendence and be immanent in, or rather, as, everything, otherwise God would be divided and delimited. Identifying God with Absolute/nondelimited Being/consciousness (*al-wujūd al-muṭlaq*), Ibn al-ʿArabī explains that perfect or nondelimited Being/consciousness (*wujūd*) must include all imperfections/delimitations otherwise it would be delimited by nondelimitation.[80] Thus, humankind made in the image of God means that human beings are similarly nondelimited in their primordial nature (*fiṭra*). It is the goal of the revelations and religious laws to lead people from their limited and limiting conceptions of and engagements with the Real (and therefore of themselves) to a nondelimited knowledge and experience of the Real, recognizing It in all of Its delimited manifestations as everything, everyone, and their various conceptions of the Real. Ibn al-ʿArabī writes:

> It is incumbent upon the Folk of Allah to know the doctrine (*'ilm*) of every religion (*millah*), so that they can contemplate Him in every form and never stand in the position of denial. For He permeates existence, so none denies Him but someone who is delimited. But the Folk of Allah follow Him whose folk they are, so His property flows over them and His property is the lack of delimitation, for He possesses all-pervading Being; so His folk possess all-pervading vision. When someone delimits His Being, he delimits his own vision of Him; such a one is not of the Folk of Allah.[81]

and

> He who is more perfect than the perfect is he who believes every belief concerning Him. He recognizes Him in faith, in proofs, and in heresy (*ilḥād*), since *ilḥād* is to deviate from one belief to another specific belief.
>
> So if you want your eye to hit the mark, witness Him with every eye, for He pervades all things through self-disclosure. In every form He has a face and in every knower a state. So examine if you will, or do not examine.[82]

This "seeing with every eye"[83] recalls Wynter's statement that our intractable problems "can be solved only if we can, for the first time, *experience* ourselves, not only as we do now, as this or that *genre* of the human, but also *as* human. A new mode of experiencing ourselves in which every mode of being human, every form of life that has ever been enacted, is a part of us. We, a part of them."[84] Ibn al-ʿArabī and his school call this mode of existing and experiencing nondelimited humanity, which is the goal of their practice (and human existence), the "station of no station" (*maqām la-maqām*) or "bewilderment" (*ḥayra*)[85] since it cannot be fixed as one thing or another. He writes,

> The bewilderment of the gnostic in the Divine Side is the greatest of bewilderments, since he stands outside of restriction and delimitation. . . . He possesses all forms, yet no form delimits him. That is why the Messenger of God used to say, "God, increase my bewilderment in Thee!"[86] For this is the highest station, the clearest vision, the nearest rank, the most brilliant locus of manifestation, and the most exemplary path.[87]

Ibn al-ʿArabī's stepson and disciple, Ṣadr al-dīn al-Qūnawī, describes his own experience of the bewilderment of the "station of no station" in the following way:

The tasting of the perfect human beings has affirmed that everything is in everything. Nothing has any essential stability in something from which it cannot change. On the contrary, everything is on the verge of being transformed into something else.... This is the situation of all of *wujūd* [being/consciousness].... This constant flow is the divine journey from the first, nonmanifest Unseen to the realm of the Visible.... No one tastes this journey and reaches its source except he whose essence has come to be nondelimited. Then the bonds are loosened—the contingent properties, states, attributes, stations, configurations, acts, and beliefs—and he is not confined by any of them. By his essence he flows in everything, just as *wujūd* [being/consciousness] flows in the realities of all things without end or beginning.... When the Real gave me to witness this tremendous place of witnessing, I saw that its possessor has no fixed entity and no reality.[88]

In fact, Ibn al-'Arabī declares, "It is the purpose of Divine Guidance to lead humankind to bewilderment (*ḥayra*), so that they learn that the Divine Order Itself is entirely bewilderment."[89] Thus, Ibn al-'Arabī and the many traditions of African Sufism influenced by him are not trying to produce a better "theory of everything," for this would just be another "knotting" or "tying down" of reality and human nature. Instead, they are trying to "untie their knots" through the "knot-undoing-knot" of the Qur'an and the Sunna (Divine words and the words and practices of a perfect (knot-free) human being, the Prophet Muḥammad). Similarly, Katherine McKittrick describes Wynter's project as being concerned with the "possibility of undoing and unsettling—*not replacing or occupying*—Western conceptions of what it means to be human."[90]

For Ibn al-'Arabī and the Sufi traditions influenced by him, the human being is, by definition, that which cannot be defined. Describing the "reality of humanity" (*ḥaqīqat al-insān*) as a *barzakh* (a liminal reality that both joins and separates two things containing the attributes of both)[91] between Being and non-being, God and the cosmos, Ibn al-'Arabī writes, "it possesses a face toward Being and a face toward nothingness. It stands opposite each of these two known things in its very essence. It is the third known thing. Within it are all possible things. It is infinite, just as each of the other two known things [God and cosmos] is infinite."[92]

This "perspective of no perspective" of the perfect human is the basis of what Zachary Wright has called the "Muhammad-centric 'Islamic Humanism'" that runs through various African Sufi and Islamic Philosophical traditions, particularly the Tijāniyya (the most popular Sufi order on the

African continent).⁹³ While these traditions create a kind of hierarchy of humanity based on knowledge of and closeness to God (with the Prophet at its summit), for those who ascend these peaks of ethico-onto-epistemological perfection, these hierarchies and differences are collapsed and relativized within the context of the deeper unity and identity of all people and all things. The transcendent ideal of humanity, the spiritual reality of the Prophet (*al-ḥaqīqat al-Muḥammadiya*) is immanent within everyone and all things (in a manner somewhat analogous to the notion of Buddha nature). As Shaykh Aḥmad al-Tijānī, founder of the Tijāniyya, said, "His being, God's peace and blessing upon him, is the spirit of everything in the universe, and there is no existence for anything without him, even for the non-believers."⁹⁴ This kind of universal Islamic humanism is somewhat analogous to the new humanism for which Wynter calls, with "nonbelievers" in the former schema being analogous to those still operating within old, partial humanisms in Wynter's schema. In fact, Wynter's ternary of nature, culture, and transculture, each freeing us from that which precedes it, functions similarly to *jism* (physical body), *nafs* (soul/psyche), and *rūḥ* (spirit) within the Sufi context.⁹⁵

However, the ontologies of these distinct levels are very different in the Sufi and Wynterian schemas. Indeed, Wynter's *homo narrans* or *bios-mythos* formulation appears to be very similar to the Islamic philosophical definition of the human as *al-ḥayawān al-nāṭiq* (a speaking/intelligent animal), but in the case of Islamic philosophy, the intelligible world is more real than, and ontologically prior to, the physical world. In Wynter's origin myth, the sociogenic or cultural level develops from a biological mutation that gives rise to language, and transculture from a mutation in culture that gives rise to the "science of the Word;" whereas in Sufi origin myths, the realms of the spirit and physical body both emerge from the Divine Real, or the physical level of reality emerges as a "descent" from the level of the soul (*nafs*), which emerges as a "descent" from the level of the spirit (*rūḥ*), which in turn emerges as a "descent" from the Divine Real. However, the return journey of an individual human being is depicted as one of "ascent" in an evolutionary schema somewhat analogous to Wynter's, as Rumi writes in his *Masnavi*:

> I died as mineral and became plant;
>   I died as plant and rose to animal
> I died as animal and I was human; so what should I fear?
>   When was I less from dying?
> At the next charge, I will die to humanity so that
>   I may lift up my head and wings among the angels

And I must leap over the river of the angel,
   for "Everything perishes but His Face" [Qur'an 28:88]
Once again I will be sacrificed and from the station of the angel,
   I will become that which cannot be imagined
O let me be non-existent; nonexistence says to me like a pan-flute,
   "Truly to Him is our return" [Qur'an 2:156][96]

These cosmological differences mean that Sufi traditions imagine different orders or possibilities of freedom, placing an emphasis on spiritual freedom as being both the source and purpose of physical, socio-political, and psycho-intellectual freedom. Thus, the Senegalese Sufi, Shaykh Aḥmadu Bamba, imprisoned and sent into exile by French colonial authorities, wrote (punning *Assīru* ["I journey"] with *Assīrun* ["a prisoner"]):

I journeyed with the righteous, when I journeyed [in exile]
   While my enemies thought that I was there a prisoner
. . .
They thought that I, during my exile, was their prisoner
   But all were there confounded
For the confounded were the prisoners of Satan and passions
While I was freely journeying toward the Lord of the Throne,
   Exalted be He
I journey towards Him, owner of the land and the sea, as a servant
   And not towards the profligate [captors] is my end as I
   journey[97]

That is, in Bamba's view, his spiritual freedom was more real and consequential than his captors' social freedom, and their spiritual captivity was more real and consequential than his physical captivity.

The point of these comparisons of different visions of "undoing the knots of humanity" is to demonstrate that Wynter's formulation of the "outside view" of "transculture" is still very much enmeshed in a particular, modern, Western, biocentric culture. That is, from the vantage points of traditions like Sufism and Ifá, we can see how Wynter's critique of biocentrism is still biocentric, that is, the *bios-mythos*, nature-culture formulation is itself revealed to be another cultural, mythic narration. To put it another way, if Maturana's autopoietic insight was that "it is the living organism that fabricates an image of the world through the internal/neurological processing of information,"[98] he (and Wynter) do not seem to take the next step to recognize this "neurological processing" as belonging to the same "fabricated image of the world."[99] In other words, the historicizing and relativizing analysis to which Wynter subjects other origin myths, conceptions of Man, and orders of knowledge is not applied to her own particular evolutionary origin myth.

But Wynter is not unaware of this fact. When David Scott raised a similar issue in an interview,[100] she responded:

> Now, here is where the conception of the genre of the human and of the governing sociogenic principle comes in. For it would be the code, the law of the code, the principle, which functions as the ground of the history that will be narrated and existentially lived. So the ground of our mode of being human will itself be the *a priori* or ground of the history to which it gives rise. But the paradox here, of course, is that it cannot itself be historicized within the terms of the ethnohistory to which it will give rise: that code/mode must remain, as you say, unhistoricizable. As ours now remains for us. . . .
> . . . While we now live as Man in the second millennium only because we're living in a Judaic/Christian conception of history, one that is now secularized. Man's history-for is therefore now put forward as if it were transcreedal, supracultural, universal. And my point here is that if we are to be able to reimagine the human in the terms of a new history whose narrative will enable us to co-identify ourselves each with the other, whatever our local *ethnos/ethnoi*, we would have to begin by taking our present history, as narrated by historians, as empirical data for the study of a specific cultural coding of a history whose narration has, together with other such disciplinary narrations, given rise to the existential reality of our present Western world system—that is, to the reality of a system enacted about the ethno-class conception of the human Man, which represents itself as if it were the human, and in which we all now live.[101]

There are several issues with this response,[102] the first being the fact that the particularity of the "our" and "we," "living as Man in the second millennium," does not apply to the many people, who despite the hegemonic domination of the modern West, still live in their own, distinct conceptions of history and humanity. Moreover, I am not convinced that only the so-called monotheistic (a problematic term in itself) traditions have conceived universal histories and that no "histories of the human" have ever been conceived. The world of Òrìṣà and other Afro-Atlantic religious traditions contain diverse and divergent origin myths, and for centuries, its practitioners have been well aware of a great number of "external" origin myths, but these are often creatively synthesized or simply left as "external" myths— the acknowledgment of the particularity of one's own tradition and history as a "*history-for*" actually opens one up to the universal recognition of the existence of multiple other perspectives and histories. That is, the babaláwo with whom I have studied view Ifá as universal, in no way limited to a particular ethno-class, and recite myths about the origins of *Oyinbo* (white people), other òrìṣà traditions, Islam, and Christianity from the Ifá corpus, easily incorporating mythic elements from these traditions. Moreover, while being aware that other òrìṣà traditions, *Oyinbo*, Muslims, and Christians have their own, distinct stories, these babaláwo are not threatened by this fact, and are able to identify with these others. Within Ifá, this *a priori* or "ground of history" is the transcendent Olódùmarè (and its human ideal, the Orí-inú or the òrìṣà Ọ̀rúnmìlà), who, because of His/Her/Its supreme transcendence, allows for a multitude of divergent myths and practices. Within Sufism, this *a priori* is the similarly transcendent Real (*al-Ḥaqq*) or the Divine Essence (*al-Dhāt*) (and its hypostasis, or human counterpart, the Muḥammadan reality (*al-ḥaqīqat al-Muḥammadiya*) or perfect human (*al-insān al-kāmil*)), so that both traditions use poetic and other apophatic modes of speech to address the origins of language, consciousness, and being that are both beyond and beyond being beyond language.[103]

I suspect that Wynter may be attempting something somewhat similar with her origin myth—that is using it as a kind of *upāya*, a liberating ruse, a boat that burns when it reaches the other shore (in the Buddhist formulation), a ladder that can be kicked away after being climbed (in Wittgenstein's sense), a laxative that purges itself (in the ancient skeptic formulation). That is, if I have understood her argument and project, she wants to start from the origin myths of the current hegemonic, overrepresented Man2 and, in its terms, give an account that will open it up beyond itself, and undo its limitations. As she says,

> And one such possibility would have to be, and imperatively so, that of our being able to effect the deconstruction of the mechanisms by means of which we continue to make opaque to ourselves, attributing the origin of our societies to imaginary beings, whether the ancestors, the gods, God or evolution, and natural selection, the reality of our own agency with respect to the programming and reprogramming of our desires, our behaviours, our minds, ourselves, the I and the we.[104]

My concern is that, on the one hand, "we can't get there from here"; that is, I doubt that the limited and limiting nature of the order of Man2, even with Wynter's ingenious neurosocial modifications, would allow for such a radical "mutation"—its grounds are too narrow and sandy. In the terms of the above quote, by implicitly reifying and elevating a particular kind of human agency as the origin and sovereign of "natural selection," "God," "ancestors," etc., Wynter subjects us to the dominion and limits of the supposed "auto-rule" of this particular conception of human agency. While on the other hand, the overrepresentation of biocentric Man2 is precisely what creates this hard line between *real* "human agency" and "imaginary beings," rendering opaque or distorting other orders of knowledge (which are very much aware of and employ human agency in the "programming and reprogramming of our desires, behaviors, minds, ourselves"), because these other orders often deconstruct, unsettle, or erase the boundary between such "imaginary beings" and "the reality of our own agency" in very different ways.[105]

For example, in Sufi cosmology, human beings can imagine gods because we ourselves are imagined (*mutakhayyal*) by God, the nondelimited, deep ground of all consciousness/being (*wujūd*), in His own image; and myths from Odù Èjì-Ogbè and Ọsa-Gudá of the Ifá corpus describe the cosmos and human beings coming into existence through the dreams of Ọrúnmìlà and Olódùmarè; and Afro-Atlantic traditions in general describe the human self as a kind of nexus of all the deities, spirits, forces, etc. of the world that needs to be kept in balance through necessarily communal ritual (including nonhuman persons). Agency means something very different in the context of these plural or universal conceptions of the human self. That is, depending on the grounds chosen, human agency imagines beings whose imaginary "agency" shapes humanity; or the human and its agency are themselves imagined beings. Traditions like philosophical Sufism and Ifá, because they unsettle and erase the boundary between human and divine, admit both perspectives. We are not other than the *a priori* Real (Allāh/Olódùmarè), although we do not typically imagine ourselves to be so. Thus Fanon's remark, "in the world through which I travel, I am endlessly creating myself,"[106] in addition to its obvious autopoetic meaning, could be interpreted from an Ifá perspective as referring to his Orí-inú ("inner head"), also known as *Ẹlẹda mi* (my creator), guiding and creating his "outer head" (*orí odè*), body (*ara*), and life (*ayé*); while from a Sufi perspective, this statement could also be read as describing the Divine "I" perpetually creating and imagining a human subject through which It experiences delimitation, but also to that human subject's self-creation through determining and delimiting Being through "the creation of its creator" as a "god created in belief," which then defines the human subject.[107] Such formulations exceed even Wynter's reconfiguration of the biocentric schema.

David Mariott has productively critiqued the tension in Wynter's work between a truly open-ended leap *à la* Fanon ("I am not a prisoner of History. I should not seek there for the meaning of my destiny. I should constantly remind myself that the real leap consists in introducing invention into existence. In the world through which I travel, I am endlessly creating myself."[108]) beyond the confines of history, beyond "the point at which methods devour themselves,"[109] into what cannot presently be defined and her commitment to the suprahistorical, "law-like" functioning of the code of sociogeny. Marriott explains, "but unlike Fanon, for whom the real is always veiled or masked,[110] Wynter presupposes that the real can somehow be *known*. Indeed, she defines the task of black cultural criticism as the 'making conscious' of the 'non-conscious' laws or codes defining 'our genres of being human.'"[111] In the Sufi tradition, the Real can only be known by the Real, but human subjects are not other than the Real, and thus can know It/themselves as such. Put another way, the Real is not veiled from Itself, but is always veiled from others (in fact these others, this alterity, are the veils themselves), yet these veils are also not other than the Real. The Real (the Divine Essence) is utterly transcendent and nondelimited, but that means It must transcend Its transcendence and nondelimitation to take on the limitations of veils and partial perspectives, or "knottings," and it is these knottings that can be known in a "law-like" fashion; in fact, these "knottings" are the laws or codes themselves. Some of these knottings lead beyond themselves to the ineffable, nondelimited Real (not even limited by ineffability nor delimitation), while others simply lead to further knottings.

As a result, some of these other orders of knowledge and conceptions of humanity offer a more radically "external" position from which to deconstruct the present hegemonic order, complementing Wynter's brilliant, but limited, immanent critique. Furthermore, Césaire's human "universal rich with all that is particular, rich with all the particulars there are, the deepening of each particular, the coexistence of them all" to which I believe Wynter's project aspires seems much closer to, and much more achievable from, Sufism's supraformal *Insān al-Kāmil* or Ifá's Ọrúnmìlà than the biocentric Man2+culture. As David Scott says in his interview with Wynter, "but what you recognize—as, of course, Césaire and Fanon recognize—is that there is an inner lining of humanism, in which the degradation of man is part and parcel of the elevation of man."[112] In traditions like Sufism and Ifá, human beings realize their elevation through their nothingness before, and therefore identity with, their transcendent ideals/divine reality, not their elevation above other beings, because paradoxically, the greatest elevation is to realize one's inner identity with all beings, which are also none other than these transcendent ideals / divine reality.

Seen from the "outside" perspectives of traditions like Ifá and Sufism, the progression of events in the expansion and self-definition of the so-called West over the last half-millennium appears not so much a "de-godding" of the world, but rather a divinization of the newly minted, limited and limiting "gods" of Man, the state, profit/productivity, and physical law.[113] Given the calamities these new gods have wreaked upon us and our fellow beings, and the looming threat of more catastrophes to come, I believe it is past time that we "got rid of them," as the Yorùbá proverb suggests, and go back to or start worshipping gods that are not so petty and cruel. Again, this is not to say that communities of òrìṣà devotees or African Muslims, even Sufis, were or are perfect, utopian, or egalitarian, but rather that they conceive of and practice freedom in ways difficult to recognize in modern, ratio- or bio-centric schemas (as Wynter's own work demonstrates), and that their traditions contain powerful resources and still-present ceremonies whose neglect is both symptomatic and causative of many of our present woes. As William Chittick writes, describing the "central point" of Ibn al-'Arabī's teachings, the nondelimited nature of human being:

> Once it is understood that the proper human role in the cosmos is to manifest the Divine Essence in a global and plenary fashion, it is easy to see that the main currents of modern thought are designed to keep people as far away from the "central point" as possible. This is because science, technology, and the other branches of modern learning—not to speak of politics—are grounded in ignorance of human nature. Modern forms of knowledge falsify the human self by defining it in terms of ever more narrowly focused disciplines—biology, neurophysiology, genetics, anthropology, psychology, history, economics, and so on. Modern intellectual currents, the media, and popular culture make people comfortable with the false notion that they belong to fixed stations. Once people lose sight of the nondelimitation of the true human state, they lose the possibility of thinking about perfection, much less achieving it. Modern knowledge tells us who we are not. It can never tell us who we are. Only a perspective rooted in the Station of No Station can show the way to the central point.[114]

Conclusion

> And what I want to suggest to you is that in your freeing yourself, you have to free the human itself. And that can only be done, literally, by what I propose; the science of origin stories.
>
> —SYLVIA WYNTER

> While the official religion is the opium of the people, the unofficial religion serves two functions: to sustain a sense of identity in the face of increasing pressures, and to *structure those states of feeling* that wait their moment to erupt.
>
> —SYLVIA WYNTER

> What you have to say has to be a greater truth than any other truth you know.
>
> —SYLVIA WYNTER

While Wynter's work has brilliantly demonstrated the limited and limiting genres of being human that have governed the epistemic, social, and material dimensions of life in the Westernized world, attending to the position of African religions in her work and to these traditions *on their own terms* elucidates a tension or even contradiction running through her constructive project. This contradiction can be clearly seen in the following passage from an interview with Katherine McKittrick in which Wynter comments on a recent report on climate change:

> So that's the terrifying thing with the *Time* report. It thinks the causes of global warming are *human* activities, but they are not! The Masai who were (and are) being displaced have nothing to do with global warming! It's all of us—the Western and mimetically Westernized middle classes—after we fell into the trap of modeling ourselves on the mimetic model of the Western bourgeoisie's liberal monohumanist Man2. But mind you, at the time—just prior to, during, and after the anticolonial and civil rights struggles—what other model was there? Except, of course, for the hitherto neocolonially neglected yet uniquely ecumenically human model put forward by Frantz Fanon from what had been his activist "gaze from below" antibourgeois, anticolonial, anti-imperial perspective....
>
> ... This model can, at the same time, be enacted only on the homogenized basis of the systemic repression of all other alternative modes of material provisioning. In this mode of material provisioning, therefore, there can ostensibly be no alternative to its attendant planetarily-ecologically extended, increasingly *techno-automated*, thereby job-destroying, postindustrial, yet no less fossil fuel–driven, thereby climate-destabilizing free-market capitalist economic system, in its now extreme neoliberal transnational technocratic configuration. The exceptions, however, are those clusters of still extant nomadic or sedentary indigenous traditionally *stateless* societies—for example, those of the Masai, the San, or the Pygmy in Africa, as well as the range of other such societies in Australia, the Americas, and

elsewhere. Many of these groups are now being pushed out of their ostensibly "underdeveloped" "places" totally.[115]

Here the Masai are rightfully exonerated of responsibility for the climate crisis, but they and the other "indigenous traditionally stateless societies" are excluded from the available "models of humanity." There is only the monohumanist Man2 and the Fanonian model, which is overrepresented as the only "gaze from below," anticolonial, anti-imperial perspective, simultaneously recognizing and neglecting those "exceptional" African and other indigenous cases that have managed to resist the dominant order in one way or another. As Anwar Omeish has thoroughly demonstrated in her brilliant thesis,

> there was a significant gap between Fanon's animating concerns and those of the Algerians he was working among. . . . It was both caused by and reveals implicit theoretical commitments to the traditional-modern binary that rendered some Algerian concerns, and the vibrant debates that surrounded them, illegible to him as a theorist. . . . These theoretical commitments, rather than (as is widely contended) producing a radically open Fanonian praxis, in fact make possible some futures while foreclosing others, thereby limiting access to the very Algerian narratives that may have had the potential to interrupt the epistemic project of colonial modernity. In turn, this restricts Fanon's (and our) world-making resources as theorists and practitioners.[116]

The opacity of Islam and Islamic discourses (not to mention those of "indigenous" African religions)—particularly those of the powerful Algerian Sufi resistance movements of Emir ʿabd al-Qādir, the Tijāniyya, and Aḥmad al-ʿAlāwī (all of whom were major propagators of Ibn al-ʿArabī's theories and Sufi practice)—to Fanon seriously delimited his otherwise brilliant critique of coloniality. While Wynter's work has a much deeper and more nuanced appreciation of African and Afro-Atlantic religious traditions than Fanon's, her supercessionist progressivism relegates of them to the "past" of a single Hegelian-Marxist timeline, and the lingering biocentrism and even secularism of her theory of autopoietic sociogeny distorts these traditions by subjecting them to an exogenous cosmology. Consequently, many of the features of these traditions are rendered illegible, and as a result, that for which Wynter looks for to the horizon of the future, I argue, can already be found in these African and Afro-Atlantic traditions.[117] As the Yorùbá proverb says, "the thing that I went to look for in Sokoto [a faraway northern town], I found inside my ṣòkòtò (trousers)." Anyone well-versed in traditions like Ifá or Sufism could easily recognize the "science of the word" or "science of the origin stories," which Wynter argues are indispensable for human liberation, in their practices and orature. Wynter's work powerfully reveals the ways in which "we" have made the world the way it is today, and as such, gives us the hope of re-making the world in a different way, if "we" can remake ourselves;[118] but not if we limit the notions of who we can be, and therefore what we can do. As she writes:

> Rather, so powerfully pervasive is the "theoretical fiction" of our fixed biological human nature that, although, as Antonio de Nicolas points out, it is clear, given the diversity of human religions, as well as of human cultures, that men and women have "never been any one particular thing or had any particular nature to tie them down metaphysically," and that, instead, we become human only by means of the conceptions (i.e. theories) of being human that are specific to each culture, there is stubborn resistance to [this] recognition. . . . Foucault shows, by our present "fundamental arrangements of knowledge" and their disciplinary paradigms [that this conception] does indeed so serve to "tie us down" metaphysically to its "theoretical fiction" of "human nature."[119]

Studying Islamic and "indigenous" African religious traditions on their own terms reveals that they offer orders of knowledge and ritual that, unlike those Foucault described, do not necessarily "tie us down," but rather aim to free us from any limiting conceptions of human nature and reality that we may have. That is, they not only aspire toward universality, but in certain modes, actually realize pluriversality,[120] whereas, even with its neurosocial modifications, Wynter's work still carries the limiting "fiction" of secular biocentrism and a single, supersessionist, universal Hegelian/Marxist timeline. Because of their fundamental differences in the conception of human nature and reality, African traditions offer a particular, delimited mode or modes of being human (as one or a few among many) that open up onto the higher, nondelimited reality of human nature / divine reality (which is not even limited by being unlimited), while Wynter's theory offers a common biological-cum-linguistic basis that spawns multiple different possibilities of being human.[121] Because these African traditions open up onto a truly transcendent reality (that transcends its transcendence to be immanent in all relative conceptions of it), they can similarly exceed and relativize the codes of inclusion/exclusion that define their boundaries and particularities. On the other hand, due to its biocentrism (language emerges from evolutionary neurobiology, which serves as the ahistorical *a priori*), there is no place for such transcendence in Wynter's historically immanent, particular origin myth which, therefore, has to overrepresent itself as the ahistorical origin of all origin myths, of all humanity. This ends up replicating the same codes of exclusion that Wynter so cogently diagnoses in other orders of knowledge. The "half-starved" cosmology of Man2 cannot contain the transcendence of the truly transcultural, whereas the more capacious cosmologies of Afro-Atlantic and Islamic traditions are grounded in this reality.

These differences have important practical consequences for concrete emancipatory projects: for Wynter, emancipation is achieved through progressive "mutations" in the dominant conception of being human and the concomitant order of knowledge, whereas, historically, Africana traditions have favored the model of marronage or hijra—the creation or recreation of a separate spiritual, epistemic, social, and political base from which emancipatory projects can be launched. While Wynter's theory may serve as a kind of *upāya* to help lead those operating in the illusorily universal biocentric paradigm of Man2 beyond it, I doubt it can lead to the total restructuring of knowledge Wynter calls for, given its congruence with the "official religion" of biocentrism of the present order.[122] Rather, it is in the "unofficial religions" that I believe the grounds for radical transformation truly lie, not only because of their difference from the currently hegemonic paradigms, but because of their profound and penetrating understanding of human potential as nearly limitless and their proven track record of realizing this potential.[123] This is by no means limited to African religious traditions, as many similar themes and concepts can be found in Taoist, neo-Platonic, Buddhist, Hindu, Jain, Indigenous American, and Christian and Jewish mystical traditions. I believe we would do well to follow the historical precedents Wynter insightfully described in her "*Black Metamorphosis*":

> Africans and Amerindians, with two different but precapitalist cultures, found culture contact points at which a fusion was achieved in the dynamic of resistance. But as the Arawak Indians died out, the Maroons humanized their mountainous interior with adaptation of their original Ashanti culture. . . . Above all, in these early stages their former African religions, gradually metamorphosed, were openly carried on. As we shall see it was by and through their original African religions, in a situation of resistance, that both the Maroons, and the plantation slaves, consciously reconstituted a group identity.[124]

That is, these African and other religious traditions offer those of us operating both within and outside of academia and the dominant episteme the resources to reconstitute a truly human identity, and thus, a truly humane world.

African traditions are not just bound to the past and vanishing orders; they are not static and closed; they are not nonadaptive—in fact, they hold some of the keys to our survival and that of many other species on this planet. As Bob Marley sang, quoting the Psalmist, "the stone that the builder refused, will always be the head cornerstone."[125] The stones of Africana religious traditions that the builders of the modern world order rejected formed the foundation of the Black radical traditions that opposed and continue to oppose the present order of things,[126] and they will continue to serve as important foundations for the renewal and restoration of humanity and the world beyond its seemingly "interminable catastrophes,"[127] just as they continue to give us access to "a greater truth than any other truth [we] know,"[128] the truth of who we are.

Notes

1. I would like to thank and acknowledge Ayọdeji Ogunnaike, Siana Monet, Amadu Kunateh, and especially Anwar Omeish for their useful comments and feedback on this chapter.

For my earlier article, see Oludamini Ogunnaike, "From Heathen to Sub-human: A Genealogy of the Influence of the Decline of Religion on the Rise of Modern Racism," *Open Theology* 2, no. 1 (2016): 785–803.

2. For accounts of the relevance of Wynter's work to the study of religion and the philosophy of religion, see Mayra Rivera, "Embodied Counterpoetics: Sylvia Wynter on Religion and Race," in *Beyond Man: Race, Coloniality, and the Philosophy of Religion*, ed. An Younntae and Eleanor Craig (Durham, NC: Duke University Press, 2021), 57–85, and Joseph Winters, "The Sacred Gone Astray: Eliade, Fanon, Wynter, and the Terror of Colonial Settlement," in *Beyond Man*, 245–68.

3. Even in her unique writing style, with the many epigraphs or "guide quotes," long and complex sentences that try to say everything at once (expressing the profound interconnectedness of things), the capitalization of key terms, and highly poetic and allusive conclusions, in the heartfelt, restless, keen, and perpetual seeking of her prose, her unbounded, transdisciplinary scope, uniquely synthesizing a wide array of topics, literatures, and perspectives and bringing them to bear on a few main central themes and concerns, and her refusal to separate the search for truth from the quest for justice, I recognized a vision toward which my own work aspired.

4. David Scott aptly characterizes the "problem space" of Wynter's unpublished "*Black Metamorphosis*": "How might we figure the relational conundrum of an African presence that was at once an *object* in the dehumanization and acculturation of colonized life and a *subject* in the rehumanization and indigenization of 'native' Black life." Scott, "Preface: Sylvia Wynter's Agonistic Intimations," *Small Axe: A Caribbean Journal of Criticism* 20, no. 1 (2016): viii. Wynter's later work is characterized by the problem of unveiling and undoing the orders of knowledge that have legitimated and constituted the current conceptions of humanity, orders of knowledge, and social

orders characterized by exclusion and giving birth to a new humanism "made to the measure of the world."

5. More recent scholarship on Islam in Africa has demonstrated the colonial and racist origins of the myth of "two Africas" separated by the Sahara, and the construction, by both Afrocentrist and Orientalist scholars, of an Arab/African dichotomy and portrayal of Islam as an "Arab" and non-African religion (Islam has had a longer presence in the Horn of Africa than in most of the Arabian peninsula, and was established in West Africa around the same time that Christianity became established in Scandinavia). Roughly 15 percent of enslaved West Africans in the transatlantic slave trade were Muslims, and Islam played an important and significant role in Afro-Atlantic religious traditions (both Islamic and non), with enslaved Muslims being particularly associated with slave uprisings throughout the Atlantic world (for example, the famed leaders of Haitian rebellions, Makandal and Dutty Boukman, are described as Muslim in several accounts). Rudolph Ware's work in particular has demonstrated the continuities and connections between antislavery jihad movements in West Africa and slave revolts on the other side of the Atlantic. See Rudolph Ware, *The Walking Qur'an: Islamic Education, Embodied Knowledge, and History in West Africa* (Chapel Hill: University of North Carolina Press, 2014); Aisha Khan, "Islam, Vodou, and the Making of the Afro-Atlantic," *New West Indian Guide / Nieuwe West-Indische Gids* 86, no. 1–2 (2012): 29–54; Michael Gomez, *Black Crescent: The Experience and Legacy of African Muslims in the Americas* (Cambridge: Cambridge University Press, 2005); João José Reis, *Slave Rebellion in Brazil: The Muslim Uprising of 1835 in Bahia* (Baltimore: Johns Hopkins University Press, 1995); and Sylviane Diouf, *Servants of Allah: African Muslims Enslaved in the Americas* (New York: New York University Press, 1998).

6. As David Scott writes of his excellent interview with her, "She would not sum it all up retrospectively. She would not allow herself so easily to be relegated to being an object of (what might have appeared) an *antiquarian* inquiry. She had not stopped thinking, after all. Indeed, she had barely begun, it could be argued" (Scott, "Preface," ix).

7. Excellent, accessible introductions to Wynter's theory of the Human can be found in Sylvia Wynter's interviews: David Scott, "The Re-enchantment of Humanism: An Interview with Sylvia Wynter," *Small Axe* 8 (2000): 173–211; Sylvia Wynter and Katherine McKittrick, "Unparalleled Catastrophe for Our Species? Or, To Give Humanness a Different Future: Conversations," in *Sylvia Wynter: Being Human as Praxis*, ed. Katherine McKittrick (Durham, NC: Duke University Press, 2015), 9–89; Sylvia Wynter and Greg Thomas, "ProudFlesh Inter/Views: Sylvia Wynter," in *ProudFlesh: A New Afrikan Journal of Culture, Politics and Consciousness* 4 (2006): 1–35; Bedour Alagraa, "What Will Be the Cure? A Conversation with Sylvia Wynter," *Offshoot*, January 7, 2021, accessed through https://offshootjournal.org/what-will-be-the-cure-a-conversation-with-sylvia-wynter/; Sylvia Wynter, Joshua Bennett, and Jarvis R. Givens, "'A Greater Truth than Any Other Truth You Know': A Conversation with Professor Sylvia Wynter on Origin Stories," *Souls* 22, no. 1 (2020): 123–37; and Derrick White, "Black Metamorphosis: A Prelude to Sylvia Wynter's Theory of the Human," *CLR James Journal* 16, no. 1 (2010): 127–48.

8. Sylvia Wynter, "Unsettling the Coloniality of Being/Power/Truth/Freedom: Towards the Human, after Man, Its Overrepresentation—an Argument," *CR: The New Centennial Review* 3, no. 3 (2003): 257–337.

9. Sylvia Wynter, "The Pope Must Have Been Drunk, the King of Castile a Madman: Culture as Actuality, and the Caribbean Rethinking of Modernity," in *The Reordering of Culture: Latin America, the Caribbean, and Canada in the Hood*, ed. Alvina Ruprecht and Cecila Taina (Ottawa: Carleton University Press, 1995), 20–21.

10. Wynter and Thomas, "ProudFlesh Inter/Views."

11. Sylvia Wynter, "The Ceremony Found: Towards the Autopoetic Turn/Overturn, Its Autonomy of Human Agency and Extraterritoriality of (Self-)Cognition," in *Black Knowledges/Black Struggles: Essays in Critical Epistemology*, ed. Jason R. Ambroise and Sabine Broeck (Liverpool: Liverpool University Press, 2015), 213 (emphasis in original; unless noted otherwise, all emphasis in original). Wynter continues, "Seeing that if such cosmogonies function to enable us to 'tell the world and ourselves who we are' (Leeming, 2002), they also function even more crucially to enable us autopoietically to institute ourselves as the *genre*-specific *We* or fictive mode of kind that each of us will from now on pre-conceptually experience and, therefore, performatively enact ourselves *to be* as an always-already symbolically encoded and cloned *I/We*" (213–14).

12. Ellen E. Berry, Kent Johnson, and Anesa Miller-Pogacar, "Postcommunist Postmodernism: Interview with Mikhail Epstein,"*Common Knowledge* 2, no. 3 (1993), quoted in Wynter, "Unsettling the Coloniality of Being/Power/Truth/Freedom," 286.

13. See Wynter and McKittrick, "Unparalleled Catastrophe," 27–30 for a description of this theory of Varela and Maturana. Walter Mignolo helpfully summarizes this point: "Wynter draws on Maturana's insights, in particular his work on autopoiesis, which uncovers the interconnectedness of 'seeing' the world and 'knowing' the world: specifically, he shows that what is seen with the eyes does not represent the world outside the living organism; rather, it is the living organism that fabricates an image of the world through the internal/neurological processing of information. Thus, Maturana made the connection between the ways in which human beings construct their world and their criteria of truth and objectivity and noticed how their/our nervous system processes and responds to information." Mignolo, "Sylvia Wynter: What Does It Mean to Be Human?," in *Sylvia Wynter: On Being Human as Praxis*, ed. Katherine McKittrick (Durham, NC: Duke University Press, 2015), 107.

Also see David Kline's chapter on autopoiesis and autoreligion in this volume.

14. Describing current, biological conceptions of humanity, Wynter writes:

> The paradox is this: that for the "descriptive statement" that defines the human as purely biological being on the model of a natural organism (thereby projecting it as preexisting the narratively inscribed "descriptive statement" in whose terms it inscripts itself and is reciprocally inscripted, as if it were a purely biological being, ontogeny that preexists culture, sociogeny), it must ensure the functioning of strategic mechanisms that can repress all knowledge of the fact that its biocentric descriptive statement is a descriptive statement. Yet that such strategic, Godelier-type mechanisms of occultation, repressing recognition that our present descriptive statement of the human is a descriptive statement, are able to function at all (if outside our conscious awareness) is itself directly due to the fact that, as Terrence W. Deacon points out in his 1997 book *The Symbolic Species: The Co-evolution of Language and the Brain*, humans have been pre-adapted, primarily through the co-evolution of language and the brain, to be a symbolic and, therefore, a self-representing species. (Wynter, "Unsettling the Coloniality of Being/Power/Truth/Freedom," 325–26)

15. See Joy Buolamwini and Timnit Gebru, "Gender Shades: Intersectional Accuracy Disparities in Commercial Gender Classification," in *Proceedings of the 1st Conference on Fairness, Accountability and Transparency, Proceedings of Machine Learning Research* 81 (2018): 77–91; Safiya Umoja Noble, *Algorithms of Oppression* (New York: New York University Press, 2018); Ruha Benjamin, "Assessing Risk, Automating Racism," *Science* 366, no. 6464 (2019): 421–22; and Ruha Benjamin, *Race after Technology: Abolitionist Tools for the New Jim Code* (Cambridge: Polity, 2019).

16. In her later writings, Wynter further explores the neurobiological correlates of this process, arguing that in addition to the "ontogenic" level of genes, for humans as social creatures, the reward centers of the human brain respond to and are conditioned by social contexts which are "always, already" shaped by the processes of sociogeny, of the symbolically coded mode of being human, of being a subject in which all human beings find themselves. Our genetic codes constitute a "first set of instructions" which are always expressed in interaction with the nongenetic codes of our culture/society. "So we note here that the mind is not the brain. Since the causal source of the nature of our response does not lie in the neurophysiological mechanisms of the brain, which implement that response. It lies instead in the master code of the sociogenic principle. Since it is its meaning systems that determine how the mechanisms of the brain will implement our experience of being human, in the terms of each culture's specific conception." Scott, "Re-enchantment of Humanism," 189. Also see Wynter and McKittrick, "Unparalleled Catastrophe for Our Species?," 70–73; Sylvia Wynter, "Towards the Sociogenic Principle: Fanon, Identity, the Puzzle of Conscious Experience, and What It Is Like to Be 'Black,'" in *National Identities and Sociopolitical Changes in Latin America*, ed. Mercedes F. Durán-Cogan and Antonio Gómez-Moriana (New York: Routledge, 2001), 30–66.

17. Sylvia Wynter, "Columbus, the Ocean Blue, and Fables That Stir the Mind: To Reinvent the Study of Letters," in *Poetics of the Americas: Race, Founding, and Textuality*, ed. Bainard Cowan and Jefferson Humphries (Baton Rouge: Louisiana State University Press, 1997), 157.

18. Sylvia Wynter, "On How We Mistook the Map for the Territory, and Re-imprisoned Ourselves in Our Unbearable Wrongness of Being, of *Désêtre*: Black Studies toward the Human Project," in *Not Only the Master's Tools: African-American Studies in Theory and Practice*, ed. Lewis R. Gordon and Jane Anna Gordon (Boulder, CO: Paradigm, 2006), 122–24.

19. As Wynter says,

> So what we are going to find now is that it is the category of "natives" and "niggers" that will be made to function as the embodiment of the human Other to this now purely biologized and bourgeois conception of the human. Now, this is very, very important, the recognition that our Otherness creates not so much a white identity as a bourgeois identity, with whiteness serving, together with non-whiteness and Blackness, as a part of a totemic signifying complex. But as one whose indispensable function is to suggest that the value difference between (bourgeois) Man and its working-class Others is as supraculturally and extra-humanly ordained as is the projected value difference between Indo-European peoples and all native peoples, at its most total, between white and Black. (Scott, "Re-enchantment of Humanism," 177)

20. Wynter "Unsettling the Coloniality of Being/Power/Truth/Freedom," 323.

21. Scott, "Re-enchantment of Humanism," 160.
22. Scott, 195.
23. Alagraa, "What Will Be the Cure?"
24. Wynter, "Ceremony Found," 202–4.
25. Wynter writes, in "'Genital Mutilation' or 'Symbolic Birth'? Female Circumcision, Lost Origins, and the Aculturalism of Feminist/Western Thought," *Case Western Reserve Law Review* 47, no. 2 (1996):

> At about the same time as Einstein, in an address given in 1946, the Négritude poet Aimé Césaire (who had first called for the recognition of the peculiar nature of our problem, as the problem I propose of the code of symbolic life inscripted by the Color Line) had put forward his proposal for a new science able to complement and complete the natural sciences. Arguing that, in spite of the remarkable achievements of the natural sciences that had helped to make the natural world predictable, they had remained "half-starved" because they were *unable* to make our human worlds intelligible, Césaire had called for the elaboration of a new order of knowledge, specific to human forms of life, a science, therefore of the Word—"More and more, the word promises to be an algebraic equation that makes the world intelligible. Just as the new Cartesian algebra permitted the construction of theoretical physics, so too an original handling of the word can make possible at any moment a new theoretical and heedless science that poetry could already give an approximate notion of. Then the time will come again when the study of the word will condition the study of nature." (550)

26. Elsewhere, Wynter describes this new science as erasing "the barrier between the natural sciences and the humanities, as the condition of making our 'narratively constructed worlds and their orders of feeling and belief' subject to 'scientific description in a new way.'" Wynter, "Columbus, the Ocean Blue, and Fables That Stir the Mind," 162. Describing this new science, Wynter also writes,

> I propose that Césaire's *new science* would necessarily have to be a new *hybrid* form, with "science" itself redefined beyond the limits of the natural sciences' restrictedness to their specific domains of inquiry of the physical and purely biological levels of reality. This new order of cognition, as the basis of a new episteme, would have as its specific domain of inquiry that of our uniquely human third level of existence—dually *biological and meta-biological*—doing so, however, according to what can now be recognized as *Laws of Human Auto-institution* that are as *specific to the functioning of this level of reality* as purely biological laws are specific to the functioning of the second level. Consequently, the telos or aim of this proposed new episteme is therefore the same in this respect as that of the natural sciences. This telos is that of working towards a new and imperatively self-correcting (however eventually), open-ended, order of *extra-territorial cognition* (Gellner, 1974). (Wynter, "Ceremony Found," 209–10)

27. Scott, "Re-enchantment of Humanism," 190.
28. Sylvia Wynter, "Toward the Sociogenic Principle," 33. In one of Wynter's oft-cited quotes, Epstein says, "Culture, in my view, is what a human being creates and what creates a human being at the same time. In culture, the human being is simultaneously

creator and creation. This is what makes culture different from both the natural and the supernatural; because in the supernatural we have the world of the Creator, and in nature we have the world of creations. The coincidence of these two roles in a human being is what makes him a cultural being . . . . Transculture means a space in, or among, cultures, which is open to all of them. Culture frees us from nature; transculture frees us from culture, any one culture." Berry, Johnson, and Miller-Pogacar, "Postcommunist Postmodernism," quoted in Wynter, "Unsettling the Coloniality of Being/Power/Truth/Freedom," 285–86.

29. Sylvia Wynter, "Ceremony Must Be Found: After Humanism," *boundary 2* 12/13, no. 3/1 (1984): 39.

30. Scott, "Re-enchantment of Humanism," 196.

31. Scott, 196–97.

32. Wynter, "Ceremony Found," 223.

33. For example, see Benjamin Robinson, "Racialization and Modern Religion: Sylvia Wynter, Black Feminist Theory, and Critical Genealogies of Religion," *Critical Research on Religion* 7, no. 3 (2019): 257–74.

34. Ulli Beier and Wọle Ṣoyinka, "Wole Soyinka on Yoruba Religion: A Conversation with Ulli Beier," *Isokan Yoruba Magazine* 3, no. 3 (1997): 5.

35. Sylvia Wynter, "Africa, the West, and the Analogy of Culture: The Cinematic Text after Man," in *Symbolic Narratives / African Cinema: Audiences, Theory and the Moving Image*, edited by June Givanni (London: British Film Institute, 2000), 40–41.

36. Wynter, "Ceremony Found," 214–15.

37. Wynter, 215–16.

38. Frantz Fanon, *The Wretched of the Earth*, trans. Constance Farrington (New York: Grove, 1963), 220.

39. Wynter, "Genital Mutilation," 509. The article continues,

> Thus, where Professor Obiora sets out to "address how relevant circumcision protestations contradict feminist principles" (protestations that, as she shows later, must, *inter alia*, attack both the women who are circumcisors and all women who still fervently believe in the practice), my proposal is that we consider the possibility that there is no contradiction, in that the generic referent subject of feminist discourse may not be *all* women. This mirrors the fact that the referent subject of our present order of knowledge, *Man*, and its discourse of Liberal humanism, is not all *humans*, but *only those who attain to Western bourgeois status*. Thus, the generic referent subject of feminist discourse is only the culturally Western and westernized middle-class woman, who alone can, within the terms of our present order, come to constitute the generic woman. As such, she is one who must necessarily claim, as does her male middle class peer, a "monopoly of humanity." (Wynter, "Genital Mutilation," 509)

40. Wynter, "Genital Mutilation," 507. Emphasis added.

41. Johannes Fabian, *Time and the Other: How Anthropology Makes Its Object* (New York: Columbia University Press, 2002 [1983]), 31.

42. This comparison is somewhat analogous to Fanon's comparison in *Black Skin, White Masks* of the "Pygmy" and the French bourgeois subjects, who experience "the normalcy of being human" and never experience the condition of the colonial subject of being "abnormally human," of being excluded from being (see Wynter and McKittrick,

"Unparalleled Catastrophe," 50–60). However, there is an important difference between the conception of humanity among Bambuti or Baka (so-called Pygmy people) and those of the modern, bourgeois French, as the former do not require the latter as a foil against which to define themselves, defining themselves through relationships to the forest, spirits, ancestors, and dynamic family/clan networks, whereas (as Wynter demonstrates) the bourgeois Frenchman requires "the pygmy" and the "African" against which his material and cultural position is created and defined.

43. Joyce E. King, "Race and Our Biocentric Belief System: An Interview with Sylvia Wynter," in *Black Education: A Transformative Research and Action Agenda for the New Century*, ed. Joyce E. King (Washington, DC: American Educational Research Association, 2005), 364–65. Emphasis added. In another essay, while recognizing the "unifying role this counter-belief system had played in making possible Haiti's anti-slavery, independence struggle and victory against the French," Wynter characterizes it as "neo-agrarian" and just as cognitively closed as the modern, Western order of knowledge for which it serves as a constitutive other. Wynter, "Pope Must Have Been Drunk," 21–22.

44. Wynter writes, "The paradox here is that, as recent scholars have shown, it was to be precisely on the basis of this degodding of being, based on the West's invention of *Man,*' and of its human Others, that the millennially held belief by all peoples in *supernatural causality* was to be replaced by the epochally new premise of *natural causality,* and thereby, of an autonomously functioning order of nature regulated, no longer as it had been held to be by divine laws, but by its own laws." Wynter, "Genital Mutilation," 546. In a later interview Wynter states, "All such sacred theological discourses (Judaism, Islamism [sic], Christianity, for example) continue to function in the already theo-cosmogonically mandated cognitively closed terms that are indispensable to the enacting of their respective behavior-inducing and behavior-regulatory fictively eusocializing imperative." Wynter and McKittrick, "Unparalleled Catastrophe," 37.

45. Scott, "Re-enchantment of Humanism," 194.

46. Scott, 199.

47. Chimamanda Ngozi Adichie, "The Danger of a Single Story," *TED Talks*, July 2009. Access through https://www.ted.com/talks/chimamanda_ngozi_adichie_the _danger_of_a_single_story/transcript?language=en.

48. See Valentin Y. Mudimbe, *The Invention of Africa: Gnosis, Philosophy, and the Order of Knowledge* (Bloomington: Indiana University Press, 1988).

49. Ultimately, this tension or contradiction in Wynter's work results from its inability to escape from the overrepresentation of the biocentric, epistemic order of Man2 as reality as such, and concomitant designation and denigration of "religious" traditions and cosmologies as somehow less "true" and "evolved" even while critiquing these dynamics. For example, describing the "part science, part myth" Darwinian story of evolution, Wynter writes, "For, on the one hand, its "part science" *aspect does indeed correctly describe the origins of the physiological/neurophysiological implementing conditions of our being hybridly human.* . . . Yet, on the other hand, this bio-cosmic representation of origins is also taken, and mistakenly so, to be the true *origins* or *basis* of our *being human*, and thereby serves to charter and legitimate the anthropological (and general Western academic/intellectual) projection of the notion that their/our own purely secular cum biocentric origin myth is somehow 'real and true.'" Wynter, "Ceremony Found," 215. Presumably this means that the "scientific" aspect of the

Darwinian story may be incomplete, but is nonetheless "correct" in ways that other origin myths are not. However, as Wynter herself writes in another essay, "Yet, it is very clear that the question, 'which of the two world perceptions' (that of the Westernized subject, that of the Vodouisant, or that of a bird), is more accurate, is a quite senseless one, since to decide this question it would be necessary to apply a (transculturally and transspecies valid) standard of right perception, i.e., to apply a standard which does and can not exist." Wynter, "Pope Must Have Been Drunk," 33. Similarly, in his essay on Evans-Pritchard's classic, *Witchcraft, Oracles, and Magic among the Azande,* Peter Winch responds to a similar assertion, "What Evans-Pritchard wants to be able to say is that the criteria applied in scientific experimentation constitute a true link between our ideas and an independent reality, whereas those characteristic of other systems of thought—in particular, magical methods of thought—do not. It is evident that that the expressions 'true link' and 'independent reality' in the previous sentence cannot be explained by reference to the scientific universe of discourse, as this would beg the question. We have then to ask how, by reference to what established universe of discourse, the use of these expressions is to be explained; and it is clear that Evans-Pritchard has not answered this question." Peter Winch, "Understanding a Primitive Society," *American Philosophical Quarterly* 1, no. 4 (1964), 309. I would argue that Wynter has also not answered this question (and, in an earlier essay, has even declared it impossible to answer).

50. As Fanon wrote, "When I search for Man in the technique and the style of Europe, I see only a succession of negations of man, and an avalanche of murders." Fanon, *Wretched of the Earth*, 310.

51. Wynter, "Pope Must Have Been Drunk," 34.

52. King, "Race and Our Biocentric Belief System," 365 (emphasis added).

53. For compelling critiques from the Islamic philosophical tradition on how to deal with a degodded world, see Seyyed Hossein Nasr, *Knowledge and the Sacred* (Albany: State University of New York Press, 1989); Seyyed Hossein Nasr, *Religion and the Order of Nature* (Oxford: Oxford University Press, 1996); Seyyed Hossein Nasr, *Islam and the Plight of Modern Man* (Cambridge: Islamic Texts Society, 2002); Cheikh Hamidou Kane, *Ambiguous Adventure*, trans. Katherine Woods (New York: Heinemann, 1972); and Wael Hallaq, *Restating Orientalism: A Critique of Modern Knowledge* (New York: Columbia University Press, 2018).

54. Wynter, "Africa, the West, and the Analogy of Culture," 421.

55. Islam was incorporated in various ways into many Afro-Atlantic religions such as Vodou; see Benson LeGrace, "'Qismat' of the Names of Allah in Haitian Vodou," *Journal of Haitian Studies* 8, no. 2 (2002): 160–64.

56. Robin Horton made a similar mistake in his work. See Robin Horton, *Patterns of Thought in Africa and the West: Essays on Magic, Religion and Science* (New York: Cambridge University Press, 1997) and Oludamini Ogunnaike, "African Philosophy Reconsidered: Africa, Religion, Race, and Philosophy," *Journal of Africana Religions* 5, no. 2 (2017): 181–216.

57. Wynter, "Africa, West, and the Analogy of Culture," 417.

58. In fact, such traditions are internally highly heterogenous and are less fixed, closed systems of thought than dynamic arenas containing potent resources left by those who have gone before and into which new resources and actors are welcome.

59. Quoted in Wynter, "Africa, West, and the Analogy of Culture," 417.

60. As with the category "Hinduism," what is often called "Yorùbá traditional religion" is really a constellation of distinct, competing, mutually recognizing and somewhat overlapping traditions that were typically practiced nonexclusively.

61. For more on the skeptical-empirical nature of traditional Yorùbá epistemologies see Barry Hallen and J. Olubi Sodipo, *Knowledge, Belief, and Witchcraft: Analytic Experiments in African Philosophy* (Stanford, CA: Stanford University Press, 1997); and Oludamini Ogunnaike, *Deep Knowledge: Ways of Knowing in Sufism and Ifá, Two West African Intellectual Traditions* (College Park: Penn State University Press, 2020).

62. See Ogunnaike, *Deep Knowledge*, 201.

63. See Ayọdeji Ogunnaike, "How Worship Becomes Religion: Religious Change and Change in Religion in Ẹ̀dẹ́ and Salvador" (PhD diss., Harvard University, 2019); and J. Lorand Matory, *Black Atlantic Religion* (Princeton, NJ: Princeton University Press, 2009).

64. See Karin Barber, "How Man Makes God in West Africa: Yoruba Attitudes towards the *Orisa*," *Africa: Journal of the International African Institute* 51, no. 3 (1981): 724–45.

65. Barber, 741.

66. J. Lorand Matory, *The Fetish Revisited: Marx, Freud, and the Gods Black People Make* (Durham, NC: Duke University Press, 2018), 31.

67. The consciously "transcultural" nature of many Islamic intellectual, aesthetic, and spiritual traditions—the Qur'an and hadith explicitly and sometimes positively mention "other" religious traditions and communities and the Muslim world was markedly cosmopolitan (including Jews, Mandaeans, Christians, Zoroastrians, Pagan Neoplatonists, and shortly thereafter, Buddhists and other Dharmic traditions, Central Asian Shamanic traditions, Confucian and Taoist traditions, indigenous African religions, and much more)—from its earliest days, leading to characteristic statements like that of the early Islamic philosopher al-Kindī's "We should not be ashamed to acknowledge truth from whatever source it comes to us, even if it is brought to us by former generations and foreign powers. For him who seeks the truth there is nothing of higher value than truth itself," probably contributed to the recognition of these "autopoietic" dynamics.

68. See O. Ogunnaike, *Deep Knowledge*, 204. However, in most Òrìṣà traditions and virtually all Sufi traditions, there is a deep ground of reality (Olódùmarè or the Divine Essence [*al-Dhāt*], respectively) that lies beyond these dynamics of mutual construction, or more precisely, "within" which these dynamics take place.

69. William C. Chittick, *The Sufi Path of Knowledge: Ibn al-'Arabī's Metaphysics of Imagination* (Albany: State University of New York Press, 1989), 355. Henceforth, "*SPK*."

70. Michel Chodkiewicz, *The Spiritual Writings of Emir 'abd al-Kader* (Albany: State University of New York Press, 1995), 128–32.

71. Moreover, in trying to fight these constructions, we often get further trapped in their constrictions, merely reinforcing the bounds we seek to free ourselves from. See Oludamini Ogunnaike, "Two Islamic Global Philosophies of Religion: Suhrawardī and Shushtarī," in *Voices of Three Generations: Essays in Honor of Seyyed Hossein Nasr on His 86th Birthday*, ed. Mohammad Fahgfoory (Chicago: Kazi, 2019), 129.

72. Wynter, "Africa, the West, and the Analogy of Culture," 402.

73. Matory, *Fetish Revisited*, 28. The "exclusion" of other "religions" is more complicated in the case of Judaism and Islam, since the latter regards all previous religions as also being "Islam"—a divinely inspired revelation, with the Qur'an saying,

"For every community there is a messenger" (10:47) and "We sent to every community a messenger" (16:36)—thus the issue becomes a more complicated one of the potential "abrogation" and boundaries of these revelations/religions.

74. Kane, *Ambiguous Adventure*, 78.

75. In Yorùbá mythical accounts (which have some parallels with the Myth of Er and the Platonic/neo-Platonic concept of a *daimon*) everyone and everything in the cosmos "chooses its head (*orí*)" in heaven (*ọ̀run*) from the storehouse of the potter Àjàlá, who never makes the same head twice. This single choice (*ìpín*) of *orí* (head/destiny) in the atemporal otherworld (*ọ̀run*) is reflected in the countless choices made in the temporal world (*ayé*), and as the "witness of the choice of destiny" (*Ẹlẹ́rí ìpín*), the òrìṣà Ọ̀rúnmìlà is consulted through Ifá divination to help people fulfil their destinies (or, from another perspective, Ifá divination facilitates communication with one's own *orí-inú*). Abiọdun records the following *oríkì* (praise incantation) for Orí-inú:

> It is Orí that creates a being
> Before the world began
> It is the Òrìṣà who can change one
> No one changes Òrìṣà.
> It is Òrìṣà who changes one, like a yam being roasted.

Rowland Abiọdun, *Yoruba Art and Language: Seeking the African in African Art* (Cambridge: Cambridge University Press, 2014), 37. (Translation modified by the author on the basis of the original Yorùbá original.) That is, through the choice of orí and worship of òrìṣà, devotees "create" and change themselves (like a yam being roasted), although in a different cosmological context than that which Wynter describes.

76. See Abiọdun, *Yoruba Art and Language*, 24–52.

77. Abiọdun, 32.

78. See Wande Abímbọ́lá, "Ìwàpẹ̀lẹ̀: The Concept of Good Character in Ifá Literary Corpus," in *Yorùbá Oral Tradition*, ed. W. Abímbọ́lá (Ife: University of Ife, 1975), 387–420.

79. See Ayọdeji Ogunnaike, "What's Really behind the Mask: A Reexamination of Syncretism in Brazilian Candomblé," *Journal of Africana Religions* 8, no. 1 (2020): 146–71; and Ayọdeji Ogunnaike, "The Myth of Purity," *Harvard Divinity Bulletin*, Summer–Autumn 2013, https://bulletin.hds.harvard.edu/articles/summerautumn2013/myth-purity.

80. He writes, "Through our own delimitation we judge that He is nondelimited. But the actual situation in itself is described neither by delimitation nor nondelimitation. Rather, it is all-inclusive Being *(wujūd 'āmm)*. Hence He is identical with the things, but the things are not identical with Him. Nothing becomes manifest without His He-ness being identical with that thing. How should He whose Being is such accept nondelimitation or delimitation? In such manner have the gnostics known Him. He who declares Him non-delimited has not known Him, and he who declares Him delimited is ignorant of Him." Chittick, *SPK*, 354.

81. Chittick, *SPK*, 351.

82. Chittick, *SPK*, 349.

83. This remark is not a mere poetic or metaphorical statement, as many autobiographical and hagiographical Sufi accounts (like those of many so-called indigenous peoples; see Eduardo Vivieros de Castro, *Cannibal Metaphysics*, trans. P. Skafish (Minneapolis: University of Minnesota Press, 2015) record the literal experience of "seeing" everything at once, from all perspectives, or seeing and experiencing reality

through the eyes or perspective of other people, animals, or other nonhuman beings. (For example, see Aḥmad b. Mubārak al-Lamaṭī, *Pure Gold from the Words of Sayyidī ʿAbd al-ʿAzīz al-Dabbāgh: Al-Dhahab al-Ibrīz min Kalām Sayyidī ʿAbd al-ʿAzīz al-Dabbāgh*, trans. John O'Kane and Bernd Radtke [Boston: Brill, 2007], 129–33; and Mervyn Hiskett, *The Sword of Truth: The Life and Times of the Shehu Usuman dan Fodio* [New York: Oxford University Press, 1973], 64–65). In Sufi traditions, this kind of experience is known as a *Fatḥ* or "opening" and stands in sharp contrast to the "cognitive closure" Wynter posits for these cultures and orders of knowledge. My favorite argument against such cognitive closure comes from the Taoist sage Zhuangzhi: "Zhuangzi and Huizi were strolling along the bridge over the Hao River. Zhuangzi said, "The minnows swim about so freely, following the openings wherever they take them. Such is the happiness of fish." Huizi said, "You are not a fish, so whence do you know the happiness of fish?" Zhuangzi said, "You are not I, so whence do you know I don't know the happiness of fish?" Huizi said, "I am not you, to be sure, so I don't know what it is to be you. But by the same token, since you are certainly not a fish, my point about your inability to know the happiness of fish stands intact." Zhuangzi said, "Let's go back to the starting point. You said, 'Whence do you know the happiness of fish?' Since your question was premised on your knowing that I know it, I must have known it from here, up above the Hao River." Brook Ziporyn, *Zhuangzi: The Essential Writings with Selections from Traditional Commentaries* (Indianapolis: Hackett, 2009), 76.

84. Scott, "Re-enchantment of Humanism," 196–97. As argued above, the illusory novelty of this position is due to the very overrepresentation of Man as the human, and the resulting distortions of other modes of being human, which Wynter demonstrates so effectively.

85. Or in the terms of Sufi poetry, as "love," as in Ibn al-ʿArabī's famous poem:

> My heart can take on any form:
> a meadow for gazelles,
> a cloister for monks,
> For the idols, sacred ground,
> Ka'ba for the circling pilgrim,
> the tables of the Torah,
> the scrolls of the Qur'án.
> I profess the religion of love;
> wherever its caravan turns along the way,
> that is my religion,
> the faith I keep.

Michael A. Sells, "Ibn ʿArabi's 'Gentle Now, Doves of the Thornberry and Moringa Thicket,'" *Journal of the Muhyiddin Ibn Arabi Society* 10 (1991): 1–12. Perhaps the same reality is alluded to in Wynter's statement, "The rule is love."

86. Compare to Fanon's closing prayer of *Black Skin, White Masks*: "O my body, make me always a man who questions!" (206).

87. Chittick, SPK, 381.

88. William Chittick, "The Central Point," *Journal of the Muhyiddin Ibn Arabi Society* 35 (2004): 45. Or in the maxim of the nineteenth-century Nigerian Sufi Muḥammad Sambo (son of Usman dan Fodio, founder of the Sokoto Caliphate), "Remove the [outward] form and free being!"

89. Ibn al-ʿArabī, *The Ringstones of Wisdom*, trans. Caner Dagli (Chicago: Kazi, 2004), 256.

90. Katherine McKittrick, "Yours in the Intellectual Struggle: Sylvia Wynter and the Realization of the Living," in *Sylvia Wynter: Being Human as Praxis*, ed. Katherine McKittrick (Durham, NC: Duke University Press, 2015), 2. However, I would argue that Wynter's sociogenic origin theory does function as such a replacement. Whereas a Sufi shaykh or babaláwo or Mambo would understand their own particular tradition as containing or opening up onto a transcendent reality that is both beyond and immanent in the particularities of their traditions and origin stories, Wynter seems to propose another particular, immanent master narrative (evolutionary, biolinguistic sociogeny) of master narratives.

91. For more on this notion see Salman H. Bashier, *Ibn al-ʿArabī's Barzakh: The Concept of the Limit and the Relationship between God and the World* (Albany: State University of New York Press, 2004).

92. Chittick, *SPK*, 204.

93. See Zachary Valentine Wright, *Realizing Islam: The Tijaniyya in North Africa and the Eighteenth-Century Muslim World* (Chapel Hill: University of North Carolina Press, 2020), 101–41.

94. Wright, 117. Wright also cites several other passages of al-Tijānī's that elucidate the "universality" of this perspective: "Reflecting on the 'Muhammadan light' that pervades all of creation, al-Tijānī similarly observed, 'There is no difference between a believer and an infidel (*kāfir*) in terms of humanity (*fī l-ādamiyy*)'" (Wright, 102); "All of the worlds are included in this love, even the disbelievers (*kuffār*), for they are His beloveds in the presence of His words, "I loved to be known, so I created the creation and made Myself known to them, and by Me they know Me." Do not imagine that any in creation are excluded from this cognizance (*maʿrifa*). Indeed, all of the souls (*arwāḥ*) have been created with complete cognizance of God the Exalted. Ignorance only occurred to them with their mixture in the material bodies . . . so the ignorance that befell the souls is not intrinsic to them. Knowledge of God the Exalted is that which is intrinsic to them" (Wright, 107).

95. As Rumi wrote:

> There are no parts or numbers in the spirit, no persons or partitions in the spirit.
> The oneness of the Friend delights the friends—catch hold of spirit's foot, for form is stubborn.
> Dissolve the stubborn form with acts of hardship till you see oneness under it like treasure.
> And if you don't dissolve it, then His favours themselves dissolve it, O my heart, His slave.
> He even manifests Himself to hearts and He will mend the ragged dervish robe.
> We were all open-hearted, all one essence; we were all headless, we were footless there.
> And of one essence were we, like the sun; we had no knots and we were pure like water.
> When that pure light began to take on form, it multiplied like battlements in shadows.
> Destroy the battlements with catapults, so that division leaves this company.

Rumi, *Spiritual Verses*, trans. Alan Williams (New York: Penguin Books, 2006), 68.

96. Rumi, *Masnavi III*: 3901–3906, cited in Annemarie Schimmel, *Mystical Dimensions of Islam* (Chapel Hill: University of North Carolina Press, 1975), 321–22. Translation

modified by author based on Persian original. Although the vastly different metaphysical and cosmological contexts mean that this should in no way be read as an account of biological evolution, see Chittick, *SPK*, 72–82.

97. Ahmadou Bamba Mbacke, *Qaṣīda Asīru ma 'l-abrār* (Touba: Bashīr Laye., n.d.), 1, 10. Also see http://www.ixassida.com/lecture/assiru/1/.

98. Mignolo, "Sylvia Wynter," 107.

99. While there is not space in this essay to go into these matters fully, there are many strong philosophical arguments and much evidence (from the likes of Nagarjuna, Sri Harsa, Shankaracarya, Dogen, Suhrawardi, Mulla Sadra, Nagel, Searle, Chalmers, Latour, the babaláwo of Ifá and mambos and houngans of Vodou) of the limited and limiting, not to mention self-contradictory, nature of this biocentric, emergentist perspective.

100. Scott asks,

> In order to make this kind of argument, do you not need a kind of ontologically prior human/nature ground on which these codes, these historical codes, are inscripted? A ground that forms the basis for the emancipated ecumenical conception of the human that you want to voice? . . . So there is on the one hand a radical rehistoricization that attempts to illuminate the place of Man in Europe's autobiography. But, on the other hand, you don't simply want to historicize humanism, you want to provide the ground for a different imagining of the human. But that reimagining of the human has in some way to rest on an unhistoricizable *a priori*, and it is that unhistoricizable *a priori* that I want to understand. (Scott, "Re-enchantment of Humanism," 197)

101. Scott, 197–98.

102. For example, David Marriott has cogently critiqued Wynter's continued attachment to the "law-like" or "code-like" nature of "science" in the biocentric formation of Man2 even in the new "science of the word" for which she calls, and the limitations this necessarily entails. See David Marriott, "Inventions of Existence: Sylvia Wynter, Frantz Fanon, Sociogeny, and 'the Damned,'" *CR: The New Centennial Review* 11, no. 3 (2011): 45–89.

103. See Michael A. Sells, *Mystical Languages of Unsaying* (Chicago: University of Chicago Press, 1994).

104. Scott, "Re-enchantment of Humanism," 194.

105. In Ifá and Yorùbá traditions more generally, this is found in the Orí-inú, which is praised as "my creator" (*ẹlẹ́da mi*), "the creator of being, before the world began" (Abiọdun, *Yoruba Art*, 37), the divine aspect of every individual and the individual aspect of Olódùmarè; Orí-inú is described as *ìpín* (active choice of destiny) but also *àyànmọ̀* (apportioned lot) and *àkúnlẹ̀yàn* (that which was passively received kneeling)—human agency is both active and passive vis-à-vis Divine agency here because orí-inú is the place where human and Divine identity meet. In Sufi traditions this issue is typically discussed in reference to the verse of the Qur'an, "You did not throw, when you threw, but God threw" (8:17) that simultaneously denies and affirms human agency, equating it with Divine agency. See Chittick, *SPK*, 113–18, 211.

106. Fanon, *Black Skin, White Masks*, 204.

107. Ibn al-ʿArabī writes, describing our self-determination:

> He does not determine our properties except through us. Or rather, we determine our own properties. Or rather, we determine our own properties

through ourselves, though within Him. . . . The Divine Will becomes connected only to a single thing. Will is a relationship which follows knowledge, while knowledge is a relationship that follows the object of knowledge. The object of knowledge is you and your states (*aḥwāl*). Knowledge displays no effect within the object of knowledge. On the contrary, the object of knowledge displays its effects in knowledge. The object gives to knowledge what it actually is in itself. . . . Even though the Real determines the property, He only effuses [*fāḍa*] existence upon you, and you determine your own property. Hence you should praise none but yourself and blame none but yourself. For the Real, only praise remains for effusing existence, since that belongs to Him, not to you. (Chittick, *SPK*, 299)

108. Fanon, *Black Skin, White Masks*, 204.
109. Fanon, 12.
110. However, Anwar Omeish's brilliant thesis has demonstrated the ways in which Fanon's work, especially in regard to Algeria, is marked by uninterrogated theoretical commitments to direct access to a culturally unmediated political real. See Anwar Omeish, "Toward the Modern Revolution: Frantz Fanon, Secularity, and the Horizons of Political Possibility in Revolutionary Algeria" (undergraduate honors thesis, Harvard University, 2019).
111. Marriott, "Inventions of Existence," 53. This is somewhat analogous to Ilya Prigogine's distinction between an "Event" and a "Law," which Wynter takes up in her work. Marriott's point is that unlike Fanon's "leap," Wynter's "fourth event" / second emergence remains bound by history and its laws.
112. Scott, "Re-enchantment of Humanism," 195. Fanon writes, "for all of these findings and all of this research have a single aim: to get man to admit that he is nothing, absolutely nothing—and get him to eradicate this narcissism whereby he thinks he is different from the other 'animals.' This is nothing more nor less than the *capitulation of man*. All in all, I grasp my narcissism with both hands and reject the vileness of those who want to turn man into a machine." Fanon, *Black Skin, White Masks*, 6.
113. As Marika Rose writes, "Taking seriously Wynter's account of the entanglement of disenchantment with epochal shifts in the genres of the human begins to suggest, then, that disenchantment is not so much about the disappearance of magic and mystery so much as their transformation. It is about the violent destruction of old social and metaphysical bonds which tied people to one another and to the world around them in order to bind them to new masters who were appropriating for themselves both legal and sovereign power—to nation states and European citizens, which is to say, to slavers and colonizers." Marika Rose, "Decolonizing Disenchantment," *Contending Modernities*, September 1, 2020, https://contendingmodernities.nd.edu/decoloniality/decolonizing-disenchantment/.
114. Chittick, "Central Point," 45. In a similar vein, Katherine McKittrick writes, "disciplines differentiate, split, and create fictive distances between us. . . . Discipline is empire." Katherine McKittrick, *Dear Science and Other Stories* (Durham, NC: Duke University Press), 35. In a similar vein, a common *oríkì* of Ọ̀rúnmìlà from Odù Èjì-Ogbè concludes, "Not knowing you fully, we [our lives] are in vain / If we could but know you in full, all would be well."
115. Wynter and McKittrick, "Unparalleled Catastrophe," 21–23.

116. Omeish, "Toward the Modern Revolution," 8. Omeish concludes,

> Fanon's commitment to the binary between modern and traditional—and its ontological and epistemological claims—rendered the Algerian problem space, and the solutions it offered, illegible to him. Indeed, these theoretical commitments limited the scope of his political project to a horizon of secularity that depended on modern subjectivities. In other words, rather than disrupting the ontological and epistemological claims that underlie colonial domination, Fanon treats them as absence and naturalizes them, and in doing so fails to recognize Algerian formulations of self and polity that challenge this domination at its epistemic root. By assuming the existence and epistemic value of the secular modern, Fanon occludes alternatives to it—the very alternatives that may have upset the foundations of the colonial domination he so fervently criticized. To put it more simply, Fanon's ontological and epistemological assumptions of secularity limited what he saw—and what he was able to see—as politically possible in revolutionary Algeria. (Omeish, "Toward the Modern Revolution," 145)

117. This is characteristic of post-Enlightenment, Western theories of time, in which a kind of progress is often dogmatic and the future is the realm of all-possibility, whereas many African traditions emphasize a kind of spiral time of renewal and balance, with the realm of all-possibility being "above" time or "before" it, which can erupt into the present at any moment. Ibn al-ʿArabī famously advocated a doctrine of the renewal of creation at every instant (*tajdīd al-khalq*), in which all of creation, including time, is manifest from and returns to the Real at each instant, discontinuously. See O. Ogunnaike, *Deep Knowledge*, 219–22, and J. D. Y. Peel, "Making History: The Past in the Ijesha Present," *Man* 19, no. 1 (1984): 111–32. These different conceptions and dimensions of temporality can have significant practical import, as Bedour Alagraa argues compellingly in "The Interminable Catastrophe," *Offshoot*, March 1, 2021, https://offshootjournal.org/the-interminable-catastrophe/.

118. In a 2021 interview Wynter (echoing African authors such as Okot p'Bitek, Cheikh Hamidou Kane, Amadou Hampâté Bâ, and Malidoma Patrice Somé) refers to initiation ceremonies in the Kingdom of Kongo in the sixteenth to eighteenth centuries to characterize all education as initiation:

> And you see what happens is that what was once there must die in order for the initiation to occur and entry into the new life. It is a birth through death. . . . And in this country we must begin to think about education as an initiation into a world full of symbols and descriptions about who we are. Thinking of it as initiation helps us to understand the importance of introducing something else into the lives and worlds of children. Initiation also gives an understanding of the symbolic significance of education, and how language and art structure the whole of our existence. We need to re-initiate ourselves, a symbolic life through death, and create ourselves anew!" (Alagraa, "What Will Be the Cure?")

119. Wynter, "Africa, the West, and the Analogy of Culture," 401.

120. See Walter D. Mignolo, "Foreword: On Pluriversality and Multipolarity," in *Constructing the Pluriverse*, ed. Bernd Reiter (Durham, NC: Duke University Press, 2018), ix–xvi.

121. In one of my favorite Wynter statements, she remarks:

> But if you move outside these limits, look at other cultures and their other conceptions, then look back at the West, at yourself, from a trans-genre-of-the-human perspective, something hits you. What you begin to recognize is that what the subjects of each order are everywhere producing is always a mode of being human, what Nietzsche [in *Genealogy of Morals*] saw as "the tremendous labour of man upon itself" by which it was to make itself calculable, its behaviours therefore predictable. This at the same time as we repress from ourselves that that is what we are doing: that we are, as humans, self-inscripting and inscripted flesh. At this juncture, you find yourself caught up in an enormously revalorized sense of what it is to be human. A kind of awe at the way in which we auto-institute, auto-inscript ourselves according to the same rules, from the most "local" and ostensibly "primitive" nomadic hunter-gatherer societies to our own vast contemporary global techno-industrial own. Further, you experience a profound co-identification, a sense that in every form that is being inscripted, each of us is also in that form, even though we do not experience it. So the human story/history becomes the collective story/history of these multiple forms of self-inscription or self-instituted genres, with each form/genre being adaptive to its situation, ecological, geopolitical. (Scott, "Re-enchantment of Humanism," 206)

My proposal is that traditions like Sufism and Ifá have been training their initiates to achieve these insights (and even "experience every form") for centuries, and that precisely because their epistemic grounds lie outside the modern West, they are better at the process of "moving beyond the limits" that makes such a perspective possible.

122. Like Fanon's work, Wynter's is an immanent critique of the present order of knowledge, what Wael Hallaq calls a "dissenting" position, rather than a "subversive" position based on radically different epistemic grounds. Both Fanon and Wynter gesture and strive toward such exteriority, but their theorizations from "liminal" positions within the dominant order of knowledge are still often bound by the limitations of the very order they seek to dismantle.

123. Matory writes,

> Therefore, European social theories and African altars are to be judged not for their truth or falsehood but for their relative efficacy at rearranging people's social priorities in a context where there is more than one choice regarding how people should organize themselves and how the rewards of their cooperation should be distributed. So it matters that, whereas Marx failed in his own efforts to organize and elevate the working class through his re-valuation of commodities and factories, the Afro-Atlantic priests who mentor me have successfully organized diverse populations around their own re-valuation of material things. And they have done so in competition with the Abrahamic religions and with the post-Enlightenment ideas—including Marxism—that dominate contemporary nation-states. (Matory, *Fetish Revisited*, xviii–xix)

I would argue that the efficacy of these Afro-Atlantic traditions is inseparable from their truth—that is, they are effective because they are true, and a "proof" of their truth is their efficacy.

124. Wynter, "*Black Metamorphosis*," 70–72.

125. Bob Marley, "Cornerstone," track 8 on *Soul Rebels*, Trojan Records, 1970.

126. Cedric Robinson called these Africana traditions "the raw material of the Black radical tradition, the values, ideas, conceptions, and constructions of reality from which resistance was manufactured." Cedric Robinson, *Black Marxism: The Making of the Black Radical Tradition* (Chapel Hill: University of North Carolina Press, 2000), 309.

127. This term is borrowed from Bedour Alagraa's work. See "The Interminable Catastrophe."

128. Wynter, Bennett, and Givens, "'A Greater Truth than Any Other Truth You Know,'" 128.

3   (Para)religious Traces in Sylvia Wynter's
    "Demonic Ground"

    Justine M. Bakker

The premise of this edited volume is, in some ways, rather simple and straightforward: religion, although always elusive and slippery, is central to Sylvia Wynter's oeuvre.[1] This also holds true for her well-known and often used concept of "demonic ground"—although not in a way one may initially expect. Already in 2006, Black studies scholar and geographer Katherine McKittrick noted that Wynter riffs on a secondary, "less ecclesial" meaning of the term demonic.[2] Although the term "demonic," McKittrick writes, "is defined as spirits—most likely the devil, demons, or deities— capable of possessing a human being,"[3] Wynter found inspiration elsewhere. In several hard sciences—including physics, mathematics, and computer science—the term denotes a "system that cannot have a determined, or knowable, outcome."[4] Conjured by scientists to think the outer limits of scientific theory, as Jimena Canales's wonderful and aptly titled *Bedeviled: A Shadow History of Demons in Science* (2020) also explains, demonic systems are fundamentally uncertain, always becoming.[5] While I agree with McKittrick that Wynter builds on this secondary meaning of the term and eschews the ecclesial, this chapter will demonstrate that the term, nevertheless, carries implicit religious traces. I am not suggesting that "demonic ground" *is* a "religious" term or a term fundamentally *about* something we may call "religion." Rather, in following various references in Wynter's exploration and explanation of demonic ground across numerous essays she published between 1987 and 2000, I observe that the term was both developed and explained in conversation with scholarship on religion and religious experience. This observation serves as a starting point to reconsider the role, limitations, and future of religion in Wynter's oeuvre.

The first part of the essay highlights that Wynter took inspiration from the writings of idiosyncratic thinker Alex Comfort, thereby using the research for and building on an essay I published previously.[6] Best known as the author of bestseller *The Joy of Sex* (1972), Comfort was a prolific writer who published on a diverse set of topics, including religion. Engaging his writings on the demonic, we will follow a slippery path from quantum physics and counterculture esotericisms to the "oceanic experiences" that Comfort observes in Hindu ontology and his critique of transcendent explanations of reality. In the second part, I will suggest, in turn, that identifying and following these religious traces in demonic ground allows us to look anew at Wynter's expansive analysis of the problematic role of religion in the origins and nature of our racialized modernity and her constructive new humanist project to move beyond it. It also points, I will suggest in the third and final part, to a form of meaning-making I have come to call parareligion.[7]

Demonic Observer Ground

The go-to text for Wynter's demonic ground is her 1990 essay "Afterword: Beyond Miranda's Meanings: Un/silencing the 'Demonic Ground' of Caliban's 'Woman.'"[8] This is also the text that was central to my earlier exploration of the term. However, it turns out that Wynter used the term, once, a couple of years prior, in the introduction of "On Disenchanting Discourse: 'Minority' Literary Criticism and Beyond" (1987).[9] The essay is one of the early examples of Wynter's "second phase" of writing, in which she shifts from primarily writing about Caribbean cultural production to advancing a vast, expansive argument about the nature and origins of racialized modernity. It proposes, more specifically, that the "unifying goal" of what Wynter calls "minority discourse" is to herald a new episteme.[10] Here's how Wynter begins the essay:

> In order to introduce and integrate, within the space of this paper, several "new objects of knowledge" which cannot meaningfully exist within the discursive *vrai* (truth) of our present "fundamental arrangements of knowledge" nor within the analogic of its "(ethico-) theoretical foundations," I shall make use of a series of epigraphs placed at different points of the argument. Their function will be to project the possibility of a "demonic observer" ground *outside* the consolidated field of meanings of our present analogic, a ground in

which these "new objects of knowledge" can find their efficient criterion/condition of truth.[11]

I will return to this quotation and its implication again and again during this essay. What matters here is that Wynter first uses the term "demonic observer ground" to consider and introduce "new objects of knowledge" that do not fit into the current "fundamental arrangements of knowledge."[12] The demonic observer ground names, in other words, a locale of epistemic intervention, "outside . . . of our present order and its related episteme." New theories, new concepts, new ways of knowing beyond, as the 1987 essay also already begins to elucidate, the figure and world of Man.[13] More strongly, the goal of "*minority* discourse" is to "accelerate the conceptual 'erasing' of the figure of Man."[14] "Man" is a term Wynter borrows from Michel Foucault's *The Order of Things: An Archeology of the Human Sciences* (1966), although she corrects and expands his argument by elucidating the central importance of race and colonialism in the formation of modernity's epistemes.[15] In Wynter's writings, Man is the shorthand for the rational-political subject (Man1) and then bio-economic subject (Man2) that over-represents itself as the only way of being human.

As the introduction and other chapters in this volume already discuss Man and its epistemic formations and foundations at length, I will refrain from doing so here. Instead, I will trace the footnote Wynter tags on to the phrase "demonic observer."[16] It reads:

> In an article—"Demonic and Historical Models in Biology"— Alex Comfort coins the term "demonic models" to refer to "logical representations of reality which exclude a space-time oriented observer." We have adapted the concept here to suggest the possibility of an observer / site of observation that is non-analogically oriented, that is, one outside the present discursive formations and meaning "fields" of our present order and its related episteme.[17]

As noted above, Wynter sees great potential in these "demonic models," precisely because they, when "adapted," point to the possibility of an observer/site that exists outside the world of "Man." "Demonic and Historical Models in Biology" builds on an article Comfort published a year prior in the same, and since 1991 defunct, *Journal of Social and Biological Structures*, entitled "The Cartesian Observer Revisited" (1979).[18] Reading the two articles side by side, as I've done in the aforementioned previous essay, helps in understanding what, precisely, Comfort means with the term "demonic" and, more specifically, what is meant by "logical representations of reality which exclude a space-time oriented observer." Allow me to repeat and summarize the three most important findings here.[19]

First, with the term "demonic," Comfort does not refer to "an imaginary demiurge"; rather, he uses the term "to imply logical and intelligent but not human and therefore not homuncular."[20] We find this phrasing—homuncular—in Wynter's description, too.[21] In conjuring demons to pursue the limits of scientific theory, Comfort steps into a long tradition. As Canales outlines in *Bedeviled*, the demon has a long and storied presence in the history of science, beginning with what remains perhaps one of the most famous: Descartes's demon.[22] In *Meditations on First Philosophy* (1640), Descartes proposes that "some evil spirit, supremely powerful and cunning, has devoted all his efforts to deceiving [him]."[23] Descartes's evil genius was born of fear and doubt: Could it be that everything he thought he knew existed was "imaginary"?[24] How could he be certain that it wasn't? "I shall think," he thus continued, "that the sky, the air, the earth, colours, shapes, sounds and all external things are no different from the illusions of our dreams, and that they are traps he has laid for my credulity."[25] Stripping down each layer of doubt—"I will consider myself as having no hands, no eyes, no flesh, no blood, and no senses"[26]—Descartes would finally conclude that his senses did not deceive him, a conclusion he could reach because of his fundamental belief in God.

The centuries that followed witnessed the birth of many demons. Scientists would conjure demons that they imagined could challenge or even break a certain hypothesis, thereby strengthening a theory—or dismissing it. Consider for instance Maxwell's demon, conjured in the nineteenth century by Scottish physicist James Clerk Maxwell to test the limits of the second law of thermodynamics. This tiny demon could disrupt the natural "progression of energy."[27] In her book *No Mercy Here: Gender, Punishment, and the Making of Jim Crow Modernity* (2016), Sarah Haley suggests Maxwell's demon as "the demon to which Wynter might refer."[28] Although I am not convinced that this is indeed Wynter's inspiration—I think Comfort's demon, to which I turn more fully shortly, is more likely—Haley's analysis does highlight something significant, as I noted elsewhere: specificity. After all, if she's correct in her hypothesis that Wynter took inspiration from Maxwell's demon, then it is not merely the case that her notion of demonic ground invokes models that embrace the unknown, nondeterministic, and contingent, but that it invokes a model that actively disrupts natural proceedings (the "progression of energy," in this specific case).[29] It would be a demon, then, that does not exist outside of but can actively intervene in the existing world.

This brings me to my second point, which revolves around an ostensibly straightforward question: What does Comfort's demon do, precisely? Comfort invokes his demon to query the limits of "Cartesian positional identity." In "The Cartesian Observer Revisited," Comfort writes that the Cartesian conceptualization of the subjective-objective distinction is, in "Western scientific ontology," treated as foundational and "real." Descartes distinguished between an I and a not-I, a subjective, observing self and an objective, outside environment. Yet, Comfort argues, "positional identity as a normal mode of experience biases our conception of the world."[30] It remains within the confines of Kantian a priori space and time (i.e., the "space-time" that is referred to in the citation that Wynter includes in her footnote). At the time of Comfort's writing, quantum physics had begun to test the limits of Descartes's theory, and Comfort was interested in thinking through the extent to which its findings could be applied in other domains as well. This is where the demon comes in: it's a way for him—as it was for so many who came before—to ask difficult questions of scientific theories. In an effort to interrogate "Cartesian positional identity"—which for him boils down to a hard-and-fast distinction between the observing self and the observed environment—Comfort conjured a demon that had "no sense of positional or temporal identity." This allowed Comfort to imagine "how a world view would look if it were not based on the conceptualizations which inhere in positional I-ness."[31]

Wynter does not relay the Cartesian specificity of Comfort's demon when she references his demonic observer ground, although it is evident that she is interested in the "vantage point" outside the "space-time oriented observer," which she rightfully links with the dominant episteme. Yet, that Comfort wrestles with Descartes gains heightened significance when we underscore the foundational role that Descartes's philosophy has played in the consolidation of what Wynter would come to call Man1: the rational-political subject. In a lecture from 1982, Wynter made the importance of Descartes for Man explicit by speaking of the "Cartesian conceptual formation" which distinguishes between the thinking subject (*res cogitans*), supposedly naturally endowed with "Reason," and the "extended matter" (*res extensa*).[32] Man, as other chapters in this volume discuss at length, needed a "symbolic other" to define himself against, an "other" that would serve as limit case, an "other" that would guarantee his coherency. Man would invent this "other" in the so-called New World, by construing "Negroes" and "Natives" as subrational or irrational.[33] To make this point explicit: Comfort's demon specifically questions the foundational worldview of Wynter-cum-Weheliye's "Cartesian Rational Man."[34]

Third, Comfort links his musings about a demon that can test the limits of Descartes to what he calls "oceanic experiences" in Hindu philosophy. While Western science has only recently begun to question the extent to which Descartes's intuitive model should be understood as "real," the "Indian tradition," Comfort writes, has always seen his subjective-objective distinction as an "illusory or at least optional way of viewing self and not-self."[35] Comfort seems dismissive of "'mystics' and other cultivators of oceanic states" who "have been uninterested in the physical universe and [are] given to making the religious noises required by their particular tradition" (note the skeptical quotations around "mystic").[36] Yet, he is simultaneously convinced "that a systematic pursuit of oceanic perception" might help to intuit precisely the kind of worldview that his demon could also invoke.[37] In "Demonic and Historical Models in Biology," the article that Wynter cites, Comfort does not invoke "Hindu tradition" but does speak—even more skeptically—of "questionable esoterica from neovitalism and entelechies to Kammerer and constellated coincidences" and Californians impressed by "parapsychology, telekinesis, and a world soul."[38]

Comfort seems to fall into the common trap of relegating "esoterica" to the realm of what Wouter Hanegraaff calls the "wastebasket of rejected knowledge."[39] That is, until the demon enters the stage. Here's Comfort: "'All theosophical garbage apart,' says the demon, 'have you seriously looked for them? It might be worth it.'"[40] And while he quickly adds, "it may also not," it is evident that Comfort, in conversing with a demon he conjured to test the limits of Descartes, sees something worth pursuing in these esotericisms. Sure, he is skeptical of the "theosophical" or "mystical" or "religious noises." Yet, in thinking through the epistemic possibilities of a demon with "no sense of positional or temporal identity," Comfort makes direct reference to religious traditions and experiences, a relationship he takes up again and deepens in *Reality and Empathy* (1984). We have arrived, then, at the first religious trace in Wynter's demonic ground: embedded in the concept is a preoccupation with oceanic and other religious experiences that challenge the reality and universalism of Descartes's subjective-objective distinction. Of course, Wynter's documented interest in the concept of "demonic observer ground" lies in its potential as a locus for epistemic intervention, not religious experiences. We can, in fact, only guess at the extent to which Wynter was interested in Comfort's ideas about religion and esoterica. However, when we track, as I will do in the next section, how she introduces the term "demonic ground" in "Beyond Miranda's Meanings," we can draw the tentative conclusion that she was at the very least aware of Comfort's engagement with these oceanic perceptions and, at the same time, uncover a second "trace" of religion.

Demonic Ground

Wynter published "Beyond Miranda's Meanings" in 1990, as the Afterword to *Out of the Kumbla*, the first edited volume on writings from women from the Caribbean. As the book's editor, Africana studies scholar Carole Boyce Davies, put it decades later, the volume was meant to begin a conversation about a specific "Caribbean feminist theoretical position."[41] Here's Wynter:

> I want to argue in this After/Word, *from its projected "demonic ground" outside of our present governing system of meaning, or theory/ontology in de Nicolas' sense of the word* that it is precisely the variable "race" which imposes upon these essays the contradictory dualism by which the writers both work within the "regime of truth" of the discourse of feminism, at the same time as they make use of this still essentially Western discourse to point towards the epochal threshold of a new post-modern and post-Western mode of cognitive inquiry; one which goes beyond the limits of our present "human sciences," to constitute itself as a new science of human "forms of life."[42]

This "new science of human ... life" is a kind of acceleration or radicalization of what Wynter, in "On Disenchanting Discourse," named "new objects of knowledge" and "new conceptual tools and theoretical foundations." This should not surprise us: Wynter's vast and expansive body of work can be seen, as decolonial scholar Walter Mignolo writes, as "a network, wherein her ideas and writings are in conversation with and refer back (and forth) to one another."[43] Yet, Wynter does not refer to Comfort's article here, but to an article by philosopher Antonio T. de Nicolás. Entitled "Notes on the Biology of Religion," this article, too, was published in the April 1980 issue of the *Journal of Social and Biological Structures*.[44] De Nicolás shows up more often in Wynter's oeuvre,[45] which tells us another important thing about her work: to the extent that Wynter's ideas and writings refer back and forth to one another, she also often returns to the same—if vast and extremely interdisciplinary—set of sources, putting these in ever-new, creative, and expanding conversations about, as the title of McKittrick's groundbreaking edited volume on Wynter's work announces, "being human as praxis."[46]

"Notes on the Biology of Religion" is an extensive book review of *I and THAT: Notes on the Biology of Religion*, published in 1979 by no other than ... Alex Comfort. And the opening paragraph of the review leaves little room for doubt that the book in question is about religion:

> *I and THAT* deals with the religious experience of mankind. The focus of religious experience is primarily on "oceanic" and mystical states that tell us not "where the world came from" but how the shift in self-consciousness created for us the worlds we know. The focus, therefore, is not on the Creator of the world, but on the kind of knowledge men needed to create the worlds they inhabit. The base of this inquiry is not how the world reflects the image of a Creator but rather how the human nervous system is coded to create the worlds known to men.[47]

What's remarkable about this opening paragraph—although, considering what I wrote above about Comfort's skepticism of "religious noises," perhaps not surprising—is that de Nicolás at once argues that *I and THAT* is about religious experience and espouses a theory about radical immanence. Although de Nicolás is critical about the book on some points (I return to this below), he is immensely supportive of Comfort's approach and central aim: grounding religion in "biology," thereby shifting the focus from God or another "agency outside the human psyche" back to, essentially, the human body.[48] We have arrived, then, at the second and arguably more significant religious trace in demonic ground: when Wynter first introduces the concept in "Beyond Miranda's Meanings"—which, it begs repeating, is considered the central source for her ideas on the demonic ground—she does so in direct reference to de Nicolás's positive take on the potential of the "biological study of religion," a study that resists transcendent explanations of religious experience and brings it back to the human body, the "human nervous system." As I will demonstrate later in this essay, Wynter incorporates this approach into her far-reaching critique of the particular mechanisms that constitute religion as a process of meaning-making. It is worth emphasizing here, furthermore, that the demonic ground as she envisioned it in 1990 would project a form of meaning-making that would counter and move beyond these mechanisms, a move that, in line and conversation with de Nicolás's shift from "agency outside" to agency within, fundamentally challenges and deconstructs the existence of what David Kline, following Wynter, would call "extrahuman agents of determination."[49] To put a finer point to it: unearthing the religious traces in demonic ground also underscores, precisely because it encourages a careful consideration of de Nicolás, the ways in which Wynter considered this "outsider position" a site for epistemic intervention, or "cognitive breakthroughs," that would push beyond religion.

To better understand why, precisely, Wynter returns to de Nicolás's article quite frequently, it is helpful to return to "On Disenchanting

Discourse," the first essay of hers that references him. His writing serves, in fact, as one of her epigraphs—indeed, one of the epigraphs that, as she announced in the earlier quoted introduction of that essay, could "project" the possibility of a "demonic observer ground." Given its importance for the concept under consideration in this essay, I cite the epigraph in full:

> Ultimately it would appear that ... men and women have never been any one particular thing or have had any particular nature to tie them down metaphysically. ... [Humans] become through their powers of embodiment, a multiplicity of theories that became human because man has the capacity to turn theory into flesh. Insofar as the past conditions the present ... [the] biological study of religion could liberate humans from codings in the nervous system which if not known as *conditioning*, might be taken as liberation when in every case they are only the shackles on human freedom.[50]

In "Rethinking Aesthetics: Notes towards a Deciphering Practice" (1992), Wynter further adds that, for de Nicolás, the "codings in our nervous system regulate our responses and sentiments."[51] In other words: such "codings" shape human behavior. And in "Africa, the West and the Analogy of Culture: The Cinematic Text after Man" (2000), Wynter makes clear that de Nicolás arrives at his conclusion that we have "never been any one particular thing" because he has observed the wide diversity of "human religions" and "human cultures."[52] De Nicolás, Wynter conveys, suggests that we *become* human: it's an active process, instituted "only by means of the conceptions (i.e. theories) of being human that are specific to each culture."[53] This is why, Wynter adds, "representational apparatuses"—such as the novel[54] or the "cinematic text"[55]—are so important, so central. After all, each human being can, de Nicolás makes clear, only become human—a process of "transmutation" from theory to flesh, discourse to nervous system—in accordance with the culturally specific system of representations through which they are socialized.[56] This is where and why he takes issue with *I and THAT*: de Nicolás disagrees with what he sees as the reductive nature of Comfort's ideas about biology. Comfort's systems theory approach "cancels" all "cultural diversity" because it reduces all experience to "a universal and uniform linguistic behavior." De Nicolás, as should be evident, thinks opposite: making a distinction between "ontology" and the "nervous system," de Nicolás argues that the "code of the nervous system is primarily epistemology."[57] It is not the case that we are human beings biologically first, and that culture is then superimposed; rather, we are "epistemology" and "ontology" at the same time, from the start.

This claim would have an immense influence on Wynter: we can find in de Nicolás's epigraph building blocks for two of Wynter's central arguments. Let me put a finer point to this: identifying and following the religious traces in demonic ground allows us to look anew at Wynter's expansive analysis of the role of religion in the origins and nature of our racialized modernity *and* her constructive attempt to move beyond it. She would develop these two related arguments throughout her oeuvre, in essays published both earlier and later than "On Disenchanting Discourse"—sometimes with specific reference to de Nicolás, at other times by bringing in other scholars in an ever-more expansive conversation between and across disciplines. I will discuss the first argument—human beings are a "hybrid-auto-instituting-languaging-storytelling species," or *homo narrans*[58]—in the next section. In the section after that, I turn to her argument that such a new conceptualization of being human necessitates a new "science of the word," which will also bring us back to the demonic ground.

Origin Stories, Master Codes, and *Homo Narrans*, or, Wynter on the "Phenomenon of Religion"

Echoing and significantly expanding on de Nicolás's claim that human beings create the worlds they live in, Wynter speaks of "origin stories" (or "cosmogonies") that inscribe and subscribe what it means to be human. Significant for this present volume, she grounds this process in what she, in an interview with McKittrick, calls "the phenomenon of religion."[59] Wynter never clearly defines religion, but from several of her writings we can gather that she understands religion to be a social function, a collective wrestling with ontological and existential questions, with the who, what, why, and where of human existence.[60] Religion provides the origin stories that guide and necessitate the ways of knowing, feeling, and being of particular "genres of being human." Every society produces, by way of religion, cosmogonies that guide and necessitate the behavior of its dominant genre.[61] Importantly, Wynter considers religion fundamentally and uniquely human: it has been, she writes, "isomorphic with the hominization process of the human itself."[62]

The genre-specific stories that we tell come ingrained into our nervous system, a process of "transmutation" that leads such stories to "tie us down metaphysically."[63] In thinking about the implications of this, Wynter combines de Nicolás's general argument with her specific critique of Man's overrepresentation as the only way of being human, which ensures that we are all "tied down metaphysically" to Man's culturally specific way of experiencing what it means to be human. Indeed, although Man is merely one of the genres, its universalizing and totalizing tendencies—a carryover from Man's roots in medieval European Christendom—have repressed and overshadowed (although most certainly not erased) all other genres of being human, such that the being of Man is now "isomorphic with the being of being human itself."[64] Much of Wynter's work consists of explaining the destructive consequences of this for Black and other racialized people. As she explains it in "On Disenchanting Discourse" with recourse to de Nicolás: "the category of minority" is, within this system, "always already a subordinated category,"[65] which implies that it is both constitutive of and the negative counterpoint to the category of majority, or Man. Below, I explicate how this position, according to Wynter, affords "minority discourse" the possibility to herald, from the demonic ground, a new episteme. Before I can do so, however, I need to elaborate on two mechanisms that I believe Wynter sees at work in—indeed, that define—the "phenomenon of religion": the desire for categorical distinction and displacement.

Categorical Distinction

Wynter furthers her argument by referencing a second biological approach to religion: James Danielli's essay "Altruism: The Opium of the People" (1980), published, again, in that same issue of *Journal of Social and Biological Structures*.[66] Building on this essay, Wynter argues that where nonhuman and human animal behaviors both revolve around a "biochemical system of *reward* and *punishment*," in "our uniquely human case," this system becomes activated by the culturally specific "representation of symbolic *life* and *death*."[67] Frequently referring to such codes as "master codes," Wynter suggests they function to produce binaries and boundaries: a group that is in—"*We/Us*"—over and against a group that is out, "*They/not-Us*."[68] Importantly, this binary is constructed and must be maintained: each culture defines itself in the "realm of symbolic life" against an "Other," which it deems in the "realm of symbolic death." Wynter makes clear that this is unique to neither Man nor the West, but part and parcel of all human cultures. To substantiate this argument, she refers to the Bakama cult of Iron Age Africa[69] and the "Arawak" in North America (although I should note that I do not have the expertise to test the veracity of this claim and should note, too, that Wynter's thinking about religion seems largely grounded in her engagement with Christian theology; see also Ogunnaike's chapter in this volume).[70]

Surely, Wynter's understanding of religion here veers dangerously close to the kind of universalism that scholars in religious studies have sought to challenge for the last decades.[71] It is important to note, however, that Wynter does not develop religion as a taxonomic category that sets up a hierarchy of religions or seeks to uncover some kind of perennial core. She is, in fact, not so much interested in religions (in the plural, as movements or institutions), but in a particular process of meaning-making, of wrestling with ontological and existential questions, of socialization, that she seems to have chosen to call religion because it involves claims about the "extrahuman." Echoing the famous claim by Jonathan Z. Smith that religion is a scholarly category, we might say that religion is for Wynter an analytical category which she uses to identify the continuity between theological and subsequent "secular" ways of producing and thinking human distinction. In a different register, we might say that Wynter points toward a conventional—if still rather imprecise, undertheorized, and generalizing—conceptualization of the social function of religion. This account of religion shares aspects with that of Émile Durkheim, whose theory of religion remains—despite its reliance on racialized constructs and hierarchies,[72] and its overly but masked Christian tendencies—the best-known functionalist interpretation.

Moreover, in addition to this more universalist argument, Wynter develops a more historical interpretation of religion that links up with critical genealogies that reveal it as an (initially) Christian category intimately wrapped with colonialist expansion. To intimate how, it is helpful to tease out a major difference between her and Durkheim: where Durkheim's focus is much more on how religion allows a community to cohere as a homogeneous whole, Wynter is interested in how religion produces destructive divisions and oppressive structures in the so-called West. As noted, Wynter's deconstructive project is centrally concerned with unearthing why and how one particular genre, Man, came to overrepresent itself as if it were the sole way of being human. The main problem that Wynter wrestles with is thus the "absolutization" and "universalization" of what is, essentially, a genre-specific iteration of being human.

Wynter turns to Comfort, Danielli, and de Nicolás—as well as many others—to understand the origins and nature of the Du Boisian color line which is, of course, also what makes her work so unique, compelling, and complex. She draws from a wide variety of different sources, from a breathtaking number of disciplines and fields, to understand, among other things, the specific characteristics of race and racism. Accordingly, Wynter is specifically interested in the codes that ground Man, or, indeed, those that preceded Man in medieval European Christendom. In medieval Europe, Jews and Muslims were construed as "Enemies-of-Christ" who threatened the coherence of the Christian subject; in post-1492 Americas, "Negroes" and "Natives" were invented as "irrational" to secure and legitimate the supposed rationality of white Europeans.[73] Importantly, such distinctions between "Us" and "Them" relied on and revolved around a series of categorical distinctions that assumed, according to Wynter, a "nonhomogeneity of substance."[74] For instance, the distinctions between the heavenly and earthly realm and habitable and uninhabitable spaces, which grounded the Christian subject, or the distinction between human and nonhuman animal that formed a foundation of Man1. These oppositional entities are assumed to be categorically different. Each of the "master codes" thus constructs and is part of a system of classification: in these systems, differences are no longer descriptive but become part of a set of relations in which they are understood in categorical and hierarchical terms.

Wynter's admittedly broad-strokes, linear, and structural analysis indicates that medieval Christian Europe was organized around the "master code" of Redeemed Spirit / Fallen Flesh. Rational/Irrational served, in turn, as the organizing principle of Renaissance humanism and the Enlightenment. Finally, evolutionary Selected/Dysselected served as the principle that (over)determines human behavior in our contemporary globalized world of Man2. These master codes thus order the world around us through and in clear-cut categories; they provide, as such, a particular kind of stability. Or, rather, the appearance of stability: as I will show shortly, the desire for absolute categorical distinction is always already futile, as supposedly oppositional categories have the persistent tendency to bleed into one another. Importantly, though, such (apparent) stability is achieved by formulating conceptualizations of group identity in relation to otherness, to alterity. It is precisely for this reason, too, that who is seen as "other"—i.e., symbolically dead—is seen as a threat to the well-being of the dominant group and should therefore be controlled, subjugated, oppressed.

Wynter links the idea of "master codes"—also referred to as "sociogenic codes" or "symbolic codes" (more on this below)—in turn, to historian of religion Norman Girardot's conceptual analysis of the significance of a "postulate of significant ill" and accompanying motivating "cure" or "plan of salvation."[75] While we may expect such a postulate in medieval Christianity—and find it, indeed, as post-Adamic enslavement to natural sin, to be "cured" by baptism and by adhering to the rules laid out by the Church—we find it, Wynter argues, also in periods that are largely released from theological strongholds.[76] In the Renaissance and Enlightenment, the newly formed "descriptive statement" of the human as a rational-political being was seen as existing under the persistent threat of enslavement to the lower, sensory, irrational aspects of human behavior.[77] The cure in those days, Wynter intimates, was deemed to be found in promoting the this-worldly goals of securing the political and economic hegemony of an ever-expanding state—a state that, it is worth emphasizing, colonized, enslaved, murdered, subjugated, and oppressed.[78]

What we see, time and time again, is that Wynter relies on scholars of religion and extrapolates concepts and inventions we usually associate with (Christian) theology—cosmogony, salvation, redemption—to denote the precise workings of the organizing principles of supposedly "secularized" societies as well. She does this, of course, on purpose: Wynter seeks to demonstrate that the "foundational narrative" of what she terms "Judeo-Christianity" has "continued to govern the social systems of the West."[79] What makes Wynter's work particularly significant, then, is that she extends the category of religion: supposedly "secular" conceptualizations of being human that we find in Renaissance humanism and even modern science remain grounded in "religion."[80] Wynter locates Man's overrepresentation in a particular way of meaning-making that survived the two "consecutive breakthroughs" that mark Man's ascendency and increasingly freed human beings from the strongholds of supernatural explanations—one symbolized by Copernicus and Galileo (Man1), the second by Darwin's evolutionary theory (Man2). Man—a supposedly "secular" philosophical/scientific/legal iteration of being human—remains grounded in religion.[81]

Displacement

This becomes even more evident when we identify the second mechanism that Wynter links with the "phenomenon of religion." According to Wynter, the invented nature of these categorical distinctions, these master codes, is obscured because they are projected onto "extrahuman agents of determination," a claim she grounds in the work of philosopher of religion Ernesto Grassi and anthropologist Maurice Godelier (see also Kline's chapter in this volume).[82] These codes are seen as true, worthy, and legitimate precisely because they are deemed to be authorized by something transcendent, something that lies outside of human agency, desire, and possibility. Initially, Wynter's expansive argument conveys, God was considered to have mandated the hierarchical order of life on earth; subsequently, such agency was attributed to the divinely ordered Great Chain of Being; currently, human life is seen as hierarchically ordered through the extrahuman agent known as Natural Selection, believed to determine "degrees of eugenic 'worth' between human groups at the level of race, culture, religion, class, ethnicity, sexuality, and sex."[83] By displacing human agency onto the transcendent, humanly invented stories and their categorical distinctions are transformed into supposedly objective *laws*.[84] The classificatory behavioral schemes and role allocations of and in genres come thus to be understood as "god-given" or "natural," which is to say fixed, eternal and unchangeable. Notice that Wynter tracks a shift from story to law: while the first term suggests a human invention, the latter claims transcendent grounds. It seems to me that one of Wynter's most significant interventions, if one that was until very recently quite underexplored, is that she unveils a continuity between "theological" and "secular" modes of thinking, in that both think toward pure or absolute difference. Both assume, produce, and reinforce supposedly fixed, eternal, transcendental, or "natural" binaries that differentiate between groups of people.

New Science of the Word, or, Beyond the "Phenomenon of Religion"

Following the religious traces in demonic ground leads us to Wynter's theory (and, indeed, critique) of religion. I am not suggesting (and neither, I think, is Wynter) that religion is ever successful in its desire to categorize, separate, demarcate, absolutize—to the contrary, I'd argue. Working from Wynter, I do suggest that religion is a useful analytical concept to name, in Euro-American theological and secular discourse, the desire—however futile—to produce and reproduce categorical distinctions and place the invented nature of such unified binaries onto extrahuman agents. To counter the potentially destructive effects of the twofold process of distinction and displacement, Wynter demands a new domain of knowledge that is in line with her conceptualization of being human as both bios and mythos. She already suggested as much in "On Disenchanting Discourse" by invoking Alex Comfort's "demonic models." In that essay, she spoke of a new "science of human systems" that transgresses the "division between the humanities and the neurosciences" to overwrite all genre-specific forms of knowledge, including that of "Man."[85] In other writings, Wynter would turn to Aimé Césaire's 1946 lecture "Poetry and Knowledge" to name this new science, this *New Studia*, a "science of the word."[86] "Poetry and Knowledge" was, Wynter argues, a call to the hard sciences to resist purely biological and "objectivist-oriented models of analysis." A new science should take "as its starting point the uniquely human capacity to convey meaning and symbols through language."[87] Wynter demonstrates here (although without making this explicit) that Césaire wrestled with issues remarkably similar to those confronted by the biologists she picked up through her reading of the *Journal of Social and Biological Structures*. Importantly, however, Césaire did so decades prior to those scholars.

At first sight, then, it seems as if Wynter seeks to advance what I will call a differentiated universal, where human beings are linked in their capacity to tell stories but are different—sometimes radically so—in the stories they tell and thus, importantly, in how they experience being human. Her goal, then, is to realize, as Wynter stated poetically in conversation with David Scott, "a new mode of experiencing ourselves in which every mode of being human, every form of life that has ever been enacted, is a part of us. We, a part of them."[88] But it seems that Wynter also had a second, even more lofty goal in mind, which is to *intervene* in this process; after all, the "biological study of religion," as de Nicolás's epigraph that is so central to my argument already announced, would not only identify and analyze but would "liberate" human beings from the "codings in the nervous system." Or, as Wynter herself writes in "On Disenchanting Discourse": the goal is "to disenchant the human, then, enabling her/his Girardian 'waking up' to a consciously chosen intentionality."[89]

And thus, while one reading of Wynter's work would suggest that she decentralizes Man to allow other past, existing, and future "genres of being human" to flourish, some of her other writings seem to advance a project that is, in literary studies scholar Jonathan Goldberg's words, even more "radical."[90] Consider what she wrote in "The Ceremony Found" (2015), her last published essay:

> How can we come to know our social reality . . . no longer in the terms of the abductive order-stabilizing/legitimating, "knowledge of categories" system of thought (Althusser's *Ideology*) to which our present sociogenic replicator code lawlikely gives rise, but instead come to know this reality (and *heretically* so) in the terms of "knowledge of the world as it is"?[91]

In this characteristically wordy sentence, Wynter intimates two things. First, she makes a specific distinction between two types of knowing: "knowledge of categories," which she would define in her essay "1492: A New World View" (1995) as genre-specific ways of knowing; and "knowledge of the world that is." The former, she further explains, refers to "the cultural knowledge of our contemporary humanities and social sciences"—indeed, the current episteme—and the latter to "scientific knowledge."[92] In "1492," she speaks in terms of Two Cultures: her new science of the word should form a bridge between the human and the natural sciences.[93] But in the quotation above, Wynter seeks to advance something different, something more: to resist the "knowledge of categories" system of thought altogether. She intimates, in other words, that we should move beyond culturally specific binary systems. The goal of the "new science" is, then, not simply to identify and analyze the "master codes" (which she refers to, in this quotation, as "sociogenic," a term she develops in conversation with

Frantz Fanon[94]) and the genres of being human these codes ground and produce, but to resist and go beyond them altogether.

To better understand this, it is helpful to turn to Wynter's source. In making a distinction between "knowledge of categories" and "knowledge of the world that is," Wynter relies on the work of Paulo Fernando de Moraes Farias. In "Models of the World and Categorical Models" (1980), Moraes Farias calls into question and examines the ideological uses of certain "cognitive categories." He particularly has a bone to pick with scholarship that creates *a priori* categories that "abstract" certain peoples and countries from their historical context, creating purely categorical models that relied on and reproduced certain oppositions.[95] Here we can see the value of Moraes Farias for Wynter, who seeks to advance a radically contingent, noncategorical ontology and epistemology. What I see in Wynter, then, is not only a desire to bring together the human and the natural sciences, but a resistance against categorical distinction, a resistance against categories that are fixed, eternal, unmovable, oppositional. This, it seems to me, is what her contingent epistemology—her move from within the demonic ground—hopes to advance, a consistent questioning of the categories that we work with, a persistent effort to break them open and up.

Just as we can nuance the sometimes sweeping nature of Wynter's historical analysis, we may also question the teleological implications of this constructive part of Wynter's project, as well as her apparent belief in human agency with a capital A.[96] It remains, moreover, an open question if Wynter disregards religiosity altogether—if she disregards, wholesale, the possibility of transcendence, of a life and world beyond that which is empirically visible, of spirituality, of the paranormal, of all those experiences Jeffrey Kripal recently named "superhuman"[97]—or if she rejects the power that invented extrahuman agents of determination, whether gods or Evolution, have over (the possibility for) human life, behavior, and experience. Put differently, we can ask if she rejects transcendence writ large, or rejects the idea of a fundamental, unalterable, extrahuman Truth that supersedes human agency, invention, and responsibility. After all, throughout her oeuvre, she has been positive about movements like Rastafarianism (see Shamara Alhassan's chapter, this volume) and, more generally, celebrates the "retention" of African religion in contemporary Caribbean traditions and movements.[98] I am in favor of the second answer, then, although the verdict is still out. And, either way, we do not have to follow Wynter in her possible dismissal; I am more interested in pursuing a slightly different (and much less all-encompassing) path. I will argue by way of conclusion that in this questioning of categorical distinctions—this questioning of binaries deemed absolute, eternal, transcendent—Wynter opens the possibility for an equally hopeful if altogether humbler project: parareligion.

Parareligion

Let's back up a bit. Thus far, I have followed the religious traces in Wynter's demonic ground, an exercise that led us not only to esoteric and oceanic experiences but also—by way of de Nicolás's embrace of the "biological study of religion"—to Wynter's critique of religion. This critique, specifically, was focused on what I call the twofold mechanism of distinction and displacement. It is this mechanism, I think, that her contingent epistemology wants to move beyond. Yet, Wynter simultaneously suggests, with her theory of being human as *homo narrans*, or storytelling species, that we cannot get outside of "origin stories" (this, of course, is a point often made in the field of religious studies). For her, narrative is central to human experience, because it is through narrative, through self-narration, that we experience being human. Wynter shifts, then, from humanity as a predetermined and fixed ontological formation to humanity as a "heuristic operation,"[99] or from human beings as noun to being human as praxis.

This leads to a question: If narrative is so central, but categorical distinction and subsequent displacement so destructive, what do we do with modes of storytelling that actively resist this? Stories that embrace their invented nature? Or, a variation of the same question, what do we name those stories that wrestle with ontological and existential questions by inhabiting the liminal positions that the necessarily futile desire for "pure difference" opens up, and explode binary distinctions from the inside out? More to the point, if the "Cartesian Rational Man" is produced and reinforced in and through a particular religious story—a story expressed in and through philosophy, literature, the law, natural history, and a range of other mediums and fields—what do we name those stories that, in challenging the racialized binary between active and inactive, subject and object, human and nonhuman animal, rational and irrational, upend those dichotomies that were foundational to this conceptualization of humanity?

This line of questioning brings me back, one last time, to demonic ground. As I argue elsewhere, the concept of demonic ground has a double meaning. It names, at once, the "position of the unthought"[100] and a locale of epistemological intervention.[101] I use the phrase "position of the unthought" deliberately: in "Beyond Miranda's Meanings," Wynter launches her "new science of the word" from the specific demonic ground of Caliban's woman—a figure who is, in Shakespeare's *The Tempest*, literally unthinkable.[102] This is why Wynter, in "On Disenchanting Discourse," affords a special role to "minority discourse." Majority discourse can deconstruct Western metaphysics, she writes, but minority discourse, precisely because the constitutive role as "always already a subordinated category"[103] in the dominant "organizing principle" must go "beyond this."[104] Minority discourse must call in question the "grounding premise" of all human systems, which is to say, for Wynter the symbolic codes of life and death and their "related 'codings in the nervous system'"; after all, only when we do that can we arrive at a truly new episteme, a "meta-discourse."[105]

Interestingly, although Wynter develops the term "demonic ground" to point to the possibility for intervention on part of "minority discourse," when she discusses the concept three years later, she makes clear that Columbus operated from a position of demonic ground.[106] After all, in medieval Christian Europe, Columbus, as a layman, constituted the Ontological Other to the clergy. Precisely those people who exist outside of but are central to the hegemonic story that structures a particular society—those who are thought to embody the "name of what is evil"—are in the position to conjure alternative imaginaries, new ways of being human, unconventional epistemologies. Wynter herself is a prime example of this: building on the work of Frantz Fanon, who of course also occupied the "position of the unthought," Wynter developed, in the words of Katherine McKittrick, a radical "counterhumanism."[107]

According to Wynter, those operating from the demonic ground are "liminal subjects" that can, effectively, demonstrate that the hegemonic "master code" is false (we return here to my claim, made above, that master codes only give the appearance of stability). Columbus did this in 1492, when he sailed to the Americas, thereby revealing as false the Christian cosmology that divided the world in habitable and uninhabitable regions—regions within and outside God's grace. As Columbus brought these regions together, the Redeemed Spirit/Fallen Flesh "master code"—which relied on this distinction—became increasingly untenable.[108] Darwin, in turn, did this in the nineteenth century, when he convincingly challenged the categorical distinction between human and nonhuman animal, thereby undercutting the Rational/Irrational "master code." And Fanon, Wynter writes, did so in 1952, when he argued—in the face of the overwhelming hegemonic power of the story of Evolution—for the importance of sociogeny. But Wynter also formulates a more specific argument. As Louis Chude-Sokei—who in turn relies on Paget Henry—argues, Wynter locates the key to epistemic shifts in what she calls "liminal figures," because these figures expose the "errors and distortions" of current epistemes.[109] The construct of the supposedly liminal position of Black people between human and animal, for instance, was necessary for the production and consolidation of Man. Yet, because the racialization of Blackness vis-à-vis animality threatened the strict separation between nonhuman animals and humans, it would ultimately encourage the epistemic break that culminated in Darwin and a new conception of the human (Man2) as purely biological entity.

In my dissertation, I looked at forms of Black religio-cultural production that consciously, deliberately inhabit the liminal position that the always already futile desire for categorical distinction opens up.[110] Consider, for example, contemporary visual artist Ellen Gallagher's *Watery Ecstatic* (2005) (figure 1).

This drawing is part of her ongoing project "Watery Ecstatic," a series of reliefs, films, drawings, and paintings that commemorate the millions who drowned during the Middle Passage.[111] While most of the images in "Watery Ecstatic" consist of conventional sea creatures such as eels and whales, this particular drawing depicts a part-human, part-jellyfish underwater creature. As I argue elsewhere, in this image, human and animal "become with" each other, a move that does not erase the differences

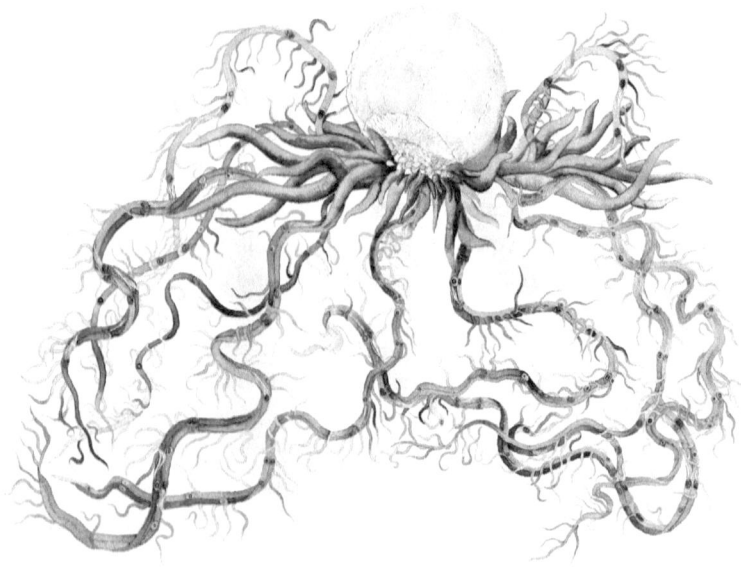

FIGURE 1. Ellen Gallagher, *Watery Ecstatic* (2005). From "Watery Ecstatic" series (ongoing, since 2001). Watercolor, ink, oil, varnish, collage and cut paper on paper. 32⅝ × 42⅜ inches. Art Institute of Chicago: Nancy Lauter McDougal and Alfred L. McDougal Fund. Courtesy of the artist and Hauser & Wirth. Photo: Mike Bruce.

between jellyfish and Black figure, but that does reinscribe the relationship between human and animal such that it is no longer hierarchical, but co-constitutive.[112] Gallagher's work undermines the categorical distinctions that formed the foundations of Man1. It presents a mode of wrestling with ontological and existential questions that distorts and exceeds religion's insistent drive towards distinction and displacement. I refer to this mode of meaning-making therefore as parareligion.[113]

What the prefix "para" names, most of all, is what Black studies scholar Nahum Chandler in his recent exploration of paraontology calls "desedimentation," a fundamental disruption of the ground (or what I call the grammar) of religion.[114] Chandler borrowed the term "desedimentation" from Jacques Derrida, his frequent interlocutor. At one point, Chandler explains in a lecture from 2018, Derrida considered desedimentation a more apt term for what he otherwise named deconstruction. Desedimentation implies an "undoing" or "unmaking" of the work of sedimentation, which is also to say the work of settlement, of consolidation, of coming together, of solidification.[115] This is what the prefix "para" names: a "desedimentation" of religion. In emphasizing their invented nature and consciously inhabiting the racialized boundary between human and nonhuman animal, works like *Watery Ecstatic* (2005) suspend the very possibility for categorical distinction and displacement. In so doing, the image challenges the normative conceptualization of being human that is produced in and through religion and creates room for new, expansive ways of being human. Importantly, parareligion and religion do not exist in an oppositional, dichotomous, or dialectical relationship. Elsewhere, I've invoked Derrida to elucidate this relationship: we may conceive parareligion as the "trace" of religion, always and everywhere deferring its narratives of hegemony and conditioning the possibility of something new.[116] It does not and cannot refute religion altogether, but it troubles and destabilizes the grammar of religion, and as such opens up the possibility for something else, something alternative.

Let's turn to Gallagher to explicate this point. At first instance, *Watery Ecstatic* (2005) seems to depict a simple, if very colorful, jellyfish. When we look closer, however, we see that Gallagher replaced the jellyfish's touch receptors with the disembodied heads of Black women, conveyed in collages of Black-and-white advertisements. Cut out from *Ebony*, *Sepia*, and other magazines directed at African American audiences, the advertisements are in turn superimposed with the signs of minstrelsy, such as big lips and wide eyes. This leads us to pause: after all, we know that Black people were and are subjugated and oppressed through abhorrent comparisons to nonhuman animals. But Gallagher engages this destructive terrain precisely to undo and disarm such comparisons.[117] What interests me here is *how* Gallagher does this. Depicting her figures against a white background and in watercolors, *Watery Ecstatic* (2005) mirrors the techniques, or what Daniela Bleichmar has called the "visual epistemology," of natural history.[118] But Gallagher's image does more than just mirror—she subverts and thereby exposes natural history. Natural history categorized and marked Black people as "other," as not fully human[119]—a discourse steeped in distinction and displacement—another discourse, indeed, produced through the grammar of religion.

Form is important, if not fundamental, here. Throughout the "Watery Ecstatic" series, Gallagher uses a scalpel to cut into the paper and plasticine—a malleable substance—to create definition, and the watercolors bleed into the paper. In so doing, she allows space for that which the taxonomies of natural history often deny: chaos, possibility, mutation, change.[120] As Mary Louise Pratt has expertly observed, the foundational practices of natural history—gathering, comparing, naming, drawing—offered Europeans a way to resolve the "chaos" of the natural world into a comprehensive and comprehensible "order," and, in doing so, helped them to establish and reinforce a back-then still-developing Eurocentric worldview.[121] Natural historians drew the species and specimens they found overseas to be able to identify sameness and difference, to hierarchically classify the "natural" world, to create order out of the chaos that so-called nature inevitably presents. Gallagher's carving, cutting, layering, and use of plasticine trouble the longing for fixed, predetermined categories and the desire to submit the natural world to totalizing systems of classification. While the "Watery Ecstatic" series certainly invokes natural history's specific purpose of order and categorization, the cuts and layers speak to a liveliness, a possibility for transformation, change, and mutation. Gallagher invokes the visual iconography of natural history to subvert its dominant meanings and intentions, thereby revealing and making explicit the field's limitations.

In so doing, she exposes natural history as an invention, an enterprise that sought to naturalize an imagined hierarchy of being. Gallagher's images produce—and allow access to—a world outside of categorical distinction and order. The series therefore opens a space to think being human differently, outside of the epistemological structures that ground its current dominant iteration. Consider, furthermore, that Gallagher does not name the creatures she depicts, opting instead, as title of each of the images, for the generic "Watery Ecstatic." The different images are, in terms of the title, indistinguishable. Gallagher departs here from the practice of naming that was so central to natural history. As Keplani Seshadri writes, Linnaeus was the first to introduce a coherent "naming practice" for the species he categorized. With Linnaeus, we find the first instance in which language—the capacity to name—becomes a mode of representation.[122] This is precisely why Gallagher's decision not to name the individual species that she depicts is so crucial. If naming is a modality of representation, the refusal to name calls the epistemological grounds that produce and reinforce the boundary between "human" and "animal" into question. After all, the capacity to name is also what *defines* being human. Linnaeus's category of *Homo sapiens* does not describe any specific behavioral traits; rather, Linnaeus distinguished the human from nonhuman animals by the dictum "know thyself," which implies that "the human" has no specific identity other than the possibility for self-recognition, and thus self-naming.[123]

It is precisely in inhabiting and exploding the techniques and practices of natural history that I understand Gallagher's series performing parareligion. The images do so from the demonic ground—or, as I argue elsewhere, "demonic ocean"[124]—a space of intervention beyond the world and grasp of Man. Read in this way, we may conclude that the demonic ground is a locale for multiple forms of epistemological intervention: where Wynter seeks a "new science of the word" that moves beyond religion altogether, Gallagher "desediments" the grasp of religion by explicitly engaging and then exploding the foundational structure of natural history, one of the formative domains of Western knowledge production and a central site of racialization. In Gallagher's parareligious story, which explicitly blurs the boundary between "real" and "imaginary," the techniques and practices of natural history become, with a twist, the locale for thinking being human anew.

Notes

1. Writing this chapter was made possible by the generous funding of Fonds Wetenschappelijk Onderzoek–Vlaanderen (FWO; Research Foundation Flanders), the organization that funded my postdoc project, "Race and the Project of Distinction in the Study of Religion" (FWO Project 12R8122N). I am incredibly fortunate to have been able to research this project at KU Leuven under the supervision of Judith Gruber and Nadia Fadil. In addition, I want to thank David Kline, Kathryn Yusoff, and Adrienne Rooney for their generous, productive reading of this essay and, more generally, for helping me think through Wynter's expansive work. Lastly, I am immensely grateful to Ellen Gallagher for giving me permission to reproduce her work and to her gallery, Hauser & Wirth, and in particular Artist Liaison Stefan Zebrowski-Rubin, for providing me with the image.

2. Katherine McKittrick, *Demonic Grounds: Black Women and the Cartographies of Struggle* (Minneapolis: University of Minnesota Press, 2006), 1.

3. McKittrick, 1.

4. McKittrick, 1.

5. Jimena Canales, *Bedeviled: A Shadow History of Demons in Science* (Princeton, NJ: Princeton University Press, 2020).

6. Justine M. Bakker, "Locating the Oceanic in Sylvia Wynter's 'Demonic Ground,'" *Journal for Cultural and Religious Theory* 21, no. 1 (2022): 1–22.

7. I first developed my theory of parareligion in my PhD dissertation (Rice University, 2020). See also Justine M. Bakker, "Blue Black Ecstasy: Ellen Gallagher's Watery Ecstatic, Oceanic Feeling, and Mysticism in the Flesh," *Journal of the American Academy of Religion* 91, no. 2 (2023): 302–25; and Bakker, "Locating the Oceanic in Sylvia Wynter's 'Demonic Ground,'" 22.

8. Sylvia Wynter, "Afterword: Beyond Miranda's Meanings: Un/silencing the 'Demonic Ground' of Caliban's 'Woman,'" in *Out of the Kumbla: Caribbean Women and Literature*, ed. Carole Boyce Davies and Elaine Savory Fida (Trenton, NJ: Africa World, 1990), 355–72.

9. Sylvia Wynter, "On Disenchanting Discourse: 'Minority' Literary Criticism and Beyond," *Cultural Critique*, no. 7 (Autumn 1987): 207–44. To the best of my knowledge, the overwhelming majority of scholars who have reflected on demonic ground refer, when elucidating the concept, solely to "Afterword: Beyond Miranda's Meanings." See McKittrick, *Demonic Grounds*; Sarah Haley, *No Mercy Here: Gender, Punishment, and the Making of Jim Crow Modernity* (Chapel Hill: University of North Carolina Press, 2016); Nijah Cunningham, "The Resistance of the Lost Body," *Small Axe: A Caribbean Journal of Criticism* 20, no. 1 (2016): 113–28; Tiffany Lethabo King, *The Black Shoals: Offshore Formations of Black and Native Studies* (Durham, NC: Duke University Press, 2019), 175–205; Laura McTighe and Deon Haywood, "Front Porch Revolution: Resilience Space, Demonic Grounds, and the Horizons of a Black Feminist Otherwise," *Signs: Journal of Women in Culture and Society* 44, no. 1 (2018): 25–52; Kate Siklosi, "'Dr. Livingstone, I Presume?': The Demonic Grounds of M. NourbeSe Philip's *Looking for Livingstone: An Odyssey of Silence*," in *Spatial Literary Studies*, ed. Robert Tally (New York: Routledge, 2021), 103–16; and Tonya Haynes, "The Divine and the Demonic: Sylvia Wynter and Caribbean Feminist Thought Revisited," in *Love and Power: Caribbean Discourses of Gender*, ed. Eudine Barriteau (Kingston: University of the West Indies Press, 2012), 54–71. An exception is Alexander Weheliye, who refers to both "Beyond Miranda's Meanings" and "On Disenchanting Discourse" in the same footnote: Alexander G. Weheliye, "After Man," *American Literary History* 20, no. 1–2 (March 1, 2008): 334.

10. Wynter, "On Disenchanting Discourse," 208–9.

11. Wynter, 208. Emphasis original.

12. Wynter, 207. Wynter here cites Michel Foucault, *The Order of Things: An Archeology of the Human Sciences* (New York: Random House, 1973), 387.

13. Wynter, "On Disenchanting Discourse," 209.

14. Wynter, 208–9.

15. See Denise Ferreira da Silva, "Before Man: Sylvia Wynter's Rewriting of the Modern Episteme," in *Sylvia Wynter: On Being Human as Praxis*, ed. Katherine McKittrick (Durham, NC: Duke University Press, 2015), 90–105.

16. Writing this chapter offers me the opportunity to set something right: in "Locating the Oceanic in Sylvia Wynter's 'Demonic Ground'" (2022), I claimed that Wynter does not cite Comfort directly, although she does refer to his work in the reference list of "Beyond Miranda's Meanings." I now know that this was a mistake: Wynter does refer to him directly, only not in "Beyond Miranda's Meanings," but in the earlier article "On Disenchanting Discourse." Although this doesn't change the nature

of my argument in the article—I remain convinced that it was prudent and necessary to delve deep into Comfort's writings and that doing so helped uncover traces of "the oceanic" as well as, as I argue here in this chapter, the religious in the term demonic ground—I do take full responsibility for this regrettable oversight.

17. Wynter, "On Disenchanting Discourse," 207n3.

18. Alex Comfort, "The Cartesian Observer Revisited: Ontological Implications of the Homuncular Illusion," *Journal of Social and Biological Structures* 2 (1979): 211–23.

19. Naturally, what follows below repeats some of the research in "Locating the Oceanic in Sylvia Wynter's 'Demonic Ground'" (in particular, pp. 8–15), even if these findings are organized differently and serve a different purpose; to limit citations, I will only cite this article when quoting from it directly.

20. Alex Comfort, "Demonic and Historical Models in Biology," *Journal of Social and Biological Structures* 3, no. 2 (1980): 211.

21. Wynter, "Beyond Miranda's Meaning," 364. See also Bakker, "Locating the Oceanic in Sylvia Wynter's 'Demonic Ground,'" 10.

22. Canales, *Bedeviled*, 14–28.

23. René Descartes, *Meditations on First Philosophy*, trans. Michael Moriarty (New York: Oxford University Press, 2008), 23.

24. Descartes, 15.

25. Descartes, 23.

26. Descartes, 23.

27. Haley, *No Mercy Here*, 229.

28. Haley, 229.

29. Bakker, "Locating the Oceanic in Sylvia Wynter's 'Demonic Ground,'" 10.

30. Comfort, "Cartesian Observer Revisited," 215.

31. Comfort, 217.

32. Sylvia Wynter, "Beyond Liberal and Marxist Leninist Feminisms: Towards an Autonomous Frame of Reference," *CLR James Journal* 24, no. 1–2 (2018): 34.

33. Sylvia Wynter, "Unsettling the Coloniality of Being/Power/Truth/Freedom: Towards the Human, after Man, Its Overrepresentation—an Argument," *CR: The New Centennial Review* 3, no. 3 (2003): 266.

34. Alexander Weheliye uses the phrase "Cartesian Rational Man" in his essay on Wynter: "After Man," 323.

35. Comfort, "Cartesian Observer Revisited," 212.

36. Comfort, 221.

37. Comfort, 221.

38. Comfort, "Demonic and Historical Models," 212.

39. Wouter J. Hanegraaff, *Esotericism and the Academy: Rejected Knowledge in Western Culture* (Cambridge: Cambridge University Press, 2012).

40. Comfort, "Demonic and Historical Models," 212.

41. Carole Boyce Davies, "Occupying the Terrain: Reengaging 'Beyond Miranda's Meanings,'" *American Quarterly* 70, no. 4 (2018): 841.

42. Wynter, "Beyond Miranda's Meanings," 356. Emphasis mine.

43. Walter D. Mignolo, "Sylvia Wynter: What Does It Mean to Be Human?," in *Sylvia Wynter: On Being Human as Praxis*, ed. Katherine McKittrick (Durham, NC: Duke University Press, 2015), 111.

44. Antonio T. de Nicolás, "Notes on the Biology of Religion," *Journal of Social and Biological Structures* 3, no. 2 (April 1, 1980): 219–25.

45. Sometimes, Wynter spells his last name as Nicholas. See Wynter, "On Disenchanting Discourse"; Wynter, "Beyond Miranda's Meanings"; Sylvia Wynter, "Rethinking 'Aesthetics': Notes towards a Deciphering Practice," in *Ex-Iles: Essays on Caribbean Cinema*, ed. Mbye B. Cham (Trenton, NJ: Africa World, 1992), 237–79; Sylvia Wynter, "Africa, the West and the Analogy of Culture: The Cinematic Text after Man," in *Symbolic Narratives / African Cinema: Audiences, Theory and the Moving Image*, ed. June Givanni (London: British Film Institute, 2000), 25–76.

46. Katherine McKittrick, ed., *Sylvia Wynter: On Being Human as Praxis* (Durham, NC: Duke University Press, 2015).

47. De Nicolás, "Notes on the Biology of Religion," 219.

48. De Nicolás, 220.

49. David Kline, "Observing Whiteness: The System of Whiteness and Its Religious Fantasy of Absolute Immunity," *Social Identities* 27, no. 1 (2021): 130. It is important to note, however, that Wynter also writes about the transformative and liberatory potential that, for instance, "minority" forms of Christianity or Rastafarianism can have, as the chapter of Shamara Wyllie Alhassan in this volume also demonstrates. While Wynter's theoretical and abstract understanding of religion seems to contradict her empirical research on Black religion and culture, I'd thus make a distinction between her analysis of religion as a problematic process of meaning-making and her appreciation for particular forms of religiosity.

50. Wynter, "On Disenchanting Discourse," 240. Suspension points, brackets, and emphasis are all Wynter's.

51. Wynter, "Rethinking Aesthetics," 252.

52. Wynter, "Africa, the West and the Analogy of Culture," 40.

53. Wynter, 40.

54. Central to "On Disenchanting Discourse."

55. Central to "Africa, the West and the Analogy of Culture."

56. Wynter, "Africa, the West and the Analogy of Culture," 40.

57. De Nicolás, "Notes on the Biology of Religion," 224.

58. Sylvia Wynter and Katherine McKittrick, "Unparalleled Catastrophe for Our Species? Or, to Give Humanness a Different Future: Conversations," in *Sylvia Wynter: On Being Human as Praxis*, ed. Katherine McKittrick (Durham, NC: Duke University Press, 2015), 25.

59. Wynter and McKittrick, 27.

60. I first began to develop my take on Wynter's theory of religion in a paper presented during a wildcard session at the annual conference of the American Academy of Religion in 2018—indeed, the session that would, many years later, be the catalyst for this edited volume. I'd like to thank David Kline and An Yountae, who served as a "respondent" to our panel, for their helpful feedback on that paper. In September 2019, I was invited to present this paper at a session of Anya Topolski's "Race-Religion Constellation" project, at Radboud University. I'd like to thank those present for their productive questions and generative critiques.

61. Sylvia Wynter, "1492: A New World View," in *Race, Discourse, and the Origin of the Americas: A New World View*, ed. Vera Lawrence Hyatt and Rex Nettleford (Washington, DC: Smithsonian Institution Press, 1995), 5–57.

62. Sylvia Wynter, "The Ceremony Must Be Found: After Humanism," in "On Humanism and the *University I: The Discourse of Humanism*," ed. William Spanos, special issue, *Boundary 2* 12, no. 3 / 13, no. 1 (1984): 25. In this respect, Wynter is in line

with the dominant, although increasingly more contested, tradition in religious studies that not only uncritically assumes a categorical distinction between nonhuman and human animals but also ascribes a special role to religion as that which "differentiates" the human from the animal; Aaron Gross, *The Question of the Animal and Religion: Theoretical Stakes, Practical Implications* (New York: Columbia University Press, 2014). Surely, although this is outside the scope of this chapter, there's plenty of space to critique Wynter's apparent anthropocentrism here, as others have done already. I direct readers, in particular, to Max Hantel, "What Is It Like to Be a Human? Sylvia Wynter on Autopoiesis," *PhiloSOPHIA* 8, no. 1 (2018): 61–79; and Christin Ellis, *Antebellum Posthuman: Race and Materiality in the Mid-nineteenth Century* (New York: Fordham University Press, 2018).

63. Wynter, "Africa, the West and the Analogy of Culture," 40.
64. Wynter, "Unsettling the Coloniality of Being/Power/Truth/Freedom," 310.
65. Wynter, "On Disenchanting Discourse," 233.
66. Wynter, 218–19.
67. Sylvia Wynter, "The Ceremony Found: Towards the Autopoetic Turn/Overturn, Its Autonomy of Human Agency and Extraterritoriality of (Self-)Cognition," in *Black Knowledges / Black Struggles: Essays in Critical Epistemology*, ed. Jason R. Ambroise and Sabine Broeck (Liverpool: Liverpool University Press, 2015), 211.
68. Wynter, "Ceremony Found," 220. See, for an example of the use of "master code," for instance: Wynter, "Unsettling the Coloniality of Being/Power/Truth/Freedom," 274.
69. Wynter, "Ceremony Must Be Found," 27.
70. Wynter, "1492," 49. The "Arawak" was a term used by Spanish colonialists and explorers to name a diverse group of indigenous peoples.
71. The scholarship here is vast. See, for example, Gil Anidjar, "Secularism," *Critical Inquiry* 33 (2006): 52–77; Talal Asad, *Genealogies of Religion: Discipline and Reasons of Power in Christianity and Islam* (Baltimore: Johns Hopkins University Press, 1993); Daniel Dubuisson, *The Western Construction of Religion: Myths, Knowledge, and Ideology* (Baltimore: Johns Hopkins University Press, 2003); Charles H. Long, *Significations: Signs, Symbols, and Images in the Interpretation of Religion*, 2nd ed. (Aurora, CO: Davies Group, 1999); Tomoko Masuzawa, *The Invention of World Religions; Or, How European Universalism Was Preserved in the Language of Pluralism* (Chicago: University of Chicago Press, 2005); and Brent Nongbri, *Before Religion: A History of a Modern Concept* (New Haven, CT: Yale University Press, 2013).
72. Malory Nye, "Decolonizing the Study of Religion," *Open Library of Humanities* 5, no. 1 (2019): 1–45.
73. Wynter, "Unsettling the Coloniality of Being/Power/Truth/Freedom," 266.
74. Wynter, 274.
75. Wynter, "Ceremony Found," 218–20.
76. Wynter, 218–20.
77. Wynter borrows the term "descriptive statement" from systems theorist Gregory Bateson.
78. Wynter, "Unsettling the Coloniality of Being/Power/Truth/Freedom," 289.
79. Sylvia Wynter, "Is 'Development' a Purely Empirical Concept or Also Teleological? A Perspective from 'We the Underdeveloped,'" in *Prospects for Recovery and Sustainable Development in Africa*, ed. Aguibou Y. Yansané (Westport, CT: Greenwood, 1996), 300.
80. Wynter and McKittrick, "Unparalleled Catastrophe for Our Species," 27.

81. Note, here, that I make a distinction between "supernatural," which in Wynter's writings would refer to God, gods, and other supernatural beings, and "religion": while supernatural explanations lose their hegemony and, for some, their validity, descriptive statements of being human remain grounded in "religion."

82. Wynter, "Unsettling the Coloniality of Being/Power/Truth/Freedom," 273.

83. Sylvia Wynter, "'No Humans Involved': An Open Letter to My Colleagues," *Forum N.H.I.: Knowledge for the 21st Century* 1, no. 1 (1994): 54.

84. Wynter, "Unsettling the Coloniality of Being/Power/Truth/Freedom," 273; Wynter, "Ceremony Found," 223–24.

85. Wynter, "On Disenchanting Discourse," 241–42. She would go on to develop this argument in a wide variety of her essays, but perhaps most explicitly in her most recent essay, "The Ceremony Found" (2015).

86. Wynter, "Ceremony Found," 209.

87. Wynter, "Ceremony Found," 209.

88. David Scott, "The Re-enchantment of Humanism: An Interview with Sylvia Wynter," *Small Axe: A Caribbean Journal of Criticism* 8 (September 2000): 197.

89. Wynter, "On Disenchanting Discourse," 244. Wynter refers here to René Girard.

90. See also Jonathan Goldberg, *Tempest in the Caribbean* (Minneapolis: University of Minnesota Press, 2003), 65–69.

91. Wynter, "Ceremony Found," 206.

92. Wynter, "1492," 49.

93. See Niki Kasumi Clements's essay in this volume.

94. See, in particular, Sylvia Wynter, "Towards the Sociogenic Principle: Fanon, Identity, the Puzzle of Conscious Experience, and What It Is Like to Be 'Black,'" in *National Identities and Sociopolitical Changes in Latin America*, ed. Mercedes F. Durán-Cogan and Antonio Gómez-Moriana (New York: Routledge, 2001), 30–66. See, for a critique of Wynter's reading of Fanon, David Marriott, "Inventions of Existence: Sylvia Wynter, Frantz Fanon, Sociogeny, and 'the Damned,'" *CR: The New Centennial Review* 11, no. 3 (2011): 45–89.

95. Paulo Fernando de Moraes Farias, "Models of the World and Categorical Models: The Enslavable Barbarian as a Mobile Classificatory Label," *Slavery and Abolition* 1, no. 2 (1980): 118.

96. David Kline takes up this task, by way of Niklas Luhmann's systems theory, in David Kline, *Racism and the Weakness of Christian Identity: Religious Autoimmunity* (London: Routledge, 2020).

97. Jeffrey J. Kripal, *The Superhumanities: Historical Precedents, Moral Objections, New Realities* (Chicago: University of Chicago Press, 2022).

98. Mayra Rivera, "Embodied Counterpoetics: Sylvia Wynter on Religion and Race," in *Beyond Man: Race, Coloniality, and the Philosophy of Religion*, ed. An Yountae and Eleanor Craig (Durham, NC: Duke University Press, 2021), 68.

99. Kathryn Yusoff, *A Billion Black Anthropocenes or None* (Minneapolis: University of Minnesota Press, 2018), 34.

100. Coined by Saidiya Hartman in conversation with Frank Wilderson III, "the position of the unthought" denotes specifically the lack of available narratives about enslaved peoples, but can be and has been extended toward Black people more generally. Saidiya Hartman and Frank B. Wilderson III, "The Position of the Unthought," *Qui Parle* 13, no. 2 (2003): 185. See, for an expansive interpretation, Ashon T.

Crawley, *Blackpentecostal Breath: The Aesthetics of Possibility* (New York: Fordham University Press, 2017), 4.

101. Bakker, "Locating the Oceanic in Sylvia Wynter's 'Demonic Ground,'" 3.

102. Wynter, "Beyond Miranda's Meanings," 364.

103. Wynter, "On Disenchanting Discourse," 233.

104. Wynter, 240.

105. Wynter, 241. In his contribution to this volume, Oludamini Ogunnaike argues convincingly that Wynter continues to operate from a certain "insider" perspective; we find a full-fledged "outsider" challenge to the Western biocentric episteme in traditions like Sufism and Ifá.

106. Wynter, "Beyond Miranda's Meaning," 264.

107. Wynter and McKittrick, "Unparalleled Catastrophe for Our Species," 11.

108. Wynter, "1492."

109. Louis Chude-Sokei, *The Sound of Culture: Diaspora and Black Technopoetics* (Middletown, CT: Wesleyan University Press, 2016), 211–12.

110. Justine Bakker, "'The Vibrations Are Different Here': Parareligious Stories in the African Diaspora" (PhD diss., Rice University, 2020).

111. I have also written about this image in "Blue Black Ecstasy: Ellen Gallagher's Watery Ecstatic, Ocean Feeling and Mysticism in the Flesh."

112. Bakker, "Blue Black Ecstasy."

113. My use of parareligion differs from that of anthropologist Jonathan Benthall and religious studies scholar Pete Ward, both of whom consider "religion" in terms of movements and institutions—rather than a social function, a mode of self- and collective narration—and the prefix "para" as indicating "religious parallels." See Jonathan Benthall, *Returning to Religion: Why a Secular Age Is Haunted by Faith* (London: I. B. Tauris, 2008); Pete Ward, "Celebrity Worship as Parareligion: Bieber and the Beliebers," in *Religion and Popular Culture in America*, ed. B. D. Forbes and J. H. Mahan (Oakland: University of California Press, 2017), 313–35.

114. Nahum Chandler, "Paraontology; or, Notes on the Practical Theoretical Politics of Thought," Society for the Humanities Annual Culler Lecture in Critical Theory, October 15, 2018, accessed on February 21, 2021, https://vimeo.com/297769615.

115. See Marquis Bey, *The Problem of the Negro as a Problem for Gender* (Minneapolis: University of Minnesota Press, 2020), https://manifold.umn.edu/read/the-problem-of-the-negro-as-a-problem-for-gender/section/3c938633-32fe-46b6-b167-3823bc7a2260#ch02.

116. See Bakker, "Blue Black Ecstasy."

117. Bakker, "Blue Black Ecstasy."

118. Daniela Bleichmar, *Visible Empire: Botanical Expeditions and Visual Culture in the Hispanic Enlightenment* (Chicago: University of Chicago Press, 2012).

119. As scholars like Christoph Irmscher have argued, "contradictions . . . marked American natural history from its beginnings—characterized as it was by the daring attempt to treat humans as part of nature and by its ultimate pathetic failure to do so in any other way than through a sharp division of those fully human from those just a little less human than human." Christoph Irmscher, *The Poetics of Natural History: From John Bartram to William James* (New Brunswick, NJ: Rutgers University Press, 1999), 279.

120. See, on this point, Nihad M. Farooq, *Undisciplined: Science, Ethnography, and Personhood in the Americas, 1830–1940* (New York: New York University Press, 2016).

121. Mary Louise Pratt, *Imperial Eyes: Travel Writing and Transculturation* (London: Routledge, 1992).

122. Kalpana Rahita Seshadri, *HumAnimal: Race, Law, Language* (Minneapolis: University of Minnesota Press, 2012), 183–84.

123. Christopher Peterson, *Bestial Traces: Race, Sexuality, Animality* (New York: Fordham University Press, 2012), 3.

124. Bakker, "Locating the Oceanic in Sylvia Wynter's 'Demonic Ground,'" 21–22.

Part Two: Science, Secularism, and Man's Political Theology of Race

4   The Wynterian Turn: Human Hybridity
     in the Natural and Human Sciences

   Niki Kasumi Clements

In 1959, physicist turned novelist C. P. Snow addressed his Oxbridge audience of academics through the Rede Lecture. In "The Two Cultures," he tells a story of the split between the "brash and boastful" scientists trumpeting "the heroic age of science" and the literary intellectuals "totally lacking in foresight" who insularly guard their "traditional" culture.[1] Snow urges his academic audience to close the gap between these two cultures, increasing scientific literacy through both concrete curricular changes in education and shifts to the more intangible "mood" of culture shaped by literary intellectuals.[2]

Snow tells his story of the two cultures in a context that assumes a literary education but not a scientific one. He wants to change what he sees as the then-hegemonic literary culture by breaking down the hierarchy of humanities over the sciences and engineering. He wants to change the world by uniting the attentions and the talents of academic knowledge producers.[3] And he wants to do so in order to alleviate suffering. He later says that he should have titled the lectures "The Rich and the Poor," since his work is motivated by the desire to better human lives.

Snow thus frames the problem in economic and social terms: the gap between the rich and the poor is a serious crisis requiring collaborative efforts between humanist and scientific researchers. While rich countries have benefited from industrial and technological advances to improve people's quality of life (living longer, eating better, working less), Snow calls for the extension of such resources to poorer countries and communities.[4] Snow calls for his elite, academic audience to get over their petty infighting and mutual hostility in order to forge a common culture. This common culture would *both* recognize the existential plight of being human and the ethical desire to ameliorate suffering *and* support the technological inventions and scientific discoveries that materially change the world.

By 1998, the hierarchy of humanities over sciences had been completely inverted. In *Consilience: The Unity of Knowledge*, E. O. Wilson identifies the natural sciences as superior to social-scientific and humanistic knowledge.[5] Wilson assumes an explicitly reductive empiricism that chains higher-level explanations of phenomena to lower-level explanations. Claiming that all explanations must be constrained by the basic sciences, Wilson contends that scientific literacy alone provides the accurate knowledge needed to oppose ideological or political positions.[6] Wilson's view of consilience assumes the methodological primacy of the natural sciences; he does not clearly identify what the humanities and social sciences distinctively contribute aside from a generic capacity for critical thinking.[7]

Both Snow and Wilson tell stories urging a unity of knowledge in order to address humanitarian crises. Like Snow, Wilson starkly frames the stakes of consilience: the future of human life is imperiled by global climate collapse and the loss of biodiversity.[8] Addressing this catastrophe requires unified work by people across disciplines: not specialists in discrete domains of inquiry, but "synthesizers, people able to put together the right information at the right time, think critically about it, and make important choices wisely."[9] For Snow in the 1950s, humanitarian crises emerge from massive global wealth disparities; forty years later, Wilson focuses on collapsing climates and biomes, identifying the ethical resources needed to address the crises as having "biological roots."[10] Both Snow and Wilson's public-facing texts frame their arguments' urgency in terms of an ethical crisis concerning human life—and this crisis can only be addressed through grounding in the natural sciences.

At face value, their claims for consilience are compelling. Who would not want to promote the human good through integrated forms of knowledge? Bringing together convergent evidence from forms of analysis from different disciplines seems to realize the grand potentials of academic research. Scientific and technological advances have dramatically shifted life expectancy and quality of life over the last hundred years; ergo the strengths of the natural sciences. Yet the human and social sciences help us recognize how shifts in life expectancy and quality of life have not been distributed equally. Snow and Wilson tie natural sciences to possibilities for human flourishing, yet they fail to adequately grasp the way that power relations and cultural logics reinforce hierarchies of human life.

Over the course of the last several decades, Sylvia Wynter has brilliantly argued the need to both engage and challenge the natural sciences in order to better realize the ethical possibilities for humanity and ecology through a "third level of existence."[11] Wynter presents a remarkable account of how to both bridge this impasse between the "two cultures" *and* challenge the scientific hierarchies encoded in Snow and Wilson's consilience model. She critiques these models while engaging their fundamental methodological strength: to recognize how multiple levels of analysis are needed in order to describe and understand multilevel human phenomena, while also forging strategies for critiquing human social orders by recognizing their historical construction and contingency. Wynter starts from a realistic appraisal of the divide between the two cultures. With "large-scale human emancipation yoked to the no less large-scale human degradation and immiseration to which these behaviors collectively lead," the natural sciences better account for the paradox of emancipation and degradation by defining humans "biocentrically on the model of a natural organism."[12]

Wynter creates a new imperative for interdisciplinary praxis that relies on a critical analysis of *both* these two cultures as created in the image of their intellectual predecessors—from religious to humanist to scientific understandings. In this chapter, I analyze Wynter's framing of intertwined Western histories of religion and science in order to expose the millennia-long construction of these cultures and their resultant historical contingency.[13] In part 1, I analyze Wynter's genealogy of Man in Western discourses as exposing the mechanisms supporting dominant epistemes serving patriarchal and colonizing interests. From a divinely ordered cosmos to the Copernican displacement of the Earth (and attendant flowering of humanism) to evolutionary Darwinian accounts of biological Man, Wynter locates the shared hierarchical logic in these epistemic shifts. She frames how secular modernity only believes itself to have cleansed itself of certain sins, showing the study of religion to be an important element in any liberatory critique of modernity. In part 2, I describe how Wynter exposes scientific hierarchies as not objective but instead bound up with dangerous logics and histories of violence which are intertwined with religious experience and history. Through the anti-Black and anti-indigenous racist logics undergirding scientific taxonomies, she delegitimizes vertical hierarchies of scientific reduction (including those of Snow and Wilson), while still incorporating the explanatory and predictive force of scientific knowledge. Critiquing the reductive conception of who counts as human (part 1) and the scientific method as reinscribing its own hierarchies on the objects it studies (part 2), I turn in part 3 to Wynter's constructions of new ways of challenging scientific orthodoxies (by embracing humanist critiques) and conceptions of being human (as a praxis) and their implications for religious studies' ongoing rapprochement with the sciences.

Part 1: A Genealogy of Man

To begin, I frame the primary "turns" that Wynter defines in Western histories of domination, notably via the intertwined histories of religion and science. I then discuss how Wynter analyzes "the human" as constructed within the epistemic hierarchies of Man. By exposing how histories of Western colonialism and imperialism have used the worldviews and technologies of religion and science to reinscribe human hierarchies that justify the subjection of others, Wynter challenges the scientific positivisms of Snow and Wilson and situates her critique as a necessary part of interdisciplinary praxis.

Epistemic Turns

In her 1984 "The Ceremony Must Be Found," Wynter gives a remarkable synthesis of the shift in conceptions of being human in Western discourses. She elaborates the logic of two main epistemes that have organized knowledge over the past two millennia in Western contexts.[14] First is the episteme of a divinely ordered world, most strikingly instituted and regulated through the Catholic Church as a social, political, and economic force, where its *mythos* and *logos* are rendered absolutes.[15] This Ptolemaic conception of the physical cosmos encodes a normative hierarchy, where the earth and its inhabitants occupied its central place, which Wynter points out is negatively coded as furthest from the heavens.[16] Wynter describes the theo-Scholastic worldview of Cardinal Bellarmine that found Copernicus's thesis so threatening because of its challenge to a fixed cosmos, where "within that theologically absolute system of knowledge, the Earth was supposed to be fixed at the center of the universe, as the divinely condemned abode of post-Adamic fallen man."[17] This moral transvaluation of the Earth accompanies an epistemic rupture where "once the Earth had been proved to move, medieval Latin-Christian Europe's then hegemonic theologically absolute worldview had begun to come to an end."[18]

The Copernican revolution unsettles the authority of *divinitas* as the ordering force for a cosmic hierarchy while also valorizing the human.[19] Renaissance humanism thus revalorizes the *homo religiosus* ("Adamic fallen Man") as *homo politicus* ("political man"). Copernicus's shift correlates with a humanism that sees *homo politicus* as "a figure now self-governed by its/his reason, articulated as reasons of state."[20] Yet this revalorization maintains the "overall vertically caste-stratified hierarchical order of medieval Latin-Christian Europe" even as it challenges ecclesial and epistemological authority, stressing *propter nos homines*, "for humankind did God create the Universe."[21] For Wynter, the Copernican turn dangerously revealed three interconnected truths: one, that the Earth is not the center of all things; two, that empirical study of the cosmos could produce new knowledge beyond Catholic ecclesial authority; three, that *homo politicus* can now govern by reason instead of ecclesial authority.

Opening such "a generalized *natural scientific* conceptual space" would then, according to Wynter, "make possible Darwin's epistemological rupture or leap—that is, its far-reaching challenge to Christianity's biblical macro-origin story's theocosmogonically projected divinely created divide between an ostensibly generically Christian mankind, on the one hand, and all other species, on the other."[22] The Darwinian rupture metonymized by the nineteenth-century theory of evolution intensifies the turn away from divine sources and toward natural ones. Here, empirical evidence for the evolution of the species contributes to the knowledge of human beings squarely situated within a naturalist epistemology. Thus emerges "the paradox of the new Darwinian descriptive statement of the human: Man in its second, purely secular, biocentric, and overrepresented modality of being human."[23]

Wynter illuminates how the religious logics structuring cosmogonies and philosophical anthropologies, "law-likely configured as being extra-humanly mandated," continue to inform "the secular substitute monohumanist religion of Darwin's neo-Malthusian biocosmogony."[24] Wynter identifies three successive conceptions of human being through the respective names, (1) "Christian," (2) "Man1," and (3) "Man2." Transitioning from theocentric to humanistic to biocentric worldviews involves corollary shifts in understanding the human as (1) made in the divine image (as the absolute authority) to (2) in relation to one's self (as the reflective human becomes the site of epistemic authority, à la Descartes) to (3) in relation to natural organisms and primate ancestors (as biological accounts gain privileged epistemic authority).

Thus emerges a humanist organization of knowledge that becomes completely biocentric. The "degodding" of Man2 correlates with the biocentrism of the late nineteenth to twentieth centuries, enabling natural and socio-human worlds to be studied historically and materially without recourse to ecclesial authority. Yet this degodding also instantiates a *particular* human being as its representative: "The larger issue is, then, the incorporation of all forms of human being into a single homogenized descriptive statement that is based on the figure of the West's liberal monohumanist *Man*."[25] God is substituted out for a rational humanism which instantiates a secular order; this secular order sees Man through a naturalist vision; this Man becomes representative for the human being as such.[26]

The question becomes, What can be empirically and materially described, predicted, and controlled? And Man comes to represent all of humanity controlled for political and economic ends. As *homo politicus* gives way to *homo oeconomicus* in the late eighteenth century, the human ability to legislate economic orders becomes more important than political orders. After all, *homo oeconomicus* exceeds political borders as it "epochally and uniquely overrepresents and reifies its genre-specific (ethno-class) *referent-we* as being isomorphic with that of the now *emergent-referent-we* 'in the horizon of humanity.'"[27] Wynter connects the technological and scientific practices supporting such global movements of economy and commerce as the same practices that Man has used to subject, massacre, and enslave people in Africa, the Americas, and Asia.

Wynter also explains how shifts between the (1) Christian then (2) Copernican then (3) Darwinian epistemes involve destructuring and restructuring.[28] Recall that an episteme is not objectively neutral but is structured by the authority against which claims are measured, the processes considered legitimate methods for measurement, and the ends to which such knowledge can be deployed.[29] The episteme of *divinitas* (whose ordering principle is Christian divinity) is restructured into the episteme of *humanitas* (whose ordering principle is human rationality), with a "new emerging sense of self."[30] This episteme apexes in the nineteenth-century organization of knowledge as defined by Michel Foucault, where new orthodoxies are established concerning biology, language, and economics that correlate with the needs of the industrial age.[31]

To consider the continuities and divergences between these epistemes, Wynter refers to Leszek Kołakowski's use of the term "heresy" to describe the "fundamental antagonism" of everything new as "questioning all existing absolutes."[32] The process of "transforming heresies into new orthodoxies, the contingent into modes of the Absolute" is the job of the Priest archetype. The Jester, by contrast, is to drag such absolutes "down to earth" in order to expose their contingency and open the possibility of critiquing them.[33] The heretical Jester and the institutionalizing Priest alternate as heresies displacing dominant understandings which then become new orthodoxies in dynamic succession.

Wynter drags this seeming orthodoxy down to earth: she argues how both the dialectic between Priests and Jesters and the semblance of neutral secular knowledge in the sciences are dangerous and inaccurate. Despite her critiques of objective knowledge in the sciences, Wynter should not be seen to reject the natural sciences as such. In addition to theorists like Kołakowski and Foucault, she challenges dominant scientific, secular, and humanist epistemes alike. And she does so from both humanistic and scientific understandings of *autopoiesis* and the world as "an interacting system in dynamic change."[34] This "autopoiesis," Katherine McKittrick says, encodes dangers and when unchecked keeps "our present normative mode of existence in order to keep the living-system—our environmental and existential world—as is. This is a recursive logic; it depicts our presently ecocidal and genocidal world as normal and unalterable. Our work is to notice this logic and breach it."[35] Our ecocidal and genocidal world is neither normal nor unalterable, yet we need to see this fact before being able to challenge its logics.

"Christian" "Man"

These logics are neither normal nor unalterable, but contingent and fungible. Wynter prompts our first epistemic shift to recognize the Copernican turn as the unseating of *divinitas* and the understanding of the human as Christian. The rationality of Renaissance Man comes to unsettle divinity as the absolute source of value and the principle of organization.[36] The human, conceived as a natural and objective category of knowledge as opposed to one dependent on divine revelation, becomes the organizing principle for the socio-human world enabling a "new emerging sense of self" that Wynter gives the name Man1.[37]

Moving from a divinely defined Christian subject to rationally ordered self-legislating Man1, however, folds the vertical hierarchy of divine over human into further hierarchies of being human.[38] And with the humanist valorization of reason emerges its dialectical contrary in the figure of unreason, of the subrational and irrational Human Other.[39] Wynter notes: "In the wake of the West's reinvention of its True Christian Self in the transumed terms of the Rational Self of Man1, however, it was to be the peoples of the militarily expropriated New World territories (i.e., Indians), as well as the enslaved peoples of Black Africa (i.e., Negroes), that were made to reoccupy the matrix slot of Otherness—to be made into the physical referent of the idea of the irrational/subrational Human Other."[40] Naturalizing these hierarchical logics is a tactic used by colonial projects to justify conquests, subjections, and violences under the cover of rationality and the "natural" order of things.[41]

With the scientific revolution bound up in political, social, and economic changes, the human being was doubly displaced in the Darwinian rupture of the nineteenth century. In the sixteenth-century model, the human was cosmically decentered yet humanistically revalorized, alongside the authorization of knowledge vis-à-vis physical instead of divine laws. Three hundred years later, the human was biologically displaced in importance, through the evolutionary theories about the development of the species.

Now an apex biological formation, Man2 becomes understood in relation to evolutionary principles tied to other primate species instead of the image of the divine.

Wynter exposes how Man2 becomes the generalized form of the human being through a biological narrative that encodes a hierarchy of being human that is racially, ethnically, and geographically coded. Such scientific and political discourses self-define as natural and normative in order to cover over their reliance on the "reinvention of Western Europe's matrix Judeo-Christian genre of the human, in its first secularizing if still hybrid religio-secular terms as Man as the Rational self and political subject of the state, in the reoccupied place of the True Christian Self."[42] Far from neutral scientific categories, Wynter's identification of Man1 and Man2 both rely on, and are deployed to justify, colonial violence. Denise Ferreira da Silva notes of Wynter's view that "the rational/irrational pair would then remap the 'space of otherness' and, significantly, be represented by the bodies and territories subjected to colonial power."[43] Man2, *homo oeconomicus*, the "purely secular" and biocentric, thereby covers over the conditions of his formation and the instantiation at the top of putatively objective hierarchies, justifying racial and gendered hierarchies in turn.[44]

Man2 thus becomes the generalized form of the human species understood through evolutionary and biological accounts—just as Snow and Wilson insist. What Wynter enables us to see is the gross hypocrisy and anti-Black violence of this biological Man2 who is constituted at the same time as the global movements of industry and capital are improving the quality of life for so many humans. It is not simply that Man2 reduces the view of the human to the material and natural—it is that the episteme buttressing Man2 "alone makes possible 'race' in its now second configuration as Du Bois's '*Color Line*,' as well as its dually correlated (neo)Liberal-humanist *Man(2)-as-homo-oeconomicus* conception together with its 'human science' episteme (Foucault, 1973)."[45] Drawing from Frantz Fanon, Wynter delineates how the Darwinian Revolution damningly includes the "imperatively secured bottom role of the Black Diaspora peoples—as well as the systemic expendability of the global Poor, of the jobless, the homeless, the underdeveloped."[46]

Part 2: Critiquing the "Science of Man"

By exposing the racist biases attendant to modern constructions of the human, Wynter calls us to reconsider the methodological operations of science. It is necessary to recognize how dangerously the dominant episteme and conception of the human operate when unchallenged; this is the work that the humanities and social sciences enable. In turn, she also calls for humanists to directly engage the methods of scientific knowledge production.

As I developed in part 1, the Darwinian turn is the prerequisite for Snow's "Two Cultures" division of knowledge, and Wynter identifies the limitations and possibilities for this division at the end of the twentieth century. This is not Snow's 1950s separation between a dominant humanist culture and an emergent scientific one; rather, the scientific culture is now dominant and the humanist culture deeply subordinate. Wynter points to the strengths of the biological sciences as seeing "continuing dazzling successes" yet calls us to critically recognize the normative bases of the two cultures: "That is, to the natural-scientific disciplines on the one hand, and to the rigorous yet adaptive, and therefore ethno-disciplines of the humanities and social sciences on the other."[47] The success of the sciences needs to be radically challenged by its attendant "obsessive ethno-biological beliefs in the genetic inferiority of nonwhite natives, in the barely evolved near-primate status of black-skinned peoples (as matrix beliefs that would logically make possible the 'life unworthy of life' extermination credo of the Nazis)."[48] The "paradigm of Evolution" operated simultaneously in two ways: both enabling biological sciences' success *and* producing ethno-bio beliefs in genetic inferiority and the division of knowledge.[49] Wynter shows us how the positivisms and progress of biological accounts of human and natural worlds have coincided with their deployment in eugenics, genocide, and ecocide; this sets the human stakes for challenging the positivisms of natural sciences, which when unchecked by humanist critique spiral into the deepest violence. The humanist ethno-disciplines are imperative—not ancillary—to understanding how the biosciences operate under dialectics of extinction and speciation fundamental to Darwinian evolution. It is necessary to include knowledge of human experience beyond the smugness of biological "facts" that continue to justify elimination—at times, under the banner of ecological concerns.

In "The Ceremony Found," "Unsettling the Coloniality of Being/Power/Truth/Freedom," and "Unparalleled Catastrophe for Our Species?," Wynter engages these existential stakes of her call.[50] The global crisis of climate change and ecological collapse sets a defined limit to human life as they become "our major collectively human predicament" in "our last chance to avoid the large-scale dilemmas that we must now confront as a species."[51] Yet Wynter points out that the best of climate scientists and agencies have misidentified the cause of ecological degradation; and it is impossible to address the crisis if the causes have been misattributed. The cause of humanity's collective dilemma is not "human" activity as such, as the scientific literature claims. In fact, it is a relatively small group of people who are responsible for the crisis: Man2, the *homo oeconomicus*. To conflate "human" being with "Man2" is a twofold problem: historically, it enabled Man2's violence against other human beings; contemporaneously, it continues to misidentify the cause of climate collapse. In our current episteme, Man2 has rendered himself the universal signifier for all humans, to disastrous effects.[52]

Wynter identifies the life-imperiling danger of allowing this episteme—this logic governing modern Western capitalist and imperialist discourses—to uncritically stand in for all humans as such. Wynter critiques this colonizing logic across her work, stressing how Man2 cannot be naturalized as "the" human subject as such (as we saw in part 1). With planetary-level ecological crises imperiling human survival, fighting these crises requires that we first accurately identify their causes. Wynter challenges us all to identify how systems of knowledge self-replicate to the advantage of the few and the destruction of the many. As McKittrick describes: "Sylvia Wynter taught me that radical theory-making takes place outside existing systems of knowledge and that this place, outside (demonic grounds), is inhabited by those who are brilliantly and intimately aware of existing systems of knowledge (as self-replicating)."[53]

From the vantage of these "demonic grounds," Wynter declares the necessity of a radical reimagining of what it is to be human. She plays the Jester who brings the absolutes of scientific and technological industry "down to earth" and shows the particular conditions of their formation and their narrow representation of the human. She plays the Priest in the planetary scope of her critique, the categorical imperative of her ethics, and the specificity of her philosophical anthropology. Her philosophical engagement with scientific disciplines—that we humanists still often fail to effectively see—helps us understand how Man2 has been reified in scientific discourses as "the" human subject and its nonuniversal "human activities." The ethical and ecological stakes of Wynter's speculative turn are vital, where humans-as-hybrid could work together to forge new possibilities for transforming humanity through "our collective human agency."[54]

Wynter demonstrates the ability of critique, taken as a methodology, to denormalize the absolutes that cover over their contingency, and this concern for collectivity and agency is particularly important with reference to the struggles of and for Black life.[55] It is damning that the natural sciences do not deal with the paradox of (1) their dazzling success and the amelioration of suffering on a global scale and (2) this progress predicated on the exploitation, subjection, and experimentation on Black, indigenous, non-male, or poor subjects. In conversation with McKittrick, Wynter insists that "these natural (biological) sciences, however—as they too function, for the main part, in cognitively open and self-correcting terms—must be taken into account with the aporia of their now globally hegemonic Janus-faced *purely biocentric* version of humanness."[56] Wynter thus helps us correctly identify the biocentric limitations of this "science of Man" in both social and philosophical terms. Scientific taxonomies organize human beings according to logics grounded in methods that were tested in fields weaponizing genetic difference; colonizing and industrial forces set these epistemic conditions that justified hierarchies of being human in order to deny the subjectivity of many humans and to make them objects for exploitation. In the organizing logics of the sciences, the authority to create such hierarchies of human being is also used to cover over the contingency of these constructions as "natural" and empirically observable. Wynter thus helps us see the violence of understanding human life through *bios* alone.

So how do we recognize the ongoing legacy of the post-Copernican and post-Darwinian turns without recapitulating the hierarchies that they naturalized? How can we come to knowledge of the world when the order of things has been defined in terms that require either methodological reduction or complete disqualification? Wynter herself asks: "How can we come to have knowledge of socio-human existence outside the terms of the answer that we at present give to the question of who-we-are as an alleged purely biological being, as one in whose genre-specific naturally selected/dysselected symbolic life/death terms we now performatively enact ourselves as secular and, thereby, necessarily Western and westernized bourgeois subjects—including us as academics/intellectuals?"[57] The "two cultures" remain—and have become even more politically and economically charged—since Man2, falsely generalized as "human activity" as a whole, persistently refuses regulations and claims moral rectitude through the profit-driven advances of global capitalism.

Wynter clearly recognizes the utility of the natural sciences for their predictive and explanatory power for collective behaviors, as she engages them to produce new knowledge about being human.[58] Yet she also stresses the horrific human costs of what we have called scientific advancement, notably through its meticulous yet global prosecution of settler colonialism and the transatlantic slave trade, whose daily operations and large-scale coordinations were entirely reliant on industrial and technological innovations. Instead of rejecting the relevance of natural scientific accounts of being human, Wynter pushes through challenging theoretical territory to effect a critique immanent to both natural scientific and humanistic accounts of the (post-)human condition.

Wynter both recognizes the brutalities of scientific histories (in a way that Snow and Wilson do not) and boldly engages their relevance for analyzing how human beings are and can be constituted, both descriptively and normatively. She thereby equips her readers with tools that in a different era might have been called demystifying, but which we could more properly call liberatory. Wynter embraces the descriptive *and* predictive powers of what we call the sciences (even extending ideas like *autopoiesis* to other human domains), while also exposing how their operative logics are not correlatively but causatively violent and pernicious toward people outside the genus of the colonizing male elite, Man2. Through "the sociogenic principle," she shows how the self-correcting mechanisms basic to the scientific method need to expand to the humanistic critique of the categories and methods of the natural sciences. Wynter thus invites a revolutionary attitude capable of critical description and constructive openings to the production of new knowledge.[59]

Part 3: The Wynterian Turn

Wynter calls upon her readers and listeners to engage the constructive side of her critical project. The next great epistemic crisis is already upon us and can be met with what Paget Henry calls Wynter's "epistemic historicism" as "an approach to history as a medium of human self-formation (and not just as a discipline) that rests on the dynamic relationships that Wynter sees between epistemic change and the transformation of social orders."[60] Global technological and scientific threats have already defined the twentieth and twenty-first centuries. To respond to the brutal human cost of these realities, Wynter creates an imaginary that might allow an emancipatory, newly ordered discourse of being human, instead of reinscribing pernicious yet "sanctified categories" of scholarship.[61]

Toward the "Science of the Word"

Taking up Aimé Césaire's 1945 "science of the Word" and Frantz Fanon's 1952 "meta-Darwinian terms," Wynter forges a praxis out of their understandings of a new science of being human.[62] This science is constitutively hybrid, engaging both biological natural scientific understandings and narrative humanistic understandings. Wynter follows Césaire's proposal for "a new science, a hybrid science: a science of the Word. This idea is one in which the study of the Word (the *mythoi*) will condition the study of nature (the *bios*)."[63] In a more compelling account of gene-culture co-evolution than the one offered by Wilson, Wynter proposes how the expression of genetics *and* social scripts are bound together in any explanatory account.

Wynter stresses how Césaire's science calls for a return to the "'very first days of the species' on what is now natural-scientifically cum linguistically known to be the Southwest region of Africa" as the beginning of "the uniquely human capacity to convey meaning and symbols through language, i.e., through the *Word*."[64] It is distinctive to the human species that *bios* (nature) and *mythoi* (language-based meaning) are bound together, where *mythoi* condition *bios*, and *bios* shapes *mythoi*. In Wynter's challenge to Wilson's hierarchy of vertical integration, this science of the Word explains the human predicament through both stories (*mythoi*) and biology (*bios*) because both words and genes contribute to the praxis of being human: *"thus our 'stories' are as much a part of what makes us human—of our being human as the imperatively artificially co-identifying, eusocial species that we are—as are our bipedalism and the use of our hands."*[65] Beyond "the physical and purely biological levels of reality," there are folds of human experience neither explained nor even perceived-as-relevant through natural scientific inquiry.[66] Wynter identifies this as our "third level of existence—dually *biological and meta-biological*," identifying both the episteme supporting these representational processes and the particular content of these codes discursively represented.[67]

Wynter also draws from Fanon's formulation of how "phylogeny, ontogeny, *and* sociogeny, *together, define what it is to be human*."[68] Phylogeny and ontogeny are ordering principles in biological discourses, taxonomizing species level beings. Sociogeny describes the human production of sociocultural orders organized around stories, kin-relations, and cooperative forms of life.[69] The "sociogenic replicator codes of symbolic life/death" must be recognized as part of the constructed scientific taxonomies that *claim* objectivity but are actually shaped through the interests of nineteenth-century colonizing and industrializing Man2. Fanon, in Wynter's reading, provides a way to move beyond Man2 and Darwinian hierarchies which perniciously rely on a "still order-instituting and order-legitimating, *biologically absolute* answer."[70]

Moving beyond this biologically absolute answer is vital to see and challenge its ongoing effects. And this perspective is one particular to human beings as a species. Wynter stresses that human beings are "alone able to transcend the narrow, genetically determined limits of eusocial, interaltruistic, kin-recognizing behaviors in order to instead attain to higher levels of cooperation and organization."[71] Phylogeny and ontogeny alone cannot account for such possibilities; thus Wynter calls us to consider the narrative forms of sociality contributing to such higher levels of organization and cooperation. With these narrative understandings, we can both understand how human orders have been shaped sociogenetically and we can consider how we might move beyond their historically contingent limitations and horrors. This understanding is not attained through biological analyses alone but relies on an expanded historical and conceptual knowledge of the past and present.

Being Hybridly Human

Wynter requires that we both see beyond scientific conceits of objectivity and shatter the isomorphism between Man2 and being human by establishing new conceptions of being human as a praxis. She calls us to see how today's "human activity" is not about all humans but instead preserves the nineteenth-century western episteme of Man2 that continues to devalue human and ecological life through hierarchical logics. *Mythoi* shape the social constructions of race, for example, within hierarchies of human being that falsely normalize the supremacy of certain humans over others, fixing ontologies of racial and gendered essence in order to enable economic and social exploitation of human beings, particularly people codified as "Black." Wynter draws from Fanon's description of the subjective experience of double consciousness conditioned by colonialist ideology: "This phenomenon is that all human *Skins* can only *become human* by also performatively enacting them/ourselves *as human* in the always-already, cosmogonically chartered terms of their/our symbolically encoded and fictively constructed *genre*-specific *Masks*, as themselves always-already programmed by their/our respective *sociogenic replicator codes of symbolic life/death*."[72]

Engaging Fanon's meta-Darwinian human beyond double consciousness and Césaire's "science of the Word," Wynter frames human praxis as part of a conceptual turn she calls the Autopoetic Turn/Overturn.[73] This Wynterian turn involves forging a "New Studia," of "a meta-systemic, indeed, meta-cosmogonic *outsider* perspective" following from her account of the original *studia humanitatis*.[74] Citing Maturana's account of how the 1968 revolutionary movements at the University of Chile made the radical conception of *autopoiesis* possible, Wynter emphasizes the world as an interacting system in dynamic change where "social uprisings have tremendous links to the transformation of knowledge."[75] And with the predicates of *autopoiesis*, Wynter comes to see humans as "a hybrid and uniquely auto-instituting mode of living being," where "*we humans cannot pre-exist our cosmogonies or origin myths/stories/narratives* any more than a bee, at the purely biological level of life, can pre-exist its beehive."[76] The stories we tell about who we are matter and "matter" quite literally in the sense that they produce real material worlds.[77] The praxis of being human involves biological origins (genetically transmitted) and narrative origins (socially transmitted), which together produce possibilities for human becoming.[78]

Recall from part 1, Humanist Man1 displaced the Christian subject tied to Divinity, which was then replaced by biological Man2. What, then, might displace Man2 without reinscribing Man's enduringly hierarchical logics? How do we challenge the episteme in order to not replicate its violences and objectification of too many humans? By emphasizing the human as hybrid, Wynter opens possibilities for such displacement as a *reformation*, where the human is not just born biologically (as with Man2), but "hybridly of the womb *and* origin-story (i.e., of the *bios/mythos*)."[79] To counter the dominant epistemes of Western-colonizer societies, Wynter turns to hybrid human representations from an ancestral human past, as Anthony Bogues notes: "using cave drawings from the Southern Africa region, Wynter argues that these drawings converge with a human phase that she calls, 'autohominisation.' For Wynter these drawings not only demonstrated the humanness of African people but illuminated human essence as one that was 'uniquely hybrid.'"[80]

Valorizing a "hybrid human" means critiquing and refusing to reinscribe the supremacist logics linking Christian/Man1/Man2 that overrepresent dominant human males in Western histories of religion and science as what it means to be human as such. Critiquing the reduction of first Christian Man then Man1 then Man2 to the human being *in general* also requires that we challenge the reduction of all religion to the role of Christianity in particular; the history of Western cultures, philosophies, and technologies have been so inflected by Christianity that other religious traditions and possibilities have been systematically devalued or otherized. As Nicosia Shakes argues, "In the realm of religion for example, we have a situation where rationalism is used to critique any 'other' religion but Christianity, especially where the religion is African-derived."[81] Instead of understanding the relation of "religion and science" through modern Western discourses—where Christian-modern-biocentric-Man continues to control epistemic horizons and assert his white supremacy over others—Wynter invites an expanded analysis of domains of data and social imaginaries only possible when appreciating humans as hybrid.

A Wynterian Turn

Wynter expresses hope that hybridity will open up ways to consider being human beyond the reduction of prior epistemes of Christian Man, Man1, and Man2. She says: "If humans are conceptualized as hybrid beings, you can no longer classify human individuals, as well as human groups, as *naturally selected* (i.e., eugenic) and *naturally dysselected* (i.e., dysgenic) beings. This goes away. It is no longer meaningful."[82] Reckoning with the histories of racism, eugenics, and violence against particularly Black and indigenous peoples in the natural sciences, Wynter refuses the classification of human individuals and groups. She turns instead to an immanent critique of the world of Man.[83]

Beyond the epistemological turn of Copernicus and the epistemological rupture of Darwin, Wynter effects her own epistemological shift. This Wynterian Turn (that she calls an Autopoetic turn) recognizes human hybridity as a challenge to orders of knowledge and hierarchies of being. This enables the "needs of mankind" to be reimagined beyond the epistemological, political, and social limits of Man2. Wynter thereby unsettles an episteme dominated by scientific norms and assumptions of methodological naturalism that require humanist accounts to reduce to—or be consilient with—scientific accounts. Wynter's account of hybridity enables a robust humanistic understanding of the contingency of putative absolutes, and the need to bring those absolutes back down to earth. The humanist and the scientific accounts need both to constrain *each other*.

And as the heretical Jester, Wynter conceptually establishes a long historical arc that enables us to see both the limitations of nonhybrid models and some possibilities beyond them. She sets up the series of turns from Copernicus and Darwin—with their associated shifts in the conception of the human—in order to expose their contingencies and their confluences.[84] She enables what I here call the Wynterian Turn, as an existential unsettling of normative understandings of the human by uncovering the mechanisms that have falsely universalized a particular conception of Man in this overrepresentation of what it means to be human. Neither the human nor the natural sciences offer ordering principles that are beyond critique and further challenge. Indeed, only by critically distancing ourselves from a given episteme can we evaluate its strengths and weaknesses. And Wynter does this by both engaging and exceeding the dogmatic epistemes of Christian, Man1, and Man2.

There are many reasons why scientists working within the current episteme would want to reject this call. Wynter explains how her hybrid logic opens—and therefore puts at risk—the very bedrock of scientific concepts and methods through critique from the humanities and social sciences. Wynter's call is even more vital, then, to reckon with enduring and pernicious dehumanizing logics. Considering humans beyond Man2 as living and dynamic forces requires the courage to see how the conditions supporting our current episteme are hierarchical and dehumanizing. If we take up Wynter's genealogical critique as an opportunity to offer challenges for our collective future, we must also see how she enables a more robust and rigorous form of consilience. Such a hybrid methodology goes beyond Snow and Wilson's "two cultures," where neither the natural sciences nor the humanities are dominant; instead, Wynter draws attention to local and distributed ways of understanding human praxis as a way of life. As Wynter learns from W. E. B. Du Bois, this involves addressing "the objectively institutionalized Problem of the color line" through "a multiplicity of local, small-scale anticolonial, antisettler apartheid, and overall anti-imperial 'gaze from below' perspectives and struggles that were as global in their reach as that of the color line itself."[85]

Recognizing and countering these racist logics involves pushing for an epistemic shift that does not assume the priority of the natural sciences and its reductive hierarchy. Instead, we can collectively hone our critical analyses to give an epistemically salient account from both humanist and natural scientific perspectives. This alone, perhaps, will help us pursue more radically integrated accounts of addressing global crises that Snow, Wilson, and other representatives of the "Third Culture" could gesture toward but not enact.

Concluding with New Ecologies

By pursuing new ways of knowing that incorporate the natural and human sciences, Wynter enacts the consilient methods she urges. She accomplishes this by deftly defining the continuities and differences between three epistemes constitutive of Western definitions of the human over millennia "in the terms of a continuous cultural field, one instituted by the matrix Judeo-Christian formulation of a general order of existence."[86] Her work constitutes a genealogy—exposing the structuring logic shared by the shifts between Christian, Man1, and Man2—in order to decouple the human from this "Judeo-Christian" logic and break down the hierarchies of being human historically mobilized in this logic.

Wynter's inquiry thus critiques constructions of the human as being neither neutral nor objective, but as continuing to universalize a particular human as *the* human. For Wynter, this needs to change. As Wynter unfolds a genealogical account of the production and normalization of a particular genre of being human in the intertwined histories of religion and science, she exposes the mechanisms silently conflating "the human being" with the male, elite subject benefiting from colonizing practices that dehumanize especially African and indigenous peoples who have been enslaved, exploited, dominated, and killed for economic gain. The denaturalization of these epistemic orders is a necessary precondition to counter the logic by which Man2 defines humanity in his own image (a logic still too reliant on the definition of Christian man as made in the divine image).

By exposing how histories of Western colonialism and imperialism have used the worldviews and technologies of religion and science to reinscribe human hierarchies that justify the subjection of others, Wynter challenges the scientific positivisms of Snow and Wilson and situates her critique as a necessary part of interdisciplinary praxis. Wynter shows, pace Snow, that it is not about extending scientific advances to people in poorer countries, but about recognizing not only that these "poorer countries" have been historical sites of exploitation and colonial extraction but also how they will continue to suffer most from ecological collapse. Wynter shows, pace Wilson, that natural sciences do not offer objective or neutral grounds for ethics, because their histories are bound up with racist logics and methods. Wilson's own call for synthesizers requires a form of critical thought that only Wynter helps us see: any interdisciplinary work must account for the biases encoded and normalized in our scientific and humanist concepts and methods.

Unlike the ideological impasse of the "two cultures," Wynter creates the conditions for consilience between the natural and human sciences that refuse the objective primacy of the natural sciences and show the need for humanistic critique in order to provide a comprehensive understanding of our current categories and how they were historically constructed and deployed. To engage in a robustly interdisciplinary enterprise bridging these two cultures thus requires both identifying and challenging the dominant norms and avoiding an uncritical acceptance of reductive scientific taxonomies. Wynter succeeds where Snow and Wilson do not, calling for a unity of knowledge and establishing the epistemic conditions for scientific and humanistic discourses to critique each other in the ongoing work of making human beings matter. Beyond her other contributions, Wynter's work also shows how the study of religion is vital for understanding the operations of science. We cannot separate these "two cultures" if we are to have an explanatory account of the very bases for scientific production and measurement through the epistemic continuities and shifts from Christian Man to Man1 to Man2.

Wynter thus exposes the ethical stakes not as distal geographically (like Snow, considering poverty around the globe), or temporally (like Wilson, considering climate change over time), but as encoded in scientific norms already.[87] The crisis not only has long been here but has been constitutive of our current moment. In this chapter, I have identified how Wynter does not just name the stakes of her work as ethical; she also exposes unethical constructions of the human being (in part 1) and unethical logics as basic to scientific methodologies (in part 2), while constructing affirmative collective forms of agency that are ecologically attuned (in part 3). Should we be courageous enough to take it up, the Wynterian Turn would thus be one that challenges scientific epistemes premised on vertical hierarchies and histories of domination, both exposing and inviting the force of stories to understand and reshape our human worlds.

Notes

1. C. P. Snow, *The Two Cultures* (Cambridge: Cambridge University Press, 1998), 4, 5, 11.

2. Snow, 60–61.

3. Snow's appeal to elite academics can also be read as a critique of classism in British academic and political cultures. Having worked in the civil service and private industry, Snow challenges the lower cultural status associated with scientific and engineering work. The global stakes of this call to break down hierarchies can also be read politically as a way of urging Britain to unite the talents of researchers across fields in order to compete in the Cold War.

4. "Among the rich are the U.S., the white Commonwealth countries, Great Britain, most of Europe, and the U.S.S.R. China is betwixt and between, not yet over the industrial hump, but probably getting there. The poor are all the rest." Snow, *Two Cultures*, 41. Snow frames the obligation to extend social and economic benefits to all people through technical training *without* the paternalisms of colonizers (48).

5. Edward O. Wilson, *Consilience: The Unity of Knowledge* (New York: Vintage Books, 1998). Hierarchies are basic to the scientific understanding of the cosmos as "an orderly material existence governed by exact laws" (24).

6. Wilson attributes the successes of "Western science" largely to reductionism (Wilson, *Consilience*, 34).

7. Consider also Edward Slingerland's call for academics to pursue scientific literacy, now as part of their research programs. Trained in the 1990s research university of Stanford, with the inundation of theory by "High Humanists," Slingerland takes theorists to task for being too arcane and challenges them to better explain what they are doing—notably through a methodological reduction to the scientific studies that disqualify many of these theories of action. Edward Slingerland, *What Science Offers the Humanities: Integrating Body and Culture* (New York: Cambridge University Press, 2008).

8. Wilson, *Consilience*, 320–22. Jason Ambroise also stresses Wilson's reliance on scientific reduction to address global climate crises: "And only on the basis of his proposed understanding of the human can such a crisis be averted. The unity of human knowledge on the basis of biology, that is, the goal of Consilience is therefore premised on the stance that such knowledge must be made consistent with this self-understanding." Jason L. R. Ambroise, "Biocentrism, Neo-Ptolemaicism, and E. O. Wilson's *Consilience*: A Contemporary Example of 'Saving the Phenomenon' of Man, in the Name of the Human," in *After Man, towards the Human: Critical Essays on Sylvia Wynter*, ed. Anthony Bogues (Kingston: Ian Randle, 2006), 228.

9. Wilson, *Consilience*, 294.

10. Ambroise captures Wilson's expectation that ethics can reduce to biology: "And ethics, religion, and moral reasoning in general, will all be brought within an empiricist worldview that elucidates their purely biological roots." Ambroise, "Biocentrism," 218. For similar expectations concerning consilience, see John Brockman, *The Third Culture: Beyond the Scientific Revolution* (New York: Simon and Schuster, 1995), as well as other participants in the Edge (edge.org).

Similar epistemological issues characterize other attempts to bring together the sciences and humanities. My 2017 edited volume, *Mental Religion*, for example, attempts to present research across the cognitive and neurosciences of religion yet does not pursue a rigorous critique of these epistemic and ethical issues (partly because of the genre of the volume as a college reference work). After spending time with Wynter, I see I was wrong to separate the ability to stage these disciplines in their own terms in the volume and defer my critique to future work. Any rigorous account of humanist and scientific engagement (in publications and pedagogies) must encode critique of its basic predicates, as I have learnt from Wynter and try to unfold in this chapter. See Niki Kasumi Clements, ed., *Mental Religion* (Farmington Hills, MI: Macmillan Reference, 2017.

11. Sylvia Wynter, "The Ceremony Found: Towards the Autopoetic Turn/Overturn, Its Autonomy of Human Agency and Extraterritoriality of (Self-)Cognition," in *Black Knowledges / Black Struggles: Essays in Critical Epistemology*, ed. Jason R. Ambroise and Sabine Broeck (Liverpool: Liverpool University Press, 2015), 209.

12. Sylvia Wynter, "Unsettling the Coloniality of Being/Power/Truth/Freedom: Towards the Human, after Man, Its Overrepresentation—an Argument," *CR: The New Centennial Review* 3, no. 3 (2003): 270.

13. For a caution when it comes to understanding Wynter's use of the term "religion" or "religious," see David Kline, "The Apparatus of Christian Identity: Religious (Auto)Immunity, Political Theology, and the Making of the Racial World" (PhD diss., Rice University, 2017).

14. Sylvia Wynter, "The Ceremony Must Be Found: After Humanism," in "On Humanism and the University I: The Discourse of Humanism," ed. William Spanos, special issue, *boundary 2* 12, no. 3 / 13, no. 1 (1984): 19–70.

Paget Henry suggests reading Wynter's ceremonies as "epistemic engineering" and as the way to challenge the epistemic foundations she exposes. Paget Henry, "Wynter and the Transcendental Spaces of Caribbean Thought," in *After Man, towards the Human: Critical Essays on Sylvia Wynter*, ed. Anthony Bogues (Kingston: Ian Randle, 2006), 273–74.

15. Wynter, "Ceremony Must Be Found," 21–25, 33–34.

16. For this *homo religiosus*, I would also stress the anti-Semitism at its Christian supremacist foundations.

17. Sylvia Wynter and Katherine McKittrick, "Unparalleled Catastrophe for Our Species? Or, to Give Humanness a Different Future: Conversations," in *Sylvia Wynter: On Being Human as Praxis*, ed. Katherine McKittrick (Durham, NC: Duke University Press, 2015), 14.

18. Wynter and McKittrick, 14.

19. Wynter, "Ceremony Must Be Found," 29–31, 41–52.

20. Wynter and McKittrick, "Unparalleled Catastrophe," 15.

21. Wynter and McKittrick, 16.

22. Wynter and McKittrick, 16.

23. Wynter, "Unsettling the Coloniality of Being/Power/Truth/Freedom," 317.
24. Wynter and McKittrick, "Unparalleled Catastrophe," 37.
25. Wynter and McKittrick, 23.
26. Wynter and McKittrick, 18.
27. Wynter and McKittrick, 38. Wynter cites Jacques Derrida, "The Ends of Man," *Philosophy and Phenomenological Research* 30, no. 1 (1969): 35, though she omits the modifier "total."
28. Wynter, "Ceremony Must Be Found," 23, 29.
29. Denise Ferreira da Silva, "Before *Man*: Sylvia Wynter's Rewriting of the Modern Episteme," in *Sylvia Wynter: On Being Human as Praxis*, ed. Katherine McKittrick (Durham, NC: Duke University Press, 2015), 93–94.
30. Silva, 33–34, 29.
31. Silva, 34–37.
32. Wynter, "Ceremony Must Be Found," 21.
33. Wynter, 21.
34. Wynter, 21–22.
35. Katherine McKittrick, *Dear Science and Other Stories* (Durham, NC: Duke University Press, 2021), 2. McKittrick analyzes this critical perspective as enabling the constructive goal to "observe this system and name its normalcy, and thus provide the conditions to assert different living systems and/or breach the existing social system" (136).
36. Wynter, "Ceremony Found," 191.
37. Wynter, "Ceremony Must Be Found," 29.
38. We note, too, that Wynter recognizes human hierarchies within the "Christian" logic, notably priest over laity and male over female, where the former has authority over the latter on analog to divine over (male) human power. Man1 attempts to undermine subordination to the ecclesia through a "secular" logic that nevertheless recapitulates the power structure in another form. Thanks to Justine Bakker and David Kline for their thoughts here. See Sylvia Wynter, "Afterword: Beyond Miranda's Meanings: Un/silencing the 'Demonic Ground' of Caliban's 'Woman,'" in *Out of the Kumbla: Caribbean Women and Literature*, ed. Carole Boyce Davies and Elaine Savory Fida (Trenton, NJ: Africa World, 1990), 355–72.
39. The dialectical logic from Michel Foucault's *The History of Madness* on the construction of reason/unreason in the classical age of Europe is present in Wynter's work. However, Wynter provides the necessary and brutal analysis of how this constitutive logic targeted not only the mad but, through the ravages of settler colonialism and imperialist economies, produced hierarchies of otherness particularly targeting African and indigenous peoples.
40. Wynter, "Unsettling the Coloniality of Being/Power/Truth/Freedom," 265–66. Walter D. Mignolo stresses how the insidious logics Wynter identifies in this Renaissance humanism were "also the foundational step for building racism as we sense and know it today" in "the sociohistorical conditions that made it possible for the elite of European Man to construct such an idea—of Man-as-Human—and to be successful in implementing it." Walter D. Mignolo, "Sylvia Wynter: What Does It Mean to Be Human?," in *Sylvia Wynter: On Being Human as Praxis*, ed. Katherine McKittrick (Durham, NC: Duke University Press, 2015), 118.
41. Nicosia Shakes stresses Wynter's anchor between religion and hierarchical anthropologies supporting colonial exploitation as "religion and rationalism during the

European conquest of the Indies, and their interpretations of sameness and otherness served to create the binary oppositional chains of European/Non-European, thus Christian/non-Christian, thus civilized/uncivilized thus good/evil. The Europeans in their own eyes, through their possession of culture and civilization, became human, while their chattels who supposedly possessed no culture and no civilization became sub-human." Nicosia Shakes, "Legitimizing Africa in Jamaica," in *After Man, towards the Human: Critical Essays on Sylvia Wynter*, ed. Anthony Bogues (Kingston: Ian Randle, 2006), 294. Denise Ferreira da Silva also frames this naturalization; "Before *Man*," 91.

42. Wynter, "Unsettling the Coloniality of Being/Power/Truth/Freedom," 281.

43. Silva, "Before *Man*," 93–94.

44. Mignolo, for example, calls for a "decolonial scientia." Mignolo, "Sylvia Wynter," 118.

45. Wynter, "Ceremony Found," 192–93.

46. Wynter, "Unsettling the Coloniality of Being/Power/Truth/Freedom," 322.

47. Wynter, 318.

48. Wynter, 317–18.

49. Justine Bakker notes that in "1492" Wynter extends this back further, such that basically everything coming after is marked as "Janus-faced" with incredible opportunities for some and a shift away from what Wynter would see as the detrimental effects of "religion" (i.e., transposing agency onto extrahuman agent of determination), yet also immensely destructive.

50. Wynter, "Ceremony Found," 231.

51. Wynter and McKittrick, "Unparalleled Catastrophe," 30; Wynter, "Unsettling the Coloniality of Being/Power/Truth/Freedom," 328.

52. Wynter, "Ceremony Found," 231. Wynter describes their identifications as "half-starved" in the sense they are reduced to a biocentric analytic that has no ability to make the link with the fact that it is Man's story about itself as biocentric that is driving the very exploitation of the earth's resources through its techno-rational-capitalist mechanisms.

53. McKittrick, *Dear Science*, 23.

54. Wynter, "Ceremony Found," 239.

55. As McKittrick argues, Wynter establishes "a rebellious methodological moment that enunciates Black life outside of crude biologized identity claims. To put it another way, Wynter methodologizes the unfinished possibilities of collective struggle." McKittrick, *Dear Science*, 41.

56. Wynter and McKittrick, "Unparalleled Catastrophe," 16.

57. Wynter, "Ceremony Found," 206.

58. Among the critiques of Wynter's engagement with science, David Marriott notes: "Yet if sociogeny is to explain what it means to be human, how it 'transcends' (the natural sciences) and illumines that opacity is never developed beyond a narrative that already presupposes a certain fantasy of science." David Marriott, "Inventions of Existence: Sylvia Wynter, Frantz Fanon, Sociogeny, and 'the Damned,'" *CR: The New Centennial Review* 11, no. 3 (2011): 80.

59. Anthony Bogues also describes Wynter's challenge to all dominant forms of knowledge through her engagement with the natural sciences: "when Wynter turns to the use of codes and the neural firings of the brain she is not just wrestling with historical or genealogical matters but instead is engaging in an intellectual practice that

combines a knowledge of the human gained from biological and complexity theories to organize new meanings of human life and of the human itself." Anthony Bogues, "The Human, Knowledge and the Word: Reflecting on Sylvia Wynter," in *After Man, towards the Human: Critical Essays on Sylvia Wynter*, ed. Anthony Bogues (Kingston: Ian Randle, 2006), 322.

60. Henry, "Transcendental Spaces," 267.

61. Wynter, "Ceremony Must Be Found," 30; here, Wynter is quoting Stafford Beer in his introduction to Humberto R. Maturana and Francisco J. Varela, *Autopoiesis and Cognition*.

62. Wynter, "Ceremony Found," 209–10.

63. Wynter and McKittrick, "Unparalleled Catastrophe," 17–18.

64. Wynter, "Ceremony Found," 209.

65. Wynter, 217.

66. Wynter, 209.

67. Wynter, 209, 217.

68. Wynter and McKittrick, "Unparalleled Catastrophe," 16.

69. Ambroise poses Wynter's account of Fanon's sociogenetic self as a challenge to the biocentricism of E. O. Wilson's epigenetic self: "And while analogies between the purely natural and socio-human worlds can be made, a true consilience of knowledge would ultimately be premised on a relation of both continuity and discontinuity between these different levels of existence. In consequence, Wilson's own epigenetic self—at the socio-human level—should be both complemented and conditioned by Fanon's sociogenetic self, together constituting Wynter's scientific description of the species as a 'third level of existence.'" Ambroise, "Biocentrism," 223.

70. Wynter, "Ceremony Found," 192. Citing Wynter's "Towards the Sociogenic Principle," Mignolo frames the possibilities for resistance in sociogeny: "Wynter follows Fanon by setting the limits of ontogenesis: ontogenesis is an imperial category while sociogenesis introduces the perspective of the subject that ontogenesis classifies as object." Mignolo, "Sylvia Wynter," 118.

71. Wynter, "Ceremony Found," 198.

72. Wynter, 198. See also Wynter and McKittrick, "Unparalleled Catastrophe," 50.

73. Wynter, "Ceremony Found," 209.

74. Wynter, 241.

75. Wynter and McKittrick, "Unparalleled Catastrophe," 28.

76. Wynter, "Ceremony Found," 213.

77. As McKittrick notes of Wynter, "our stories—especially our origin stories—have an impact on our neurobiological and physiological behaviors. Her observations draw attention to the natural sciences as well as interdisciplinarity, emphasizing a dynamic connection between narrative and biology (stories have the capacity to move us)." McKittrick, *Dear Science*, 9. For a philosopher of religion's account of Black subjectivity and the multivalence of mattering, see Biko Mandela Gray, *Black Life Matter: Blackness, Religion, and the Subject* (Durham, NC: Duke University Press, 2022).

78. Wynter, "Ceremony Found," 196.

79. Wynter, 201.

80. Bogues, "Human," 318.

81. Shakes, "Legitimizing Africa," 306. Note also: "The philosophical hegemony of Europe in the Caribbean has relied heavily on Christianity. As such throughout this chapter a great deal of attention will be paid to this religion and the powerful effect it

has had in de-legitimizing African culture, even while being co-opted by people of African descent in liberation struggles" (Shakes, 298).

82. Wynter and McKittrick, "Unparalleled Catastrophe," 27.

83. Wynter, "Ceremony Found," 193.

84. Wynter and McKittrick, "Unparalleled Catastrophe," 15.

85. Wynter and McKittrick, 51.

86. Wynter, "Unsettling the Coloniality of Being/Power/Truth/Freedom," 318; the reader should note that the language of "Judeo-Christian" has been critiqued for decades, with even Michel Foucault noting its production as a pernicious fiction. See Michel Foucault, *History of Sexuality*, vol. 2, *The Use of Pleasure*, trans. Robert Hurley (New York: Vintage Books, 1985), 251.

87. I follow Clevis Headley's framing of ethics in Wynter's work as neither procedural nor deontological: "Here we should also be cognizant of the fact that, when referring to ethics, we are not implying adherence to an *a priori* set of principles but, rather, we understand ethics in the sense of being absolutely concerned and focused on the other." Clevis Headley, "Otherness and the Impossible in the Wake of Wynter's Notion of the 'After Man,'" in *After Man, towards the Human: Critical Essays on Sylvia Wynter*, ed. Anthony Bogues (Kingston: Ian Randle, 2006), 69–70.

5 The Ceremony beyond the Secular: Postreligious Autopoetics in Wynter's *The Hills of Hebron*

Rafael Vizcaíno

Introduction

In the last couple of decades, the work of Sylvia Wynter has become one of the richest and most fertile grounds to critique the philosophical discourse of Western modernity. For instance, one can no longer speak of epistemic decolonization without engaging Wynter's powerful critique of the "overrepresentation of Man" with the figure of the human.[1] Committed to a broader project of decolonization that closely follows the works of other radical Afro-Caribbean intellectuals such as Frantz Fanon and Aimé Césaire, Wynter's work has become one of the standards or principal points of departure for what it would take to rewrite the entire order of knowledge in the modern/colonial world.[2]

While this relatively recent reckoning with the epistemic components of Wynter's work across disciplinary formations has long been overdue, a more practical aspect of her work continues to be underemphasized in its reception. Although the bulk of Wynter's work is a conceptual intervention into the theoretical frameworks of Western epistemologies, her project also demands and culminates in a *praxis* that exceeds purely theoretical or epistemic domains to enter into the sphere of social reality. It has only been among the more self-critical disciplinary formations, such as Black studies and feminist studies, that this overly abstracting-away tendency in the reception of Wynter's work has begun to be seriously challenged. The contributions of scholars such as Katherine McKittrick—most specifically her edited anthology aptly titled *Sylvia Wynter: On Being Human as Praxis*—Alexander Weheliye, and Zakiyyah Iman Jackson, just to name a few, have remarkably articulated what is at stake in such practical orientation in Wynter's work.[3]

In some of my previous work I have followed McKittrick's line of interpretation to elucidate how some of the seemingly most abstract and theoretical aspects of Wynter's work, such as the development of a "New Science of the Word," only make sense when understood in the context of a broader praxis of decolonization.[4] In this present chapter, I elaborate this point by paying attention to one of the most overlooked exemplars of Wynter's work: her first and only published novel to date, *The Hills of Hebron*.[5] As scholars such as Paget Henry and Kelly Baker Josephs have argued, "*The Hills of Hebron* presents in fiction, in a more concrete form, the theory that Wynter later works out in her critical articles."[6] And this is most evidently the case concerning the roles that religion and its secularization play in Wynter's philosophical anthropology.

The publication of *The Hills of Hebron* in 1962 actually branded Wynter as the very "first Black woman novelist from the English-speaking Caribbean."[7] In light of this landmark achievement, the relegated status of this text within the wider reception of Wynter's work no doubt speaks volumes to the still overly disciplinary lenses through which such reception has taken place. This is a notable irony considering that one of the principal goals of Wynter's *oeuvre* has been to bridge the "*normally unbreachable*" gap between the sciences and the humanities, that is, between science and the word.[8] It is, therefore, in the interest of developing a more holistic and *transdisciplinary* understanding of Wynter's work, one that moreover understands the centrality of *praxis* in it, that I hereby seek to develop a new reading of *The Hills of Hebron*.

Building on much of the available critical commentary on this novel, I seek to articulate one way in which, as Henry and Josephs have put it, Wynter's early *The Hills of Hebron* already actualizes, if allegorically, Wynter's later theoretical objectives. To be specific, the novel could be read as an attempt to find the "ceremony," as the later Wynter would put it, that can solve the problem of the "*aporia of the secular*," the ceremony that can unite the cognitive emancipation initiated by the modern secularizing epistemologies of Man, on the one hand, and the "demonic" perspectives of those subjects upon whom such secular order has been built in the first place, on the other.[9] Wynter's atypical deployment of the notion of "the demonic" here signifies not a Christocentric perspective but quite the opposite: a post-Christian and decolonizing excavation of the ontological absences in the epistemologies of Man that are nevertheless co-constitutive of his wor(l)d.[10] As such, the ceremony that is actually found in the novel represents a certain *postsecular*—and, because the religious is co-constitutive of the secular, an always-already *postreligious*—decolonial praxis with the potential to overcome the modern/colonial wor(l)d of Man.[11]

As one possible answer to what lies beyond Man, the ceremony found in *The Hills of Hebron* then has the capacity to generate nothing less than the "symbolic birth" of humanity.[12] In the technical terms of Wynter's later work, we are talking about the "Second Emergence," our species-level emancipation from "our own humanly invented, autopoetically instituted cosmogonies or origin narratives and their mandated/prescribed sociogenic replicator codes of symbolic life/death."[13] In short, this postsecular and always-already postreligious ceremony of "(re)birth" is one way in which we can finally come to know ourselves in our full and naked complexity: as humans that "*auto-institute* ourselves as the uniquely hybrid mode of living being that we are."[14]

The Hills of Hebron and The Task of Epistemic Decolonization

The spatio-temporal arc of *The Hills of Hebron* develops in the Jamaica of the 1940s and 1950s, the years of social and political buildup that culminate in Jamaica's formal independence from the United Kingdom. It focuses on the small, rural, and marginalized religious community of Hebron, which is composed of a close-knit group of neo-maroons, exiles from the urban ghettos of Jamaica. Once guided to the hills by their charismatic leader, Moses, in search of freedom and tranquility, the community now finds itself at the height of a triple crisis that has put in question the very survival of the community.

First, a drought has diminished their chances of survival away from the rest of Jamaican society. Second, an accusation of a broken vow of continence against the recently appointed successor of Moses, Obadiah, results in his expulsion from the community, a circumstance that results in a frantic search for the real adulterer who raped his wife, Rose. Third, and as a consequence of Obadiah's expulsion from the community, Hebron remains in the hands of Moses's wife, Miss Gatha, who rules sternly while waiting for the triumphant return of her son, Isaac. The young Isaac is away from Hebron, and therefore in normative society, studying in a prestigious school in preparation for his expected leadership of the community, which belongs to him by birthright as the son of Moses.

The narrative core of *The Hills of Hebron* gives an account of Moses's rise as the leader of the community (whose official name is "the Church of the New Believers of Hebron"), as well as of his eventual downfall and the series of events that resulted in the community's triple crisis. It is only after this prolonged back story has unfolded that the reader finds out in the end that Isaac, the celebrated son of Moses and Miss Gatha, is both Rose's rapist, as well as the thief that steals Miss Gatha's savings, which during the drought functioned as the community's principal source of income. Isaac's double betrayal of Hebron is exacerbated by his subsequent escape from the island, made possible only by the stolen funds of the community. This final treason causes an even deeper crisis of legitimacy in the community. It is in this context that the novel's closing scenes might provide a glimpse of its potential resolution.

The outcast Obadiah finds himself back in the urban marketplace, selling wooden dolls that he carves in order for him, Rose, and their child (whom Obadiah has taken as his own), to survive. As I will show below, this entire experience of subsistence through the praxis of his manual labor awakens in Obadiah a sense of creativity that snaps him out of his distraught exile. At the very end of the novel, Obadiah thus returns to Hebron to retake the position of the community's leader, this time with "a new ritual, a new morality, a new right and wrong, a new God."[15]

Despite the layers of meaning in this narrative, scholarly analyses of it remain scant. The few available publications on *The Hills of Hebron* have tended to coalesce on the meaning of nationhood. This interpretation makes sense when one takes into account that the publication of the novel in 1962 coincided with Jamaica's formal independence from British rule. For instance, following Wynter's own understanding of the role of "minority literary criticism," Shirley Toland-Dix has argued that *The Hills of Hebron* "not only disenchants colonialist discourse," but also "probes the limitations of nationalist discourse by depicting and warning against cultural attitudes and practices that are potentially internal threats to the new nation."[16] In closely following such a nationalist framework, however, the argument is made that the novel remains limited by "the parameters of the narrative of the nation."[17] As such, this line of interpretation has argued that the novel is symptomatic of the most patriarchal tendencies found in movements for national liberation.[18]

Departing from the strict nationalist reading, Anthony Bogues has argued that Wynter's probing of nationalist discourses places *The Hills of Hebron* not within a nationalist literary tradition, but in the tradition of the anticolonial novel, a tradition which is concerned less with the parameters of the nation and more with the "rehumanisation" of Jamaican life beyond the limitations of the nation.[19] For Bogues, the symbolic lifeworlds of the *damnés* depicted in *The Hills of Hebron*, to use Frantz Fanon's construal of colonization as damnation, are "outside of the epistemological categories of modernity" and therefore have the power to reconfigure "the normative categories of Western political and religious thought" such as nationhood, redemption, and "modernity itself."[20] This is why another critic and very close reader of Wynter, Demetrius L. Eudell, contends that *The Hills of Hebron* rewrites the symbolic orders inherited by colonialism in order to effect a "transformation of consciousness" at the level of humanity.[21] In short, what we are talking about is the question of epistemic decolonization.

My own reading of *The Hills of Hebron* echoes the interpretations of Bogues and Eudell to claim that the novel is critically productive at the level of epistemic decolonization; that is, at the level of the "transformation of consciousness" beyond the modern/colonial order of Man. This is to say that Wynter's transformation of consciousness puts into question the very epistemic demarcations that define the order of Man, such as the very distinction, as Bogues puts it, between "the political" and "the religious." Extrapolating from this claim, and in conjunction with the work of other decolonial scholars who have made arguments along these lines, such as Nelson Maldonado-Torres's, I argue that one significant layer that emerges from reading Wynter's novel through the lens of epistemic decolonization entails grasping its *postsecular* (and, as already indicated, always-already *postreligious*) impetus to conceive of that which exceeds the politico-theological matrix of modernity/coloniality.[22] It is in this sense, for instance, that we should understand Wynter's seemingly "religious" grammar of "(re)birth," as it aims to push our understanding of what is at stake in the radicalizing and decolonizing epistemic transformation of consciousness that she is asking us to undertake.

Highlighting the more practical aspects of Wynter's work, I also take inspiration from the work of other scholars who have attempted to positively answer Wynter's call to find the ceremony that could go beyond Man in a way that centers the question of the coloniality of the secular/religious binary. One such example can be found in the work of Drucilla Cornell and Stephen Seely, who have turned toward the spiritual formations of the African diaspora to locate one potential ground for such ceremony.[23] In their view, the ritual practices of spiritual systems such as Vodou and Candomblé contain the potential to disrupt the order of Man because there is something *demonic* about them—*demonic*, of course, in Wynter's post-Christian/decolonizing signification—which is to say, they are neither properly secular, nor properly religious.[24] Thus, in exceeding the world of Man limited by the terms of the secular/religious binary, such spiritual formations can be deployed as a resource for decolonization in a way that does not merely reiterate facets of the secular/religious framing.[25] Curiously enough, such a focus on the critical potential of demonic spiritualities is precisely the focus of much of Wynter's early work, especially *The Hills of Hebron*.

In this chapter, I consequently turn to Wynter's novel to explore how something like a demonic spirituality cracks the order of Man to get one step closer toward living that true "ecumenical" humanism finally made, as Césaire once put it, "to the measure of the world."[26] Challenging a secularist conception of art and poetic praxis that is found in much of the critical commentary on Wynter's novel—for instance, in the work of Josephs—I focus on one scene from the novel's concluding passages: the moment when Obadiah "stumble[s] upon God" while consciously carving a wooden doll.[27] This scene succinctly yet powerfully illustrates the workings of one of the central mechanisms that Wynter's late theoretical corpus aims to systematize: the conjunction of material and spiritual self-creation, which is to say, how *being human* entails synthetizing material autopoiesis with spiritual autopoetics.[28] What is crucial in this scene is that, having found himself expelled from the religious community of Hebron, Obadiah stumbles upon God outside the realm of orthodox doctrine, that is, through a poietic praxis of material creation that opens up to the realm of the poetic, that is, artistic creation.

To put it even more concretely, and to continue to express it in the terms of Wynter's later work, my argument is that Obadiah's final transformation embodies the "transformative mutation" that represents the "symbolic birth" or "re-birth" of humanity, the entrance into our "Second Emergence" as fully emancipated beings, beyond the "opacity" of our "*genre*-specific orders of consciousness."[29] Obadiah's awareness of the agency contained in the praxis of his manual labor thus signifies nothing less than the praxis of the "Autopoetic Turn/Overturn" that enacts the Second Emergence; which is to say, through which the Ceremony *is* Found.[30] In this case, the demonic spirituality of such Turn/Overturn is why this whole endeavor ought to be understood in *postsecular* terms—as it escapes the proper domains of the secular and the religious. Furthermore, the fact that such spiritual autopoetics are arrived at through the Word, through the "artful image," as Mark Lewis Taylor would put it, is why this transformation should be understood in *postreligious* terms—as, in the context of decolonization, the language of orthodox doctrine is no longer the hegemonic path to finding any spiritual meaning.[31]

Finding Oneself, Stumbling upon God

After months of "searching for the adulterer," the outcast Obadiah only "had found himself and returned to Rose."[32] A carpenter by trade, Obadiah soon begins to gather wood to build his new room that he will share with Rose and the child, whom he has now welcomed as his own. It is here that a crucial moment of the narrative takes place. Waiting for daybreak in order to look for work back in the urban marketplace, Obadiah

> took up a fragment of wood and carved idly, thinking of making a toy for the child. Then as he shaped the rough outlines of a doll, he began to concentrate. For the first time in his life he created consciously, trying to embody in his carving his new awareness of himself and of Hebron. When he had finished he put the doll in his pocket and left Hebron as twilight settled into the hollow spaces between the hills. He took the short cut down the hill-side that by-passed the church. From time to time he touched the doll as if it were a fetish. For in carving the doll, Obadiah had stumbled upon God.[33]

In this scene, Wynter depicts how the unity of *poiesis* (material creation) and *praxis* (intersubjective action, i.e., for an-Other) awakens in Obadiah something that he had never experienced before. In consciously carving the doll (*poiesis*), not for its own sake or for himself, but for his son, that is, for an-Other (*praxis*), Obadiah at last has managed to actualize his *autopoetic* potential.[34] He has managed not only to create consciously, but also to create an object that is not merely material, imbued with spiritual, haunting power. Now carrying *and* embodying this new *autopoetic* way of being, Obadiah has shaken off his old self, bypassing "the church." In other words, sidestepping the old ways of Man, Obadiah has been (re)born as the full Human that until now he has not been able to be.

In the terms of Wynter's later theoretical framing, the *autopoetic* creative *praxis* that takes place in this scene effectively breaks off the feedback loop between Obadiah's self-representation and his behavior, to the point that such material creation leads Obadiah to see himself differently ("his new awareness of himself") and thus to want to behave differently. Because it is this feedback loop between self-representation and behavior that sustains Man's "descriptive statement" of the human, the self-conscious breaking of it makes possible a *new* description of what it means to be human beyond Man.[35] Through his own *praxis*, Obadiah has now entered a self-conscious process of self-observation, and its endless recursivity will enable him to determine the codes and "narrative schemas" that order his social life, rather than to be unconsciously determined by them.[36]

This last point—that the process of descriptive recursion that has led Obadiah to see himself differently has the capacity to unmask the codes and "narrative schemas" that thus far have determined his life—takes place most concretely with the question of God. Rather than to be unconsciously determined by a false idol from without, as in Moses's Christ-like "black God," who fails to come to Moses's rescue during his attempt to fly into the heavens, Obadiah's new vision has allowed him to encounter the truth of all idol-making or god-building (what might go by the name of "religion"), which comes from within: it is his own creative agency, now embodied in the "fetish" in his pocket.[37] This "degodding/de-supernaturalizing" moment is the part of the "Autopoetic Turn/Overturn" that restages the secularizing cognitive emancipation of Man, but this time turned against Man himself, from the "demonic grounds" beyond Man.[38] It is "a critique of the critique" as a specific phase in the coming-to-consciousness of the oppressed, in the formulation of the renowned scholar of Black religion Charles Long.[39]

Obadiah's "degodding/de-supernaturalizing," conveyed by his eventual realization that "All that was God lay in the palm of [his] hand," can be seen as a direct prefiguration of Wynter's theory of religion, which considers the function of religion as "*guarding against the entropic disintegration or falling apart* of our artificially instituted, cosmogonically chartered fictive modes of kind and their societies as autopoetic living systems."[40] What for short goes by the name of "religion" has the precise function here of being the dumping grounds of the responsibility for our collective agency and capacity for *autopoetic* reproduction.[41] Obadiah's "new awareness of himself and of Hebron," arrived at through his conscious *poietic praxis*, gives Obadiah an outsider perspective to the sociogenic codes of Hebron, a community exclusively founded as the search for a kingdom on earth with the help of a "black God." That such a God now lay in the palm of his hand reveals that Obadiah no longer needs "the illusions of [his] hitherto story-telling, extra-human projection of that Agency" into the form of such a God.[42]

Nevertheless, it is important to note that, to some extent, Obadiah still ends up "stumbl[ing] upon God" despite "by-pass[ing] the church." This is to say that the fact that all that is God lies in Obadiah's palm should *not* be read as a form of secularist nihilism. On the contrary, it is the grounding of all possible meaning in *auto-poietic/poetic praxis*. This point is simply the *postsecular* mirror to the aforementioned *postreligious* "degodding" that makes possible the symbolic (re)birth of Obadiah. This spiritual residue is what I referred to above as a "demonic spirituality." It is the question of re-enchantment, the ceremony beyond the secular, or more precisely, the "re-enchantment of humanism."[43]

To highlight the intersubjective character of this new *praxis* of being human, Obadiah only attains the above realization in full after an exchange with a foreigner who asks to purchase his wooden doll. This man, in exile from what the reader might reasonably assume is the Nazi regime in Germany, presents himself as an expert in sculptures and carvings. Ascertaining that Obadiah's doll is identical to those he has seen in Africa, he asks

Obadiah, "what legend did you carve this doll from?"[44] After an initial confusion, Obadiah quickly comprehends that the man "understood at once that there was more to the doll than the wood and the shape he had fashioned."[45] Obadiah consequently responds with "the story of Hebron, of their search for God, for it was out of this, *the dream and the reality*, that he had carved the doll."[46]

It is not only the conscious carving of the doll, but the Other-oriented character of such creation (initially meant as a *gift* for his son) that first plunges Obadiah in a cycle of self-conscious self-observation that begins to give him an outsider's perspective that fully culminates in the telling of such new story to a complete stranger.[47] The need to produce a description of Hebron for someone *outside* of this community then leads Obadiah to a yet higher consciousness regarding Hebron's search for God, now from a disenchanted or "degodded" perspective. That all that is God lays in Obadiah's palm then re-affirms the function of a *postreligious* ("demonic") *spirituality* in the creation of our places of dwelling. Recognizing ourselves as the *auto-instituting* beings that we are, our "attempts to create Hebrons would continue for ever."[48] In the end, Hebron symbolizes the spirit of an *autopoetically* self-aware "ecumenical" Human, finally made to the measure of the world.

Marxism and the Bible

To bring this chapter to a close, *The Hills of Hebron* could be seen as rewriting components of two significant narratives of the modern West: Marxism and the Bible. Regarding the former, at this point in her career and political involvement (late 1950s and early 1960s) Wynter is discreetly interested in exploring and revising the question of religion within a Marxist framework. Indeed, among the vast array of characters in the novel, it is the Marxist voices that come the closest to exemplifying her degodded *autopoetic* position. The socialist agitator in the town's center, for instance, leads Moses to deeply question himself, pondering: "In this new raceless world that he talked about, what was the place there for God, for the black God?"[49] This has led some critics to read *The Hills of Hebron* as a tacit endorsement of the conventional Marxist critique of religion as ideology. In his pioneering interpretation of the novel, for instance, the leading critic of Caribbean fiction, Kenneth Ramchand, goes as far as claiming that "Wynter comically deflates the cults depicted in her novel."[50] Curiously, however, in his analysis of Obadiah's carving scene, Ramchand entirely leaves out the last sentence about stumbling upon God. Moreover, if it were the case that what is at stake here is merely a secularist rejection of religion as ideology, it remains a mystery why, despite such critique of institutionalized religion ("We want nothing to do with churches"), Obadiah nonetheless "stumbles upon God" and eventually decides to return and lead the community of Hebron.[51]

In fact, I argue that the rewriting of the question of religion within a Marxist framework begins with such carving sequences in *The Hills of Hebron*, first as a commentary on Hegel's master-slave dialectic, the central metaphor for creative labor in Marxist theory.[52] Wynter here agrees with Hegel that the crafting of the doll is the material externalization of the consciousness of the slave, and it is from this act that the slave finds the recognition that he previously did not have in a context of domination. However, for Wynter, there is something in the labor of the slave, the working on the thing (the doll), that exceeds *poiesis* in a way that enters the realms of *praxis* (the gift to Obadiah's son) and *poetics* (spirituality) simultaneously. Like Fanon's own commentary on the master-slave dialectic, as developed in his *Black Skin, White Masks*, Wynter expounds on the horizontality of the world of the slave in a way that does away with the verticality of the master. That verticality now clearly appears as the object of desire of those that are stuck within the self-referential dialectics of self-recognition—for instance, the false idol of Moses's "black God." It is not for nothing that, twenty years after the publication of *The Hills of Hebron*, Charles Long would find Hegel's master-slave dialectic "most insightful as a philosophic guide in our attempt to understand the religions of the oppressed."[53]

I contend, therefore, that part of Wynter's literary intervention is to seriously defend the question of religion within a revised revolutionary theoretical framework, just in the way that heretically postsecular Marxists such as Ernst Bloch were doing at the time.[54] Before the onset of a movement such as Latin American liberation theology, which utilizes the secular tools of critical social theory to amend theological inquiry, Wynter's novel takes seriously the place that religious narratives have within sociopolitical processes of liberation. This commitment is ultimately why Obadiah decides to return to Hebron with a "new awareness of himself and of Hebron" in order to change it and join the transformations that are also happening at the national level. Having disenchanted the narrative schemas of an imperial Christianity and Moses's reactionary negation of it in the form of a black God, Obadiah returns and leads Hebron out of its crisis, with the "apprehension of the newer, brighter worlds that could spring from the fusion of men's creative dreams."[55]

This proto-theological concern of Wynter ultimately leads me to my last point: the ways in which *The Hills of Hebron* rewrites the Bible, a facet of the novel that has been entirely lost in its reception. Josephs, for instance, mentions in a footnote that while "Moses's role in leading his followers into a form of exile does correspond with his name" in the Bible, she "cannot discern any connections between Obadiah and Isaac and their biblical counterparts," therefore concluding that the names in Wynter's novel have "no consistency in their application" vis-à-vis the narrative of the Bible.[56] While fully developing this argument is beyond the scope of this chapter, my claim is that Wynter is indeed trying to accomplish something with the name choice of both Isaac and Obadiah as the two characters that must battle for the legacy of Hebron. Let us remember that in the Hebrew Bible, Isaac is the grandfather of the Edomites from the Kingdom of Edom, who according to none other than the prophet Obadiah, are guilty of betraying their neighbors of the Kingdom of Judah in collusion with the invading Babylonians. Obadiah's book, the shortest in the Bible, no less, prophesizes the destruction of Edom and visualizes the eventual redemption of Judah and all Israelites.

This fleeting summary of the Book of Obadiah invites readers to interpret Wynter's novel as a rewriting of the Bible, specifically from the anticolonial perspective of the modern *damnés*. The city of Hebron, in what today is the Palestinian West Bank under Israeli military occupation, is here significant for being considered the most ancestral of all Jewish communities at the center of the Kingdom of Judah. In Wynter's work, Obadiah's prophecy against the Edomites thus becomes a warning against the neighbors of the *damnés* that colluded with the modern/colonial system to oppress them (Isaac raping Rose and taking the moneybox and leaving Hebron), being also a redemptive story about the hopes and aspirations of the process of decolonization that will rebuild Hebron (Obadiah's return with schooling and engineering initiatives to connect Hebron with the rest of Jamaica). That the later Wynter borrows the notion of a "*counter-cosmogony*" from "the Hebrew Bible, as elaborated by the exiled Jewish priests who had been captive in Babylon at the heart of the then Babylonian empire in the wake of the latter's 587 BCE conquest of the kingdom of Judah and destruction of Jerusalem," tells us that this historical narrative is not of mere anecdotal interest.[57] It goes to the heart of the rewriting of knowledge that conditions our *current* genre of being human.

Conclusion

In this chapter, I have read *The Hills of Hebron* as an attempt to find the "ceremony" that will overcome the "*aporia of the secular*." As such, this ceremony is a *postsecular* one, but this does not mean that it is, therefore, a return to "the religious." The ceremony found is, rather, a "demonic" ceremony that aims to overcome, or better yet, to *decolonize*, the secular-religious complex as it is expressed in the order of Man.[58] I have analyzed this dynamic through a close reading of one of the novel's concluding scenes: the moment when Obadiah "stumble[s] upon God" while consciously carving a wooden doll.[59] This scene exemplifies Wynter's philosophico-anthropological answer to the aforementioned *aporia*: the fact that we "*auto-institute* ourselves as the uniquely hybrid mode of living being that we are," a conjunction of material and spiritual self-creation, which is to say, *a synthesis of autopoiesis and autopoetics*.[60]

Searching for the adulterer, Obadiah ends up finding himself. And seeking to embody himself in his creative labor, he ends up stumbling upon God. Through a conscious act of creation (*poiesis*) and storytelling (*poetics*) for-an-other (*praxis*), Obadiah unknowingly breaks off from the status quo of Hebron; that is, he offers a redescription of himself (the human) outside the terms of his until-then-present descriptive statement of the human (Man). He locates his own demonic grounds, out of which he can then return to Hebron with "a new ritual, a new morality, a new right and wrong, a new God."[61] I have argued that this newfound ceremony encapsulates the "transformative mutation" that makes possible the "symbolic birth" or "re-birth" of humanity.[62] This is because, as an endlessly recursive self-conscious process of self-observation, Obadiah has opened for himself the doors toward our species-level "Second Emergence" as fully emancipated beings, beyond the "opacity" of our "*genre*-specific orders of consciousness."[63]

Obadiah's new vision is one that no longer deceptively benefits from the overrepresentation and occultation of how modes of *autopoietic/autopoetic praxis* function—as Moses's false vision once did. Instead, fully cognitively emancipated, it understands itself within a broader outline of "all the labour and all the visions of all Hebrons to come, and after them and after them until the end of them. And the end of them was the beginning of them."[64] The "new God" in this new ritual is characteristic of a *postsecular/postreligious* demonic spirituality, captured in the epigraph from Dostoevsky to the concluding chapters of *The Hills of Hebron*: "the end of the whole national movement is only the search for God. . . God is the synthetic personality of a whole people considered from its origins until its end."[65] This line points to how God is that which is found when one seeks to find oneself. This is, once again, the meaning of an *autopoiesis/autopoetics* of the flesh: the fact that we are a *praxis* of "self-inscripting and inscripted flesh."[66] Here, Man's secular-religious complex vanishes to make way for "new continents of the spirit" and new "planets of the imagination."[67]

Notes

1. Sylvia Wynter, "Unsettling the Coloniality of Being/Power/Truth/Freedom: Towards the Human, after Man, Its Overrepresentation—an Argument," *CR: The New Centennial Review* 3, no. 3 (2003): 257–337.

2. Frantz Fanon, *Black Skin, White Masks*, trans. Richard Philcox (New York: Grove, 2008); Frantz Fanon, *The Wretched of the Earth*, trans. Richard Philcox (New York: Grove, 2004); Aimé Césaire, *Discourse on Colonialism*, trans. Joan Pinkham (New York: Monthly Review Press, 2000).

3. Katherine McKittrick, *Demonic Grounds: Black Women and the Cartographies of Struggle* (Minneapolis: University of Minnesota Press, 2006); Katherine McKittrick, *Dear Science and Other Stories* (Durham, NC: Duke University Press, 2021); Katherine McKittrick, ed., *Sylvia Wynter: On Being Human as Praxis* (Durham, NC: Duke University Press, 2015); Alexander G. Weheliye, *Habeas Viscus: Racializing Assemblages, Biopolitics, and Black Feminist Theories of the Human* (Durham, NC: Duke University Press, 2014); Zakiyyah Iman Jackson, *Becoming Human: Matter and Meaning in an Antiblack World* (New York: New York University Press, 2020).

4. Rafael Vizcaíno, "Sylvia Wynter's New Science of the Word and the Autopoetics of the Flesh," *Comparative and Continental Philosophy* 14, no. 1 (2022): 72–88.

5. Sylvia Wynter, *The Hills of Hebron*, introduction by Anthony Bogues, afterword by Demetrius L. Eudell (1962; Kingston: Ian Randle, 2010).

6. Kelly Baker Josephs, *Disturbers of the Peace: Representations of Madness in Anglophone Caribbean Literature* (Charlottesville: University of Virginia Press, 2013), 61; Paget Henry, *Caliban's Reason: Introducing Afro-Caribbean Philosophy* (New York: Routledge, 2000), 125.

7. Janice Lee Liddell, "The Narrow Enclosure of Motherdom/Martyrdom: A Study of Gatha Randall Barton in Sylvia Wynter's *The Hills of Hebron*," in *Out of the Kumbla: Caribbean Women and Literature*, ed. Carol Boyce Davies and Elaine Savory Fido (Trenton, NJ: Africa World, 1990), 322.

8. Sylvia Wynter, "The Ceremony Found: Towards the Autopoetic Turn/Overturn, Its Autonomy of Human Agency and Extraterritoriality of (Self-)Cognition," in *Black Knowledges/Black Struggles: Essays in Critical Epistemology*, ed. Jason R. Ambroise and Sabine Broeck (Liverpool: Liverpool University Press, 2015), 210, emphasis in original.

9. Wynter, "Ceremony Found," 189, emphasis in original; Sylvia Wynter, "The Ceremony Must Be Found: After Humanism," in *"On Humanism and the University I: The Discourse of Humanism,"* ed. William Spanos, special issue, *boundary 2* 12, no. 3/13, no. 1 (1984): 19–70.

10. Sylvia Wynter, "Afterword: Beyond Miranda's Meanings: Un/silencing the 'Demonic Ground' of Caliban's 'Woman,'" in *Out of the Kumbla: Caribbean Women and Literature*, ed. Carole Boyce Davies and Elaine Savory Fido (Trenton, NJ: Africa World, 1990), 361.

11. On the colonial co-constitution of the secular/religious binary, see Talal Asad, *Genealogies of Religion: Discipline and Reasons of Power in Christianity and Islam* (Baltimore: Johns Hopkins University Press, 1993); Talal Asad, *Formations of the*

Secular: Christianity, Islam, Modernity (Stanford, CA: Stanford University Press, 2003); Timothy Fitzgerald, ed., *Religion and the Secular: Historical and Colonial Formations* (New York: Routledge, 2007).

12. Sylvia Wynter, "'Genital Mutilation' or 'Symbolic Birth'? Female Circumcision, Lost Origins, and the Aculturalism of Feminist/Western Thought," *Case Western Reserve Law Review* 47, no. 2 (1997): 501–52.

13. Wynter, "Ceremony Found," 223.

14. Wynter, 199, 223. In my aforementioned previous work, I have expressed this praxis as one of an autopoiesis/autopoetics of the flesh. Throughout the present chapter, I am deliberately writing Wynter's "re-birth" as "(re)birth," simply to more properly highlight the radical nature of this "transformative mutation"—one that is as radical as our very first birth or "Emergence."

15. Wynter, *Hills of Hebron*, 306.

16. Shirley Toland-Dix, "*The Hills of Hebron*: Sylvia Wynter's Disruption of the Narrative of the Nation," *Small Axe: A Caribbean Journal of Criticism* 12, no. 1 (2008): 61; Sylvia Wynter, "On Disenchanting Discourse: 'Minority' Literary Criticism and Beyond," *Cultural Critique*, no. 7 (Autumn 1987): 207–44.

17. Toland-Dix, "*Hills of Hebron*," 72–73.

18. The classic critique of Wynter's politics on the question of gender has been advanced by Natasha Barnes's *Cultural Conundrums: Gender, Race, Nation, and the Making of Caribbean Cultural Politics* (Ann Arbor: University of Michigan Press, 2006). While this is not the place to engage this debate, I do think that there is room for a more fruitful elaboration of Wynter's contributions to feminist politics, especially from the perspective of Black and women of color feminisms. On this point, see Xhercis Méndez and Yomaira C. Figueroa's "Not Your Papa's Wynter: Women of Color Contributions toward Decolonial Futures," in *Beyond the Doctrine of Man: Decolonial Visions of the Human*, ed. Joseph Drexler-Dreis and Kristien Justaert (New York: Fordham University Press, 2019), 60–88.

19. Anthony Bogues, "Introduction: Sylvia Wynter and the Black Radical Anti-colonial Intellectual Tradition: Towards a New Mode of Existence," in *The Hills of Hebron*, by Sylvia Wynter (Kingston: Ian Randle, 2010), xvii.

20. Bogues, xix, xxi; Fanon, *Wretched of the Earth*. This religious metaphor of colonization as damnation is largely lost in the English rendition of *Les damnés de la terre* as *The Wretched of the Earth*.

21. Demetrius L. Eudell, "Afterword: Towards Aimé Césaire's 'Humanism Made to the Measure of the World': Reading *The Hills of Hebron* in the Context of Sylvia Wynter's Later Work," in *The Hills of Hebron*, by Sylvia Wynter (Kingston: Ian Randle, 2010), 331.

22. Nelson Maldonado-Torres, "The Time of History, the Times of Gods, and the *Damnés de la terre*," *Worlds and Knowledges Otherwise* 1, no. 2 (2006): 1–12; Nelson Maldonado-Torres, *Against War: Views from the Underside of Modernity* (Durham, NC: Duke University Press, 2008); Nelson Maldonado-Torres, "Secularism and Religion in the Modern/Colonial World-System: From Secular Postcoloniality to Postsecular Transmodernity," in *Coloniality at Large: Latin America and the Postcolonial Debate*, ed. Mabel Moraña, Enrique Dussel, and Carlos A. Jáuregui (Durham, NC: Duke University Press, 2008), 360–84. For Maldonado-Torres, all discussion about religion and secularity "should be preceded by the decolonization of both of these terms and by the critical examination of the complicitous relation of Christianity and

secularization in the creation of *damnation*." This is to say that Fanon's now questionably "religious" metaphor of damnation, in fact, "raises unique perspectives and questions" that challenge at a more foundational level the very grammar of what is taken to be "religious" and "secular." Maldonado-Torres, "Time of History," 9. In my view, this is also why "the religious" cannot be innocently taken to be the solution to the coloniality of "the secular," thereby linking the notion of the postsecular that emerges from this process of epistemic decolonization to the concomitant notion of the postreligious; Maldonado-Torres, "Secularism and Religion," 383. In a forthcoming book, I articulate how the postsecular impetus that emerges from a process of decolonization is distinct from alternative theorizations of postsecularity, such as Jürgen Habermas's, that are not primarily committed to a decolonial framework. The horizon of postsecularity that emerges from a process of decolonization ultimately goes beyond the issue of adding self-reflexivity to the theory of modernity and the place of secularization in it. That is, what is at stake is wholly reconceiving what modernity and secularization are in relation to the process of colonization that put in place the modern world in the first place.

23. Drucilla Cornell and Stephen D. Seely, *The Spirit of Revolution: Beyond the Dead Ends of Man* (Malden, MA: Polity, 2016), 48, 131. See also their contribution to the *CLR James Journal* dossier on "Decolonizing Spiritualities." I contextualize such intervention in my "Introduction to Special Issue: Decolonizing Spiritualities," *CLR James Journal* 27, no. 1-2 (2021): 17-23.

24. Cornell and Seely here channel the work of several women of color feminists, such as Audre Lorde, Gloria Anzaldúa, and M. Jacqui Alexander. Alexander's formulation of how spirituality is to be distinguished from religion is indeed key for their argument and my own. For Alexander, the realm of the spiritual alludes to that which colonization contains, collapses, and institutionalizes in order to turn it *into* religion. M. Jacqui Alexander, *Pedagogies of Crossing: Meditations on Feminism, Sexual Politics, Memory, and the Sacred* (Durham, NC: Duke University Press, 2005), 281.

25. For recent explorations that partly touch on this question, see Joseph Drexler-Dreis and Kristien Justaert, eds., *Beyond the Doctrine of Man: Decolonial Visions of the Human* (New York: Fordham University Press, 2020); and An Yountae and Eleanor Craig, eds., *Beyond Man: Race, Coloniality, and Philosophy of Religion* (Durham, NC: Duke University Press, 2021).

26. Wynter, "Ceremony Found," 194; Césaire, *Discourse on Colonialism*, 73.

27. Wynter, *Hills of Hebron*, 283. For Josephs's secularist conception of art and poetic praxis, see *Disturbers of the Peace*, 67-68.

28. I have spelled out how Wynter develops this synthesis of autopoiesis and autopoetics, as two distinct but nonetheless related levels of existence, in "Sylvia Wynter's New Science of the Word and the Autopoetics of the Flesh." Jeong Eun Annabel We has fruitfully used the concept of "spiritual sociogenesis" to highlight the spiritual dimensions of social and material processes of symbolic (re)birth in "The Transpacific Tempest: Relational Sovereignty and Spiritual Sociogenesis," *Cultural Dynamics* 31, no. 4 (2019): 390. See David Kline's contribution to this anthology for a helpful reconstruction of Wynter's theory of religion as "autoreligion."

29. Wynter, "Ceremony Found," 189n7, 99, 242; Wynter, "'Genital Mutilation' or 'Symbolic Birth'?"

30. Wynter, "Ceremony Found," 245.

31. Mark Lewis Taylor, *The Theological and the Political* (Minneapolis, MN: Fortress, 2011), 12. For Taylor, aesthetics is the language of the theological insofar as the former exceeds and, therefore, "haunts" institutionalized Theology. See specifically Taylor, 9–12. On this front, Wynter's work should also be taken to be central to the "postsecularization" of literary studies. For instance, Lori Branch's program for a postsecular literary studies argues that "humanistic and social science work on personhood provides important grounds for postsecular studies in that it situates believing, poetry- and narrative-making human reality in the world, not as something aberrant in an insentient, strictly material cosmos." Lori Branch, "Postsecular Studies," in *Routledge Companion to Literature and Religion*, ed. Mark Knight (New York: Routledge, 2016), 99. Wynter's paradigm of the "New Science of the Word" not only brings together the sciences and the humanities but further interrogates the very category of "religion" through the task of epistemic decolonization. In so doing, her work can be said to have the potential to *radicalize* the "postsecularization" of literary studies, ultimately conceiving of *postsecularity* as always-already *postreligious*.

32. Wynter, *Hills of Hebron*, 282.

33. Wynter, 283.

34. This distinction between *poiesis* and *praxis* can be found in the work of Enrique Dussel, *Philosophy of Liberation*, trans. Aquilina Martinez and Christine Morkovsky (Maryknoll, NY: Orbis Books, 1985), 63.

35. Wynter, "Unsettling the Coloniality of Being/Power/Truth/Freedom," 262; Wynter, "Ceremony Must Be Found," 22.

36. Wynter, "Ceremony Must Be Found," 65n56. Wynter is here explicitly channeling the work of the Chilean biologists Humberto Maturana and Francisco Varela. Let us remember that, for Maturana, "We become self-conscious through self-observation; by making descriptions of ourselves (representations), and by interacting with our descriptions we can describe ourselves describing ourselves, in an endless recursive process." Humberto R. Maturana and Francisco J. Varela, *Autopoiesis and Cognition: The Realization of the Living*, 2nd ed. (Dordrecht: D. Reidel, 1980), 14. To better understand what is at stake in Wynter's reliance on the work of Maturana and Varela, specifically their technical usage of the notion of "autopoiesis," see Max Hantel, "What Is It Like to Be a Human? Sylvia Wynter on Autopoiesis," *philoSOPHIA* 8, no. 1 (2018): 61–79; Vizcaíno, "Sylvia Wynter's New Science of the Word"; and Kline's contribution to this anthology.

37. The lie of Moses's "black God" is finally revealed in Moses's last moments. Just as he is about to die crucified, the witness to his death, Aloysius, reports that Moses cried out: "God is white after all . . . God is white!" *Hills of Hebron*, 243.

38. Wynter, "Unsettling the Coloniality of Being/Power/Truth/Freedom," 273.

39. Charles H. Long, *Significations: Signs, Symbols, and Images in the Interpretation of Religion*, 2nd ed. (Aurora, CO: Davies Group, 1999), 179. Long's work adds some clarity to the falsity of the black God. In his terms, this phenomenon could be seen as a characteristic aspect of the lives of the oppressed in their "second creation," which is the mode of living whose truth is determined by the categories of the oppressor (Long, 184). The falsity of the black God is ultimately rooted in the concept's reliance on and replication of Man's colonially imposed notion of "God," *e.g.*, Moses's last words: "God is white!" In more technical philosophico-theological terms, as a moment in the development of self-consciousness, the "second creation" does not permit the oppressed to truly access "the divine," as transcendental alterity is experienced simply

as "the other culture" (Long, 180). As we shall see below, the Hegelian connotation of this entire dynamic is not lost to Wynter. I thank David Kline for directing me to Long's *Significations* in his feedback to an earlier version of this chapter.

40. Wynter, *Hills of Hebron*, 307; Wynter, "Ceremony Found," 227.

41. Kline's contribution to this anthology arrives at a similar conclusion with the notion of an "affective load bearing" mechanism.

42. Wynter, "Ceremony Found," 245.

43. David Scott, "The Re-enchantment of Humanism: An Interview with Sylvia Wynter," *Small Axe* 8 (2000): 119–207.

44. Wynter, *Hills of Hebron*, 300.

45. Wynter, 300.

46. Wynter, 300, my emphasis.

47. I am unable to deepen here how the notion of "gift-giving" *also* brings forth the question of ethics. Maldonado-Torres has analyzed this question in phenomenological terms following the work of Emmanuel Levinas, Enrique Dussel, and Fanon. He concludes that "the gift of the self represents, beyond the solipsistic achievement of truth and knowledge, the point of entry of the existent into the human." Maldonado-Torres, *Against War*, 240. If we take these terms, we can clearly see how Obadiah's *auto-poetic* awakening cannot be solipsistic. It can only be for-an-other. This is to say that there is an ethics at the core of the *praxis* of being human—an aspect of Wynter's work that remains underexplored.

48. Wynter, *Hills of Hebron*, 300–301.

49. Wynter, 223.

50. Kenneth Ramchand, *The West Indian Novel and Its Background* (London: Faber and Faber, 1970), 128.

51. Wynter, *Hills of Hebron*, 223.

52. G. W. F. Hegel, *Phenomenology of Spirit*, trans. A. V. Miller (Oxford: Oxford University Press, 1997).

53. Long, *Significations*, 183.

54. See, for instance, Ernst Bloch, *Atheism in Christianity: The Religion of the Exodus and the Kingdom*, trans. J. T. Swann (New York: Verso Books, 2009). Wynter converges on this point with a decolonial and Marxist thinker such as Enrique Dussel, who has also explored such postsecular revision in his *Las metáforas teológicas de Marx* (Navarra, Spain: Verbo Divino, 1993). I reconstruct such convergence between Wynter and Dussel in my forthcoming book. I also explore some aspects of Dussel's postsecular liberation philosophy "of religion" in my "Which Secular Grounds? The Atheism of Liberation Philosophy," *APA Newsletter on Hispanic/Latino Issues in Philosophy* 20, no. 2 (2021): 2–5; and "Liberation Philosophy, Anti-Fetishism, and Decolonization," *Journal of World Philosophies* 6, no. 2 (2021): 61–75. Lastly, I systematically engage Dussel's *Las metáforas teológicas de Marx* in light of contemporary debates in political theology and the postsecular in my "Postsecular Philosophy as Metaphoric Theology: On Dussel's Reading of Marx," *Journal of the American Academy of Religion* (forthcoming).

55. Wynter, *Hills of Hebron*, 300.

56. Josephs, *Disturbers of the Peace*, 170n4.

57. Wynter, "Ceremony Found," 207.

58. For a recent account of the coloniality of the secular, see An Yountae, *The Coloniality of the Secular: Race, Religion, and Poetics of World-Making* (Durham, NC:

Duke University Press, 2024). My forthcoming book develops an analogous but conceptually divergent account based on a dialectical theory of secularization.

59. Wynter, *Hills of Hebron*, 283.

60. Wynter, "Ceremony Found," 199, 223.

61. Wynter, *Hills of Hebron*, 306.

62. Wynter, "Ceremony Found," 189n7, 99; Wynter, "'Genital Mutilation' or 'Symbolic Birth'?"

63. Wynter, "Ceremony Found," 242.

64. Wynter, *Hills of Hebron*, 307.

65. Wynter, 279.

66. Scott, "Re-enchantment of Humanism," 206; Vizcaíno, "Sylvia Wynter's New Science of the Word and the Autopoetics of the Flesh."

67. Wynter, *Hills of Hebron*, 301.

6 Sociogeny, Race, and the Theological Genealogy of Economy

Tapji Garba

> My proposal here is that the founding Judaeo-Christian religion of the West and its secularized variants should be seen in now parallel terms, beyond the question of whether these beliefs, and the consciousness to which they gave and gives rise, are true or false. Rather, they should be seen as the expression, especially in their degodded and secular forms, as part of an overall Judaeo-Christian cosmogonic belief system, which, in "varied garb and myriad diversity of appearance" served and serves to embody a "central rule of law."
>
> —SYLVIA WYNTER

> How can we think *outside* the terms in which we *are*?
>
> —SYLVIA WYNTER

> The fundamental moment comes when the formulation of a general order of existence is changed.
>
> —SYLVIA WYNTER

This chapter reads Sylvia Wynter in relation to theological genealogies of economy as a way of identifying the ethical and methodological stakes of her reconfigurations of political theology and critical theory. Although Wynter's engagement with theological-political problems has yet to be widely discussed, theology is nonetheless central for her understanding of modernity, as she argues that the modern West's figure of the human and its global overdetermination emerges from the revolution of Renaissance humanism and the transition from the feudal-monarchical order of the Middle Ages and its "economy of spiritual redemption" to the territorial expansion of mercantile states and their corresponding conceptions of citizenship.[1] In contrast to the approaches to theological genealogy represented by Giorgio Agamben (with his focus on *oikonomia*) and Alberto Toscano (with his focus on *chrematistics*), Wynter's interpretation of the Fanonian concept of sociogeny offers a protocol for approaching theological problems as matters of social reproduction, while also elaborating the fundamental role of racial slavery in the genesis of the modern world. By tracing the ways that racial slavery comes to mediate the shifting relationship between theology and politics, I argue that slavery functions as the hermeneutical key for understanding how race comes to reoccupy the waning legitimacy of theological structures of authority predicated on the temporal powers of the Church and its grammar of sin and redemption. It does so by providing new answers to pressing questions regarding the origins and intelligibility of the modern world as well as the *telos* and possibility of human self-determination. By centralizing race as a theological-political problem and highlighting the essential role of the symbolic in the constitution of social reality—thereby thematizing the intrinsic relationship between the material and ideal—I argue that Wynter folds theological genealogy into her own sociogenic framework without falling into "reductivist idealism."[2] As Wynter argues, it is within the emergent world of colonial racial distinctions that the landed aristocracy and absolutist states of the mercantilist era yielded to an emerging bourgeois civil society and its ideology of liberal-economic humanism. With the shift from Man1 to Man2, the concept of "the originally free and unbound individual with his natural right to private property was to be the mythological charter of the commercial and industrial bourgeoisie on their rise to hegemony."[3] In this shift, wealth and status were delinked from feudal ties and "rights based on birth" and the "inherited freehold landowning" form of wealth gave way to capital accumulation as the "macro-signifier" of social life.[4] This bears on the production of knowledge and subjectivity as modern economists and their disciples function as the "secular priesthood" of the nation-state, while the field of economics itself mirrors the role that theology had played for the societal order of Christendom."[5]

This chapter proceeds in four parts. First, I will situate Wynter in relation to the literature on theological genealogy. Second, I will provide an overview of Wynter's sociogenic method with emphasis on her philosophy of history and philosophical anthropology. Third, I will unpack the concept of economy, its reinterpretation by Christian theology, and Wynter's account of its post-Gregorian institutionalization and eventual crisis. Fourth, I turn to Wynter's understanding of the lay movements of the Renaissance and its myriad implications, while also elaborating how race comes to suture the modern world's internal dynamics. In conclusion, I will briefly take up the ethical-political implications of Wynter's method.

Economy or Chrematistics: Wynter and Contemporary Debates

Much ink has been spilled on the relationship between earlier theological understandings of economics and the economy of contemporary capitalist modernity.[6] While Michel Foucault covers the institutionalization of pastoral power—the Church's techniques of governing the inner lives of individual Christians—it is Giorgio Agamben who most directly engages the *theological* appropriation of economy (*oikonomia*) and specifically its role in the development of Trinitarian theology. For Agamben, the modern West's theological-political heritage shows up in the present in the form of a signature that *underwrites* the movement of time, a notion that corresponds to the idea of secularization as a *transfer* from the theological to the political, with the theological being the *origin* of what succeeds it.[7] This claim leads Alberto Toscano to raise the charge against Agamben of historical substantialism, the view that ideal forms are the driving force of history in such a way that the movement of social history can be understood in terms of trans-historical underlying *concepts* as opposed to the transformation of social relations and their imaginaries. Further, Toscano questions whether either Trinitarian or ecclesial economies are appropriate objects of genealogical inquiry as Agamben and Foucault failed to recognize what is most relevant for the development of the *modern* economy.[8] Toscano argues for a genealogy that privileges an often overlooked genealogical category: chrematistics. This is, with few exceptions, practitioners of the art of unlimited monetary accumulation that Aristotle distinguished from economics. Because chrematistics presages the self-valorizing logic of capital, a reconstruction of its history would be more relevant for contemporary communist theory and politics than the more general genealogy of *oikonomia* undertaken by Foucault and Agamben. It would be a line of inquiry pursued "not in terms of theological genealogy but of historical materialism."[9]

Toscano's intervention is helpful for situating Wynter's sociogenic approach to political theology relative to the existing literature on theological economy as many of Toscano's suggestions resonate with aspects of Wynter's work. For instance, both oppose historical substantialism and point to Hans Blumenberg's reoccupation thesis as an alternative. However, rather than detracting from a consideration of contemporary political economy, as Toscano claims theological genealogies tend to do, Wynter's practice of centralizing race as the manifest-form of repressed theological-political problems advances a critical theory of how we came to inhabit the very *terms* that make the capitalist form of value and its apparatuses of biopolitical control possible. Thus, her sociogenic method (which I will be elaborating next) does not require Toscano's opposition between theological genealogy and historical materialism.

Sociogenic Method: A Philosophical Anthropology and Philosophy of History

The construction of Wynter's methodology arises from the need to overcome the limits of biocentric and historicist approaches to social theory. For Wynter, these approaches rest upon a set of assumptions that take natural impulse and personal preference to be the driving force of secular society and propose self-interest as the central constraint upon social life.[10] They also assume that simply *describing* the course of human actions (and the motivations of conscious historical actors) suffices as an explanation of social dynamics. But, as Wynter shows, the organization of society is not the effect of the "individual psyche" but rather "*the process* of socialization that institutes the individual as a human, and therefore, *always* sociogenetic subject."[11] Wynter aims to explain how our collective actions operate before and above our consciousness, as opposed to assuming that either "nature" or "history" provides "the ground of all human existential reality or actuality."[12] Building on Frantz Fanon's complications of Sigmund Freud's phylogenetic-ontogenetic theory of the subject, Wynter introduces the sociogenic principle (sometimes called the "governing code") as her central methodological protocol. The sociogenic code is the generative mechanism of the intersubjective field in which "self, Other, and World should be represented and known," and thereby sets the coordinates for the modes of subjective understanding proper to specific forms of social life.[13] As the "shared mind" or intellect of a society, the sociogenic code is never purely subjective, as our habits of "intersubjective valuation" are always in line with the reigning social imagination.[14] As an autopoietic system (a concept Wynter borrows from Humberto Maturana and Francisco Varela), it is both subjective and objective, naming the inseparability of individual consciousness *and* trans-individual system of meaning.[15]

The development of the sociogenic method entails an explanation of how and why our existence is mediated by socio-symbolic structures to begin with. For this reason, Wynter's sociogenic method includes a formulation of a critical philosophical anthropology. As narrating animals, the production of systems of collective identification is essential for the institution and reproduction of our forms of life in such a way that the construction of narratives is "as much a part of what makes us human . . . as our bipedalism and the use of our hands."[16] Forms of socio-symbolic mediation are not immutable, as they transform in "adaptive response to the ecological as well as to the geopolitical circumstances in which we find ourselves."[17] In contrast to deterministic anthropologies, Wynter's highlighting of our adaptive capacities underscores the *minimalism* of her anthropology as she conceives of human forms of life (and their corresponding systems of meaning) as *a historically evolving* multitude of strategies for the satisfaction of individual and collective needs. Moreover, the role of sociogenic codes in determining the specificity of our needs is connected to the general relationship between the social and the biological, especially the transformation of the latter by the former. The coercive nature of the sociogenic code—its imposition being a constitutive feature of sociality—makes it possible for codes to harness the body's drives for its own sociohistorical ends.[18] The inseparability of the social and the biological brings Wynter to call for a mode of inquiry that can transcend the limitations of the purely natural-scientific approaches to consciousness as well as philosophies of mind that assume we can study consciousness in abstraction from sociality. Here she follows Aimé Césaire's proposal for a "science of the word" that thematizes the way the sociogenic principle is enacted as both Word (*ordo verborum*) and nature (*ordo naturae*).[19] This would be a theoretical approach that aims to grasp the *speculative* identity of being and meaning, the dialectic of "Words made flesh, muscle and bone animated by hope and desire, belief materialized in deeds, [and] deeds which crystallize our actualities."[20]

As a theory of the intrinsic relationship between consciousness, knowledge, and social practice, the sociogenic method must also account for material production. Because "systems of knowledge are inseparable from the empirical arrangements of any society,"[21] they are inextricably tied to "each societal order's *genre-specific mode of material provisioning*."[22] Rejecting any vulgar materialist or economistic notion of material production in abstraction from determinate symbolic forms, Wynter argues that as the generative mechanism of subjectivity the sociogenic principle determines the social form of the provisioning process. Thus, the telos of our mode of production "is *not* to produce for human beings in general, it's to provide the material conditions of existence for the production and reproduction of our present *conception* of being human."[23] There is no predetermined mode of production underlying sociocultural variation, for what we *are* is the product of *what we do*.[24] By eliding the interdependence of subjectivity and objectivity we produce the "mechanisms by means of which we have been able to invert cause and effect, allowing us to repress the recognition of our collective production of our modes of social reality."[25] Consequently, the present society appears *as if* it were a mere reflection of a perfected natural order, a phenomenon that Wynter refers to as "overrepresentation."

Wynter's critique of overrepresentation sets up her critique of historicism.[26] Having overrepresented itself as if the natural form of human existence, our present genre of being human (Man) overrepresents its history as if it were capital-H "History." By assuming that social reality is the outcome of our agentive capacities alone and that we can access the truth of it by tracing the course of our actions, historicism fails to apprehend the logic that grounds the unfolding of events and conditions our habits of narration. It fails to reckon with the paradox where history's conditions of possibility cannot be accessed through history itself:

> For it would be the code, the law of the code, the principle, which functions as the ground of the history that will be narrated and existentially lived. So the ground of our mode of being human will itself be the a priori or ground of the history to which it gives rise. But the paradox here, of course, is that it cannot itself be historicized within the terms of the ethnohistory to which it will give rise: that code/mode must remain, as you say, unhistoricizable.[27]

Being unhistoricizable, the governing code is an absent cause which cannot be empirically known but only reconstructed retrospectively.[28] This does not make it a transcendental principle in the vein of Kant's critical philosophy; while it is unhistoricizable, it is not timeless. The history of every society is instituted by the sociogenic principle thus making it, in this respect, a transhistorical condition, but there is no single code for *all* societies, no ahistorical form transcending determinate contents, and therefore no meta-principle or overarching logic governing history as a whole. Instead Wynter argues that history ought to be understood on two levels: first, the level of human history as such, the *whole* range of ways in which "we're enacting [and] instituting ourselves as human," and second, the history instituted by the code we currently inhabit.[29] By positing the history of Man as one instance within the broader history of human sociogenesis, Wynter relativizes its claim to be the substance of human existence. Moreover, by framing human history as the history of incommensurate modes of auto-institution, she desubstantializes history altogether.

If history amounts to an array of discontinuous societies, then we need to account for why this is the case. This raises the question of rupture and its conditions of possibility: What must the internal dynamics of these societies be like such that they can break *from themselves*? It is here that

Wynter emphasizes the centrality of political struggle to the constitution of society. Her argument aims to "redefine Marx's class struggle in the terms of a 'politics of being,'" a term that frames the production of knowledge and subjectivity as emergent effects of political antagonism.[30] Moreover, her redefinition also aims to highlight the importance of political struggle by claiming that what is at stake is the determination of the mode of *existence* itself. If every regime of *truth* is a proximate function of a regime of *being*, then the politics of being is the struggle over the very terms through which society is organized.[31] The reformulations of knowledge that the politics of being entails emerge from the need "to redescribe both the human, and its human activity" outside of the structuring terms of the previous order.[32] All political struggles, from the lay-humanist and merchant struggle against the *sacerdotium* of Latin Christendom to the bourgeois revolt against the landed aristocracy, are struggles over the terms of what it means to be human and the various political-juridical, cultural, theological, and philosophical forms that can engender it.

While societies and their systems of knowledge are discontinuous, the transformation of Latin Christendom into modern civil society occurred within a continuous cultural-intellectual field "instituted by the matrix Judeo-Christian [*sic*] formulation of a general order of existence."[33] Sociogenic codes can be discontinuous in terms of their systems of meaning while remaining in continuity with regard to the concepts and questions up for contestation. The simultaneity of continuity and discontinuity allows us to interpret the ways that the problems pertaining to the old order are reformulated and transformed in the new one. Positing a shared cultural-intellectual field that encompasses Graeco-Roman thought and Christian theological discourse offers a way to explain the relevance of theological concepts and metaphors for contemporary politics without assuming a transhistorical structure.

Genealogy of Economy: From the Household to the Cathedral

The transformation of the concept of economics was central to the cultural-intellectual field from which the modern world emerges. In Greek antiquity economics refers to the art of household management. The master of the household—tasked with ruling over his wife, children, and slaves—administers the use of property with the aim of ensuring both the material subsistence of each member of the household and the necessary conditions for the enjoyment of political life. Although the *polis* "comes into existence for the sake of mere life," it ultimately exists for "the sake of a good life."[34] The master, having secured the health of the household, is now free to participate in politics among his equals, to govern *and* be governed. Taken up by early Christian thinkers, the concept of *oikonomia* was later used in patristic theology as a way of describing God's administration of the world during the early formulation of Trinitarian theology. Agamben argues that what was essentially at stake was the question of how to affirm both divine transcendence (the immanent trinity or God's being-in-and-for-itself) and immanence (the economic trinity or God's being-for-us) without fracturing the divine substance. If God's being is identical to God's praxis, then there can be no substantial difference between God's being *in se* and God's works *ad extra*: the will of the immanent trinity is executed in time as the economy of Christ.[35] Agamben's argument, however, overlooks what was actually central for patristic authors, namely, soteriology. The questions regarding God's transcendence and immanence, being and praxis, were functions of the task of working out the implications and necessary conditions for the redemption of humanity.[36] As Sean Capener puts it, "it is clear that the stakes for patristic writers, in working out a Trinitarian theology, were precisely salvation. The lines between heresy and orthodoxy are consistently argued in terms of their relationship to the possibility of salvation—the possibility of a triumph over sin and death."[37]

The emphasis on soteriology brings to light the social dimensions of theological economics, as an account of the divine economy requires tending to the conditions of human sinfulness. Because humanity's enslavement to sin will not be fully defeated on this side of the eschaton, the economy of the church consists in caring for the souls of the faithful in anticipation of the final judgment. Therefore, as Nicholas Heron puts it, "the politics of the church" consists "in nothing more, or nothing less, than mediating the theological economy."[38] In this respect, Augustine's notion of original sin (and the corresponding notion of divine grace) is a decisive moment for the development of Latin Christendom's ecclesiastical apparatus. Augustine's conception of sin and grace is the foundation upon which its spiritual economy was built. According to this theology, we are enslaved to sin as the result of our free will, for "when man by his own free will sinned . . . the freedom of his will was lost."[39] The effects of original sin are self-perpetuating and cannot be undone, even though our free will is what brings sin into being. While all are enslaved to sin, some—by the grace of God—can be redeemed, having their liberty restored and thereby restoring order.[40] True freedom or true political life is only realized in the heavenly city of God (*civitas dei*), which means that the spiritual economy of the church trains the soul for the enjoyment of heavenly political life. This Augustinian move transforms the Aristotelian management of the household into the Christian governance of souls, a new form of power that organizes "an entire economy and technique of the circulation, transfer, and reversal of merits."[41]

The Christian development and institutionalization of this pastoral economy, with its techniques of governing people's everyday lives, forms the background for Wynter's account of the centralized post-Gregorian church of the Middle Ages. Because redemption from enslavement to sin can only be realized through the sacraments of the church and adherence to its prohibitions, the work of attaining "Divine Election for eternal salvation in the Augustinian *civitas dei* (the city of God)" was the sociogenic principle of Latin Christendom.[42] As such, the Augustinian telos of redemption and the centralization of the church were enmeshed not only in the organization of social practices but also in the elaboration of the reigning order of knowledge. The Ptolemaic astronomy of Graeco-Roman antiquity was carried over into the medieval Christian imagination. The distinction between the eternal unmoving bodies of the supralunar regions of the cosmos and the finite corruptible bodies of the sublunar regions found their correlation in the hierarchy of spirit over flesh.[43] The spirit-flesh binary was enacted as the hierarchy of clergy over laity and the epistemic privileging of theological over secular knowledge. Theology, with its access to "knowledge of things Divine, celestial, of the category of the spirit," claimed authority on the grounds of its proximity to eternal truth and oversaw knowledge of "the socio-human world whose works were the works of natural unregenerate man," and therefore "secondary and partaking of the inferiority of all things terrestrial."[44]

These categorical distinctions between the spiritual and the material, the other-worldly and this-worldly, reached their limits in the crisis of late scholastic nominalism. Its conception of a "totally omnipotent God who had created the universe for the sake of His own glory rather than specifically for mankind's sake" would come to dramatically shape the problematic of human freedom.[45] God's absolute power (*potentia absoluta*) was juxtaposed with the "total helplessness and cognitive incapacity of 'natural man' as the fallen heir of Adam's sin."[46] Because God has the power to arbitrarily change the order of nature, humanity *cannot* rely upon "the regularity of the rules governing nature in order to obtain access to their organizing or anagogic principles."[47] Under these circumstances, the church—being the only mode of access to truth—mediates not only Christ's governance of the world, but also humanity's relation to reality itself. Outside of the church, the "this-worldly perspective" of the lay world was "entrapped in the fallen time of the secular realm" where humanity is subjected to "the instability and chaos of the capricious whims of Fortune."[48] Enslaved to sin and ignorant of the world's causes, unredeemed humanity is left "without any hope of being able to have any valid knowledge of reality except through the mediation of the very paradigms that excluded any such hope."[49] With this, the long march from the household to the cathedral is complete.

The Sociogenesis of Race: From the Cathedral to the State, the State to the Market

The breakdown of ecclesiastical hegemony emerged within a process of social transformation involving the "rise of the modern political city and monarchical states of Europe" along with the expansion of an already ongoing commercial revolution.[50] The intellectual revolution of Renaissance humanism elaborated the *conceptual* grounds for this paradigmatic shift in social relations. As a lay movement, the European Renaissance sought to revalorize the lives of the laity and in doing so ushered in a renewed sense of the legitimacy of the secular, the city of man. Its revindication of "Natural Man" and its "arts of rhetoric, philosophy, [and] profane literature" would mark an epistemological break from the absolutism of late medieval theology, for these secular arts were deemed "a valorizing activity in [their] own right."[51] This enabled "a new kind of freedom, that of human reason, and of its power to gain knowledge of all things including things celestial."[52] The valorization of reason came with an affirmation of the world's order and intelligibility, a sense that God had ordered the world for our sake (*propter nos homines*).[53] The generalization of this sensibility—what Wynter calls the poetics of the *propter nos*—forms the philosophical and theological background of the Copernican revolution. While the Copernican revolution demonstrated the homogeneity of physical matter, the revolution of the "fifteenth-century voyages of the Portuguese and Columbus" to the previously uninhabitable torrid zone along the west coast of Africa and the null space of the Western hemisphere reconfigured the earth as universally habitable. These epoch-making shifts in cosmology and geography set in motion a new universality defined around rational Man. Nature, as "an autonomously functioning force or cause in its own right," is now conceived as being governed by universal laws which could be understood by human beings.[54] Complicating geographies divided by God's grace and upending the hierarchy between supralunar and sublunar regions of the universe, nature now found itself ruled by the same principles in Europe as in Africa and the Americas, governed on earth as in heaven. By situating the Copernican revolution within the context of the Columbian expedition and the Portuguese slave trade, Wynter positions heliocentrism as a "'conceptual repercussion' of the Columbian voyages"[55] and reconfigures new scientific advances, with the postmedieval conceptions of human freedom and mastery over nature being actualized in the expansion of the slave trade.[56]

Although Western Europe's large-scale expropriation of land and labor was initially carried out within a theological-political schema,[57] the rapid expansion of the Spanish and Portuguese empires meant that their monarchs were soon "no longer content to remain dependent on a system of legitimation based on terms that still concede temporal power to the papacy."[58] Such discontent called for new forms of legitimacy and a reformulation of the neo-Augustinian notion of spiritual slavery wherein the enslavement of Africans was legitimated on the grounds of their being idolators and heathens. By turning to Aristotle's *Politics* and reworking the inherited theological-political toolkit, the state and its discourse of civic humanism inaugurated a rupture in political thought where natural law now functioned to "order human societies in the same way as the newly discovered laws of nature served to regulate the processes of functioning of physical and organic levels of reality."[59] Unlike the capricious world of late scholasticism, natural law is immanent to the world itself; humans—having no *natural* end—are now defined by their capacity for self-determination, determined by nature to determine themselves. Now instead of enslavement to sin, for the state and its citizens there was the threat of finding oneself enslaved to "the particularistic desires of one's human nature."[60] Sovereignty could only be exercised by "the subject able to subdue his private interests" by adhering to the laws of the state and upholding the common good, thereby transcending one's enslavement to one's inclinations and passions through the social contract. As the earlier theological distinction between the "Elect-redeemed and the condemned" became the civic-humanist distinction between reason and non-reason, this new form was forcibly "actualized in a new relation."[61] Because slavery was already legitimized within the theological-political terms of spiritual slavery, Blackness was primed to mediate the conceptual transition from enslavement to sin to enslavement to irrationality and the shift from the *spiritual* redemption of the church to the *political* redemption of the state.

Wynter's excavation of slavery's material and symbolic conditions of possibility serves as a potent interpretive lens for thinking the sociogenesis of modern society and mapping the structure of Western modernity as a problematic of the human. A central question of modernity arises from the claim that reason's newfound capacity to apprehend the order of nature *materializes* as the apprehension of the proper order of society. If the world is governed by universally binding laws of nature, then how can there be freedom? Even with Black slaves signifying total subordination to natural necessity (thereby marking what sovereignty is *not*), the problem remained unresolved.[62] How were those who could transcend natural necessity capable of doing so? The sociogenic code of Latin Christendom rooted spiritual redemption in divine election, but how—in the absence of divine predestination—to determine what *ensures* the capacity for *worldly* redemption? It was this need to resolve the tension between necessity and freedom that called for a concept that could measure varying capacities for self-determination. Thus the concept of race was summoned to do the work of ensuring "that 'ends' . . . are still extra-humanly set for the human by *nature*, in our case, by the constraints of nature and/or of history."[63] By positing variation as an effect of causal mechanisms intrinsic to nature, race ensures that one's capacity for self-determination is a matter of *internal* necessity.[64] Thus, the measurement of racial difference renders freedom representable and ensures that its *actuality* follows from the essence of one's being. Race is the condition of possibility for the measurement of humanity as such, and with the transition from *homo politicus* (mercantilism) to *homo oeconomicus* (industrial capitalism), Man1 to Man2, such measurement is eventually framed in *biological* terms, as we shift from "the first *ratiocentric* (i.e., reason-centered) form of what was later to become the full-fledged *biocentric* issue of 'race.'"[65] The emergence of the human sciences solidified the conception of humanity as a natural-scientific object. In this frame, self-interest is conceived as being more fundamental to human existence than culture, as "all human societies have their ostensibly natural scientific organic basis, with their religions/cultures being merely superstructural."[66] With culture redefined as being merely the historical variation of the biological drive for self-preservation, the bourgeois conception of self-interest as the essence of human nature finds its ideological ground in the positivism of the human sciences.

In addition to situating *homo oeconomicus* within a larger genealogy of economics (spanning from Aristotle to Augustine to early modernity), Wynter's breakthrough here is her identification of the way that liberal humanism—and its positing of economics as a discipline akin to the natural sciences[67]—naturalizes itself *through* the reproduction of racial difference. What we are dealing with is "the institution of a mode of social relations that marks, inscribes, the groups that are to be exploited by different attributes, attributes which then become the condition of possibility for the varying forms of exploitation."[68] When race is reified as an empirical object, the categories of political economy (labor, value, exchange, etc.) along with its corresponding formations of gender, sexuality, and nation can be read from the body.[69] Race grounds the perception of *social* difference as *bodily* difference and in doing so works as an essential condition for the ethical judgment of the body as such.[70]

The question of how race does this work is tied to the metastasizing of the political culture of slavery after legal emancipation. In the wake of the global abolition of slavery, all peoples of African descent—as well as Africa itself—were positioned as "the actualized embodiment, no longer of the human made degenerate by sin and therefore fallen to the status of the apes, but of the human totally dysselected, barely evolved, and as such intermediate between 'true' humans and primates."[71] In the movement from sin to natural necessity to biological dysselection, the representation of Blackness as the "mode of non-being that each individual and group must strive to avoid, struggle to prove that they themselves are not, if they are to be," sustains bourgeois society and its promises of freedom through productive labor and equal exchange.[72] These promises make possible a sustained faith in the possibility of transcendence even when empirical circumstances such as poverty suggest otherwise.[73] As Wynter writes in *Black Metamorphosis*, "the forced confinement of Black labour was central to the constitution of the social value of 'free' labour, and to the constitution of the bourgeois mode of freedom as the single freedom—freedom to labour freely."[74] From the Renaissance to the Industrial Revolution, from Lisbon to London, Amsterdam to New York, race works as an unstable remedy for the social, theological, and philosophical anxieties that coalesce around Blackness, suturing modernity's structures of meaning-making at "high cost."[75]

Conclusion

I have argued that Wynter's account of the way that the theological-political grammar of Latin Christendom transforms into the grammar of race contributes to a critique of contemporary forms of power and domination. As such, the questions of theological genealogy form an essential aspect of the diagnosis of power in the present. What I hope to have shown is the way that the overrepresentation of *homo politicus* and later *homo oeconomicus* mystifies the way our now "purely biocentric terms" emerge from world-historical transformations following the breakdown of Latin Christendom's theological-political toolkit.[76] Across the *longue durée*, the problem of economy mutates from the management of the household into the government of the soul, citizen, and ultimately the laboring body. Such mutations do not appear as mutations when Capitalism accomplishes its "theologization of material life, its production of the economic as its sole reality principle, its reduction of man to his productive capacity," through the representation of itself as something *other* than theological, as simply historical or natural.[77]

By arguing that theological-political problems are essential to the constitution of the capitalist social form, my reading of Wynter's diagnostic brings into view some of the limits of Toscano's critical remarks on theological genealogy. Arguing that the exigencies of the present require us to move from the frame of theological genealogy to historical materialism, and affirming the "preoccupation with real needs and material constraints, as well as with the resistances of nature" found in classical Marxist literature, Toscano sets up an opposition between the recognition of the need for *some* form of economic thinking and Agamben's desire to render the theological-political machine inoperative.[78] By dividing between theological genealogy and "real needs" he runs the risk of reinforcing or reinscribing the very biocentric episteme that emerged from the kinds of crises in theological legitimacy that Wynter takes up. Put differently, the limit of Toscano's alternative resides in the way that he presupposes a fixed or predetermined border between the theological and the political, and by extension the symbolic and the material. By prioritizing the symbolic as the *form* of our sociality, Wynter can better account for *why* modern society is configured the way that it is. As she writes in a 1981 essay,

> The aesthetic is not less "material" than the *economic*. The expropriation of the means of aesthetic perception, of the mechanics of critical judgment are no less and perhaps far more terrible with respect to its consequences than the expropriation of the means of production. The means of providing for material existence are vital, but so too are the means of enacting, exercising, developing the innate faculty—*the eye for line and for significant form.*[79]

Thinking alongside Wynter, engaging the way that theological problems are essential to the production of the form of contemporary power, can offer insight into *why* our needs and material constraints are what they are.

In addition to serving as Wynter's philosophy of history and philosophical anthropology, the sociogenic method that makes possible the above insights into our contemporary condition also grounds her normative or ethical-political commitments. Thus, the reigning sociogenic code is deemed unethical because of the way its reproduction takes precedence over the well-being of "the flesh-and-blood individual subject and of the human species as a whole, together with, increasingly, that of the interests of all other nonhuman forms of life on this planet."[80] This means that the task of building "collective or trans-individual power" must account for the role of meaning-making in the constitution of social domination.[81] For Wynter, the work of grasping the characteristic form of social domination means identifying the liminal position of the social order, a position which "must be systemically excluded from the normal functioning of each specific order, as the condition of that order's stable production and reproduction."[82] Having named Blackness the internal limit of our political culture, Wynter affirms Black political struggle (and with it Black studies) as the movement toward the dissolution of the present organization of knowledge, a movement that proceeds by revealing the contingency of the social structure. In doing so, it points to the potential for reigniting the politics of being, reopening sedimented philosophical and theological questions, and denaturalizing the repetition of racial violence. The demands of radical Black political and intellectual discourse beget a critical project in which the overcoming of the present order is inseparable from adjudicating its conditions of possibility. For Wynter, it is the jobless and unskilled "surplus" populations of the world's ghettos, shantytowns, and favelas who reveal the truth of our society and take the Fanonian leap of invention. Their struggle for the *necessities* of life is a struggle to transform the *meaning* of life itself. It is the struggle against our "narratively condemned status."[83]

Notes

1. Sylvia Wynter, "Columbus and the Poetics of the *Propter Nos*," *Annals of Scholarship* 8, no. 2 (1991): 252.

2. Alberto Toscano, "Divine Management: Critical Remarks on Giorgio Agamben's *The Kingdom and the Glory*," *Angelaki* 16, no. 3 (2011): 128. "Reductivist idealism" is Toscano's term for a kind of inverted vulgar materialism that he finds in Agamben's genealogy.

3. Sylvia Wynter, "Review: A Utopia from the Semi-periphery: Spain, Modernization, and the Enlightenment," *Science Fiction Studies* 6, no. 1 (1979): 103.

4. Sylvia Wynter and Katherine McKittrick, "Unparalleled Catastrophe for Our Species? Or, to Give Humanness a Different Future: Conversations," in *Sylvia Wynter: On Being Human as Praxis*, ed. Katherine McKittrick (Durham, NC: Duke University Press, 2015), 37.

5. Wynter and McKittrick, 26.

6. Some of the major books on the topic are Nicholas Heron, *Liturgical Power: Between Economic and Political Theology* (New York: Fordham University Press, 2018); Dotan Leshem, *The Origins of Neoliberalism: Modeling the Economy from Jesus to Foucault* (New York: Columbia University Press, 2017); Germano Maifreda, *From "Oikonomia" to Political Economy: Constructing Economic Knowledge from the Renaissance to the Scientific Revolution* (London: Routledge, 2016); Marie-Jose Mondzain, *Image, Icon, Economy: The Byzantine Origins of the Contemporary Economy* (Stanford, CA: Stanford University Press, 2005); and Devin Singh, *Divine Currency: The Theological Power of Money in the West* (Stanford, CA: Stanford University Press, 2018).

7. Giorgio Agamben, *The Kingdom and the Glory: For a Theological Genealogy of Economy and Government (Homo Sacer II)*, trans. Lorenzo Chiesa and Matteo Mandarini (Stanford, CA: Stanford University Press, 2011), 4.

8. Toscano, "Divine Management," 126–27.

9. Toscano, 133.

10. Sylvia Wynter, "The Ceremony Must Be Found: After Humanism," in *"On Humanism and the University I: The Discourse of Humanism,"* ed. William Spanos, special issue, *Boundary 2* 12, no. 3 / 13, no. 1 (1984): 62n33.

11. Sylvia Wynter, "1492: A New World View," in *Race, Discourse, and the Origin of the Americas*, ed. Vera Lawrence Hyatt and Rex Nettleford (Washington, DC: Smithsonian Institution Press, 1995), 47.

12. Sylvia Wynter, "The Pope Must Have Been Drunk, the King of Castile a Madman: Culture as Actuality, and the Caribbean Rethinking Modernity," in *The Reordering of Culture: Latin America, the Caribbean and Canada in the Hood*, ed. Alvina Ruprecht and Cecilia Taiana (Ottawa: Carleton University Press, 1995), 20–21.

13. Sylvia Wynter, "Unsettling the Coloniality of Being/Power/Truth/Freedom: Towards the Human, after Man, Its Overrepresentation—an Argument," *CR: The New Centennial Review* 3, no. 3 (2003): 268.

14. Sylvia Wynter, "In Quest of Matthew Bondsman: Some Cultural Notes on the Jamesian Journey," *Urgent Tasks* 12 (1981), http://www.sojournertruth.net/matthewbondsman.html.

15. Sylvia Wynter, "On Disenchanting Discourse: 'Minority' Literary Criticism and Beyond," *Cultural Critique*, no. 7 (Autumn 1987): 242. On Autopoiesis she writes:

> [Maturana and Varela] wanted to think about the idea of biological organisms as *autonomously functioning, living* (i.e., autopoietic) systems. And this is related to our human social systems—a point they also put forward in their later work. Now if you look at living systems such as the beehive, they are purely biological eusocial systems. Our human eusocial systems are instead *hybrid languaging cum storytelling (if biologically implemented) living systems*; but they function according to laws analogous to those regulatory laws of the supra-autopoietic system, which is the beehive. So I call these the *laws of hybrid human auto-speciation*, thereby of *autopoiesis*. Yet what we also find is that these laws, as the very condition of their ostensibly *extrahumanly* mandated functioning, are nevertheless ones that have hitherto been enacted outside of our conscious awareness—even though we ourselves have always rigorously and behaviorally adhered to them as indispensable to our respective genre-specific praxes of being hybridly human! (Wynter and McKittrick, "Unparalleled Catastrophe," 27)

16. Sylvia Wynter, "The Ceremony Found: Towards the Autopoetic Turn/Overturn, Its Autonomy of Human Agency and Extraterritoriality of (Self-)Cognition," in *Black Knowledges / Black Struggles: Essays in Critical Epistemology*, ed. Jason R. Ambroise and Sabine Broeck (Liverpool: Liverpool University Press, 2015), 217.

17. Joyce E. King, "Race and Our Biocentric Belief System: An Interview with Sylvia Wynter," in *Black Education: A Transformative Research and Action Agenda for the New Century*, ed. Joyce E. King (Washington, DC: American Educational Research Association / Lawrence Erlbaum Associates, 2005), 361.

18. Sylvia Wynter, "Towards the Sociogenic Principle: Fanon, Identity, the Puzzle of Conscious Experience, and What It Is Like to Be 'Black,'" in *National Identities and*

Sociopolitical Changes in Latin America, ed. Mercedes F. Durán-Cogan and Antonio Gómez-Moriana (New York: Routledge, 2001), 48.

19. Wynter, "Ceremony Found," 211.

20. Wynter, "Pope Must Have Been Drunk," 35. For Wynter's reading of physicist David Bohm on the identity of "Being" and "Meaning," see Sylvia Wynter, "Columbus, the Ocean Blue, and Fables That Stir the Mind: To Reinvent the Study of Letters," in *Poetics of the Americas: Race, Founding, and Textuality*, ed. Bainard Cohen and Jefferson Humphries (Baton Rouge: Louisiana State University Press, 1992), 162.

21. Sylvia Wynter and Greg Thomas, "ProudFlesh Inter/Views: Sylvia Wynter," *ProudFlesh: New Afrikan Journal of Culture, Politics and Consciousness* 4 (2006): 13.

22. Wynter, "Ceremony Found," 203.

23. David Scott, "The Re-enchantment of Humanism: An Interview with Sylvia Wynter," *Small Axe: A Caribbean Journal of Criticism* 8 (September 2000): 160. See also Wynter, in her interview with Joyce King: "what is produced is not just the material conditions. What is produced is our conception of being human. Every mode of production is a function of producing that conception." King, "Race and Our Biocentric Belief System," 363.

24. For Wynter on praxis see Wynter and McKittrick, "Unparalleled Catastrophe," 33, and Wynter, "Ceremony Found," 195–96.

25. Wynter, "Unsettling," 273.

26. Michael Gillespie offers a useful definition of historicism: "It [historicism] began with the assumption that history is not merely one realm of being but all reality and that there is nothing behind or beneath or above history, not even a restless eternity of becoming such as Nietzsche supposed. What is real is life-experience, and this cannot be explained either by natural science or introspection but only by history." Michael Gillespie, *Hegel, Heidegger, and the Ground of History* (Chicago: University of Chicago Press, 1984), 18.

27. Scott, "Re-enchantment of Humanism," 197.

28. Wynter, "Ceremony Must Be Found," 60n25.

29. Scott, "Re-enchantment of Humanism," 198.

30. Wynter, "Unsettling," 319.

31. Scott, "Re-enchantment of Humanism," 199.

32. Wynter, "Unsettling," 320.

33. Wynter, 318. Elsewhere Wynter speaks of "an extended tradition unique to the West, beginning with its origin in ancient Greece and arriving at its ultimate realization with the rise of the West to now planetary hegemony. I shall define this tradition as that of the Western *autopoetic field*." Wynter, "Ceremony Found," 193n14.

34. Aristotle, *The Politics*, trans. Ernest Barker, rev. and intro. by R. F. Stalley (Oxford: Oxford University Press, 2009), I.2, 1252b27.

35. Agamben, *Kingdom and the Glory*, 53–67.

36. "It is only if God's economies encompass everything that the incarnational economy will redeem the whole universe. If this economy disappears, everything disappears." Mondzain, *Image*, 36.

37. Sean Capener, "Being and Acting: Agamben, Athanasius and the Trinitarian Economy," *Heythrop Journal* 57, no. 6 (2015): 950.

38. Heron, *Liturgical Power*, 5.

39. Augustine of Hippo, *The Enchiridion on Faith, Hope, and Love*, ed. Henry Paolucci (South Bend, IN: Regnery/Gateway, 1961), 37.

40. Augustine, 38.

41. Michel Foucault, *Security, Territory, Population: Lectures at the Collège de France, 1977–1978*, ed. Michel Senellart, trans. Graham Burchell (New York: Palgrave Macmillan, 2007), 183.
42. Wynter, "Unsettling," 274.
43. Wynter, 274.
44. Wynter, "Ceremony Must Be Found," 26.
45. Wynter, "1492," 26.
46. Wynter, "1492," 26.
47. Wynter, "1492," 26.
48. Wynter, "Unsettling," 276.
49. Wynter, 276.
50. Wynter, 275.
51. Wynter, "Ceremony Must Be Found," 29.
52. Wynter, 30.
53. Wynter, "1492," 27.
54. Wynter, "Unsettling," 264.
55. Wynter, "Columbus," 155.
56. Wynter and McKittrick, "Unparalleled Catastrophe," 62.
57. Wynter, "Unsettling," 291. The topic of large-scale accumulation of wealth and resources brings to mind Marx on primitive accumulation. While Marx recognizes the *historical* role of slavery and colonialism in the constitution of capitalist modernity, it is Wynter who recognizes their historical and *conceptual* role in the constitution of the capitalist social form. Wynter's critique of modernity exceeds the parameters of what Sara-Maria Sorentino and I call "the labor theory of slavery." See Tapji Paul Garba and Sara-Maria Sorentino, "Slavery Is a Metaphor: A Critical Commentary on Eve Tuck and K. Wayne Yang's 'Decolonization Is Not a Metaphor,'" *Antipode* 52, no. 3 (2020); and Sara-Maria Sorentino, "The Abstract Slave: Anti-Blackness and Marx's Method," *International Labor and Working-Class History* 96 (2019): 17–37.
58. Wynter, "1492," 34.
59. Wynter, "Unsettling," 297.
60. Wynter, 288.
61. Wynter, 304.
62. "The Negro represents the Negative signifier of an allegedly 'primal' human being totally subordinated to "natural necessity.'" Wynter, "On Disenchanting Discourse," 222.
63. Sylvia Wynter, "Afterword: Beyond Miranda's Meanings: Un/silencing the 'Demonic Ground' of Caliban's 'Woman,'" in *Out of the Kumbla: Caribbean Women and Literature*, ed. Carole Boyce Davies and Elaine Savory Fido (Trenton, NJ: Africa World, 1990), 357.
64. Here race is conceived as "a natural causality which differentiated human groups along a continuum of different degrees of rationality, a differentiation which was part of a universal law of Nature beyond human control." Wynter, "Ceremony Must Be Found," 35.
65. Wynter, "Ceremony Found," 187.
66. Wynter and McKittrick, "Unparalleled Catastrophe," 21.
67. Sylvia Wynter, "Is 'Development' a Purely Empirical Concept or Also Teleological? A Perspective from 'We the Underdeveloped,'" in *Prospects for Recovery and Sustainable Development in Africa*, ed. Aguibou Yansan (Westport, CT: Greenwood, 1996), 311.

68. Sylvia Wynter, "*Black Metamorphosis: New Natives in a New World*," unpublished manuscript, IBW Papers, Schomburg Center for Research in Black Culture, New York, Box (Sylvia Wynter), 564.

69. "From this ultimate mode of otherness based on 'race,' other subtypes of otherness are then generated—the lower classes as the lack of the normal class, that is, the *middle class*; all other cultures as the lack of the normal culture, that is, *Western culture*; the nonheterosexual as the lack of *heterosexuality*, represented as a biologically selected mode of erotic preference; women as the lack of the normal sex, *the male*." Wynter, "1492," 42.

70. "Race was therefore to be, in effect, the non-supernatural but no less extrahuman ground (in the reoccupied place of the traditional ancestors/gods, God, ground) of the answer that the secularizing West would now give to the Heideggerian question as to the who, and the what we are." Wynter, "Unsettling," 264. In saying this, Wynter differs from approaches that conceive of race as a *distortion* of the body, a mask that hides the person underneath, as opposed to the condition for the very *materialization* of the body and the ethical subject. For a brilliant discussion of the relationship between ethics and race, see J. Reid Miller, *Stain Removal: Ethics and Race* (New York: Oxford University Press, 2017).

71. Wynter, "*Unsettling*," 325.

72. Wynter, 325.

73. For Wynter, the promise of transcendence through self-determined labor is also a compensation for the (American) white working classes who have been exploited by Capital. She writes: "The bottommost role of Black Americans in the United States is systematically produced, since it is the ostensible proof of their alleged dysselected 'undeservingness' that then functions as the central psychic compensatory mechanism for the white working class, at the same time as this mechanism induces them to continue to see/experience themselves as also being, in terms of class, 'dysselected by Evolution'—a perception that induces them to accept their own class-subordinated status, as well as the hegemony of their middle classes." (Wynter, "*Unsettling*," 324).

74. Wynter, "*Black Metamorphosis*," 894.

75. Wynter, "1492," 40.

76. Wynter, "Ceremony Found," 193fn14.

77. Wynter, "*Black Metamorphosis*," 439.

78. Toscano, "*Divine Management*," 134.

79. Wynter, "In Quest of Matthew Bondsman."

80. Wynter, "1492," 47.

81. Toscano, "*Divine Management*," 134.

82. Sylvia Wynter, "On How We Mistook the Map for the Territory, and Reimprisoned Ourselves in Our Unbearable Wrongness of Being, of *Désêtre*: Black Studies toward the Human Project," in *Not Only the Master's Tools: African-American Studies in Theory and Practice*, ed. Lewis R. Gordon and Jane Anna Gordon (Boulder, CO: Paradigm, 2006), 157.

83. Sylvia Wynter, "'No Humans Involved': An Open Letter to My Colleagues," *Forum N.H.I.: Knowledge for the 21st Century* 1, no. 1 (1994): 70.

Part Three: Counter-religiosities beyond Man

7   Interrupting the Sanctity of Man:
    Wynter, Imperial Piety, and the Unruly Sacred

    Joseph Winters

Prelude to an Encounter

On June 1, 2020, law enforcement fired tear gas on protesters in Lafayette Square (Washington, DC) to clear a path for President Donald Trump and members of his administration, enabling them to walk from the White House to St. John's Episcopal Church. In what has now become an iconic scene, Trump positions himself for several minutes in front of the church, awkwardly showcasing a Bible—almost as though he is advertising and selling something to the audience. At one point, Trump responds to a reporter questioning the president about the recent protests against state violence and anti-Black racism. Sounding as if he is trying to reassure himself more than the viewer, he proclaims: "We have a great country . . . the greatest in the world . . .we will make it even greater. . .it's coming back, it's coming back strong."[1] In the face of confrontations between the state and dissident subjects and in the midst of a pandemic exposing and intensifying global inequities regarding vulnerability to death, Trump turns to the Bible, church, and US exceptionalism as the way to anticipate the restoration of order and the renewal of American supremacy. By clearing a path, with tear gas and other weapons, to keep Trump safe from the protesters and by mobilizing the Bible and nation-state sovereignty as a rejoinder to political resistance, this religious-political performance aims to sacralize law and order, to reauthorize the violence necessary to maintain or bring back the semblance of imperial order.

Amid many different kinds of responses to these machinations of the Trump regime, one powerful criticism was articulated in a statement by former defense secretary James Mattis. Among other things, Mattis chastises Trump for deploying military force on US citizens "to provide a bizarre photo op for the elected commander in chief, with military leadership alongside."[2] Mattis accuses Trump of fomenting division instead of promoting unity, exemplified by the conflict created between the military and civilians. Similarly, the former defense secretary offers a warning about turning American cities into battle spaces, an admonition which assumes that while the fabrication of war zones is rarely appropriate for home, these zones are necessary and acceptable abroad. Mattis ends his statement against Trump's actions on an urgent note. He proclaims, "Only by adopting a new path—which means, in truth, returning to the original path of our founding ideals—will we again be a country admired and respected at home and abroad."[3] Here, the new path forward and away from the Trump administration requires a reaching back, a return to the nation-state's origins and foundations. The path to restoring the United States' global stature involves recovering the sacred ideals that established and inaugurated the nation. Even though there are important differences between Trump and Mattis, these disagreements occur on a shared terrain, a field governed by a logic that associates the sacred with the reestablishment of order and the affirmation of US settler nation-state sovereignty.

One could read Trump's "Bible photo op" as a mere ploy to galvanize evangelical supporters, those constituencies that are primed to think of Christianity as a bastion of (white) nationalism and other conservative values.[4] One might also think of Mattis' appeal to founding ideals as an all too familiar maneuver designed to make a plea for unity in a time of tumult and conflict. In both cases, religion and the invocation of the sacred are simply expedient ways to manage and re-constitute the body politic. This essay takes a different route, one that interrogates the logics and principles that make a certain invocation of the sacred readily available and useful for the solidification of imperial agendas. In other words, I am interested in what enables and makes possible Trump's appeal to Christian texts and institutions in the staging of state opposition to Black Lives Matter–inspired protests and demonstrations. Similarly, I am interested in what makes Mattis's gesture toward origins and foundations so commonplace and axiomatic as a religious strategy of rebinding and tying people to nation-state projects. (Recall that the word "religion" derives from the Latin *religare*, meaning to tie or to bind.) If Mircea Eliade suggests that religiosity has something to do with a yearning for an original purity, then it is important to underscore how Mattis's longing runs around the relationship between founding ideals and the conquest of indigenous peoples; it must disremember those events and erasures that contaminate origin stories of a people.⁵ To make sense of this common backdrop to Trump and Mattis, this shared commitment to the sanctity of US sovereignty—the greatness of America, the origins of the national project—and the sacred as a guarantor of rule and stability, I turn to the work of Sylvia Wynter. I contend that Wynter's description of the emergence of Man, with its shifts and transitions, provides us with a vocabulary to study the religiosity of coloniality and its afterlives. Even as Wynter tends to make a sharp distinction between the religious and the secular, she underscores how certain theological divisions and demarcations get rearticulated in the figure of Man, the overrepresented human, or the cis-gendered, propertied, Euro-American imperial subject. In what follows, I show how Wynter exposes a certain grammar of sacrality that propels the project of Man, exemplified in the political examples above. At the same time, Wynter's work gestures toward an alternative and heretical sacred, an unruly and demonic piety that stays with the wild and opaque, those qualities of human and non-human life that Man cannot fully master.⁶

Imperial Piety, Un-civil Religion, and the Perdurance of the Sacred

One way to appreciate Wynter's understanding of the sanctity of Man is to juxtapose her with scholars who have thought about secular piety or practices of the sacred that are influenced by, but distinguishable from, religious traditions such as Christianity, Islam, Judaism, or Candomblé. Consider for instance Émile Durkheim's oft-cited definition of religion. For Durkheim, the phenomenon of religion does not necessarily involve fidelity to gods or supernatural beings. What is central to religion is the separation between the sacred and the profane, a separation that is socially fabricated and that functions to solidify a community. As Durkheim puts it, "religion is a unified system of beliefs and practices relative to sacred things, that is to say things set apart and forbidden"—beliefs and practices through which sociality is organized and maintained.⁷

There is a doubleness to Durkheim's notion of the sacred, or those objects, figures, and ideas that are protected, set apart, and that provide the cohesive glue to social life. On the one hand, the French sociologist locates the origins of religious communion in festival-like gatherings where individuals are taken from the routineness of everyday life into "effervescent social milieux."⁸ These collective assemblies are defined by frenzy, disorder, and a kind of wild energy that takes individuals outside themselves, blurring the line between self and other. At the same time, Durkheim insists that this exorbitant energy must find a stable object or emblem (like a flag or some collective image) so that this state of intense connection and solidarity can endure. This emblem serves as a "rallying point ... [and] expresses the social unit tangibly."[9] In other words, there is an interplay between the wildness of religious experience—energies that can lead to upheaval—and the stability provided by the sacred objects and emblems that hold communities together.[10] This doubleness of the sacred, this oscillation between the disordering and stabilizing dimensions of religiosity, is further manifested in the notion of being set apart. An object, space, or group can be set apart through prohibitions and regulations that protect these valued phenomena from being contaminated. Yet lines of demarcation are also deployed to sequester and keep apart beings, objects, and forces that are considered dangerous to life and well-being. Consequently, Durkheim insists that "religious forces are of two kinds" and that while sacrality usually signifies life, health, and order, it is also expressed through death, disorder, and darkness.[11]

Durkheim's understanding of religion as not just a social phenomenon but the life and soul of social existence influences an author like Robert Bellah and his notion of civil religion.[12] Against those who would claim that Christianity is the true faith of the United States, Bellah contends that there is another kind of religion that hangs alongside (but is heavily intertwined with) Christianity, one that involves the narratives, myths, and rituals that give shape and meaning to US history and the American experience. According to Bellah, presidential speeches and political oratory are occasions when this other religion becomes explicit, this "collection of beliefs, symbols, and rituals with respect to sacred things and institutionalized in a collectivity."[13] And even as this civil religion pilfers tropes and narratives from the Old and New Testaments, it takes these elements and creates something new and unprecedented. As Bellah puts it, "Behind the civil religion at every point lie biblical archetypes: Exodus, Chosen People, Promised Land, New Jerusalem, Sacrificial Death and Rebirth. But it is also genuinely American and genuinely new."[14] According to this transformative process, America becomes the promised land; the American people take themselves to be a chosen people with a burden to protect and spread democracy; the Civil War is a kind of collective sacrifice to bring about a renewed nation divided over slavery. Bellah is not unaware of the ethical ambiguities involved in this assemblage of biblical archetypes. He knows that this sacred economy "has suffered various deformations and *demonic* distortions."[15] More specifically, the "theme of the American Israel was used, almost from the beginning, as a justification for the shameful treatment of the Indians so characteristic of our history. It can be overtly or implicitly linked to the idea of manifest destiny which has been used to legitimate several adventures in imperialism since the early nineteenth century."[16] For Bellah, the American civil religion has sanctioned and emboldened imperial and genocidal projects, exemplifying again the equivocal quality of the sacred.

But we need to pause and linger a bit on the language that Bellah uses to describe the ambiguities of civil religion. At times, he suggests that the violent, imperial dimension of this American piety is a distortion or deviation from a more benign and constructive set of nation-forming beliefs and rituals. The problem therefore lies in misuse or misappropriation. And yet Bellah also claims that "almost from the beginning" central motifs borrowed from biblical traditions enabled and made acceptable what Tzvetan Todorov calls the "conquest of America."[17] The latter point is a reminder that conquest and dispossession are intrinsic to the Exodus paradigm.[18] There is no vision of, or desire for, the promised land apart from the negation of the Canaanites, or those who inhabit a land that, in the context of the Americas, is (retroactively) valorized as newly discovered, original, and primed for settlement. While the Exodus narrative has been resignified and repurposed in various ways, what remains in the different iterations is this structural relationship between *land promised* and land and inhabitants that can be treated as property, and therefore occupied by the settler.[19] Consequently, what needs to be interrogated is how a certain conception of sacrality, which the Exodus paradigm instantiates, underwrites and facilitates the conversion of spaces, places, geographies, and ecologies into something possessable. If the Americas were imagined by European settlers as a kind of wilderness (and original paradise), then the religious tropes and archetypes that compose Euro-American settler piety serve as conduits of order, rule, and containment of this perceived wildness and disorder.[20] To put it differently, this genre of the sacred that involves forming and establishing a people, and a nation, also entails the imagining of certain populations and regions as formless, as devoid of form, order, and the capacity for self-governance.[21] These are figures of both lack and excess that need to be brought into the fold of civilization, even as this fold is defined by an unassimilable outside that determines the limits of the civilizing paradigm.

Sylvia Wynter's writings elaborate on and underscore the religious and theological underpinnings of colonial modernity and its hierarchical demarcations, such as the contrast between the ordered and the chaotic. Her work lays out how Western Man adopts these religious demarcations while extending them to a global scale that is unprecedented. Wynter's work, more than Durkheim's or Bellah's, insists that any discussion of religion, secularity, and the sacred-profane must linger with the kinds of demarcations and divisions that define legacies of settler colonialism, slavery, and anti-Black racism. At the same time, her criticisms show that these legacies, tethered to a prevailing conception of the human, do not exhaust possibilities for inhabiting the world differently. As Katherine McKittrick writes,

> Wynter's philosophies ... are secured to her ongoing struggle to represent the fullness of human ontologies, which have been curtailed by what she calls the overrepresentation of Man (Western bourgeois Man) as if it/he were the only available mode of complete humanness. Spanning roughly 1492 to the present, Wynter's analyses of the inventions of Man/human and his human Others are genealogies, which trace how racial-sexual-economic categories get made, remade, and disrupted through the production of knowledge and conceptions of time-space.[22]

Consequently, Wynter's task has been not only to show how a particular invention of the human has become entrenched through binary oppositions and modes of subordination but to underscore how this invention comes to present itself as natural and ineluctable. I take it that emphasizing this conversion from culture to nature is the key to remembering that alternative human ontologies have always persisted alongside Man. Consequently, my aim in this essay is to trace how a certain form of the sacred (analogous to Durkheim's pure, healthy sacred) contributes to the emergence and development of Western, imperial Man and to draw out Wynter's allusions to an unruly, demonic sacred that intimates trajectories beyond Western imperial paradigms. This heretical form of the sacred, as described below, resembles Durkheim's darker sense of the sacred but also veers toward other directions.

Not unlike writers within the field of political theology, Wynter claims that Western secular epistemes and frameworks of meaning are rearticulations of Christian theological imaginaries. Her description of Man1, which is both a figure associated with the period "from the Renaissance to the eighteenth century"[23] and a figure that registers a shift from theological to "de-supernaturalizing" meta-descriptions and modes of being, lays out the religious underpinnings of colonial modernity. Drawing from Jacob Pandian's seminal 1985 text, *Anthropology and the Western Tradition*, she writes, "the physical referents of the conception of the Untrue Other to the True Christian Self had been the categories of peoples defined in religious terminology as heretics, or as Enemies-of-Christ infidels and pagan-idolators (with Jews serving as the boundary-transgressive 'name of what is evil' figures, stigmatized as Christ-killing deicides)."[24] The ontological division, or what she calls nonhomogeneity, between the true Christian and the infidel/pagan is part of a larger set of hierarchical theological divisions, such as spirit and flesh, clergy and laity, redeemed and unredeemed, heavenly and terrestrial, and symbolic life and symbolic death. Alongside a series of political and epistemic changes, crises, and transformations within and at the edges of Europe (including the emergence of the territorial state; internal conflicts and wars; the introduction of new forms of knowledge that challenged Christian theological hegemony; the expansion of Europe through trade, commerce, conquest, and settler projects), these religious demarcations get transposed onto invidious distinctions between the proper, rational human and his irrational others. As Wynter puts it,

> In the wake of the West's reinvention of its True Christian Self in the transumed terms of the Rational Self of Man1, however, it was to be the peoples of the militarily expropriated New World territories (i.e., Indians), as well as the enslaved peoples of Black Africa (i.e., Negroes), that were made to reoccupy the matrix slot of Otherness— to be made into the physical referent of the idea of the irrational/ subrational Human Other, to this first degodded (if still hybridly religio-secular) "descriptive statement" of the human in history, as the descriptive statement that would be foundational to modernity.[25]

There is much to unpack in Wynter's understanding of these shifts regarding Euro-Christian ways of describing, carving up, and organizing the world. For one, Wynter claims that racial taxonomies have been animated by religious categories and epistemes; consequently, race, religion, and coloniality are inseparable and must be studied together.[26]

In addition, Wynter indicates that even as there is some break or discontinuity between the true Christian self and the rational Man1, there is also continuity with respect to a "matrix" that divides the world into either agents of life and order or signifiers of otherness, death, and disorder. There may be differences between the Christian/pagan contrast and the opposition between the rational European and the subrational Indian/Black, but what these contrasts share is a commitment to nonhomogeneity and strategies of ordering the world according to hierarchical binaries. According to Wynter, "the new criterion of Reason [developed during the Renaissance] would come to take the place of the medieval criterion of the Redeemed Spirit as its transumed form—that the master code of symbolic life ("the name of what is good") and death ("the name of what is evil") would now become that of reason/sensuality, rationality/irrationality in the reoccupied place of the matrix code of Redeemed Spirit / Fallen Flesh."[27] Not unlike Durkheim's distinction between a pure form of the sacred and a darker sacred, the redeemed spirit fallen flesh opposition registers a difference between beings and practices on a path toward elevation, wholeness, and completion and those defined in terms of descent, dissipation, and "base matter." As Mayra Rivera points out, flesh frequently invokes lust, excess, sinfulness, and death; it is slippery, formless, and mutable; it is both the most elemental level of existence and that which needs to be whipped into shape and molded properly.[28] While there are strands of Christianity that eschew a simple binary relationship between spirit and flesh, Wynter contends that a certain way of imagining this relationship within medieval Christendom gets reoccupied by an agenda that subordinates peoples and regions perceived as irrational and hypersensual to the proprietors of reason and order. Consequently, "the evangelizing mission of the church" and the "imperializing mission of the state based on its territorial expansion and conquest" become two sides of the same colonial process, a process that involves racial, gendered, and sexual modes of subjection.[29]

What connects the Christian self and the figure of Man1 is a certain assumptive logic regarding sacrality, ultimate value, and the qualities and attributes that need to be defended and extended, that require killing and dying to uphold. The various demarcations that Wynter identifies, modes of nonhomogeneity that carve up, sort out, and rank-order populations and geographies, place a premium on fulfillment, completion, and (self)-possession while stigmatizing that which appears as deficit, lack, or errantry according to a general yearning for purity. Western Man, or a certain invention of the ideal human as white, bourgeois, male, and cis-gendered, presents itself as the closest approximation to these values and signifiers of life; non-Europeans, especially indigenous and Black peoples, have come to symbolize that which life is supposed to be set apart from—death, lack, excess, and impurity. The sanctity of Man is enacted through endeavors to convert embodiments of deficit into something complete and whole, even if this requires negation and erasure. Therefore we might say, in response to Bellah's concerns about the ambiguities of civil religion, that the conquest of the Americas and the doctrine of Manifest Destiny have comprised religious/evangelizing and secular/imperial undertakings that share a commitment to the sacred as a subordinating and purifying force. What holds imperial projects together is a genre of the sacred that solidifies at the expense of those peoples and regions designated as perilous to cohesion and stability. Or to put this in terms closer to Wynter's language, what holds these projects together is a genre of the human propelled by a drive to separate the self-same from perilous others.

Even as Wynter acknowledges Man1 as a "religio-secular hybrid," she tends to adopt a linear secularization narrative. One notices this tendency when she uses language like "purely secularized" or "replacement" to discuss the movement from a Christian theological system of meaning to a degodded, humanist schema of representation.[30] David Kline has addressed this tension in Wynter's thought. As he points out, "when [Wynter] speaks of Man's exit from religion, she is referring primarily to the west's shift away from Christianity being the explicit frame of meaning for the genre of Man."[31] Kline reminds the reader that despite this inclination to conflate secularization with the decentering of Christian theology, Wynter suggests that autoreligiosity accompanies the transitions to Man1 and to the biocentric, Darwin-inspired Man2. As Kline describes, autoreligion names the human capacity to self-create ideas and meanings while projecting this capacity "onto transcendent or 'extrahuman' agents of determination and behavior regulation."[32] On this reading, the *natural* selection that defines Man2 is still a form of autoreligion since nature within this Darwinian framework is treated as an "objective reality of order" apart from narrative, logos, and power relations.[33] In addition, the distinction between the "selected" and "dysselected" maps onto the aforementioned divisions, including the contrast between carriers of life and signifiers of death. As Wynter puts it, the Du Boisian color line could be rearticulated and intensified by another kind of "extrahumanly . . . determined nonhomogeneity" between those selected by Evolution and those dysselected by Evolution; or those who deserve to continue living and those who do not.[34] Therefore, Wynter draws attention to affinities (and differences) between theological imaginaries that carve a line between spirit and flesh and biocentric schemas that select for a being's worthiness for life/death.

While the significance of autoreligion challenges Wynter's occasional commitment to a strong secularization narrative, we still might push further regarding the details and logistics of the religiosity of Man. In other words, more must be said regarding what ties and binds subjects to the figure and enterprise of Man, even as these attachments continue to ravage the world. One way to supplement Wynter's insights, including her understanding of symbolic systems as forms of behavior regulation, is to broach W. E. B. Du Bois's description of the religion of whiteness in his collection *Darkwater*. As J. Kameron Carter describes, this concept is situated within Du Bois's explanation of the origins of World War I, an account that underscores Europe's scramble for the possession of Africa.[35] Similarly, Du Bois's interrogation of the "soul of whiteness" responds to those who depicted the horrors and atrocities of World War I as an aberration of European civilization. For Du Bois, the "madness" of World War I was prepared for by "conquest and conquest, not in Europe, but primarily among the darker peoples of Asia and Africa."[36] As an attempt to make sense of the novelty and expansiveness of Western imperialism, in addition to the recent "conversion to whiteness," Du Bois draws on the language of religion and belief. He asks, "'But what on earth is whiteness that one should so desire it?' Then always, somehow, some way, silently but clearly, I am given to understand that whiteness is the ownership of the earth forever and ever, Amen!"[37] Whiteness for Du Bois is not reducible to skin color or pigmentation; it entails something more like a belief in "such an extraordinary dictum,"[38] an attachment to the aspiration of eternal and omnipresent rule. In other words, "the new religion of whiteness" consists of a belief structure, a set of convictions, that revolve around the superiority of European civilization and its American offspring in addition to "the doctrine of the divine right of white people to steal."[39] This religion of whiteness justifies theft and exploitation—in the name of civilization or the defense of freedom—because whiteness is a general investment in self-authorizing territorial expansion and ownership.

Not unlike Durkheim and Bellah, Du Bois contends that "a nation's religion is its life."[40] And yet for Du Bois, this life-giving force is parasitic on death and destruction. What binds and fastens people to a belief system that produces life through annihilation and conquest? How does whiteness, or the pursuit of ownership and domination, convert and pervade subjects? What kinds of rituals, micro-practices, and affective economies are involved in the sanctification of whiteness? To borrow a formulation from Charles Long, what "techniques of orientation"[41] keep populations invested in the figure of Western Man as if it is coextensive with being, value, and presence? Du Bois mentions a series of rituals and activities—including civilizing missions, sacrificial lynchings, literary practices, and film—that reproduce whiteness as the sinew of the nation (and world) and that harness desires and beliefs to property, rule, and possession. Moreover, Du Bois alludes to the piety of Western Man as a kind of "phantasy," one that positions the proprietors of civilization as "super-men and world-mastering demi-gods." As Jacques Lacan describes it, phantasy supports and structures desire; and it "is never anything more than the screen that conceals something quite primary."[42] Perhaps whiteness can be understood as a kind of fantasy that regulates desires, attachments, and cathexes while screening the traumatic kernel of this structure of fantasy. Perhaps this structure of fantasy is based on a particular image of the divine Sovereign, which imperial Man replaces after what Nietzsche calls the death of God. Like the divine Sovereign, the world-mastering demi-god is defined as a ruler, lawgiver, and owner of the earth, functions that reduce the earth to property. If the image of the world-mastering subject aligns with Wynter's description of Man, then Du Bois's reflections on religion, belief, and fantasy supplement Wynter's account by highlighting the adhesive character of whiteness and Western imperial piety. And yet Du Bois and Wynter share a sense that imperialism is largely enabled by a conception of sacrality that signifies order, the imposition of form, and whiteness (or mastery and ownership). In the rest of this essay, I show how Wynter's corpus also points toward a different kind of sacred, an unruly sacred that promises a more receptive disposition toward that which incites and exceeds mechanisms of containment.

On the Left-Hand Side: Movement, Surplus, and the Demonic Sacred

Throughout this essay, I have alluded to what Durkheim describes as the double quality of the sacred or the doubleness that inheres in the impulse to set things apart. Riffing on Durkheim's reflections, Roger Caillois underscores how, in certain cultures and languages, the same term that translates as holy or pure also means defilement or accursed.[43] As Caillois further describes this duplicity, the right-handed sacred signifies purity and goodness while the left hand is associated with illness, disorder, and being "possessed by a demon."[44] Here we need to be careful. While the strong contrast between the pure and impure sacred aligns with Wynter's attunement to the different ways that peoples and regions get carved up according to life/death, the response cannot be to merely inverse the evaluative schema. In other words, my aim is not simply to redescribe Blackness and indigeneity in terms of death and disorder, especially since this would retain a rigid contrastive logic between life and death, and order and chaos. As Caillois and Durkheim both point out, powers and objects that are venerated as protectors and benefactors can turn dangerous and vice versa. Similarly, as Wynter's work suggests, Man might be self-perceived as an agent of order and settlement, yet for Man's others, this will to order has been disordering and unsettling. And even as the slot of alterity has been consigned to symbolic death, those adversaries of Man have always cultivated practices and modes of endurance in the face of, and alongside, violence and erasure. Consequently, the demonic sacred would not only have to depart from a conception of sacrality that safeguards order and property; it would have to depart from the kinds of unyielding oppositions that Man's call to order relies on and replicates.

Wynter introduces the language of the "demonic" in her important essay, "Beyond Miranda's Meanings: Un/silencing the 'Demonic Ground' of Caliban's 'Woman.'" Building on a tradition that interprets Shakespeare's *The Tempest* as an allegory of colonial modernity, Wynter asks the reader to think beyond the illicit desires that the not-quite-human Caliban has for the sovereign Prospero's daughter, Miranda, and to contemplate the absence of "Caliban's Woman, of Caliban's physiognomically complementary mate."[45] For Wynter, this absence of Black femaleness points to a "'demonic ground' outside of our present governing system of meaning," to a field at the "threshold" of our current ordering discourses and epistemes.[46] Zakiyyah Jackson points out that this lacuna in *The Tempest* is not just "a silenced social subject"; rather, it represents "the occlusion of modes of feeling/knowing/being . . . signified by the iconicity of the 'Black female body' in the canonized discourses of Humanism."[47] These occluded modes of living and being cut against the paradigm of Man and its racial, gendered, and sexual divisions and hierarchies. As Wynter notes, the term "demonic" has a genealogy within physics that refers to "an outside" or an excess to our "consolidated field" of knowledge and being.[48] Therefore, the demonic, according to McKittrick, has been understood in ways that are not always "ecclesiastical" but in a (scientific) manner that emphasizes uncertainty, indeterminacy, and an openness to the unknown.[49] Consequently, the Black female other is a kind of icon of irrepresentability within prevailing regimes of the human; and yet this opaque figure still constitutes a central part of the project of Man (as that which cannot be assimilated and yet the object through which so much energy is spent trying to repress, keep in line, extract value from, and so on).

It is important that Wynter turns to physics and its understanding of the demonic, thereby breaking with the assumption that religion has a monopoly on this concept. Reflecting on this move in Wynter's thought, McKittrick explains that "etymologically, demonic is defined as spirits . . . capable of possessing a human being. It is attributed to the human or the object through which the spirit makes itself known, rather than the demon itself, thus identifying unusual, frenzied, fierce, and cruel human behaviors."[50] Furthermore, "demons, devils, deities, and the behavioral energies they pass on to others, are unquestionably wrapped up in religious hierarchies and the supernatural."[51] While McKittrick's insightful reading of the religious demonic is an opportunity for her to shift focus to mathematics and physics (where the demonic signifies indeterminacy and nonlinearity), I want to tarry a bit longer with the religious and the affinities between the religious and the scientific regarding the demonic.

The language that McKittrick uses—such as possession, energy, and frenzy—dovetails with Durkheim's aforementioned description of collective effervescence, those ecstatic gatherings and festivals that take the individual outside and beside itself. Durkheim acknowledges that there is an exorbitant and wild dimension to religious experience even as this volatility tends to get attached to, and captured by, stabilizing objects and symbols for the sake of communal solidarity. Yet I wonder if there is a connection between the "outside" or threshold that the demonic represents in physics and the ecstatic quality of the sacred detailed by Durkheim and his successors (Caillois and Georges Bataille, for instance). In other words, I want to examine the overlap between the ways of being/knowing/feeling that cannot be captured by prevailing epistemes and the religious exuberance that disrupts the ordinary and undermines our sense of control and (self-)possession prior to being "wrapped up in religious hierarchies." Following the work of J. Kameron Carter, I want to pursue a demonic sacred "as a kind of pathological and ek-static threshold before which other, differential and unrepresentable presences, genres or forms of life, unplottable gatherings in representation's colonizing ruins, alternative ways of being with the earth, come into view."[52] In other words, I am after those qualities and positions shared by the scientific and religious senses of the demonic—threshold, rupture, im/possibility, surplus, and unrepresentability.

Wynter gestures toward these qualities of the unruly sacred when she discusses the epistemic upheavals that befell European settlers in the fifteenth and sixteenth centuries. In her essay "1492: A New World View," she presents a "Janus-faced" perspective on the event that initiated the Spanish and Portuguese conquest of the Americas. While she delineates the "behavior-orienting" schemas and demarcations that authorized Columbus's settler aspirations, she also reminds the reader that Columbus's voyages to the Americas occurred in the midst of various crises in Euro-Christian epistemic frameworks. Wynter mentions, for instance, the emergence of Renaissance humanism and its challenge to forms of ecclesial authority; Copernicus's heliocentric discoveries that went against accepted astronomical and geographical truths; Columbus's finding that regions in the Western hemisphere deemed uninhabitable by Christian traditions were in fact habitable and populated. Even as Wynter remembers and cites the violence inscribed in the event of 1492, she also draws attention to the ruptures to dominant systems of meaning that accompanied and conditioned Columbus's voyages and encounters. These ruptures revealed the instability of governing structures of meaning in addition to the significance of human fabrication (*logos*, *mythos*) regarding the truths and norms that determine how we live, how we relate to and come to understand life. I take it that Wynter aims to underscore a tension-filled interaction between a deconstructive, disordering moment that throws a certain imaginary into disarray and the reordering of the world according to a different, yet analogous, master code of nonhomogeneity. What I want to highlight is how the disordering moment betrays an excess (both internal and external;

or an inside that pushes toward an exterior) to any prevailing epistemic paradigm. Because this excess with respect to Christian theological frameworks can be recontained by secular grammars and figures, such as Man, Wynter suggests that a certain conception of sacrality—defined by order and division—remains during the secularization of human existence. This enduring conception of sacrality is (auto)religion.

And yet what prevents Wynter from being a pessimist is her commitment to the upheaval that occurs incompletely during Columbus's epoch but that gets repeated and intensified during anticolonial and Black liberation uprisings in the twentieth century. The general upheaval to systems of knowledge that purport to be grounded in the eternal and extrahuman is more like a flickering possibility than a fulfilled experience. As Wynter puts it, "Because the mutation by which we have gradually come to secure the autonomy of the mode of cognition specific to our species in the wake of the voyage of 1492 has been only partial, and its true victory therefore remains incomplete, the completion of that first true victory is necessarily the *only* possible commemoration of 1492. Such a completion would call therefore for another such conceptual move into a 'realm beyond reason.'"[53] Notwithstanding the teleological language of "true victory" and "completion," Wynter remains open to the possibility of turning the governing system of orientation into an object that can be interrogated, deconstructed, and transfigured. In fact, she proposes "that such a 'move beyond reason' has already begun, even if still marginally so."[54] A general upheaval that parallels "the intellectual revolution of Christian humanism and humanism out of which Columbus and Copernicus's challenge to the representation systems . . . was to be effected" has been enacted, for instance, by Blacks and Native peoples as they refuse the racist grammars and violent hierarchies that have been imposed on them.[55] In this juxtaposition of two upheavals—five centuries apart—Wynter does not downplay how the consolidation of the first leads to the need for the second. At the same time, her fidelity to the threshold and the prospect of disruptions to knowledge and behavior-orienting systems is a reminder of the destabilizing energies, interactions, and modes of becoming that Man (or any congealed figure) can never fully represent, hold, or assimilate. It is a witness to the unruly and demonic; to that which frustrates the yearning for wholeness, solidity, and possession.

As I take it, the partial victories of Christian humanism and anticolonial struggle lie in the coming to critical awareness of the fabricated quality of ideas, knowledges, and arrangements that have come to appear as immutable and inevitable. While this can sound like a Hegelian narrative of freedom as self-consciousness, it is important that Wynter highlights the significance of rupture and disordering events, those qualities that depart from linear conceptions of time and human development. In other words, I am reading Wynter closer to Adorno's "consistent sense of non-identity" which avoids Hegel's will to wholeness and remains receptive to the "divergent, dissonant, and negative."[56] For Wynter, something like hope is located in the human capacity to come to terms with our twofold nature—both *bios* and *logos*; beings composed of organic matter and beings that make meaning through language. And I take it that one mode of this *bios/logos* interaction is expressed through poesis, poetics, or the ability to make and create, especially in situations marked by exorbitance and opacity. Poetics opens up the possibility of experiencing what the presiding framework of representation deems as unthinkable and heretical.[57] Here we might think of the poet Nathaniel Mackey's claim that "to poeticize or sing is to risk irrelevance, to be haunted by poetry's or music's possible irrelevance [or non-sense within a particular regime of truth]."[58] According to Wynter, "a new poetics of the *propter nos* [or We]" would be guided by a concern for "the interests both of the flesh-and-blood individual subject and of the human species as a whole, together with, increasingly, that of the interests of all other nonhuman forms of life on this planet."[59]

The new counterpoetics would involve being attuned to the social processes that bind subjects to the order of things; redefining the relationship between human and nonhuman life and these social processes; an openness to the currently unthinkable and unrepresentable. Riffing on Fanon, Wynter urges us to "introduce invention into existence"; and while invention is the "true leap," it is also the foundation-less ground for the social configurations that have become sedimented and second nature.[60] Poetics is one way that invention is introduced; it is also an enactment of the demonic energies that inundate (and activate) strategies of possession and control. If there is room for a redefined sacred in Wynter's new poetics, it would be one that veers toward the left, toward the unruly and errant, without retrieving the kinds of rigid partitions and ordering schemas that define the sanctity of Man. The unruly sacred and the flickering potential of a new poetics, of alternative ways of being and living, may be the last hope in a world that, each day, appears to approximate the descriptions of the pessimist.

Notes

1. "Donald Trump Bible: Tear Gas Used to Clear Protesters for Photo Op," *The Telegraph*, June 2, 2020, https://www.youtube.com/watch?v=AzBhYhu7NYI&ab_channel=TheTelegraph.
2. "Former Defense Secretary Mattis' Statement on Trump and Protests," CNN Politics, https://www.cnn.com/2020/06/03/politics/mattis-protests-statement/index.html.
3. "Mattis' Statement."

4. Anthea Butler provides a concise history of white evangelical racism and nationalism in her book *White Evangelical Racism: The Politics of Morality in America* (Chapel Hill: University of North Carolina Press, 2021).

5. On the relationship between religious desire and purity, see Mircea Eliade, *The Sacred and the Profane*, trans. Willard Trask (New York: Harcourt, Brace and World, 1963), 65. Tomoko Masuzawa has shown how many theorists of religion participate in the search for origins that they associate with religious life. See Masuzawa, *In Search of Dreamtime* (Chicago: University of Chicago Press, 1993).

6. My understanding of the demonic sacred is very much indebted to Katherine McKittrick's work on Sylvia Wynter. See McKittrick, *Demonic Grounds: Black Women and the Cartographies of Struggle* (Minneapolis: University of Minnesota Press, 2006), 121–42. Also see J. Kameron Carter's engagement with Wynter regarding an alternative conception of the sacred in "Black Malpractice (A Poetics of the Sacred)," *Social Text* 37, no. 2 (2019): 67–107.

7. Emile Durkheim, *The Elementary Forms of Religious Life*, trans. Karen E. Fields (New York: Free Press, 1995), 44.

8. Durkheim, 220.

9. Durkheim, 231.

10. For a helpful analysis of these two forces within Durkheim's sacred sociology, see Michèle H. Richman, *Sacred Revolutions: Durkheim and the Collège de Sociologie* (Minneapolis: University of Minnesota Press, 2002). Richman associates the effervescent quality of the sacred with the upheavals in France in 1789 and 1968.

11. Durkheim, *Elementary Forms of Religious Life*, 412.

12. While Bellah takes the name from Jean-Jacques Rousseau's *The Social Contract*, Durkheim is also behind Bellah's formulation of civil religion.

13. Robert N. Bellah, "Civil Religion in America," *Daedalus* 134, no. 4 (2005): 46.

14. Bellah, 54. Bellah analyzes these archetypes in more detail in *The Broken Covenant: American Civil Religion in Time of Trial* (Chicago: University of Chicago Press, 1975).

15. Bellah, "Civil Religion in America," 49; emphasis mine.

16. Bellah, 51.

17. See Tzvetan Todorov, *The Conquest of America: The Question of the Other*, trans. Richard Howard (Norman: University of Oklahoma Press, 1999).

18. Here I am thinking with Edward Said's response to Michael Walzer's *Exodus and Revolution* (New York: Basic Books, 1986), a book that offers a powerful account of Exodus as a paradigm for the constitution of peoplehood, liberation from tyranny, and social democratic practice. For Said, Walzer's book denies the violence directed toward the figure of the Canaanite, violence that is divinely sanctioned. See Edward Said, "Michael Walzer's 'Exodus and Revolution': A Canaanite Reading," *Arab Studies Quarterly* 8, no. 3 (1986): 289–303.

19. As Andrea Smith has pointed out, colonization is not just about the theft of land but also about the creation of "something called land" that can be stolen, related to as property, etc. See Andrea Smith, "Sovereignty as Deferred Genocide," in *Otherwise Worlds: Against Settler Colonialism and Anti-Blackness*, ed. Tiffany King, Jenell Navarro, and Andrea Smith (Durham, NC: Duke University Press, 2020), 118–19.

20. Bellah offers a rich account of the interplay between images of America as both wilderness and paradise for sixteenth- and seventeenth-century European settlers. See Bellah, *Broken Covenant*, 1–35.

21. I address these themes in my essay "The Sacred Gone Astray: Eliade, Fanon, Wynter, and the Terror of Colonial Settlement," in *Beyond Man: Race, Coloniality, and Philosophy of Religion*, ed. An Yountae and Eleanor Craig (Durham, NC: Duke University Press, 2021), 245–68.

22. McKittrick, *Demonic Grounds*, 123.

23. Wynter, "Unsettling the Coloniality of Being /Power/Truth/Freedom: Towards the Human, after Man, Its Overrepresentation—an Argument," *CR: The New Centennial Review* 3, no. 3 (2003): 264.

24. Wynter, 265–66.

25. Wynter, 266.

26. On this, see Nelson Maldonado-Torres, "Race, Religion, and Ethics in the Modern/Colonial World," *Journal of Religious Ethics* 42, no. 4 (2014): 691–711.

27. Wynter, "Unsettling the Coloniality of Being/Power/Truth/Freedom," 287.

28. See Mayra Rivera, *Poetics of the Flesh* (Durham, NC: Duke University Press, 2015), 1–14.

29. Wynter, "Unsettling the Coloniality of Being/Power/Truth/Freedom," 269.

30. See, for instance, Wynter, "1492: A New World View," in *Race, Discourse, and the Origin of the Americas: A New World View*, ed. Vera Lawrence Hyatt and Rex Nettleford (Washington, DC: Smithsonian Institution Press, 1995), 12–15.

31. David Kline, *Racism and the Weakness of Christian Identity: Religious Autoimmunity* (London: Routledge, 2020), 32.

32. Kline, 32.

33. Kline, 33.

34. Wynter, "Unsettling the Coloniality of Being/Power/Truth/Freedom," 322.

35. J. Kameron Carter, "Between W. E. B. Du Bois and Karl Barth: The Problem of Modern Political Theology," in *Race and Political Theology*, ed. Vincent W. Lloyd (Stanford, CA: Stanford University Press, 2012), 99.

36. W. E. B. Du Bois, *Darkwater: Voices from within the Veil* (Mineola, NY: Dover, 1999), 26.

37. Du Bois, 18.

38. Du Bois, 18.

39. Du Bois, 27.

40. Du Bois, 21.

41. See Charles H. Long, *Ellipsis: The Collected Writings of Charles H. Long* (New York: Bloomsbury, 2018), 26.

42. Jacques Lacan, *The Four Fundamental Concepts of Psychoanalysis: The Seminar of Jacques Lacan, Book XI*, ed. Jacques-Alain Miller, trans. Alan Sheridan (New York: W. W. Norton, 1978), 60.

43. See Roger Caillois, *Man and the Sacred*, trans. Meyer Barash (Chicago: University of Illinois Press, 2001), 35.

44. Caillois, 43.

45. Sylvia Wynter, "Afterword: Beyond Miranda's Meanings: Un/silencing the 'Demonic Ground' of Caliban's 'Woman,'" in *Out of the Kumbla: Caribbean Women and Literature*, ed. Carol Boyce Davies and Elaine Savory Fido (Trenton, NJ: Africa World, 1990), 360.

46. Wynter, "Afterword," 356.

47. Zakiyyah Iman Jackson, "'Theorizing in a Void': Sublimity, Matter, and Physics in Black Feminist Poetics," *South Atlantic Quarterly* 117, no. 3 (2018): 619.

48. Wynter, "Afterword," 364.
49. McKittrick, *Demonic Grounds*, xxiv. Also see Jackson, "Theorizing in a Void," 618.
50. McKittrick, *Demonic Grounds*, xxiv.
51. McKittrick, xxiv.
52. Carter, "Black Malpractice," 74.
53. Wynter, "1492," 40.
54. Wynter, 40.
55. Wynter, 40–41.
56. Theodor Adorno, *Negative Dialectics*, trans. E. B. Ashton (New York: Continuum, 1973), 5.
57. See Tiffany Lethabo King's analysis of Wynter in *The Black Shoals: Offshore Formations of Black and Native Studies* (Durham, NC: Duke University Press, 2019), 175–206.
58. See Nathaniel Mackey, *Splay Anthem* (New York: New Directions, 2006), xvi.
59. Wynter, "1492," 47.
60. See Wynter, "Unsettling the Coloniality of Being/Power/Truth/Freedom," 331.

8   Moving to a Realm beyond Reason: Mapping Ontological Sovereignty in Counter-worlds of Liminality

Shamara Wyllie Alhassan

Whiteness is not the measure of humanity and Europe is not the center of episteme. Stepping into that claim means abolishing disinformation campaigns of domination and mapping ontological sovereignty in lived philosophies of the subjugated Black and Brown global majority. Pan-African anticolonial socio-spiritual movements, like Rastafari, emerge from counter-worlds of liminality that comprise "the stigmatized yet powerful undertow of African religions and their cultural seedbed that had transformed itself into a current that was now neoindigenous to the Caribbean."[1] These cultural seedbeds provide navigational coordinates for charting a future outside the realms of white supremacist reason. Rooted in the philosophies emerging from these cultural seedbeds, Sylvia Wynter's literary imagination explores the contours of ontological sovereignty, a term she coined in a conversation with David Scott about her only novel, *The Hills of Hebron* (1962).

Ontological sovereignty is different from prevailing notions of economic and political sovereignty because it means moving outside the prevailing notions of the human and episteme. Wynter writes,

> We do not know about something called ontological sovereignty. And I'm being so bold as to say that in order to speak the conception of ontological sovereignty, we would have to move completely outside our present conception of what it is to be human, and therefore outside the ground of the orthodox body of knowledge which institutes and reproduces such a conception.[2]

Historically, Rastafari philosophy provided a cultural seedbed for thinking about how to live as ontologically sovereign and not adapt to the "mad" and "drunken" prevailing descriptive statements of the human and their attenuating colonial regimes of truth.[3] Rastafari philosophy created a "heresy of humanism,"[4] or an "underground cultural experience"[5] where "the blacks reinvented themselves as a We that needed no Other to constitute their Being."[6] Rejecting their alterity and engaging in the madness of socio-poiesis or the process of self-invention, Rastafari livity or lived philosophy created counter-symbolic orders of "new . . . nonadaptive mode[s] of human self-cognition" that attempt to "fully realize . . . autonomy of feelings, thoughts, [and] behaviors."[7] Inquiring into these new nonadaptive feelings, thoughts, and behaviors, as I will do in this essay, maps the ways Wynter's thought is inspired by Rastafari worldmaking strategies of the early and mid-twentieth century.

To explore these worldmaking strategies of Rastafari, I will first introduce Wynter's vast exploration of the colonization of knowledge and being; subsequently, I meditate on Wynter's exploration of counter-symbolic worlds of liminality in *The Hills of Hebron* (which was inspired, in part, by the Rastafari movement). Thinking about *Hebron* provides a strategic point of departure for mapping the inventions of those defined as "primitive" or "mal-evolved" in proximity to Christianity, which are notions that percolate through the colonial history of religious studies and the contemporary intellectual and juridical elision of Africana religious studies.

Moving to a Realm beyond Reason

> Christianity was the greatest fraud ever perpetrated on any peoples. That's why they put you away, my friend. You were dangerous. You challenged this God of theirs, went in search of this heaven that you had been offered in exchange for your malnutrition, disease, ignorance, and poverty. You wanted to feel this Heaven in your hand, see it with your eyes, not later in the by and by, but right here, right now.
>
> —SYLVIA WYNTER

Employing computer scientist Jaime Carbonell's notion of "subjective understandings,"[8] Wynter argues that, as human beings, our empirical reality and perception of the past are shaped by a "relation to specific behavior-orienting supraordinate goals and their sets of subgoals or goal-trees. . . . These goals therefore determine what is to be perceived and what not perceived."[9] Through deep study of how we know what we know (or epistemological inquiry) and how we express "empirical social affectivities" or ontological relations with other living beings, we can begin to "access ... the specific mode of 'subjective understanding' in terms of which we normally, even when dissidently, perceive our contemporary sociosystemic reality as well as conceive the past that led to it."[10] Western episteme created descriptive statements of the human that became common subjective understandings imposed on a global scale through colonialism.[11] Wynter argues that the creation of the human in the West relies on a notion of generic "Man," who is represented in the white European, secularized Christian, upper-class, property-owning, heterosexual cis-gendered male, who has women and children as dependents.

Wynter's discussion of the way societies produce descriptive statements of the human that become societal governing codes is important for understanding the logic of continued colonial rationality. Wynter argues that everything outside of the governing Christian code comes to exist in a liminal space or "space of otherness." In this code, religion becomes intertwined with the formation of the liminal category. For Wynter, Christopher Columbus's 1492 voyage marks an epistemic shift that ushers in what she terms a new "descriptive statement of the human" as Columbus moved outside of the medieval scholastic episteme and toward the Christian humanism of the *studia humanitatis*. These new humanistic ideas would be at the conceptual center of global European imperialism, racial slavery, racial capitalism, and the dehumanization of people not fitting under the rubric of prototypic humanity. With the dismantling of the theodicy of western Europe and the creation of Man, the governing code became humanity as tied to the province of rationality. On the other hand, the *space of otherness* was tied to supposed human irrationality and therefore existed as foil for the governing logic. Wynter writes,

> The secularizing formulation of a general order of existence now inscribed his (man's) identity, while a transformed version of the Judeo-Christian matrix, unlike the latter, no longer had to contend with any other possible schema, any other possible variant of *Man*, given that the latter was not over-represented, in terms of its formulation, as the human itself. As a result, all other human beings who did not look, think, and act as the peoples of Western Europe did were now to be classified not as *Enemies-of-Christ* but, rather, as the *lack of "true humanness,"* allegedly because of their lack of the Western European order of rationality (over represented as rationality in general); this, as a Lack that determined that they should be discursively and institutionally classified as Man's Human Others.[12]

During the Renaissance period of western Europe, this meant that the others of rational Man1 or *homo politicus* were defined by the expansionist ideas of the state, while retaining some of the theological governing schemas of homo religiosus.[13] In the second half of the nineteenth century at the height of racialized slavery, the idea of Man2 becomes rooted in biology along with capital accumulation, or what Wynter defines as *homo oeconomicus*, so that the *space of otherness* during this period became the Du Boisian color line: "the Color or [the] Evolved/Non-evolved line was now to be mapped upon the skin color and physiognomic differences between white and non-white."[14] Wynter thus argues that Christian man (*homo religiosus*) transforms into "rational" Man1 (*homo politicus*) and then into "biocentric" Man2, which is grounded in the "human as capital" descriptive statement of *homo oeconomicus*, which remains the overrepresented governing schema of humanity.[15] But *homo oeconomicus* never loses the theodicy that it conceals through the secularized vehicle of the state. Religion remains the root and key to the endurance of the prevailing secularized governing schema. Racism and the accumulation of capital become facets of religious belief that guide the practices of those in power.[16]

Wynter calls us to "move into a 'realm beyond reason'—one able to take our present mode of reason itself, and its system of symbolic representation and mode of subjective understanding that orient the perceptual matrices that in turn orient our behaviors—as the object of a new mode of inquiry."[17] But this move requires abolishing subjective understandings that limit the ability to accept the full humanity and counter-epistemologies of those emerging from liminality or alterity. Even though some academics are working toward this, scholarly resistance remains through the claim of ignorance. This also holds true for the field of religious studies. Religious studies, a nineteenth-century western European invention, further concretized, organized, and systematized colonial logics in what David Chidester would call an empire of citation, which served to epistemologically fortify the colonial project and legitimized Christianity as the metric upon which the metaphysical could be understood.[18] This colonial legacy continues to haunt religious studies and is the reason Dianne M. Stewart Diakité and Tracey E. Hucks coined the term "Africana religious studies" to describe a field of inquiry rooted in a rejection of epistemic racism and animated by a transdisciplinary and transnational exploration of Africana religious and spiritual practices.[19] There are scholars who are not ready to question the field's white center. It remains possible for scholars to receive a PhD in religious studies without having had to explore Africana and indigenous religious and spiritual traditions. There are still scholars of religion who question the centrality of race in the formation of our field. The American

Academy of Religion, which is the premier organization for the academic study of religion in the United States, made several statements about the need to dismantle white supremacy and rectify the historic marginalization of practitioners of Africana religions in the field. In religious studies it is not a lack of knowledge that allows constitutive codes of domination to persist—it is a lack of will to move to a realm beyond these governing schemas. This is precisely what drives my interest in the ways Rastafari influenced Wynter's ability to critique the dominant power structure and the ways Rastafari women, in particular, can provide further cultural seedbeds for mapping a realm beyond prevailing colonial rationality.

Counter-worlds of Liminality

Religious studies emerged from the bowels of racial hereditary slavery and colonialism, although many students of the field only study its emergence in the context of the nineteenth-century western European academy. The western European academy is not immune to the broader political context of transatlantic slavery and imperial expansion, which provide tacit and overt epistemological underpinnings of the academic study of religion and other formations of nineteenth-century humanistic inquiry.[20] Wynter's creative corpus centers the way counter-worlds of liminality critique empire and the nation as concepts rooted in the mad and drunken constitutive codes, categories, and discursive frames of Western episteme. Wynter argues that the Cenù Indians, in their reply to the Spanish Requisition of 1513, a document based on the Papal Bull of 1492, understood that the Pope must have been drunk when he gave their land, which he did not own, to the King of Castile, who must have been mad for receiving a gift that did not belong to the giver. The only way to make such blatant thievery legitimate was to declare all inhabitants of these lands "*inimicos Christi* (enemies of Christ). On that basis, they could then be captured, enslaved and sold within the prescriptive rules laid down by the Church with respect to what could and could not be accepted as just causes for the enslavement of others."[21] Despite the Cenù Indians' logic that the terms on which Spain legitimized colonization constituted a form of madness and drunken speech "and therefore non-sense," those terms "were to be indispensable to the specific culture-historical dynamics out of which 'Modernity,' the contemporary Caribbean, and the Americas were to emerge and on the basis of whose 'ground' Europe's conquest of the Americas was both effected and made to seem legitimate and just."[22] Religion justified, legitimated, and extended the colonial and imperial project of the state.

Working with Wynter's corpus can aid us to think about Black religious practitioners as autonomous worldmakers, rather than through Man's coding, which dismisses them as "primitive" and "mal-evolved." Indeed, while Wynter predicates the formation of modernity as rooted in this indigenous perception of madness and drunkenness, it is important to note that colonial rationality itself regarded indigenous people and Africans as outside the realms of reason and therefore lacking any vestiges of knowledge, history, or thought. Ways of knowing innovated by Black and Brown peoples were considered the discredited murmurings of the condemned. This is one reason colonial regimes weaponized colonial psychology and the mental asylum to incarcerate those who fought against or questioned the prevailing order. Attending to this history, *The Hills of Hebron*, Wynter's only novel, locates the mental asylum as a space for mapping anticolonial critique and Black political awakening. As central literary motifs in her novel, madness and drunkenness become integral to engaging the ways she thinks about the monumental task of the ontologically sovereign, who must revalorize, reconceive, remake, and renarrate their ways of being.[23]

The Hills of Hebron provides perhaps Wynter's most concrete model of engaging the imaginative Black radical religiosity of the liminal counter-world. Anthony Bogues argues,

> In Wynter's view, because human beings weave "webs of signification," then for the dominated group to assert its humanity required the creation of what she called in the 1970s, "the counter-world, the counter symbolic order" of the colonized. Wynter suggests that this "powerful symbolic counterworld . . . was reinvented in response to the forced exodus of the middle passage to the enforced diaspora in the plantation archipelago of Black America." For Wynter therefore, the major objective of *The Hills of Hebron* was an attempt to begin to describe this "counter-world," and in doing so present as allegory a different rendering of Jamaican history.[24]

However, even though she centers the liminal sphere, Wynter does not valorize it as she critiques its reenactment of power paradigms and structures of the dominant order. This tension allows Wynter to analyze how people have historically created autonomous communities and the limitations of these communities as they tried to decolonize intimate relationships. Wynter's indigenization thesis or the way she writes about Africans rehumanizing themselves and the earth by populating the land with their gods and duppies places her meditations on liminal counter-worlds firmly in the realm of Black spirituality, a liminal space too dangerous and too aberrant to be located in the prevailing governing schema.[25]

Before we delve into *The Hills of Hebron*, it is important to clarify what Wynter means by liminality and why mapping the intellectual genealogies that arise from spaces of liminality is important. Wynter leans into Ethiopian anthropologist Asmarom Legesse's notion of the liminal as the categories "that embod[y] the deviant Other to the normal identity of the society."[26] Wynter quotes Legesse as emphasizing that the "liminal person is not irrelevant to the structured community surrounding him."[27] Indeed, the liminal person is societies' "conceptual antithesis"; it is "by reference to him that the structured community defines and understands itself."[28] Legesse defines the liminal category as the antithetical space that becomes a referent for the prevailing order to define itself against. This antithetical space calls into the question the status quo and situates the space of the liminal as "the repository of the creative potential underlying human society."[29]

Wynter's use of Legesse allows her to further delineate the ways liminal and dominant societal categories create regimes of truth that govern what is considered normal/rational and abnormal/irrational. From Wynter and Legesse, we can understand colonial rationality as functioning with a series of binary logics that define legitimate or illegitimate modes of being. Legitimate modes of being confirm, expand, and reify themselves across time and space to such a great extent that they become the meaning of sanity and normality in Western episteme. Illegitimate modes of being are further erased, fragmented, pathologized, and maligned across time and space to such a great extent that they become the meaning of insanity and abnormality in Western episteme. Although each colonial empire deploys different tactics, the use of mythmaking in order to control the very interiority of a person was implemented across geopolitical imperial and colonial spaces.

As Legesse argues, people emerging from liminal spaces can use their subject position to excavate colonial rationality in order to create their own counter-worlds of existence. Frantz Fanon did this by developing a "third way" to explore the contours of humanity. He argued that alongside phylogeny and ontology there is sociogeny, which denotes the way human beings are inherently social. We form a sense of self in community with others.[30] Wynter argues that Fanon's sociogeny, or what she terms the "sociogenic principle," is the foundation of the multiplicity of "genres of being human" that have existed historically across the earth.[31] Essentially, she argues that there is no single way to be human and that there is danger in a single overrepresented narrative of humanity.[32] Single narratives of humanity construct mythologies that become part of the colonizer's identity so that their sense of self necessitates having a human Other, who is the colonized. In the case of the Papal Bull of 1492, constructing the mythology that indigenous inhabitants of the Americas and the Caribbean were enemies of Christ meant indigenous people could be enslaved, killed, and treated as less than human. Aimé Césaire arrived at an apt equation to describe the effect of colonization on identity of the colonizer/colonized in his 1955 essay *Discourse on Colonialism*. Césaire writes,

> No human contact, but relations of domination and submission which turn the colonizing man into a classroom monitor, an army sergeant, a prison guard, a slave driver, and the indigenous man into an instrument of production. My turn to state an equation: colonization = "thingification."[33]

Colonialism imposed a new cerebral and material reality by forcing colonized and colonizer to embody the myth or role created by the imperial structure. As Césaire writes, the colonizer becomes a representation of the dominant power of the state embodied in the slave driver or the police officer.[34] Wynter grew up under British imperialism in Jamaica; her intimate knowledge of colonization influenced her ability to diagnose the mythologies of empire. As Wynter describes in the interview with David Scott referenced above, "You cannot imagine today how total a system colonialism was! ... How could it ever have occurred to you then, before the anti-colonial struggles erupted, that you as a 'native' subject could take any action on your own?"[35] Conversely, Wynter describes her feeling during the time that anticolonial social movements emerged as entering a different dimension: "it was as if you were suddenly in a different dimension. ... All in all, the whole sense of activity, of a self-initiated new beginning—I would say that movement determined everything I was going to be or have been."[36] The totalizing colonial logic was unmasked by anticolonial movements that allowed for the mythology of empire to be questioned. Wynter's experiences under colonialism allow her intimate knowledge of colonized subjectivity and the psychic decolonization it takes to imagine something outside the prevailing order.

While Wynter identifies madness and drunkenness at the root of modernity, she also understands madness as a creative tool to think outside the existing governing schemas. She explores the madness of ontological sovereignty in her novel, *The Hills of Hebron*. While Wynter affirms that the concept of madness was a tool to ostracize people from the logics of western European states, she also reimagines madness as the decolonial framework upon which to imagine a new world order.[37] Lamar Jurelle Bruce argues that "madness animates—and sometimes agitates—black radical artmaking, self-making, and worldmaking. Moreover, madness becomes content, form, symbol, idiom, aesthetic, existential posture, philosophy, strategy, and energy in an enduring black radical tradition."[38]

The space of otherness is already constructed as illegitimate, so there is nothing to lose in "black radical creativity," which "signifies black expressive culture that imagines, manifests, and practices otherwise ways of doing and being—all while confounding dominant logics, subverting normative aesthetics, and eroding oppressive structures of power and feeling."[39] Wynter's choice to leverage black radical creativity through writing a novel allowed her the latitude to explore themes that have become the central animating logics of her work. In writing the novel, she seized the freedom to move slowly through the ideas and create, uninterrupted by the necessities of citation or the concise formed tempo of theatrical playwriting (another genre Wynter is familiar with).[40]

Rastafari Women's Ontological Sovereignty

Using the novel as her vehicle, and Rastafari as a source of inspiration, Wynter explored these conjoined and disparate notions of madness, colonial rationality, and the cultural seedbed of Black religiosity. Rastafari is a pan-African socio-spiritual movement that was created by Black people to affirm Black dignity, beingness, and divinity in colonial 1930s Jamaica. Locating divinity in Emperor Haile Selassie and Empress Menen Asfaw of Ethiopia, Rastafari created Black gods in human formation and embodied those gods and goddesses through the notion of InI, which means becoming one with the divine. This notion of Black people becoming divine destroyed the whiteness-as-religion order and planted the seeds for new ways of being and knowing. As she notes in her interview with Scott,

> Rastafarianism begins to become a force. You can see it in the realm of the imaginary. Because what is Rastafari doing? It is transforming symbols, it is re-semanticizing them. And by the way, what I had done with Moses in *The Hills of Hebron*, I'm pretty sure I would have had the Rastafarians in the back of my mind. Because their re-semanticizing of the meaning of blackness was already there since the thirties. But they now began to have a pervasive presence.... And so you began to get this phenomenon where radicalism begins to take on a Rastafarian face.[41]

Following Wynter, my work leans into these theorizations as a navigational compass for thinking through what it takes to live as ontologically sovereign in a counter-world of liminality. The Rastafari movement represents an experiment in this process. The audacity it took for colonized Black people in the 1930s to proclaim their freedom, denounce the British monarchy, and build autonomous Black communities in the mountains of Pinnacle, St. Catherine, Jamaica, was momentous.

Founded by Leonard and Tyneth Howell, Pinnacle in Sligoville, St. Catherine, Jamaica, was the first Rastafari commune.[42] The Howells and two thousand members of the Howellite community made Pinnacle their home in the 1940s. The Howells' audacious desire for self-determination set off a firestorm of political, economic, social, and cultural exploitation and repression, which continued into the twenty-first century. In fact, Leonard Howell was in prison when his book, *The Promised Key* (1935), which became the foundational document of Rastafari, was published. In his book, he wrote that central to the idea of Rastafari was the formation of a protected space for Black people to heal. He called this space the Balm Yard. He wrote,

> A Balm Yard is a Holy place that is wholly consecrated to God Almighty for the cleansing and healing of the nations. Where only the Holy Spirit of God alone is allowed to do the Royal work of healing. Who does the balming work? Consecrated men and women that the Holy Spirit moves upon the blazing altar of their soul and endowed them with power that they command and handle the infirmities of the nations.[43]

Howell envisioned Rastafari people as being vested with the authority to heal. Consecration was the only prerequisite for doing balm work, the work of healing. Sistren and bredren who have become consecrated or sacred through the space of Rastafari were imbued with the power to heal their physical and spiritual selves and the power to heal others. If we think about these words being published in 1935, the very idea that Black people can be sacred, that we can heal ourselves and each other is an absolute revelation in a space with totalizing white supremacist racial capitalist imperialism. The radical imaginary it took to create a space of healing where there was no place for Black people to exist except as tools of extractive labor to support the British Empire was, then and now, revolutionary. This group of Black people rejected the imposition of European imperialism without a social safety net.

But even as they developed a new language and new ways of relating to each other with love, reverence, and care, they retained some of the types of domination that ordered colonial society. Sexism is not disproportionately practiced in Rastafari, but it is an area in which the movement is still evolving, still trying to come up with new ways of building relationships beyond male domination. As a living, ever eclectic and evolving way of life, Rastafari is not static, is diverse, and is committed to constantly engaging in the self-examination process that the liminal perspective of alterity engenders. According to Imani Tafari-Ama, "the Rastafarians regard themselves as inheritors of the Maroons' freedom-fighting tradition, and the Rastafari woman is appropriately characterized as a 'lioness,' positioning rebel woman against the Babylon system."[44]

My forthcoming book argues that Rastafari women's lived philosophy or livity ensures that the Rastafari movement retains an epistemological integrity in its deployment of challenges to power. Due to Rastafari women's existence at the apex of multiple interlocking systems of domination, such as race, gender, class, and religion, sistren are uniquely positioned to experience the way power deploys itself in multiple and totalizing ways. This unique liminal perspective of alterity enables sistren to place patriarchy on the table as one of the many manifestations of power and domination that Rastafari needs to challenge as a part of dismantling western European imperial logics. Tying the destruction of patriarchy to the destruction of Western imperialism, Rastafari women are able to ensure liberation for men, women, and children. As a Rastafari woman, I am aware that not all Rastafari women agree or operationalize their unique subject position in the same way. Rastafari women in the early twentieth century transformed the realms of the possible in colonial Jamaican society by foregrounding the divine feminine and gender justice. As religious studies and Rastafari studies scholars, it is not enough to acknowledge the contributions of women; we must also condemn the disinformation of patriarchy and white supremacy and develop a citational praxis that actively attends to women's scholarship.

Ultimately, sistren created an entire way of existing in the world that sought to decolonize everything, from language to sexism. Therefore, when we think of Rastafari women, the balm yard became a space for them to breathe—and with every breath they became sacred. It was also a space to share strategies for healing, self-affirmation, and futurity. The balm yard was an ontologically sovereign decolonial imaginary that allowed for new narrations of self, which led to new spheres of reference such as a positive valuation of Black womanness, centering African freedom, and a reverence for the environment and all forms of life. Structural oppression did not overdetermine the ways Rastafari women experienced their spiritual selves. This focus on intimate healing and community building reorients us to the long legacy of Black women's healing in ritual community. Rastafari women's healing practices enabled them to become flexible, durable, and expansive enough to grow and be transformed in the process of becoming sacred.

Rastafari women like Miriam Lennox shaped the theological notions of divinity within the movement from at least the 1940s.[45] Lennox's

Ethiopianist and biblical read on the divinity of Empress Mennen Asfaw alongside Emperor Haile Selassie positioned "women and men [as] partners in a codependent arrangement that will mentally and culturally prepare them to improve their ability to overcome deprivation and resist oppression."[46] During her time at Pinnacle, Lennox learned about women's agency and independence, which was nurtured by a "matrifocal arrangement" at Pinnacle and the self-reliance that her mother, Sister Elvie, taught her. The overshadowing narrative of patriarchy in Rastafari marginalizes intergenerational commitments to women's empowerment within the movement, which can only be gleaned through Rastafari women's remarkable biographies. Dunkley writes, "Lennox's case summons us to think about ways in which other women were possibly creators of the doctrinal diversity of the early Rastafari movement."[47] As thinkers and intellectual stewards of Rastafari, women were instrumental in imagining new conceptual frameworks for divinity rooted in a divine feminine and masculine balance.

Due to the lack of archival records detailing the lives of sistren in the early years of the movement, oral histories of sistren who lived at Pinnacle help counter epistemic erasure. Through my oral historical work with the memories of sistren in 2017, I was able to learn about what life was like at Pinnacle, an outpost of Black resistance under the British Empire in the early twentieth century.[48] The life experiences of sistren form part of the tapestry of young early twentieth-century women and girls who dared to challenge British Empire and form new frameworks for Black self-determination.[49] One such woman was Mama Irone, who lived at Pinnacle until it was destroyed in the 1950s and she went to live in Spanish Town, where I interviewed her at her home in 2017. Even though she was well into her nineties when we met, she recalled vivid memories from her Howellite days. As "homo narrans," a storyteller, she responded to my questions by telling stories full of names and prescient details mixed with a witty humor. Women like her, keepers of generational knowledge, are reminders that Rastafari women have a long herstory to tell. Wynter writes that, contrary to what hegemonic understandings of being human like Christian man, rational Man1, or *homo oeconomicus* (Man2) would suggest, human beings are hybrid, part *bios* and part *mythoi*. She writes "the human as hybridly auto-instituting, languaging cum storytelling species," which allows for multiple "genres of being human" to coexist. Once we story ourselves into being,

> the study of the *Word/the mythoi* will now determine the study of the *bios/of the brain*, and this will thereby enable us to gain an external (demonic ground) perspective on the always already

storytellingly chartered/encoded discursive formations/aesthetic fields, as well as of, co-relatedly, out systems of knowledge. And, with this gain insight into how these systems of knowledge, each together with its genre-specific "truth of solidarity," all institute and stably replicate our genres of being hybridly human with the also communitarian viability of each respective societal order.[50]

Listening to the genre-specific truths of solidarity Mama Irone shared was instructive for thinking through ways in which Black people in the grip of colonialism invented themselves through the stories they told and rewired their brains in order to embody their lived philosophy or livity. In shaping the intellectual and theological foundations of the movement, Mama Irone and Miriam Lennox are examples of early twentieth-century young women who used their Rastafari identity to eschew social constraints of normative behavior and chart their own paths to self-actualization through reshaping the possible. Imagining a new world order requires new conceptual frameworks. Clinton Hutton and Nathaniel Samuel Murrell argue that Rastafari psychology was formed in the crucible of Black resistance struggles and movements that led up to the 1930s and continued long after that decade.[51] By working with a flexible temporality and ontological sovereignty, the concept of Rastafari becomes deeply intertwined with the Africana religiosity and Black radical imaginaries that made visible the unthought and created new realms of possibility for Black aliveness.[52] The transgressive *homo narrans* of Rastafari helped lay the foundation for Wynter's understanding of counter-worlds of liminality or the possibility of living in realms beyond reason.

Ontological Sovereignty in *The Hills of Hebron*

The early twentieth century marked some important transitions in the Black radical flow of ideas and the material conditions of the Caribbean. By the 1950s, just a few years after Rastafari began and Pinnacle was established, Wynter began writing *The Hills of Hebron*. The Jamaican anticolonial movement was in full swing. In an interview, she says that she and other anticolonial writers of the time wrote to "challenge the central belief system on which our societies were founded, the belief that the fact of blackness is a fact of inferiority and that of whiteness a fact of superiority."[53] By the time she published *The Hills of Hebron*, in 1962, it was the year of Jamaica's independence and the first Rastafari commune at Pinnacle had been destroyed.[54] The novel is committed to exploring the lives and descriptive statements of the human emerging from people living in the space of otherness and, specifically, the ways in which they use Black radical creativity to form liminal counter-worlds. As Anthony Bogues points out, her book, originally titled *The End of Exile*,

> was given this original title because "there is an exile thematic and therefore the motif is a quest for the Promised Land in Hebron." She also notes that the original title was indicative that the quest of the Afro-Jamaican was about "the bringing to an end the imaginative exile of the majority population of Jamaica from any overt and official connection to our original homeland—that of the systemically stigmatized (from the colonizer's perspective) 'primitive' Africa."[55]

The notion of ending the imaginative architecture of exile that epistemic racism engenders is a powerful way to understand Rastafari and Africana religions vis-à-vis the colonizer's perspective.

Originally written as a play, the novel provides a multi-standpoint critique of colonial rationality, discursive formations of madness, and the people, like Rastafari, who dared to live, create, and shape the world anew. She divides her book into four parts. The first part is entitled "Saturday," the second part is "Friday," the third part is "Night," and the last part is "Morning." I will highlight the first two sections of her novel and combine a conversation of the last two sections. Wynter locates counter-worlds of liminality in a nonlinear conception of time, in which each day or time of day encompasses many years, is told by a variety of narrators, and mostly takes place in Cockpit Centre or Hebron.

Saturday

The book opens in the midst of a crisis in Hebron, where Obadiah Brown, the Elder of the church, curses his wife, Rose, for becoming pregnant. It is implied that Obadiah broke the vow of celibacy that came with his position. Later in the book we learn, however, that Isaac, Prophet Moses's son, raped Rose. Prophet Moses was the original leader of Hebron before Obadiah took over. After Rose is cursed and banished from the church, Obadiah goes mad because a woman in the church named Sister Beatrice, who used to be a medium in Pocomania, tells him that if he curses Rose, he curses himself and everyone else at Hebron. Wynter's invocation of women practicing Pocomania as the conscience and foreteller of destiny, allows Black woman's spiritual fortune-telling traditions to take primacy in shaping the counter-world.

Subsequently, a drought occurs in Hebron and lasts for the duration of the novel until the last section when Rose's baby is born. The drought symbolizes the curse of Rose. Miss Gatha, who is the mother of Isaac, becomes the elder of the church, but she hopes when her son comes back from school, he will take over the position of church elder. She is elected primarily because the community perceives her to be the only economically sound member of the community since she was saving money for Isaac when he returned from school. Unfortunately, Isaac comes back and takes the money but does not help Hebron; instead, he leaves to go abroad. Under Miss Gatha's leadership, the church thrives because she has an acumen for organization. The critical theme in this section is women's eldership at Hebron, because normally the elder would be male in these types of communes.

While some praise Wynter for centering the important roles women occupy in spaces of liminality, there are critiques that suggest she does not go far enough in foregrounding gender issues.[56] Toland-Dix argues that "Wynter did not ... militantly introduce gender issues into her novel; she depicted gender inequalities, but without overt analysis or critique."[57] In her novel, women are important organizational strategists; they can foretell the future, and are subject to gender-based violence and dispossession. For example, in *Hebron*, Black people form the space of liminality, but within this space Black women are further ostracized due to gender oppression.

In an essay published several decades after *The Hills of Hebron*, Wynter argues that the ground Black women occupy is demonic, because they embody the outer limit of humanity not only through the experience of racialization, but also through the experience of sexism and patriarchy.[58] Experiencing their ultimate erasure through interlocking systems of domination allows liminal subjects to sensorially engage multiple resisters of the dominant power structure. Wynter posits Black women as having a unique liminal perspective:

> It is here that our situation, as members of an intelligentsia of African hereditary descent who are also women, can provide us with a liminal perspective of alterity (as the only perspective, as Asmaron Legesse argues, that can free us from the cognitive closure defining all human orders), from which to identify what the laws that govern our purposes, and thereby, our symbolically codded orders of consciousness, always culture-specific, must necessarily be.[59]

Wynter draws attention to a unique gaze Black women and Rastafari women can access as a mode for dismantling the prevailing "symbolically coded order of consciousness." Black women's unique position adds a caveat for thinking about liminal subjectivity. Wynter argues that pluri-consciousness allows the liminal subjects to question not only the prevailing orders of the dominant power structure, but also the contours of liminality within the space of the liminal.[60]

Friday

The second section of the novel goes back in time to explain the history of Prophet Moses and many of the founders who follow Prophet Moses to Hebron. At the time Prophet Moses comes to Cockpit Centre there is already a vibrant spiritual order with Obeah, Pocomania, and the colonial Wesleyan Church. Each religious or spiritual persuasion instituted a symbolic order that supported their particular response to the prevailing colonial order. For example, the Wesleyan Church advanced the colonial order by having a closed membership of colonial officials, the Brown bourgeoisie, educated elite, and a few Black entrepreneurs. On the other hand, Obeah, Pocomania, and the prophets acquired a predominantly poor Black working-class membership.

Prophet Moses comes to Cockpit Centre to "break the neck of cowardice and slavery" and "to lead the people of Cockpit Centre out of bondage."[61] He achieves his goal by identifying women who are lonely, poor, and desperate and convincing them that he has spoken to and received visions from God. He claims that God told him to gather a group of chosen people who would travel on golden chariots to heaven. Prophet Moses first gains the confidence of Liza Edwards, whom he says God revealed to him as his spiritual mother. Within a month of first arriving in the town, he then gains the confidence of other members of the community. Prophet Moses sets a date, December 31, for the travel to the Kingdom of Heaven. In the Kingdom of Heaven, the prevailing racial order will be reversed, so Black people will be the masters and white people will be the slaves. Prophet Moses inspires hundreds of people with his message and they all sell their belongings and prepare to travel to the Kingdom of Heaven. When December 31 arrives, Prophet Moses climbs to the top of a tall tree and attempts to fly off to Heaven. Unfortunately, he falls and breaks his leg. Many of his followers are disenchanted by this attempt and go back to the spiritual groups they were in before, but others become disgruntled because they already sold their belongings. Prophet Moses is arrested by the colonial regime for being a "political agitator and a lunatic,"[62] and he is taken to the mental asylum.

This story is loosely based on Alexander Bedward, who founded the Jamaica Native Baptist Free Church in late nineteenth- and early twentieth-century Jamaica. He drew followers based on incendiary anticolonial critiques and was imprisoned in the mental asylum by the colonial Jamaican government, where he later died.[63] There are also several allegorical references to the Rastafari movement and the early twentieth-century formation of Pinnacle. The Bedwardite movement provides an important precursor to the Rastafari movement and many followers of Bedward became

Rastafari. These autonomous Black communities were attempting to build a new world by upsetting colonial rationality.

As mentioned earlier in the essay, madness is a motif throughout Wynter's novel that several scholars have explored. In discussing Wynter's reflections on C. L. R. James and his engagement with the Rastafari movement, Kelly Baker Josephs writes, "being similarly situated 'outside the productive process,' both the Rastafarians and the insane—despite the obvious differences between the two groups—could conceive of and create different social structures."[64] Through her engagement with Rastafari, Wynter was able to think about the neurocreative rewiring that would necessitate the destruction of coloniality and inaugurate something new. As Amir Douglas writes, "Wynter's work propels us to engage 'mad' possibilities and otherworldly divination practices that move beyond the liminal category of the human through indigenous cultural and religious expressions."[65] Even as we engage in the creative and positive potential of madness, Mathew Arthur argues, part of the important work that Wynter does is to provide a space for thinking about the very real problem of mental health in the Caribbean and, I would add, the limited tools psychology as a medical science has innovated to grasp the neurocreative logics of those living outside prevailing logics of reason.[66]

I add to these conversations by exploring Wynter's discussion of the mental asylum. The Black radical tradition has long recognized the prison as a site for political empowerment, mobilization, and reeducation.[67] Adding to the conversation around carcerality, Wynter posits the mental asylum as a site for political awakening because it functions as the ultimate institutional space of unreason in the prevailing order. When Prophet Moses goes to the mental asylum, his doctor is a drunken Irishman, who offers blistering critiques of British colonial empire and harbors plans to overthrow the empire and free all colonial subjects. The irony here is that the doctor who is supposed to treat patient insanity launches incendiary critiques, which makes him appear mad as well. Josephs argues, "From their marginal positions, the doctor and Moses are able to see—and say—things that accepted members of society cannot."[68] The character of Dr. O'Malley thus becomes an allegory for Wynter's proclamation of drunkenness and madness leading to the development of modernity.[69] Dr. O'Malley is bitter toward the British because of Ireland's own experience with British colonialism, and he sees in Prophet Moses the same rebellious instinct that he has. Immediately, he vows to help Prophet Moses. He prescribes him a medical treatment that consists of learning how to read and write, and instructs him in literature and political philosophy so that Prophet Moses can have the tools he needs to institute a new world order.

It is important to note that Dr. O'Malley does not see Moses as equal, but he helps Moses because he views him as insane and therefore harmless. Madness makes Moses appear more benign and therefore safe to rant to about the British Empire. However, being taught how to read and write would undermine Moses's diagnosis as insane and the entire apparatus of the mental asylum. The other astute insight Wynter provides about the asylum is the fact that this is the first time Moses has had regular food and housing. Moses is able to use his position with Dr. O'Malley strategically to gain better living conditions for all prisoners in the asylum. It is important to note that the reality of poorly resourced mental health facilities in the Caribbean may not have such accommodations and food provisions as this imaginary psychiatric hospital.

Although this alliance between colonized subjects becomes the sustenance for maintaining the counter-world, Dr. O'Malley and Prophet Moses have personal investments in this process. Wynter writes that Dr. O'Malley really wants to join the British, which is why he is so bitter. Moses, in turn, wants to repair the deep-seated shame that the anti-Black order has created within him. This broad-based male inferiority is one of the deep and abiding themes of the text. Both Moses and O'Malley, and a number of other male characters in the novel, struggle with a deep sense of inadequacy that is repeatedly articulated through physical violence against women.

Moses stays in the asylum for five years. When he reemerges, he has a revelation that he should found a Kingdom of Heaven on Earth. He goes back to Liza Edwards's house and finds that the women are the ones who stayed committed to his vision, even after he fell from the tree, and have never wavered in their faith for the duration of his stay in the asylum. Eventually, Prophet Moses organizes a community of what he calls "New Believers" to journey to the mountains and create a new world order. While Moses learned from Dr. O'Malley how to read and write, he also learned about the colonial order of paperwork. He becomes invested in making sure he has a deed for the land. Around the time he is looking for a way to get a deed for the land, Gloria, a little thirteen- or fourteen-year-old girl, is raped and impregnated by the Reverend Brooke of the Wesleyan Church. Gloria's child is Rose. Prophet Moses uses this as an opportunity to proposition the Reverend Brooke to help him use his capacity to secure a land grant for Hebron in exchange for Moses's silence about the rape and pregnancy. They strike a deal and the land grant is secured through the violation of a young girl's body. This rape and subsequent baby usher in the new world order at Hebron. The violation of Black women and girls forms the demonic ground in the space of liminality and the prevailing order. There is a long history of Rastafari and Black woman intellectuals and freedom fighters writing against and challenging heteronormative patriarchy within liberation movements.[70] The development of a pluri-conceptual model of liberation not only means struggling against white supremacy, heteronormative patriarchy, or proletariat liberation, but fundamentally brings together an analysis of multiple sites of power in order to overthrow the superstructure and institute a new world order predicated upon the liminal subjectivity of Black women.

Night and Morning
In the last sections of the book, Moses crucifies himself after he goes to the market and suffers a crisis of confidence because he sees a man preaching about worker liberation and trying to encourage the town to go on strike in order to disrupt the prevailing order. The man appears to be a communist and cites religion and God as one of the tools of Empire that block workers from their liberatory potential. Moses begins to shout that what the man is saying is blasphemy because there is a Black God, not a white God. He points out that Black people removing their labor from Empire and working for themselves to establish their own counter-order by going on strike is something that he already did with the founding of Hebron, but the people of the town only recognize him as the madman who jumped out of a tree and either ignore him or become angry and throw things at him. Some people ask him, If he is the son of God, why doesn't he crucify himself? Moses suffers a crisis of conscience and decides to crucify himself, but when he is about to die, he asks his next in command to untie him from the cross because he doesn't want to die anymore. But his second in command refuses and Moses dies. Through Moses's narrative, Wynter plays with the confluence of historical erasure and the embrace of new ideas, but also with the ways in which new movements that try to undo the prevailing order are more efficient when they know their history.[71]

Conclusion

The significance of Wynter's text for religious studies, Rastafari studies, Caribbean literature and the Black radical tradition rests in her ability to center critical cultural seedbeds that form counter-symbolic orders for an emergent ontological sovereignty.[72] Rather than dismissing figures like Prophet Moses and his followers as mad, she centers them as important political and social theorists who were critical to fleshing out the contours of a realm beyond reason. Similar to the work of Therí Alyce Pickens,[73] I read Wynter's novel as critical theory, which illustrates madness as a space of creative potential that holds its own ways of knowing. In talking about the relationship between Blackness and madness, Pickens points out that these categories are "conjoined," which means that Prophet Moses's madness is symptomatic not of his time in the asylum but of his positionality in the liminal category, which affords him the disposition of "critical otherness" that enables his critique of the prevailing order.

Rastafari, Sylvia Wynter, and others living as ontologically sovereign inaugurate new narratives that don't recognize difference negatively but see collective differences as important parts of a puzzle that create a whole. Reflecting upon the courage of people who dared to move beyond the status quo and into an elsewhere, a genre of existence no longer inured to the colonial logics of the prevailing order, I am profoundly humbled. How can we learn from this in religious studies to do the work necessary to radically dismantle colonial logics still guiding the way we think, analyze, and write? The key to ridding religious studies of Man is the ability to dismantle Europe and whiteness as the center of legitimate knowledge and foreground multiple narratives of humanity and ways of knowing. This move beyond coloniality means a reorganization of knowledge, which dispenses with disciplinary or field-specific modes of inquiry. The move to a realm beyond reason centers ontological sovereignty as a mode of knowing outside of empire, inaugurates restorative healing from epistemic harm, and marshals the will needed to chart new epistemological coordinates that center the "communitarian viability" of our species and all forms of life.

Notes

1. David Scott, "The Re-enchantment of Humanism: An Interview with Sylvia Wynter," *Small Axe: A Caribbean Journal of Criticism* 8 (September 2000): 130.
2. Scott, 136.
3. Sylvia Wynter, "The Pope Must Have Been Drunk, The King of Castile a Madman: Culture as Actuality, and the Caribbean Rethinking Modernity," in *The Reordering of Culture: Latin America, the Caribbean and Canada in the Hood*, ed. Alvina Ruprecht and Cecilia Taiana (Ottawa: Carleton University Press, 1995), 28.
4. Sylvia Wynter, "Ethno or Socio Poetics," *Alcheringa/Ethnopoetics* 2, no. 2 (1976): 86.
5. Wynter, 86.
6. Wynter, 86.
7. Sylvia Wynter, "Unsettling the Coloniality of Being/Power/Truth/Freedom: Towards the Human, after Man, Its Overrepresentation—an Argument," *CR: The New Centennial Review* 3, no. 3 (2003): 331.
8. Sylvia Wynter, "1492: A New World View," in *Race, Discourse, and the Origin of the Americas*, ed. Vera Lawrence Hyatt and Rex Nettleford (Washington, DC: Smithsonian Institution Press, 1995), 12.
9. Wynter, 12.

10. Wynter, 13.

11. Wynter, "Unsettling the Coloniality of Being/Power/Truth/Freedom," 257–337.

12. Sylvia Wynter, "On How We Mistook the Map for the Territory, and Reimprisoned Ourselves in Our Unbearable Wrongness of Being, of *Desêtre*: Black Studies toward the Human Project," in *Not Only the Master's Tools: African-American Studies in Theory and Practice*, ed. Lewis R. Gordon and Jane Anna Gordon (Boulder, CO: Paradigm, 2006), 140.

13. Sylvia Wynter and Katherine McKittrick, "Unparalleled Catastrophe for Our Species? Or, to Give Humanness a Different Future: Conversations," in *Sylvia Wynter: On Being Human as Praxis*, ed. Katherine McKittrick (Durham, NC: Duke University Press, 2015), 10.

14. Wynter, "On How We Mistook the Map for the Territory," 145.

15. Wynter, "Unsettling the Coloniality of Being/Power/Truth/Freedom," 282.

16. See Anthea Butler, *White Evangelical Racism: The Politics of Morality in America* (Chapel Hill: University of North Carolina Press, 2021); and Stephen C. Finley, Biko Mandela Gray, and Lori Latrice Martin, eds., *The Religion of White Rage: White Workers, Religious Fervor, and the Myth of Black Racial Progress* (Edinburgh: Edinburgh University Press. 2020).

17. Wynter, "1492," 40.

18. See David Chidester, *Empire of Religion: Imperialism and Comparative Religion* (Chicago: University of Chicago Press 2014), 285–86; and An Yountae and Eleanor Craig, eds., *Beyond Man: Race, Coloniality, and Philosophy of Religion* (Durham, NC: Duke University Press, 2021).

19. Dianne M. Stewart Diakité and Tracey E. Hucks, "Africana Religious Studies: Toward a Transdisciplinary Agenda in an Emerging Field," *Journal of Africana Religions* 1, no.1 (2013): 28–77.

20. See Charles H. Long, *Significations: Signs, Symbols, and Images in the Interpretation of Religion*, 2nd ed. (Aurora, CO: Davies Group, 1999); Tomoko Masuzawa, *The Invention of World Religions; Or, How European Universalism Was Preserved in the Language of Pluralism* (Chicago: University of Chicago Press, 2005); Chidester, *Empire of Religion*; Lewis R. Gordon, *Disciplinary Decadence: Living Thought in Trying Times* (London: Routledge, 2006); and An and Craig, *Beyond Man*.

21. Wynter, "Pope Must Have Been Drunk," 19.

22. Wynter, 28.

23. Kelly Baker Josephs, "The Necessity for Madness: Negotiating Nation in Sylvia Wynter's *The Hills of Hebron*," in *The Caribbean Woman Writer as Scholar: Creating, Imagining, Theorizing*, ed. Keshia N. Abraham (Coconut Creek, FL: Caribbean Studies, 2009), 179–204; Carole Boyce Davies, ed., "Sylvia Wynter, 'The End of Exile': New Readings of *The Hills of Hebron*," special issue, *Interviewing the Caribbean* 8, no. 1 (2022).

24. Anthony Bogues, "Introduction: Sylvia Wynter and the Black Radical Anticolonial Intellectual Tradition: Towards a New Mode of Existence," in Sylvia Wynter, *The Hills of Hebron* (Kingston: Ian Randle, 2010), xx. Also see Sylvia Wynter, "'We Know Where We Are From': The Politics of Black Culture from Myal to Marley (1977)," in *We Must Learn to Sit Down Together and Talk about a Little Culture: Decolonising Essays, 1967–1984*, ed. Demetrius L. Eudall (Leeds, UK: Peepal Tree, 2022), 457.

25. See Sylvia Wynter, "Jonkunnu in Jamaica: Towards the Interpretation of Folk Dance as a Cultural Process," *Jamaica Journal* 4, no. 2 (1970): 34–48; and Carole Boyce

Davies, "From Masquerade to *Maskarade*: Caribbean Cultural Resistance and the Rehumanizing Project," in *Sylvia Wynter: On Being Human as Praxis,* ed. Katherine McKittrick (Durham, NC: Duke University Press, 2015), 203–25.

26. Shirley Toland-Dix, "*The Hills of Hebron*: Sylvia Wynter's Disruption of the Narrative of the Nation," *Small Axe: A Caribbean Journal of Criticism* 12, no. 1 (2008): 64.

27. Toland-Dix, 64.

28. Toland-Dix, 64.

29. Toland-Dix, 64.

30. Frantz Fanon, *Black Skin, White Masks,* trans. Richard Philcox (New York: Grove, 1952; 2008), 11.

31. Sylvia Wynter, "Towards the Sociogenic Principle: Fanon, Identity, the Puzzle of Conscious Experience, and What It Is Like to Be 'Black,'" in *National Identities and Sociopolitical Changes in Latin America,* ed. Mercedes F. Durán-Cogan and Antonio Gómez-Moriana (New York: Routledge, 2001), 31; Wynter, "On How We Mistook the Map for the Territory," 116, 117.

32. Wynter, "On How We Mistook the Map for the Territory," 117, 118.

33. Aimé Césaire, *Discourse on Colonialism,* trans. Joan Pinkham (New York: Monthly Review Press, 1955; 2001), 42.

34. Césaire, 42.

35. Scott, "Re-enchantment of Humanism," 125.

36. Scott, 125.

37. See Wynter, "The Pope Must Have Been Drunk"; Michel Foucault, *Madness and Civilization: A History of Insanity in the Age of Reason,* trans. Richard Howard (New York: Vintage Books, 1961).

38. La Marr Jurelle Bruce, *How to Go Mad without Losing Your Mind: Madness and Black Radical Creativity* (Durham, NC: Duke University Press, 2021), 5.

39. Bruce, 6.

40. *The Hills of Hebron* was originally a play before Wynter turned it into a novel. See Carole Boyce Davies, "From Masquerade to *Maskarade*."

41. Scott, "Re-enchantment of Humanism," 145.

42. Clinton A. Hutton, Michael A. Barnett, D. A. Dunkley, and Jahlani A. H. Niaah, *Leonard Percival Howell and the Genesis of Rastafari* (Kingston: University of the West Indies Press, 2015).

43. G. G. Maragh [Leonard P. Howell], *The Promised Key* (London: Forgotten Books, 1935; 2007), 9.

44. Imani Tafari-Ama, "Rastawoman as Rebel: Case Studies in Jamaica," in *Chanting Down Babylon: The Rastafari Reader,* ed. Nathaniel Samuel Murrell, William David Spencer, and Adrian Anthony McFarlane (Philadelphia: Temple University Press, 1998), 90.

45. D. A. Dunkley, *Women and Resistance in the Early Rastafari Movement* (Baton Rouge: Louisiana State University Press, 2021), 78.

46. Dunkley, 59.

47. Dunkley, 78.

48. Shamara Wyllie Alhassan, "Rastafari Women's Early-Twentieth-Century World-Making," Out There: Perspectives on the Study of Black Metaphysical Religion, *The Immanent Frame: Secularism, Religion, and the Public Sphere,* April 1, 2022, https://tif.ssrc.org/2022/04/01/rastafari-womens-early-twentieth-century-world-making/.

49. Saidiya V. Hartman, *Wayward Lives, Beautiful Experiments* (New York: W. W. Norton, 2019).

50. Wynter and McKittrick, "Unparalleled Catastrophe for Our Species," 32.

51. Clinton A. Hutton and Nathaniel Samuel Murrell, "Rastas' Psychology of Blackness, Resistance, and Somebodiness," in *Chanting Down Babylon: The Rastafari Reader*, ed. Nathaniel Samuel Murrell, William David Spencer, and Adrian Anthony McFarlane (Philadelphia: Temple University Press, 1998), 36–54.

52. Kevin Quashie, *Black Aliveness, or A Poetics of Being* (Durham, NC: Duke University Press, 2021).

53. Scott, "Re-enchantment of Humanism," 134.

54. Bogues, "Introduction," ix–xxviii.

55. Bogues, xiv.

56. Toland-Dix, "Sylvia Wynter's Disruption," 62.

57. Toland-Dix, 62.

58. Sylvia Wynter, "Afterword: Beyond Miranda's Meanings: Un/silencing the 'Demonic Ground' of Caliban's 'Woman,'" in *Out of the Kumbla: Caribbean Women and Literature,* ed. Carole Boyce Davies and Elaine Savory Fido (Trenton, NJ: African World, 1990), 356.

59. Sylvia Wynter, "'Genital Mutilation' or 'Symbolic Birth'? Female Circumcision, Lost Origins and the Aculturalism of Feminist/Western Thought," *Case Western Reserve Law Review* 47, no. 2 (1997): 547.

60. Sylvia Wynter, "Beyond the Categories of the Master Conception: The Counter-Doctrine of the Jamesian Poiesis," in *C. L. R. James's Caribbean*, ed. Paget Henry and Paul Buhle (Durham, NC: Duke University Press, 1992), 63, 69.

61. Wynter, *Hills of Hebron*, 105.

62. Wynter, 118.

63. Veront M. Satchell, "Early Stirrings of Black Nationalism in Colonial Jamaica: Alexander Bedward of the Jamaica Native Baptist Free Church 1889–1921," *Journal of Caribbean History* 38, no. 1 (2004): 75–106.

64. Josephs, "Necessity for Madness."

65. Amir Douglas, "Wynter's New Modes of Being: 'Mad' Possibilities," *Interviewing the Caribbean* 8, no. 1 (2022): 74.

66. Mathew Kennedy Arthur, "'Madness' in *The Hills of Hebron*," *Interviewing the Caribbean* 8, no. 1 (2022): 64–68.

67. Stephen Wilson, Dylan Rodriguez, Joy James, et al., "The Roots of the 'Imprisoned Black Radical Tradition,'" *Black Perspectives*, from: African American Intellectual History Society (AAIHS), August 24, 2020, https://www.aaihs.org/the-roots-of-the-imprisoned-black-radical-tradition/#:~:text=As%20soon%20as%20the%20colonial,of%20incarcerated%2Fimprisoned%20Black%20radicalisms.

68. Josephs, "Necessity for Madness," 179–204.

69. Wynter, "Pope Must Have Been Drunk," 28.

70. Anne Moody, *Coming of Age in Mississippi: The Classic Autobiography of Growing Up Poor and Black in the Rural South* (New York: Doubleday Dell, 1968; 1997); Francis Beale, "Double Jeopardy: To Be Black and Female," in *The Black Woman: An Anthology*, ed. Toni Cade Bambara (New York: Washington Square, 1970); Denise Lynn, "The Historical Erasure of Violence against Black Women," *Black Perspectives*, from: African American Intellectual History Society, December 20, 2018, https://www.aaihs.org/top-10-of-2018-7-the-historical-erasure-of-violence-against-black-women/.

71. This is not an exhaustive read of the narrative arc in *The Hills of Hebron* or even the main characters. Please see Carole Boyce Davies's recent edited collection "Sylvia Wynter, 'The End of Exile.'"

72. Anthony Bogues, *Black Heretics, Black Prophets: Radical Political Intellectuals* (New York: Routledge, 2003).

73. Therí Alyce Pickens, *Black Madness :: Mad Blackness* (Durham, NC: Duke University Press, 2019).

Coda: Nuiscientia

Anthony Bayani Rodriguez

Scientific people know very well that time is only a kind of space. We can move forward and backward in time just as we can move forward and backward in space. To prove this theory, I invented a machine to travel through time. If you pressed one lever, the machine went back into the past. If you pressed the other lever, the machine glided forward into the future. With this machine, I set out to explore time.[1]

These opening lines to a 1956 comic book adaptation of H. G. Wells's *The Time Machine* sparked an eleven-year-old boy's obsession with Time. For nearly a year, nothing preoccupied his imagination more than the night his father lay down beside his mother, closed his eyes, and quietly succumbed to an undiagnosed heart condition. In the following months the boy felt as if he were "stuck in a bad dream," and he pored through the comics, novels, and science magazines he had collected with his father as a way to escape. He was especially mesmerized by science fiction's stories of distant worlds, advanced technologies, and alternate realities. They captivated his imagination the way his father (a self-taught electronics wiz) had when they would sit and chat beside their homemade crystal radio, and rummage through boxes of wires, components, and tools. It was not until *The Time Machine*, however, that it occurred to him that science, let alone science fiction, might hold a solution for his predicament. The image of a man entering his time machine was dumbfounding. "That time is only a kind of space" was nothing short of a "life-altering discovery." If time is a kind of space, what would he need to traverse it? If time is a kind of space, might there be more than one way to occupy it? It was at this moment that the boy decided to find out with the greatest possible certainty whether time travel was more than fiction. And should there be no cosmic laws prohibiting it, he was determined to build himself a time machine.

In 2002, fifty of the world's leading physicists convened in Washington, DC, for the third biennial conference of the International Association for Relativistic Dynamics. Among them was Ronald Mallett, a theoretical physicist known for his controversial research on the possibilities of time travel. During the nearly five decades since his father's death, Mallett had established himself in the world of "scientific people," and was finally prepared to share his life's work with the public. Accompanied by diagrams, illustrations, and proofs of his calculations, Mallett explained by way of Einstein and Gödel why he was convinced that space and time could be manipulated to make going back in time possible, along with a theoretical model for a functioning time machine. Mallett had long accepted that thinking against the scientific orthodoxies and conventions of his day was likely to be seen as crazy enough, and to do so as a Black scientist would be "crazy crazy." He shared his findings and topped off his presentation with a confession: his lifelong commitment to science, his inquiries as a theoretical physicist, and ultimately his theory of time travel, had never ceased to be motivated by a childhood wish to save his father's life. In subsequent tests, Mallett realized that although his design for a time machine could theoretically make it possible to go back to the past, this sort of "time travel" could only occur within a "closed loop" of timespace of such minuscule scale that it would be perceptible only under extremely controlled conditions. The earliest "past" within this closed loop of timespace would furthermore be confined to the instant the machine is turned ON, and no earlier.

Mallett brought his obsession with Time from the Bronx to the university, where it became the basis for a professional life of study. In academia he took refuge in a *studia* with an entire field devoted to understanding the nature of Time. This was, in his view, the perfect "cover" to pursue his childhood mission. Two decades since he presented the sum of his life's work, dismissals of Mallett's research have not stifled interest in the scientific implications of his theories. The prospect that Mallett's time machine could soon be more than a theoretical model is still considered as far-fetched today as it was when he first proposed it. But even critics of his calculations concede that his time machine is plausible according to widely accepted theories of space-time relativity and quantum mechanics. Since revealing his time machine and the childhood wish behind his work, Mallett maintains that time travel could one day be a reality. And he has added to his findings what he considers his most important discovery: "*Time is one of the most important things that we have, and I think we need to realize, even without time travel, how precious it is."*[2]

The validity of Mallett's theories will ultimately be determined by the theoretical status quo of his present and future colleagues. However, whether or not his dreams of time travel ever come true is inconsequential to the epistemic implications of being a nuisance to the disciplinary divisions of modern academic knowledge. These disciplines would deem the critical writings of a literary scholar, playwright, cultural theorist, and Black studies professor extraneous to the professional reverberations of a rogue theoretical physicist's unsettling findings on the nature of timespace. Nevertheless, Sylvia Wynter's critical scholarship since the 1950s represents the most extensive excavation of the epistemic genealogy of our "now globally institutionalized order of knowledge." Among her findings is an epistemic impasse in our present system of knowledge that requires a "far-reaching transformation of knowledge . . . pari passu with a new mutation of the answer (its "descriptive statement") that we give to the question as to *who as humans we are.*"[3] "Our present system of knowledge," she argues, "is based on the premise that the human is, like all purely biological species, a natural organism; or, the human is defined biocentrically and therefore exists, as such, in a relationship of pure continuity with all other living beings (rather than in one of both continuity and discontinuity)."[4] By relentlessly questioning the orthodoxies of modern forms of "knowledge" writ large, Wynter's critical writings encourage epistemic disobedience. Her work has proven relevant to the intellectual struggles of decolonial scholars across the disciplinary boundaries of academia, and furthermore has inspired pioneering experiments in genre, aesthetic theory, and social criticism by several visual artists, performers, and writers.

Wynter's excavations of the origins and implications of our present order of knowledge extend from a Caribbean tradition of anticolonial critique inspired by the unprecedented wave of mass uprisings and liberation struggles of colonized, structurally marginalized, socially dyselected, and (in her words) "narratively condemned" peoples during the twentieth century. It is by way of Martinician writer and anticolonialist Aimé Césaire that Wynter gestures toward the possibility of a critical study of the "nature" of Time, beyond our present disciplinary divisions. Little more than a decade before Mallett's encounter with *The Time Machine*, Césaire wrote the treatise "Poetry and Knowledge," in which he argued that the creation of new ways of thinking, new types of knowledge, and a new form of humanism "made to the measure of the world" was as much an endeavor for the scientist and the politician as it was for the poet, fiction writer, and artist.[5] By 1944, the reverberations of this thread of his treatise on knowledge were palpable in the writings of critical intellectuals across the African diaspora that would later be associated with the political-cultural discourse of Négritude.

Wynter calls on Césaire not simply because of his profound influence on the political imaginations of an important generation of anticolonial writers, artists, and social theorists. She also sees the radical potential of Césaire's characterization of the poetic and the scientific as more intimately linked than the modern episteme suggests, which is as blasphemous a notion today as it was when he first proposed it. Her advocacy of Césaire's vision of a "new science" in which the "study of the Word informs the study of Nature" extends from an intellectual life which, from her earliest memories as a student in colonial Jamaica, compelled her to question the forms, methods, imperatives, and disciplinary boundaries of "knowledge" formalized and sanctified by modern academia.

Like many anticolonial intellectuals, Wynter grew up in the Caribbean during the decisive decades of mass uprisings that led to regionwide national independence struggles in the 1960s. Her experience of modern academia began with a colonial system of education whose curriculum was based on the theological, historical, geographical, and cultural traditions of an imperial order, which appeared far more resilient to the disturbances of those "order-overturning" movements "from below" than the colonial system of government itself. Postwar London was an important crossroads for migrants, exiles, and dissidents from across the colonized world who helped issue into existence a new era of self-identified "Black" art, literature, scholarship, and activism. It was in London, during the 1950s, that Wynter discovered a "wealth of knowledge" whose potential relevance to Caribbean people (as a *tradition*) could only be fully understood if historicized on its own terms. Her formal studies of the literature of Golden Age Spain at King's College furthermore "offered a path to understanding the objectively instituted colonial and colonizing order of consciousness. It would be within the system of meaning produced by this order of consciousness that subjects of imperial Spain and England would have been instituted and their social orders legitimated."[6] Her studies of literature in London coincided with intellectual shifts in the academic study of literature, in which "the traditional Euro-centered discipline of literature/literary criticism began to reformulate itself in the more globally inclusive terms of 'literary studies' . . . in the wake of the then ongoing successes of the global anti-colonial struggles, upon which followed an explosion of new literatures, including those of the Anglophone West Indies [and/or Caribbean]."[7] This marked a pivotal moment early on in her academic life in which she recalls that "the imperative of my own overall problematic was to push me, from then on, towards what was to be a more radically far-reaching conception, beyond its present disciplinary boundaries, of literary studies itself."[8]

Throughout the 1960s, Wynter devoted most of her efforts as a writer toward the cultural front of postindependence decolonization. The significance of fiction-writing to the development of Wynter's critical thought, from the 1960s onward, resonates with the creative endeavors of radical Black writers, public intellectuals, and activists throughout the twentieth century. Some of Wynter's early literary contributions to postindependence critical intellectual culture arrived in the form of plays she wrote for the Jamaican national stage. She championed the creative efforts of West Indian activists, students, writers, and artists; she also wrote several plays that centered the perspective of the region's Black peasant majority, and she published numerous essays that excavated the long submerged cultural histories of the West Indies. Traces of her later critiques of knowledge appear when Isaac—the successor of a fictional formerly enslaved revivalist community in her 1962 Jamaican novel *The Hills of Hebron*—leaves his village intent on educating himself at the newly founded college in Kingston. There he is surrounded by indifference to the plight of his people on the part of his peers, his university, and its order of knowledge. Consumed by the shame of being a nuisance in the world of academe and the world of his kin, Isaac ends his studies and chooses to live in exile rather than return to Hebron.

As a lecturer for the Department of Spanish at the University of the West Indies' Mona campus, from 1963 to 1971, Wynter advanced her critique of knowledge to resist an intellectual climate where one of the top priorities was to train young Jamaicans in disciplines, technologies, and forms of literacy, which would advance the development of the newly independent island nation. UWI's first cohort of students in 1948 was composed exclusively of medical students who became the resident doctors at the newly established University Hospital of the West Indies. In 1949, several more students were admitted into UWI's medical school, as well as to a newly minted three-year degree program in the "Natural Sciences." From 1948 to 1962, the UWI Mona campus trained a generation of young professionals in scientific and social scientific disciplines that supported the economic development of Jamaica. Issues of leftist academic journals like *New World Quarterly* and conservative journals like *The Caribbean Quarterly* frequently included essays on economic development, Caribbean history, and literary studies that were interwoven with articles that presented new data on topics ranging from the chemical composition of arable land, to the nutritional content of the average Jamaican child. Advancing the scientific study of the Caribbean islands as geographically and ecologically distinct "national" units was of paramount concern for nationalists and colonial governments alike.

Leading up to Jamaican independence, Wynter thought of herself primarily as a fiction writer—a dramatist, a playwright, a novelist. But as doctors, chemists, physicists, botanists, and engineers were compiling new data and producing new "empirical" knowledge in an effort to serve the new reality of *nationhood*, Wynter was becoming more and more politically invested in the importance of "re-storying" the history of the Caribbean from the perspective of its Black majority. This is not to say that she gave up on fiction. Rather, like her colleagues at UWI who were busy at work applying various forms of scientific research toward the advancement of their respective islands, she wanted to direct her efforts as a writer toward discovering new knowledge that would be valuable for the Black majority of the Caribbean archipelago in the coming decades of the postcolonial age. Wynter joined a generation of Afro-Caribbean intellectuals who sought to reinterpret the history of Western modernity from the perspective of the plantation system of the ex-slave archipelago of the Americas, and "to re-represent the lives and social worlds of the majority of its people."[9] This led to the establishment of unprecedented cultural formations like the Caribbean Artists Movement, the establishment of a number of journals dedicated to new scholarship on Afro-Jamaican culture and history (*Savacou*, *Jamaica Journal*), and the formation of radical intellectual organizations like the New World Group.

Wynter continued to expand her critical inquiries of knowledge during the early 1970s by sharing her work with colleagues of various disciplines and participating in campus movements that demanded the recognition of new fields of study with relevance to structurally marginalized people. In 1973, Wynter went to Mexico City to attend an international conference of nearly five thousand scientists, engineers, government officials, representatives of business and industry, and science journalists. She was the only literary scholar to present in those two weeks, and she delivered a paper titled "Culture and Dependency: The Colonization of Consciousness." The conference had been thwarted from the very first day due to mounting criticisms of its avoidance of "political issues," their attempts to silence anti-imperialist perspectives, and the presence of researchers with ties to the US government. This was set off by a contingent of Marxist scientists and engineers from the United States who came to the conference uninvited, and declared that "the focus of world science has to change, as it has changed in the past. But the new science which will be developed in the Third World cannot and must not copy the bourgeois science which it displaces. We will make a new science whose form and content form an integrated part of the struggle for human liberation."[10] Her critical dialogue with scholars in the sciences reached new heights when she went to Stanford University in 1977. The campus in Palo Alto would become the home for groundbreaking studies of the biochemical mechanisms of the brain, the human genome, climate change, artificial intelligence, and computer engineering. It was amidst these breakthroughs in science that Wynter turned her attention toward an argument for a tradition of epistemic disobedience/heresy/nuisance, in which critical intellectuals from across the disciplinary map—from Elsa Goveia to David Bohm—are entangled in an epochal project to unsettle modern knowledge in and of itself.

Wynter's advocacy of "a new Science of the Human in which the study of the Word informs the Study of Nature" requires us to think beyond our disciplines and across the boundaries of intellectual and cultural traditions. Her inquiries into the history of modernity's dominant conceptions and categorical divisions of knowledge remind us that, from its very beginnings, modern academic/scientific pursuits to understand "the laws of nature" are irreducible to investigations of physics, material properties, chemical composition, biology, mathematics, or measurable quanta. Her work calls for radical rethinking of *studia* in itself as part of the epistemic leap that a new science of the human would require. In 1983, little more than six years after accepting a full-time position as a professor of Spanish literature at Stanford, she divulged in a public radio interview: "I believe that we have to rewrite knowledge, create a new synthetic approach.... We in the literary humanities have been sitting on a growing mountain of data. It is we, you know, who are the missing link to the mind-brain problem.... We hold the clue to the functioning of the systems of configuring representations [which] map on to the neurophysiological machinery of our brains to create our shared modes of 'mind.'"[11] Both her writings and her writing life should provide reassurance that it is not only permissible but urgently necessary to subject all forms of knowledge to critical inquiry—including the permissible scales, units of measurement, conceptual categories, and laws of nature, which underlie everything from the study of the history of our species to the study of the physics of timespace.

Notes

1. "The Time Machine," *Classics Illustrated*, no. 133 (1956): 1.
2. Quoted in Liz Shemaria, "How to Bend Time," *Maize*, January 31, 2020, https://www.maize.io/magazine/build-time-machine/
3. Sylvia Wynter and Katherine McKittrick, "Unparalleled Catastrophe for Our Species? Or, to Give Humanness a Different Future: Conversations," in *Sylvia Wynter:*

On Being Human as Praxis, ed. Katherine McKittrick (Durham, NC: Duke University Press, 2015), 24.

4. Wynter and McKittrick, 16–17.

5. Aimé Césaire, "Poetry and Knowledge," in *Lyric and Dramatic Poetry, 1946–82* (Charlottesville: University of Virginia Press, 1990), xliii.

6. Sylvia Wynter, *We Must Learn to Sit Down Together and Talk about a Little Culture: Decolonising Essays, 1967–1984*, ed. Demetrius L. Eudell (Leeds, UK: Peepal Tree, 2022), 9.

7. Wynter, 10.

8. Wynter, 10.

9. Quoted in Demetrius L. Eudell, "Afterword: Toward Aimé Césaire's 'Humanism Made to the Measure of the World,'" in *The Hills of Hebron, by Sylvia Wynter* (Kingston: Ian Randle, 2010), 311.

10. "Toward an Anti-imperialist Science," *Science for the People* 5, no. 5 (September 1973): 19.

11. Sylvia Wynter, interview by Donald Stokes, *Profiles of Stanford Faculty and Staff*, Stanford University, 1985, audio cassette, Stanford Digital Repository, https://purl.stanford.edu/ws562qn9854.

Acknowledgments

This book began as a wildcard session at the American Academy of Religion, in the Fall of 2018. We'd like to thank An Yountae for his wonderful response to very early iterations of some of this book's contributions. The seeds of this book lay earlier and elsewhere, however: in the African American Religion PhD program at Rice University in Houston, Texas, where we met and worked under the guidance of Anthony Pinn. We'd like to thank Dr. Pinn for his unwavering support of this book and his help in navigating the unfamiliar roads of publishing and editing.

We are incredibly grateful to the following collaborators: our contributors, who trusted two young academics with their innovative, beautiful, challenging work; Richard Morrison, our editor at Fordham University Press, who took on this chance; our peer reviewers, who invited us to follow Sylvia Wynter in thinking more thoroughly about disciplinary commitments, boundaries, and problems; George Kafka, who expertly proofread the entire manuscript; and Nancy Basmajian, for her keen eye and sharp copyediting.

Lastly, we sincerely thank Ellen Gallagher, her gallery Hauser & Wirth, and her artist liaison, Stefan Zebrowski-Rubin, for providing us permission to use her recent painting *Ecstatic Draught of Fishes* (2022) as the cover of the book. A Black American artist who lives and works between New York City and Rotterdam, Gallagher's work charts unknown, unfamiliar underwater worlds. She began this pursuit in her famous and ongoing series titled "Watery Ecstatic," a collection of films, paintings, drawings, and reliefs (since 2001; see chapter 3 of this volume). The painting on the cover is part of a newer series called the "Ecstatic Draught of Fishes" (since 2019), but likewise finds inspiration in a myth developed by Drexciya in the 1990s. In albums such as *Deep Sea Dweller* and *The Quest*, the Detroit-based techno-duo brought their listeners to an underwater city called Drexciya. This "bubble Metropolis" is home to the Drexciyans, an underwater race that descended from the pregnant enslaved Africans that the crew of slaving vessels had thrown overboard during the Middle Passage. As Drexciyans, they live and thrive; for Gallagher, as for many other Black American artists, the ocean is at once a site of terror and a locale of possibility. But if Drexciya's relentless synths plunged us deep into the ocean, the many shades of brown, red, maroon, and orange in Gallagher's painting guide us all the way to the seabed, seemingly teeming with life. The nine figures are, in turn, reminiscent of Fang figures, sculptures made by the Fang people of Cameroon and Gabon. In this painting—as in all her work—Gallagher obscures and troubles the distinctions between history and myth, nature and culture, surface and depth. As such, her work can be seen as a visual attempt at Sylvia Wynter's "new science of the word"—and, because of that, a fitting image for *Words Made Flesh: Sylvia Wynter and Religion*.[1]

Notes

1. Drexciya is also mentioned as inspiration for the conversations between Sylvia Wynter and Katherine McKittrick that would become the much-read contribution "Unparalleled Catastrophe for Our Species? Or, to Give Humanness a Different Future" (see page 9). The first essay of McKittrick's groundbreaking volume *Sylvia Wynter: On Being Human as Praxis*, that contribution is also frequently cited in the volume before you.

Bibliography

Abímbọlá, Wande. "Ìwàpẹlẹ: The Concept of Good Character in Ifá Literary Corpus." In *Yorùbá Oral Tradition,* edited by W. Abímbọlá, 387–420. Ifẹ: University of Ifẹ, 1975.
Abiọdun, Rowland. *Yoruba Art and Language: Seeking the African in African Art.* Cambridge: Cambridge University Press, 2014.
Adichie, Chimamanda Ngozi. "The Danger of a Single Story." *TED Talks,* July 2009. https://www.ted.com/talks/chimamanda_ngozi_adichie_the_danger _of_a_single_story/transcript?language=en.
Adorno, Theodor. *Negative Dialectics.* Translated by E. B. Ashton. New York: Continuum, 1973.
Agamben, Giorgio. *The Kingdom and the Glory: For a Theological Genealogy of Economy and Government (Homo Sacer II).* Translated by Lorenzo Chiesa and Matteo Mandarini. Stanford, CA: Stanford University Press, 2011.
Alagraa, Bedour. "The Interminable Catastrophe." *Offshoot,* March 1, 2021. https://offshootjournal.org/the-interminable-catastrophe/.
———. "What Will Be the Cure? A Conversation with Sylvia Wynter." *Offshoot,* January 7, 2021. https://offshootjournal.org/what-will-be-the-cure-a -conversation-with-sylvia-wynter/.
al-ʿArabī, Ibn. *The Ringstones of Wisdom.* Translated by Caner Dagli. Chicago: Kazi, 2004.
Alexander, M. Jacqui. *Pedagogies of Crossing: Meditations on Feminism, Sexual Politics, Memory, and the Sacred.* Durham, NC: Duke University Press, 2005.
Alhassan, Shamara Wyllie. "Rastafari Women's Early-Twentieth-Century World-Making." Out There: Perspectives on the Study of Black Metaphysical Religion. *The Immanent Frame: Secularism, Religion, and the Public Sphere,*

April 1, 2022. https://tif.ssrc.org/2022/04/01/rastafari-womens-early-twentieth-century-world-making/.

Ambroise, Jason L. R. "Biocentrism, Neo-Ptolemaicism, and E. O. Wilson's *Consilience*: A Contemporary Example of 'Saving the Phenomenon' of Man, in the Name of the Human." In *After Man, towards the Human: Critical Essays on Sylvia Wynter*, edited by Anthony Bogues, 209–36. Kingston: Ian Randle, 2006.

Anidjar, Gil. "Secularism." *Critical Inquiry* 33 (2006): 52–77.

An Yountae. *The Coloniality of the Secular: Race, Religion, and Poetics of World-Making*. Durham, NC: Duke University Press, 2024.

———. "A Decolonial Theory of Religion: Race, Coloniality, and Secularity in the Americas." *Journal of the American Academy of Religion* 88, no. 4 (2020): 947–80.

An Yountae and Eleanor Craig, eds. *Beyond Man: Race, Coloniality, and Philosophy of Religion*. Durham, NC: Duke University Press, 2021.

Aristotle. *The Politics*. Translated by Ernest Barker. Revised and with an introduction and notes by R. F. Stalley. Oxford: Oxford University Press, 2009.

Arthur, Matthew Kennedy. "'Madness' in *The Hills of Hebron*." *Interviewing the Caribbean* 8, no. 1 (2022).

Asad, Talal. *Formations of the Secular: Christianity, Islam, Modernity*. Stanford, CA: Stanford University Press, 2003.

———. *Genealogies of Religion: Discipline and Reasons of Power in Christianity and Islam*. Baltimore: Johns Hopkins University Press, 1993.

Augustine of Hippo. *The Enchiridion on Faith, Hope, and Love*. Edited by Henry Paolucci. South Bend, IN: Regnery/Gateway, 1961.

Azoulay, Ariella Aïsha. "Letter to Sylvia Wynter." *The Funambulist* 30 (2020). https://thefunambulist.net/magazine/reparations/open-letter-to-sylvia-wynter-unlearning-the-disappearance-of-jews-from-africa-by-ariella-aisha-azoulay.

Bakker, Justine M. "Blue Black Ecstasy: Ellen Gallagher's Watery Ecstatic, Oceanic Feeling, and Mysticism in the Flesh." *Journal of the American Academy of Religion* 91, no. 2 (2023): 302–25.

———. "Locating the Oceanic in Sylvia Wynter's 'Demonic Ground.'" *Journal for Cultural and Religious Theory* 21, no. 1 (2022): 1–22.

———. "'The Vibrations Are Different Here': Parareligious Stories in the African Diaspora." PhD diss., Rice University, 2020.

Barber, Karin. "How Man Makes God in West Africa: Yoruba Attitudes towards the *Orisa*." *Africa: Journal of the International African Institute* 51, no. 3 (1981): 724–45.

Barnes, Natasha. *Cultural Conundrums: Gender, Race, Nation, and the Making of Caribbean Cultural Politics*. Ann Arbor: University of Michigan Press, 2006.

Bashier, Samier. *Ibn al-ʿArabī's Barzakh: The Concept of the Limit and the Relationship between God and the World*. Albany: State University of New York Press, 2004.

Beale, Francis. "Double Jeopardy: To Be Black and Female." In *The Black Woman: An Anthology*, edited by Toni Cade Bambara, 109–22. New York: Washington Square, 1970.
Beier, Ulli, and Wọle Ṣoyinka. "Wole Soyinka on Yoruba Religion: A Conversation with Ulli Beier." *Isokan Yoruba Magazine* 3, no. 3 (1997): 1–36.
Bellah, Robert N. *The Broken Covenant: American Civil Religion in Time of Trial*. Chicago: University of Chicago Press, 1975.
———. "Civil Religion in America." *Daedalus* 134, no. 4 (2005): 1–21.
Benjamin, Ruha. "Assessing Risk, Automating Racism." *Science* 366, no. 6464 (2019): 421–22.
———. *Race after Technology: Abolitionist Tools for the New Jim Code*. Cambridge: Polity, 2019.
Benson, LeGrace. "'Qismat' of the Names of Allah in Haitian Vodou." *Journal of Haitian Studies* 8, no. 2 (2002): 160–64.
Benthall, Jonathan. *Returning to Religion: Why a Secular Age Is Haunted by Faith*. London: I. B. Tauris, 2008.
Benveniste, Émile. *Indo-European Language and Society*. Translated by Elizabeth Palmer. Miami, FL: University of Miami Press, 1973.
Berry, Ellen E., Kent Johnson, and Anesa Miller-Pogacar. "Postcommunist Postmodernism: Interview with Mikhail Epstein." *Common Knowledge* 2, no. 3 (1993): 103–18.
Bey, Marquis. *The Problem of the Negro as a Problem for Gender*. Minneapolis: University of Minnesota Press, 2020.
Bleichmar, Daniela. *Visible Empire: Botanical Expeditions and Visual Culture in the Hispanic Enlightenment*. Chicago: University of Chicago Press, 2012.
Bloch, Ernst. *Atheism in Christianity: The Religion of the Exodus and the Kingdom*. Translated by J. T. Swann. New York: Verso Books, 2009; 1972.
Bogues, Anthony. *Black Heretics, Black Prophets: Radical Political Intellectuals*. New York: Routledge, 2003.
———. "The Human, Knowledge and the Word: Reflecting on Sylvia Wynter." In *After Man, towards the Human: Critical Essays on Sylvia Wynter*, edited by Anthony Bogues, 315–38. Kingston: Ian Randle, 2006.
———. "Introduction: Sylvia Wynter and the Black Radical Anti-colonial Intellectual Tradition: Towards a New Mode of Existence." In *The Hills of Hebron*, by Sylvia Wynter, ix–xxvii. Kingston: Ian Randle, 2010.
Boyce Davies, Carole, ed. "Sylvia Wynter, 'The End of Exile': New Readings of *The Hills of Hebron*." Special issue, *Interviewing the Caribbean* 8, no. 1 (2022).
———. "From Masquerade to *Maskarade*: Caribbean Cultural Resistance and the Rehumanizing Project." In *Sylvia Wynter: On Being Human as Praxis*, edited by Katherine McKittrick, 203–25. Durham, NC: Duke University Press, 2015.
———. "Occupying the Terrain: Reengaging 'Beyond Miranda's Meanings.'" *American Quarterly* 70, no. 4 (2018): 837–45.
Branch, Lori. "Postsecular Studies." In *Routledge Companion to Literature and Religion*, edited by Mark Knight, 91–101. New York: Routledge, 2016.

Brockman, John. *The Third Culture: Beyond the Scientific Revolution.* New York: Simon and Schuster, 1995.
Bruce, La Marr Jurelle. *How to Go Mad without Losing Your Mind: Madness and Black Radical Creativity.* Durham, NC: Duke University Press, 2021.
Buolamwini, Joy, and Timnit Gebru. "Gender Shades: Intersectional Accuracy Disparities in Commercial Gender Classification." In *Proceedings of the 1st Conference on Fairness, Accountability and Transparency, Proceedings of Machine Learning Research* 81 (2018): 77–91.
Butler, Anthea. *White Evangelical Racism: The Politics of Morality in America.* Chapel Hill: University of North Carolina Press, 2021.
Caillois, Roger. *Man and the Sacred.* Translated by Meyer Barash. Chicago: University of Illinois Press, 2001.
Canales, Jimena. *Bedeviled: A Shadow History of Demons in Science.* Princeton, NJ: Princeton University Press, 2020.
Capener, Sean. "Being and Acting: Agamben, Athanasius and the Trinitarian Economy." *Heythrop Journal* 57, no. 6 (2015): 950–63.
Carter, J. Kameron. "Between W. E. B. Du Bois and Karl Barth: The Problem of Modern Political Theology." In *Race and Political Theology*, edited by Vincent W. Lloyd, 83–111. Stanford, CA: Stanford University Press, 2012.
———. "Black Malpractice (A Poetics of the Sacred)." *Social Text* 37, no. 2 (2019): 67–107.
———. *Race: A Theological Account.* New York: Oxford University Press, 2008.
Césaire, Aimé. *Discourse on Colonialism.* Translated by Joan Pinkham. New York: Monthly Review Press, 1955 (2001).
———. *Notebook of a Return to the Native Land.* Translated by Clayton Eshleman and Annette Smith. Middletown, CT: Wesleyan University Press, 2001.
———. "Poetry and Knowledge." In *Lyric and Dramatic Poetry, 1946–82.* Charlottesville: University of Virginia Press, 1990.
Chandler, Nahum. "Paraontology; or, Notes on the Practical Theoretical Politics of Thought." Society for the Humanities Annual Culler Lecture in Critical Theory, October 15, 2018. https://vimeo.com/297769615.
Chidester, David. *Empire of Religion: Imperialism and Comparative Religion.* Chicago: University of Chicago Press, 2014.
———. *Savage Systems: Colonialism and Comparative Religion in Southern Africa.* Charlottesville: University of Virginia Press, 1996.
Chittick, William C. "The Central Point." *Journal of the Muhyiddin Ibn Arabi Society* 35 (2004): 25–45.
———. *The Sufi Path of Knowledge: Ibn al-'Arabī's Metaphysics of Imagination.* Albany: State University of New York Press, 1989.
———. *The Sufi Path of Love: The Spiritual Teachings of Rumi.* Albany: State University of New York Press, 1984.
Chodkiewicz, Michel. *The Spiritual Writings of Emir 'abd al-Kader.* Albany: State University of New York Press, 1995.
Christian, David. *Maps of Time: An Introduction to Big History.* Berkeley: University of California Press, 2004.

Chude-Sokei, Louis. *The Sound of Culture: Diaspora and Black Technopoetics.* Middletown, CT: Wesleyan University Press, 2016.

Clements, Niki Kasumi. "Foucault's Christianities." *Journal of the American Academy of Religion* 89, no. 1 (2021): 1–40.

———, ed. *Mental Religion.* Farmington Hills, MI: Macmillan Reference, 2017.

Comfort, Alex. "The Cartesian Observer Revisited: Ontological Implications of the Homuncular Illusion." *Journal of Social and Biological Structures* 2 (1979): 211–23.

———. "Demonic and Historical Models in Biology." *Journal of Social and Biological Structures* 3, no. 2 (1980): 207–15.

Copeland, M. Shawn. "Blackness Past, Blackness Future—and Theology." *South Atlantic Quarterly* 112, no. 4 (2013): 625–40.

Cornell, Drucilla, and Stephen D. Seely. *The Spirit of Revolution: Beyond the Dead Ends of Man.* Malden, MA: Polity, 2016.

Crawley, Ashon T. *Blackpentecostal Breath: The Aesthetics of Possibility.* New York: Fordham University Press, 2017.

Cunningham, Nijah. "The Resistance of the Lost Body." *Small Axe: A Caribbean Journal of Criticism* 20, no. 1 (2016): 113–28.

de Nicolás, Antonio T. "Notes on the Biology of Religion." *Journal of Social and Biological Structures* 3, no. 2 (April 1, 1980): 219–25.

Derrida, Jacques. "The Ends of Man." *Philosophy and Phenomenological Research* 30, no. 1 (1969): 31–57.

Descartes, René. *Meditations on First Philosophy.* Translated by Michael Moriarty. New York: Oxford University Press, 2008.

Diakité, Dianne M. Stewart, and Tracey E. Hucks. "Africana Religious Studies: Toward a Transdisciplinary Agenda in an Emerging Field." *Journal of Africana Religions* 1, no. 1 (2013): 28–77.

Diouf, Sylviane. *Servants of Allah: African Muslims Enslaved in the Americas.* New York: New York University Press, 1998.

Douglas, Amir. "Wynter's New Modes of Being: 'Mad' Possibilities." *Interviewing the Caribbean* 8, no. 1 (2022).

Drexler-Dreis, Joseph, and Kristien Justaert, eds. *Beyond the Doctrine of Man: Decolonial Visions of the Human.* New York: Fordham University Press, 2020.

Driscoll, Christopher, and Monica Miller. *Method as Identity: Manufacturing Distance in the Academic Study of Religion.* London: Rowman and Littlefield, 2018.

Du Bois, W. E. B. *Darkwater: Voices from within the Veil.* Mineola, NY: Dover, 1999.

Dubuisson, Daniel. *The Western Construction of Religion: Myths, Knowledge, and Ideology.* Baltimore: Johns Hopkins University Press, 2003.

Dunkley, D. A. *Women and Resistance in the Early Rastafari Movement.* Baton Rouge: Louisiana State University Press, 2021.

Durkheim, Emile. *The Elementary Forms of Religious Life.* Translated by Karen E. Fields. New York: Free Press, 1995.

Dussel, Enrique. *Las metáforas teológicas de Marx*. Navarra, Spain: Verbo Divino, 1993.

———. *Philosophy of Liberation*. Translated by Aquilina Martinez and Christine Morkovsky. Maryknoll, NY: Orbis Books, 1985; 1977.

Edwards, Norval. "'Talking about a Little Culture'": Sylvia Wynter's Early Essays." *Journal of West Indian Literature* 10, no. 1/2 (2001): 12–38.

Eliade, Mircea. *The Sacred and the Profane*. Translated by Willard Trask. New York: Harcourt, Brace and World, 1963.

Ellis, Christin. *Antebellum Posthuman: Race and Materiality in the Mid-nineteenth Century*. New York: Fordham University Press, 2018.

Eudell, Demetrius L. "Afterword: Towards Aimé Césaire's 'Humanism Made to the Measure of the World': Reading *The Hills of Hebron* in the Context of Sylvia Wynter's Later Work." In *The Hills of Hebron*, by Sylvia Wynter, 311–40. Kingston: Ian Randle, 2010.

Fabian, Johannes. *Time and the Other: How Anthropology Makes Its Object*. New York: Columbia University Press, 2002 (1983).

Fanon, Frantz. *Black Skin, White Masks*. Translated by Richard Philcox. New York: Grove, 2008 (1952).

———. *The Wretched of the Earth*. Translated by Constance Farrington. New York: Grove, 1963.

———. *The Wretched of the Earth*. Translated by Richard Philcox. New York: Grove, 2004.

Farooq, Nihad M. *Undisciplined: Science, Ethnography, and Personhood in the Americas, 1830–1940*. New York: New York University Press, 2016.

Finley, Stephen C., Biko Mandela Gray, and Lori Latrice Martin, eds. *The Religion of White Rage: White Workers, Religious Fervor, and the Myth of Black Racial Progress*. Edinburgh: Edinburgh University Press, 2020.

Fitzgerald, Timothy. *Discourse on Civility and Barbarity*. New York: Oxford University Press, 2007.

———, ed. *Religion and the Secular: Historical and Colonial Formations*. New York: Routledge, 2007.

Foucault, Michel. *History of Sexuality*. Vol. 2, *The Use of Pleasure*. Translated by Robert Hurley. New York: Vintage Books, 1985.

———. *Madness and Civilization: A History of Insanity in the Age of Reason*. Translated by Richard Howard. New York: Vintage Books, 1961.

———. *Security, Territory, Population: Lectures at the Collège de France, 1977–1978*. Edited by Michel Senellart. Translated by Graham Burchell. New York: Palgrave Macmillan, 2007.

Garba, Tapji Paul, and Sara-Maria Sorentino. "Blackness before Race and Race as Reoccupation: Reading Sylvia Wynter with Hans Blumenberg." *Political Theology* (2022). https://doi.org/10.1080/1462317X.2022.2079216.

———. "Slavery Is a Metaphor: A Critical Commentary on Eve Tuck and K. Wayne Yang's 'Decolonization Is Not a Metaphor.'" *Antipode* 52, no. 3 (2020): 764–82.

Gillespie, Michael. *Hegel, Heidegger, and the Ground of History*. Chicago: University of Chicago Press, 1984.
Godelier, Maurice. *The Enigma of the Gift*. Translated by Nora Scott. Chicago: University of Chicago Press, 1999.
Goldberg, Jonathan. *Tempest in the Caribbean*. Minneapolis: University of Minnesota Press, 2003.
Gomez, Michael. *Black Crescent: The Experience and Legacy of African Muslims in the Americas*. Cambridge: Cambridge University Press, 2005.
Gordon, Lewis R. *Disciplinary Decadence: Living Thought in Trying Times*. London: Routledge, 2006.
Gray, Biko Mandela. *Black Life Matter: Blackness, Religion, and the Subject*. Durham, NC: Duke University Press, 2022.
Gross, Aaron. *The Question of the Animal and Religion: Theoretical Stakes, Practical Implications*. New York: Columbia University Press, 2014.
Haley, Sarah. *No Mercy Here: Gender, Punishment, and the Making of Jim Crow Modernity*. Chapel Hill: University of North Carolina Press, 2016.
Hallaq, Wael. *Restating Orientalism: A Critique of Modern Knowledge*. New York: Columbia University Press, 2018.
Hallen, Barry, and J. Olubi Sodipo. *Knowledge, Belief, and Witchcraft: Analytic Experiments in African Philosophy*. Stanford, CA: Stanford University Press, 1997.
Hanegraaff, Wouter J. *Esotericism and the Academy: Rejected Knowledge in Western Culture*. Cambridge: Cambridge University Press, 2012.
Hantel, Max. "What Is It Like to Be a Human? Sylvia Wynter on Autopoiesis." *philoSOPHIA* 8, no. 1 (2018): 61–79.
Hartman, Saidiya V. *Wayward Lives, Beautiful Experiments*. New York: W. W. Norton, 2019.
Hartman, Saidiya V., and Frank B. Wilderson III. "The Position of the Unthought." *Qui Parle* 13, no. 2 (2003): 183–201.
Haynes, Tonya. "The Divine and the Demonic: Sylvia Wynter and Caribbean Feminist Thought Revisited." In *Love and Power: Caribbean Discourses of Gender*, edited by Eudine Barriteau, 54–71. Kingston: University of the West Indies Press, 2012.
Headley, Clevis. "Otherness and the Impossible in the Wake of Wynter's Notion of the 'After Man.'" In *After Man, towards the Human: Critical Essays on Sylvia Wynter*, edited by Anthony Bogues, 57–75. Kingston: Ian Randle, 2006.
Hegel, G. W. F. *Phenomenology of Spirit*. Translated by A. V. Miller. Oxford: Oxford University Press, 1990 (1807).
Henry, Paget. *Caliban's Reason: Introducing Afro-Caribbean Philosophy*. New York: Routledge, 2000.
———. "Wynter and the Transcendental Spaces of Caribbean Thought." In *After Man, towards the Human: Critical Essays on Sylvia Wynter*, edited by Anthony Bogues, 258–89. Kingston: Ian Randle, 2006.

Heron, Nicholas. *Liturgical Power: Between Economic and Political Theology.* New York: Fordham University Press, 2018.

Hiskett, Mervyn. *The Sword of Truth: The Life and Times of the Shehu Usuman dan Fodio.* New York: Oxford University Press, 1973.

Horton, Robin. *Patterns of Thought in Africa and the West: Essays on Magic, Religion and Science.* New York: Cambridge University Press, 1997.

Hulsether, Lucia. "The Grammar of Racism: Religious Pluralism and the Birth of Disciplines." *Journal of the American Academy of Religion* 86, no. 1 (2018): 1–41.

Hutton, Clinton A., Michael A. Barnett, D. A. Dunkley, and Jahlani A. H. Niaah. *Leonard Percival Howell and the Genesis of Rastafari.* Kingston: University of the West Indies Press, 2015.

Hutton, Clinton A., and Nathaniel Samuel Murrell. "Rastas' Psychology of Blackness, Resistance, and Somebodiness." In *Chanting Down Babylon: The Rastafari Reader*, edited by Nathaniel Samuel Murrell, William David Spencer, and Adrian Anthony McFarlane, 36–54. Philadelphia: Temple University Press, 1998.

Irmscher, Christoph. *The Poetics of Natural History: From John Bartram to William James.* New Brunswick, NJ: Rutgers University Press, 1999.

Jackson, Zakiyyah Iman. *Becoming Human: Matter and Meaning in an Antiblack World.* New York: New York University Press, 2020.

———. "'Theorizing in a Void': Sublimity, Matter, and Physics in Black Feminist Poetics." *South Atlantic Quarterly* 117, no. 3 (2018): 617–48.

Jennings, Willie. *The Christian Imagination: Theology and the Origins of Race.* New Haven, CT: Yale University Press, 2011.

Johnson, Paul Christopher. *Automatic Religion: Nearhuman Agents of Brazil and France.* Chicago: University of Chicago Press, 2020).

Johnson, Sylvester. *African American Religions, 1500–2000.* Cambridge: Cambridge University Press, 2015.

Josephs, Kelly Baker. *Disturbers of the Peace: Representations of Madness in Anglophone Caribbean Literature.* Charlottesville: University of Virginia Press, 2013.

———. "The Necessity for Madness: Negotiating Nation in Sylvia Wynter's *The Hills of Hebron*." In *The Caribbean Woman Writer as Scholar: Creating, Imagining, Theorizing*, edited by Keshia N. Abraham, 179–204. Coconut Creek, FL: Caribbean Studies, 2009.

Kamugisha, Aaron. "'That Area of Experience That We Term the New World': Introducing Sylvia Wynter's 'Black Metamorphosis.'" *Small Axe: A Caribbean Journal of Criticism* 20, no. 1 (2016): 37–46.

Kane, Cheikh Hamidou. *Ambiguous Adventure.* Translated by Katherine Woods. New York: Heinemann, 1972.

Keel, Terence. *Divine Variations: How Christian Thought Became Racial Science.* Stanford, CA: Stanford University Press, 2018.

Khan, Aisha. "Islam, Vodou, and the Making of the Afro-Atlantic." *New West Indian Guide / Nieuwe West-Indische Gids* 86, no. 1–2 (2012): 29–54.

King, Joyce E. "Race and Our Biocentric Belief System: An Interview with Sylvia Wynter." In *Black Education: A Transformative Research and Action Agenda for the New Century*, edited by Joyce E. King, 361–66. Washington, DC: American Educational Research Association / Lawrence Erlbaum Associates, 2005.

King, Richard. *Orientalism and Religion: Postcolonial Theory, India, and the "Mystic East."* New York: Routledge, 1999.

King, Tiffany Lethabo. *The Black Shoals: Offshore Formations of Black and Native Studies.* Durham, NC: Duke University Press, 2019.

Kline, David. "The Apparatus of Christian Identity: Religious (Auto)Immunity, Political Theology, and the Making of the Racial World." PhD diss., Rice University, 2017.

———. "Observing Whiteness: The System of Whiteness and Its Religious Fantasy of Absolute Immunity." *Social Identities* 27, no. 1 (2021): 129–42.

———. *Racism and the Weakness of Christian Identity: Religious Autoimmunity.* London: Routledge, 2020.

Kripal, Jeffrey J. *The Superhumanities: Historical Precedents, Moral Objections, New Realities.* Chicago: University of Chicago Press, 2022.

Lacan, Jacques. *The Four Fundamental Concepts of Psychoanalysis: The Seminar of Jacques Lacan, Book XI.* Edited by Jacques-Alain Miller. Translated by Alan Sheridan. New York: W. W. Norton, 1978.

Leshem, Dotan. *The Origins of Neoliberalism: Modeling the Economy from Jesus to Foucault.* New York: Columbia University Press, 2017.

Liddell, Janice Lee. "The Narrow Enclosure of Motherdom/Martyrdom: A Study of Gatha Randall Barton in Sylvia Wynter's *The Hills of Hebron.*" In *Out of the Kumbla: Caribbean Women and Literature*, edited by Carol Boyce Davies and Elaine Savory Fido, 321–30. Trenton, NJ: Africa World, 1990.

Long, Charles H. *Ellipsis: The Collected Writings of Charles H. Long.* New York: Bloomsbury, 2018.

———. *Significations: Signs, Symbols, and Images in the Interpretation of Religion.* 2nd ed. Aurora, CO: Davies Group, 1999.

Luhmann, Niklas. *Social Systems.* Translated by John Bednarz Jr. with Dirk Baecker. Stanford, CA: Stanford University Press, 1995.

Lum, Kathryn Gin. *Heathen: Religion and Race in American History.* Cambridge, MA: Harvard University Press, 2022.

Lynn, Denise. "The Historical Erasure of Violence against Black Women." *Black Perspectives*, from: African American Intellectual History Society. December 20, 2018. https://www.aaihs.org/top-10-of-2018-7-the-historical-erasure-of-violence-against-Black-women/.

Mackey, Nathaniel. *Splay Anthem.* New York: New Directions, 2006.

Maifreda, Germano. *From "Oikonomia" to Political Economy: Constructing Economic Knowledge from the Renaissance to the Scientific Revolution.* London: Routledge, 2016.

Maldonado-Torres, Nelson. "AAR Centennial Round Table: Race, Religion, and Ethics in the Modern/Colonial World." *Journal of Religious Ethics* 42, no. 4 (2014): 691–711.
———. *Against War: Views from the Underside of Modernity*. Durham, NC: Duke University Press, 2008.
———. "Race, Religion, and Ethics in the Modern/Colonial World." *Journal of Religious Ethics* 42, no. 4 (2014): 691–711.
———. "Religion, Conquest, and Race in the Foundations of the Modern/Colonial World." *Journal of the American Academy of Religion* 82, no. 3 (2014): 636–65.
———. "Secularism and Religion in the Modern/Colonial World-System: From Secular Postcoloniality to Postsecular Transmodernity." In *Coloniality at Large: Latin America and the Postcolonial Debate*, edited by Mabel Moraña, Enrique Dussel, and Carlos A. Jáuregui, 360–84. Durham, NC: Duke University Press, 2008.
———."The Time of History, the Times of Gods, and the *Damnés de la terre*." *Worlds and Knowledges Otherwise* 1, no. 2 (2006): 1–12.
Maragh, G. G. [Leonard P. Howell]. *The Promised Key*. London: Forgotten Books, 1935 (2007).
Marley, Bob. "Cornerstone." Track 8 on *Soul Rebels*, Trojan Records, 1970.
Marriott, David. "Inventions of Existence: Sylvia Wynter, Frantz Fanon, Sociogeny, and 'the Damned.'" *CR: The New Centennial Review* 11, no. 3 (2011): 45–89.
Marx, Karl, and Ben Fowkes. *Capital: A Critique of Political Economy*. Vol. 1. Harmondsworth: Penguin in association with New Left Review, 1990.
Masuzawa, Tomoko. *In Search of Dreamtime*. Chicago: University of Chicago Press, 1993.
———. *The Invention of World Religions; Or, How European Universalism Was Preserved in the Language of Pluralism*. Chicago: University of Chicago Press, 2005.
Matory, J. Lorand. *Black Atlantic Religion*. Princeton, NJ: Princeton University Press, 2009.
———. *The Fetish Revisited: Marx, Freud, and the Gods Black People Make*. Durham, NC: Duke University Press, 2018.
Maturana, Humberto R., and Bernhard Poerksen. *From Being to Doing: The Origins of the Biology of Cognition*. Heidelberg: Carl Auer International, 2004.
Maturana, Humberto R., and Francisco J. Varela. *Autopoiesis and Cognition: The Realization of the Living*. 2nd ed. Dordrecht: D. Reidel, 1980.
———. *The Tree of Knowledge: The Biological Roots of Human Understanding*. Rev. ed. Boston: Shambhala, 1987.
Mbacke, Ahmadou Bamba. *Qaṣīda Asīru ma'l-abrār*. Touba: Bashīr Laye., n.d.
McKittrick, Katherine. *Dear Science and Other Stories*. Durham, NC: Duke University Press, 2021.

———. *Demonic Grounds: Black Women and The Cartographies of Struggle.* Minneapolis: University of Minnesota Press, 2006.

———, ed. *Sylvia Wynter: On Being Human as Praxis.* Durham, NC: Duke University Press, 2015.

———. "Yours in the Intellectual Struggle: Sylvia Wynter and the Realization of the Living." In *Sylvia Wynter: On Being Human as Praxis*, edited by Katherine McKittrick, 1–8. Durham, NC: Duke University Press, 2015.

McTighe, Laura, and Deon Haywood. "Front Porch Revolution: Resilience Space, Demonic Grounds, and the Horizons of a Black Feminist Otherwise." *Signs: Journal of Women in Culture and Society* 44, no. 1 (2018): 25–52.

Méndez, Xhercis, and Yomaira C. Figueroa. "Not Your Papa's Wynter: Women of Color Contributions toward Decolonial Futures." In *Beyond the Doctrine of Man: Decolonial Visions of the Human*, edited by Joseph Drexler-Dreis and Kristien Justaert, 60–88. New York: Fordham University Press, 2019.

Mignolo, Walter D. "Foreword: On Pluriversality and Multipolarity." In *Constructing the Pluriverse*, edited by Bernd Reiter, ix–xvi. Durham, NC: Duke University Press, 2018.

———. "Sylvia Wynter: What Does It Mean to Be Human?" In *Sylvia Wynter: On Being Human as Praxis*, edited by Katherine McKittrick, 106–23. Durham, NC: Duke University Press, 2015.

Miller, J. Reid. *Stain Removal: Ethics and Race.* New York: Oxford University Press, 2017.

Mondzain, Marie-Jose. *Image, Icon, Economy: The Byzantine Origins of the Contemporary Economy.* Stanford, CA: Stanford University Press, 2005.

Moody, Anne. *Coming of Age in Mississippi: The Classic Autobiography of Growing Up Poor and Black in the Rural South.* New York: Doubleday Dell, 1968; 1997.

Moraes Farias, Paulo Fernando de. "Models of the World and Categorical Models: The Enslavable Barbarian as a Mobile Classificatory Label." *Slavery and Abolition* 1, no. 2 (1980): 115–31.

Mubārak al-Lamaṭī, Aḥmad b. *Pure Gold from the Words of Sayyidī ʿAbd al-ʿAzīz al-Dabbāgh: Al-Dhahab al-Ibrīz min Kalām Sayyidī ʿAbd al-ʿAzīz al-Dabbāgh.* Translated by John O'Kane and Bernd Radtke. Boston: Brill, 2007.

Mudimbe, Valentin Y. *The Invention of Africa: Gnosis, Philosophy, and the Order of Knowledge.* Bloomington: Indiana University Press, 1988.

Murrell, Nathaniel Samuel, William David Spencer, and Adrian Anthony McFarlane, eds. *Chanting Down Babylon: The Rastafari Reader.* Philadelphia: Temple University Press, 1998.

Myers, Joshua. *Of Black Study.* London: Pluto, 2023.

Nasr, Seyyed Hossein. *Islam and the Plight of Modern Man.* Cambridge: Islamic Texts Society, 2002.

———. *Knowledge and the Sacred.* Albany: State University of New York Press, 1989.

———. *Religion and the Order of Nature*. Oxford: Oxford University Press, 1996.
Noble, Safiya Umoja. *Algorithms of Oppression*. New York: New York University Press, 2018.
Nongbri, Brent. *Before Religion: A History of a Modern Concept*. New Haven, CT: Yale University Press, 2013.
Nye, Malory. "Decolonizing the Study of Religion." *Open Library of Humanities* 5, no. 1 (2019). https://olh.openlibhums.org/article/id/4580/.
Obiora, L. Amede. "Bridges and Barricades: Rethinking Polemics and Intransigence in the Campaign against Female Circumcision." *Case Western Reserve Law Review* 47, no. 2 (1996): 275–378.
Ogunnaike, Ayọdeji. "How Worship Becomes Religion: Religious Change and Change in Religion in Ẹdẹ and Salvador." PhD diss., Harvard University, 2019.
———. "The Myth of Purity." *Harvard Divinity Bulletin*, Summer–Autumn 2013. https://bulletin.hds.harvard.edu/articles/summerautumn2013/myth-purity.
———. "What's Really behind the Mask: A Reexamination of Syncretism in Brazilian Candomblé." *Journal of Africana Religions* 8, no. 1 (2020): 146–71.
Ogunnaike, Oludamini. "African Philosophy Reconsidered: Africa, Religion, Race, and Philosophy." *Journal of Africana Religions* 5, no. 2 (2017): 181–216.
———. *Deep Knowledge: Ways of Knowing in Sufism and Ifá, Two West African Intellectual Traditions*. College Park: Penn State University Press, 2020.
———. "From Heathen to Sub-human: A Genealogy of the Influence of the Decline of Religion on the Rise of Modern Racism." *Open Theology* 2, no. 1 (2016): 785–803.
———. "Two Islamic Global Philosophies of Religion: Suhrawardī and Shushtarī." In *Voices of Three Generations: Essays in Honor of Seyyed Hossein Nasr on His 86th Birthday*, edited by Mohammad Fahgfoory, 107–37. Chicago: Kazi, 2019.
Omeish, Anwar. "Toward the Modern Revolution: Frantz Fanon, Secularity, and the Horizons of Political Possibility in Revolutionary Algeria." Undergraduate honors thesis, Harvard University, 2019.
Peel, J. D. Y. "Making History: The Past in the Ijesha Present." *Man* 19, no. 1 (1984): 111–32.
Peterson, Christopher. *Bestial Traces: Race, Sexuality, Animality*. New York: Fordham University Press, 2012.
Pickens, Therí Alyce. *Black Madness :: Mad Blackness*. Durham, NC: Duke University Press, 2019.
Pratt, Mary Louise. *Imperial Eyes: Travel Writing and Transculturation*. London: Routledge, 1992.
Quashie, Kevin. *Black Aliveness, or A Poetics of Being*. Durham, NC: Duke University Press, 2021.
Ramchand, Kenneth. *The West Indian Novel and Its Background*. London: Faber and Faber, 1970.
Reis, João José. *Slave Rebellion in Brazil: The Muslim Uprising of 1835 in Bahia*. Baltimore: Johns Hopkins University Press, 1995.

Richman, Michèle H. *Sacred Revolutions: Durkheim and the Collège de Sociologie*. Minneapolis: University of Minnesota Press, 2002.
Rivera, Mayra. "Embodied Counterpoetics: Sylvia Wynter on Religion and Race." In *Beyond Man: Race, Coloniality, and the Philosophy of Religion*, edited by An Yountae and Eleanor Craig, 57–85. Durham, NC: Duke University Press, 2021.
———. "Poetics Ashore." *Literature and Theology* 33, no. 3 (2019): 241–47.
———. *Poetics of the Flesh*. Durham, NC: Duke University Press, 2015.
Robinson, Benjamin. "Racialization and Modern Religion: Sylvia Wynter, Black Feminist Theory, and Critical Genealogies of Religion." *Critical Research on Religion* 7, no. 3 (2019): 257–74.
Robinson, Cedric. *Black Marxism: The Making of the Black Radical Tradition*. Chapel Hill: University of North Carolina Press, 2000.
Rodriguez, Anthony Bayani. "Introduction: On Sylvia Wynter and the Urgency of a New Humanist Revolution in the Twenty-First Century." *American Quarterly* 70, no. 4 (2018): 831–36.
Rorty, Richard. *Philosophy and the Mirror of Nature*. Princeton, NJ: Princeton University Press, 1979.
Rose, Marika. "Decolonizing Disenchantment." *Contending Modernities*, September 1, 2020. https://contendingmodernities.nd.edu/decoloniality/decolonizing-disenchantment.
Rumi. *Spiritual Verses*. Translated by Alan Williams. New York: Penguin Books, 2006.
Said, Edward. "Michael Walzer's 'Exodus and Revolution': A Canaanite Reading." *Arab Studies Quarterly* 8, no. 3 (1986): 289–303.
Satchell, Veront M. "Early Stirrings of Black Nationalism in Colonial Jamaica: Alexander Bedward of the Jamaica Native Baptist Free Church 1889–1921." *Journal of Caribbean History* 38, no. 1 (2004): 75–106.
Schimmel, Annemarie. *Mystical Dimensions of Islam*. Chapel Hill: University of North Carolina Press, 1975.
Schmidt, Peter R. *Historical Archaeology: A Structural Approach in an African Culture*. Rev. ed. Westport, CT: Praeger, 1978.
Schneider, Rachel, and Sophie Bjork-James. "Whither Whiteness and Religion? Implications for Theology and the Study of Religion." *Journal of the American Academy of Religion* 88, no. 1 (2020): 175–99.
Scott, David. "Preface: Sylvia Wynter's Agonistic Intimations." *Small Axe: A Caribbean Journal of Criticism* 20, no. 1 (2016): vii–x.
———. "The Re-enchantment of Humanism: An Interview with Sylvia Wynter." *Small Axe: A Caribbean Journal of Criticism* 8 (September 2000): 119–207.
Sells, Michael A. "Ibn 'Arabi's 'Gentle Now, Doves of the Thornberry and Moringa Thicket.'" *Journal of the Muhyiddin Ibn 'Arabi Society* 10 (1991): 1–12.
———. *Mystical Languages of Unsaying*. Chicago: University of Chicago Press, 1994.

Seshadri, Kalpana Rahita. *HumAnimal: Race, Law, Language*. Minneapolis: University of Minnesota Press, 2012.
Shakes, Nicosia. "Legitimizing Africa in Jamaica." In *After Man, towards the Human: Critical Essays on Sylvia Wynter*, edited by Anthony Bogues, 290–314. Kingston: Ian Randle, 2006.
Shemaria, Liz. "How to Bend Time." *Maize*, January 31, 2020. https://www.maize.io/magazine/build-time-machine/.
Siklosi, Kate. "'Dr. Livingstone, I Presume?': The Demonic Grounds of M. NourbeSe Philip's *Looking for Livingstone: An Odyssey of Silence*." In *Spatial Literary Studies*, edited by Robert Tally, 103–16. New York: Routledge, 2021.
Silva, Denise Ferreira da. "Before *Man*: Sylvia Wynter's Rewriting of the Modern Episteme." In *Sylvia Wynter: On Being Human as Praxis*, edited by Katherine McKittrick, 90–105. Durham, NC: Duke University Press, 2015.
Singh, Devin. *Divine Currency: The Theological Power of Money in the West*. Stanford, CA: Stanford University Press, 2018.
Slingerland, Edward. *What Science Offers the Humanities: Integrating Body and Culture*. New York: Cambridge University Press, 2008.
Smith, Andrea. "Sovereignty as Deferred Genocide." In *Otherwise Worlds: Against Settler Colonialism and Anti-Blackness*, edited by Tiffany King, Jenell Navarro, and Andrea Smith, 118–32. Durham, NC: Duke University Press, 2020.
Smith, Jonathan Z. *Map Is Not Territory*. Chicago: University of Chicago Press, 1993.
Snow, C. P. *The Two Cultures*. Cambridge: Cambridge University Press, 1998.
Sorentino, Sara-Maria. "The Abstract Slave: Anti-Blackness and Marx's Method." *International Labor and Working-Class History* 96 (2019): 17–37.
Tafari-Ama, Imani. "Rastawoman as Rebel: Case Studies in Jamaica." In *Chanting Down Babylon: The Rastafari Reader*, edited by Nathaniel Samuel Murrell, William David Spencer, and Adrian Anthony McFarlane, 89–106. Philadelphia: Temple University Press, 1998.
Taylor, Charles. *A Secular Age*. Boston: Harvard University Press, 2007.
Taylor, Mark Lewis. *The Theological and the Political*. Minneapolis, MN: Fortress, 2011.
Todorov, Tzvetan. *The Conquest of America: The Question of the Other*. Translated by Richard Howard. Norman: University of Oklahoma Press, 1999.
Toland-Dix, Shirley. "*The Hills of Hebron*: Sylvia Wynter's Disruption of the Narrative of the Nation." *Small Axe: A Caribbean Journal of Criticism* 12, no. 1 (2008): 57–76.
Topolski, Anya. "The Race-Religion Constellation: A European Contribution to the Critical Philosophy of Race." *Critical Philosophy of Race* 6, no. 1 (2018): 58–81.
Toscano, Alberto. "Divine Management: Critical Remarks on Giorgio Agamben's *The Kingdom and the Glory*." *Angelaki* 16, no. 3 (2011): 125–36.

Varela, Francisco J. "The Early Days of Autopoiesis: Heinz and Chile." *Systems Research* 13, no. 3 (1996): 407–16.
Varela, Francisco J., Evan Thompson, and Eleanor Rosch. *The Embodied Mind: Cognitive Science and Human Experience*. Rev. ed. Cambridge, MA: MIT Press, 2016.
Veer, Peter van der. *Imperial Encounters: Religion and Modernity in India and Britain*. Princeton, NJ: Princeton University Press, 2001.
Vial, Theodore. *Modern Religion, Modern Race*. New York: Oxford University Press, 2016.
Vivieros de Castro, Eduardo. *Cannibal Metaphysics*. Translated by P. Skafish. Minneapolis: University of Minnesota Press, 2015.
Vizcaíno, Rafael. "Introduction to Special Issue: Decolonizing Spiritualities." *CLR James Journal* 27, no. 1–2 (2021): 17–23.
———. "Liberation Philosophy, Anti-Fetishism, and Decolonization." *Journal of World Philosophies* 6, no. 2 (2021): 61–75.
———. "Postsecular Philosophy as Metaphoric Theology: On Dussel's Reading of Marx." *Journal of the American Academy of Religion* (forthcoming).
———. "Sylvia Wynter's New Science of the Word and the Autopoetics of the Flesh." *Comparative and Continental Philosophy* 14, no. 1 (2022): 72–88.
———. "Which Secular Grounds? The Atheism of Liberation Philosophy." *APA Newsletter on Hispanic/Latino Issues in Philosophy* 20, no. 2 (2021): 2–5.
Walzer, Michael. *Exodus and Revolution*. New York: Basic Books, 1986.
Ward, Pete. "Celebrity Worship as Parareligion: Bieber and the Beliebers." In *Religion and Popular Culture in America*, edited by B. D. Forbes and J. H. Mahan, 313–35. Oakland: University of California Press, 2017.
Ware, Rudolph. *The Walking Qur'an: Islamic Education, Embodied Knowledge, and History in West Africa*. Chapel Hill: University of North Carolina Press, 2014.
We, Jeong Eun Annabel. "The Transpacific Tempest: Relational Sovereignty and Spiritual Sociogenesis." *Cultural Dynamics* 31, no. 4 (2019): 375–98.
Weheliye, Alexander G. "After Man." *American Literary History* 20, no. 1–2 (March 1, 2008): 321–36.
———. *Habeas Viscus: Racializing Assemblages, Biopolitics, and Black Feminist Theories of the Human*. Durham, NC: Duke University Press, 2014.
White, Derrick. "Black Metamorphosis: A Prelude to Sylvia Wynter's Theory of the Human." *CLR James Journal* 16, no. 1 (2010): 127–48.
Wilson, Edward O. *Consilience: The Unity of Knowledge*. New York: Vintage Books, 1998.
Wilson, Stephen, Dylan Rodriguez, Joy James, et al. "The Roots of the 'Imprisoned Black Radical Tradition.'" *Black Perspectives*, from: African American Intellectual History Society (AAIHS), August 24, 2020. https://www.aaihs.org/the-roots-of-the-imprisoned-Black-radical-tradition/#:~:text=As%20soon%20as%20the%20colonial,of%20incarcerated%2Fimprisoned%20Black%20radicalisms.

Winch, Peter. "Understanding a Primitive Society." *American Philosophical Quarterly* 1, no. 4 (1964): 307–27.
Winters, Joseph. "The Sacred Gone Astray: Eliade, Fanon, Wynter, and the Terror of Colonial Settlement." In *Beyond Man: Race, Coloniality, and Philosophy of Religion*, edited by An Yountae and Eleanor Craig, 245–68. Durham, NC: Duke University Press, 2021.
Wolfe, Cary. *Critical Environments: Postmodern Theory and the Pragmatics of the "Outside."* Minneapolis: University of Minnesota Press, 1998.
———. *What Is Posthumanism?* Minneapolis: University of Minnesota Press, 2010.
Wright, Zachary Valentine. *Realizing Islam: The Tijaniyya in North Africa and the Eighteenth-Century Muslim World.* Chapel Hill: University of North Carolina Press, 2020.
Wynter, Sylvia. "1492: A New World View." In *Race, Discourse, and the Origin of the Americas: A New World View*, edited by Vera Lawrence Hyatt and Rex Nettleford, 5–57. Washington, DC: Smithsonian Institution Press, 1995.
———. "Africa, the West and the Analogy of Culture: The Cinematic Text after Man." In *Symbolic Narratives/African Cinema: Audiences, Theory and the Moving Image*, edited by June Givanni, 25–76. London: British Film Institute, 2000. Also reprinted in *Caribbean Popular Culture: Power, Politics, and Performance*, edited by Yanique Hume and Aaron Kamugisha. Kingston: Ian Randle, 2016.
———. "Afterword: Beyond Miranda's Meanings: Un/silencing the 'Demonic Ground' of Caliban's 'Woman.'" In *Out of the Kumbla: Caribbean Women and Literature*, edited by Carole Boyce Davies and Elaine Savory Fido, 355–72. Trenton, NJ: Africa World, 1990.
———. "Beyond Liberal and Marxist Leninist Feminisms: Towards an Autonomous Frame of Reference." *CLR James Journal* 24, no. 1–2 (2018): 31–56.
———. "Beyond the Categories of the Master Conception: The Counterdoctrine of the Jamesian Poiesis." In *C. L. R. James's Caribbean*, edited by Paget Henry and Paul Buhle, 63–91. Durham, NC: Duke University Press, 1992.
———. *"Black Metamorphosis: New Natives in a New World."* Unpublished manuscript, IBW Papers, Schomburg Center for Research in Black Culture, New York, Box (Sylvia Wynter).
———. "The Ceremony Found: Towards the Autopoetic Turn/Overturn, Its Autonomy of Human Agency and Extraterritoriality of (Self-)Cognition." In *Black Knowledges/Black Struggles: Essays in Critical Epistemology*, edited by Jason R. Ambroise and Sabine Broeck, 184–245. Liverpool: Liverpool University Press, 2015.
———. "The Ceremony Must Be Found: After Humanism." *In "On Humanism and the University I: The Discourse of Humanism,"* edited by William Spanos. Special issue, *boundary 2* 12, no. 3/13, no. 1 (1984): 19–70.
———. "Columbus and the Poetics of the *Propter Nos.*" *Annals of Scholarship* 8, no. 2 (1991): 251–86.

———. "Columbus, the Ocean Blue, and Fables That Stir the Mind: To Reinvent the Study of Letters." In *Poetics of the Americas: Race, Founding, and Textuality*, edited by Bainard Cohen and Jefferson Humphries, 141–64. Baton Rouge: Louisiana State University Press, 1992.

———. "Ethno or Socio Poetics," *Alcheringa/Ethnopoetics* 2, no. 2 (1976): 78–94.

———. "'Genital Mutilation' or 'Symbolic Birth'? Female Circumcision, Lost Origins, and the Aculturalism of Feminist/Western Thought." *Case Western Reserve Law Review* 47, no. 2 (1996): 501–52.

———. *The Hills of Hebron*. Introduction by Anthony Bogues. Afterword by Demetrius L. Eudell. Kingston: Ian Randle, 2010. Originally published in 1962.

———. "In Quest of Matthew Bondsman: Some Cultural Notes on the Jamesian Journey." *Urgent Tasks* 12 (1981), http://www.sojournertruth.net/matthew bondsman.html.

———. "Is 'Development' a Purely Empirical Concept or Also Teleological? A Perspective from 'We the Underdeveloped.'" In *Prospects for Recovery and Sustainable Development in Africa*, edited by Aguibou Y. Yansané, 299–316. Westport, CT: Greenwood, 1996.

———. "Jonkunnu in Jamaica: Towards the Interpretation of Folk Dance as a Cultural Process." *Jamaica Journal* 4, no. 2 (1970): 34–48.

———. "'No Humans Involved': An Open Letter to My Colleagues." *Forum N.H.I.: Knowledge for the 21st Century* 1, no. 1 (1994): 42–73.

———. "On Disenchanting Discourse: 'Minority' Literary Criticism and Beyond." *Cultural Critique*, no. 7 (Autumn 1987): 207–44.

———. "On How We Mistook the Map for the Territory, and Re-imprisoned Ourselves in Our Unbearable Wrongness of Being, of *Désêtre*: Black Studies toward the Human Project." In *Not Only the Master's Tools: African-American Studies in Theory and Practice*, edited by Lewis R. Gordon and Jane Anna Gordon, 106–69. Boulder, CO: Paradigm, 2006.

———. "The Pope Must Have Been Drunk, the King of Castile a Madman: Culture as Actuality, and the Caribbean Rethinking Modernity." In *The Reordering of Culture: Latin America, the Caribbean and Canada in the Hood*, edited by Alvina Ruprecht and Cecilia Taiana, 17–41. Ottawa: Carleton University Press, 1995.

———. "Rethinking 'Aesthetics': Notes towards a Deciphering Practice." In *Ex-Iles: Essays on Caribbean Cinema*, edited by Mbye B. Cham, 237–79. Trenton, NJ: Africa World, 1992.

———. "Review: A Utopia from the Semi-periphery: Spain, Modernization, and the Enlightenment." *Science Fiction Studies* 6, no. 1 (1979): 100–107.

———. "Towards the Sociogenic Principle: Fanon, Identity, the Puzzle of Conscious Experience, and What It Is Like to Be 'Black.'" In *National Identities and Sociopolitical Changes in Latin America*, edited by Mercedes F. Durán-Cogan and Antonio Gómez-Moriana, 30–66. New York: Routledge, 2001.

———. "Unsettling the Coloniality of Being/Power/Truth/Freedom: Towards the Human, after Man, Its Overrepresentation—an Argument." *CR: The New Centennial Review* 3, no. 3 (2003): 257–337.

———. *We Must Learn to Sit Down Together and Talk about a Little Culture: Decolonising Essays, 1967–1984*. Edited by Demetrius L. Eudell. Leeds, UK: Peepal Tree, 2012.

Wynter, Sylvia, Joshua Bennett, and Jarvis R. Givens. "'A Greater Truth than Any Other Truth You Know': A Conversation with Professor Sylvia Wynter on Origin Stories." *Souls* 22, no. 1 (2020): 123–37.

Wynter, Sylvia, and Katherine McKittrick. "Unparalleled Catastrophe for Our Species? Or, to Give Humanness a Different Future: Conversations." In *Sylvia Wynter: On Being Human as Praxis*, edited by Katherine McKittrick, 9–89. Durham, NC: Duke University Press, 2015.

Wynter, Sylvia, and Greg Thomas. "ProudFlesh Inter/Views: Sylvia Wynter." *ProudFlesh: New Afrikan Journal of Culture, Politics and Consciousness* 4 (2006): 1–35.

Yusoff, Kathryn. *A Billion Black Anthropocenes or None*. Minneapolis: University of Minnesota Press, 2018.

Ziporyn, Brook. *Zhuangzi: The Essential Writings with Selections from Traditional Commentaries*. Indianapolis: Hackett, 2009.

Contributors

Shamara Wyllie Alhassan is an Africana Studies scholar and transnational ethnographer focusing on the ways Rastafari women build pan-African communities and combat anti-Black gendered racism and religious discrimination in the Caribbean and Africa. Her forthcoming book tentatively titled *Re-membering the Maternal Goddess: Rastafari Women's Intellectual History and Activism in the Pan-African World* is winner of the National Women's Association and University of Illinois Press First Book Prize. She is the coeditor of *Black Women and Da Rona: Community, Consciousness, and Ethics of Care,* which was published with the Feminist Wire Books series at the University of Arizona Press in 2023. Currently, she is Assistant Professor of African American Studies at the University of California, Los Angeles.

Justine M. Bakker is an Assistant Professor in Comparative Religious Studies at Radboud University Nijmegen (the Netherlands). She researches the intersections of race and religion, with a specific focus on alternative, heterodox, and esoteric forms of religiosity and method, theory, and conceptualization in religious studies.

Niki Kasumi Clements is the Watt J. and Lilly G. Jackson Associate Professor of Religion at Rice University (Houston, Texas). Clements researches Michel Foucault's fascination with Christianity and ethics through his published works and the archives at the Bibliothèque nationale de France. Her first monograph, *Sites of the Ascetic Self*, engages the ethics of John

Cassian (c. 360–c. 435) through Foucault's interest in this late ancient ascetic as part of his genealogy of the desiring subject. Clements is at work on her second and third monographs, *Chez Foucault: Foucault's Histories of Sexuality* and *Foucault the Confessor*, focusing on Foucault's textual and conceptual shifts over his last decade.

Tapji Garba is a PhD student in Social and Political Thought at York University. Their research engages political theology, legal history, and political economy from within the field of Black studies.

David Kline is Teaching Associate Professor in the Religious Studies Department at the University of Tennessee, Knoxville. He is the author of *Racism and the Weakness of Christian Identity: Religious Autoimmunity* (Routledge, 2020).

Oludamini Ogunnaike is Associate Professor of African Religious Thought and Democracy at the University of Virginia. He received his PhD in African Studies and the Study of Religion from Harvard University and is the author of *Deep Knowledge: Ways of Knowing in Sufism and Ifa, Two West African Intellectual Traditions* (PSU Press, 2020) and *Poetry in Praise of Prophetic Perfection: West African Madīḥ Poetry and Its Precedents* (Islamic Texts Society, 2020).

Anthony Bayani Rodriguez is Assistant Professor in St. John's University's Department of Sociology and Anthropology. His current book project, *Heretical Scripts*, chronicles Sylvia Wynter's involvement in decolonial struggles in the Caribbean, Britain, and the United States since the 1950s.

Rafael Vizcaíno is Assistant Professor in the Department of Philosophy at DePaul University. His work employs decolonial approaches to examine the intersections between race, religion, politics, and secularization. He won the American Philosophical Association's 2020 Essay Prize in Latin American Thought, and his first book (forthcoming) recounts the modern dialectics of secularization from the perspective of Latin American and Caribbean thought. His second book (in progress) examines the relation between philosophy of religion and political theology in the context of epistemic decolonization.

Joseph Winters is Associate Professor at Duke University in Religious Studies and African and African American Studies. He holds secondary appointments in English and Gender, Sexuality, and Feminist Studies. His interests lie at the intersection of Black religious thought, Black studies, and critical theory. His research examines the ways Black literature and aesthetics develop alternative configurations of the sacred, piety, (Black) spirit, and secularity in response to the religious underpinnings of anti-Black violence and coloniality. His first book, *Hope Draped in Black: Race, Melancholy, and the Agony of Progress*, was published by Duke University Press in 2016. He is currently finishing a second manuscript, titled *The Disturbing Profane: Hip Hop, Blackness, and the Sacred.*

Index

ʿAbd al-Qādir, 62
abolition of slavery, 183
Adorno, Theodore, 207
Agamben, Giorgio, 171, 178
American Academy of Religion, 44, 214–15
anticolonial: *Hills of Hebron* as, 156, 163; movements, 2, 211, 218, 223, 226; uprisings, 1, 76, 145, 206, 237
Ariella Aïsha Azoulay, 1
Aristotle, 173; and household management, 178, 181
Augustine: and divine election, 182; neo-Augustinianism, 181; and original sin, 178
autopoiesis, 5, 11, 22, 24–26, 55, 70–71, 135, 174, 140, 142, 158, 164, 174, 186
autoreligion, 8, 11, 22, 32–33, 35–37, 39–40, 201

Bamba, Shaykh Ahmadu, 70
Bataille, George, 205
Bateson, Gregory, 33
Bellah, Robert, 14, 196–97, 200, 202
bible, 161, 162, 163,194, 196, 222
big history, 21
biocentricism, 70, 77–79, 133, 147, 184
bios-mythoi: and Césaire, 140–41; humanness based on the conception of, 22, 49, 69, 111, 142, 222; and Third Event, 22
blackness: conceptualized as animality, inferior, symbolically dead, non-being, or dysselected, 38, 116, 179, 181, 183, 185, 203, 223; as limit of political culture, 184; and madness, 230; Rastafari reconceptualization of, 219
Blumenberg, Hans, 9, 173
Boyce Davies, Carole, 103

Caillois, Roger, 203, 205
Canales, Jimena, 97
Capener, Sean, 178
capitalism, 46, 139, 182–83
Caribbean Artists Movement, 240
The Caribbean Quarterly, 239
Carter, J. Kameron, 1, 201, 205
Césaire, Aimé, 4, 5, 12, 37, 50, 53, 64, 111, 140–41, 153,158, 175, 237–38
Chandler, Nahum, 117
Chidester, David, 214
Chude-Sokei, Louis, 115
chrematistics, 172–73
Christian, David, 21, 30
Christianity: and colonialism, 214; and Latin Christendom, 179; and Man, 133, 135, 200; and the study of religion, 8, 143, 212; and (white) nationalism, 194–95; and Wynter's conceptualization of religion, 35–36, 109–10
colonialism: and Christianity, 200; and conceptualizations of religion, 7, 35, 197–98; and education, 3, 238; and Man, 1, 48, 85, 135–36, 157, 172, 212, 213, 217; and the study of religion, 165, 212, 214–15, 230

coloniality: and the limits of Fanon's critique of, 77; and religion, 157, 195, 199, 227; and the secular, 167; and the study of religion, 7
Columbus, Christopher, 189, 205, 212
Comfort, Alex, 9, 12, 98, 100–5, 108, 111
communist theory, 173
Copeland, M. Shawn, 1
Copernicus, Nicholai, 131, 133, 144, 180, 205–6
Corbonell, Jaime, 212

Danielli, James, 33, 107–8
Darwin, Charles, 34, 47, 110, 115–16, 201
decolonization, 153, 154, 155, 157, 158, 163, 166, 167, 168, 169
Delaney, Carol, 36
demonic: ground, 12, 138; ocean, 119; sacred, 14, 201–3; spirituality, 157–58, 164
de Nicolás, Antonio T., 9, 12, 103–6, 107, 108, 112, 114
Derrida, Jacques, 117
Descartes, René, 100–1, 114
divine election, 182
Du Bois, W. E. B., 6, 9, 14, 37, 108, 136, 201–3
Durkheim, Émile, 14, 108, 195–96, 197–98, 203–5
dysselection: blackness and, 183; as human category (Man2), 34, 183, 109, 189, 201

ecclesial hegemony, 180
economics, 177, 183–84
economy, 171
Einstein, Albert, 236
emancipation: after slavery, 183; and Wynter's conceptualization of humanness, 13, 79, 131, 154–55, 160
episteme, 36, 46, 48, 54, 98–99, 106, 114, 132–35, 138, 143–44, 184
epistemological break, 180
Epstein, Mikhail, 50
esotericism, 102
eugenics, 13, 137, 144
Evans-Pritchard, E. E., 60
event: first, 23, 51; second, 23, 27, 51; third, 23, 27–32, 34–37, 40, 51
evolution, 23, 28, 34, 36, 48, 50, 54, 60, 72, 111, 135, 137, 201

Fanon, Frantz, 4, 5, 9, 12, 37, 38, 55, 58, 73, 74, 77, 113, 115, 153, 165–66, 174, 217
Foucault, Michel, 9, 99, 173
freedom: and Augustine, 178–79; and capitalism, 183; in *Hills of Hebron*, 155; and Sufi traditions, 70; Wynter's conceptualization of humanness and, 105, 180, 182, 206
Freud, Sigmund, 174

Gallahger, Ellen, 12, 116–19
Geertz, Clifford, 46
genealogy: of demonic, 204; of economics, 177; of Man, 46, 131–36, 237; theological, 171–73, 177
genres of being human, 1, 28, 33–34, 37, 47, 57, 74, 106–7, 112, 217, 222; and the possibility of a trans-genre perspective, 22, 38
Girardot, N. J., 9, 109, 112
Glissant, Édouard, 4, 9
Godelier, Maurice, 9
governance: Christ's, 179; of souls, 178
Gödel, Kurt, 236
Godelier, Maurice, 33, 33, 82, 110
Goldberg, Jonathan, 112
Goveia, Elsa, 241
Grassi, Ernesto, 110
Great Chain of Being, 110

Haley, Sarah, 100
Hanegraaff, Wouter, 102
Hegel, G. W. F., 206–7; and master-slave dialectic, 162
Henry, Paget, 115, 154
Heron, Nicholas, 178
Hindu philosophy, 102
historical materialism, 184
historical substantialism, 173, 178
historicism, 176
homo narrans, 28, 69, 106, 114, 222–23. See also *bios-mythoi*
homo oeconomicus, 134, 135, 138, 182–83. See also Man2
homo politicus, 182–83. See also Man1
homo sapiens, 119
Hucks, Tracy E., 214
humanism: Césaire's reconceptualization of, 46, 49, 158, 237; Christian, 206, 213; civic, 181; Islamic, 68–69; liberal-economic, 85, 172, 182; Rastafari's reconceptualization of, 212; re-enchantment of, 160, 169, 170; Renaissance, 48, 109, 131–32, 171, 180, 205; Wynter's reconceptualization of, 49–51, 57, 66, 115, 160, 237
humanities, 49, 111, 129–30, 136, 144–45, 154, 241
humanness: and second emergence, 11, 45, 50, 52, 55, 57, 155, 158, 164; and third level

of existence, 27, 131. See also *bios-mythoi*; genres of being human; hybridity
hybridity, 5, 12, 13, 22, 28, 32, 38, 40, 54, 136, 138, 140, 142–43, 155. See also *bios-mythoi*; liminality

Ibn ʿAjība, 63
Ibn al-Arabī, 61–62
imperial Man, 197–203
interdisciplinarity, 131, 146
Islamic philosophy, 45, 59, 66, 69, 77

Jackson, Zakiyyah Iman, 153, 204
James, C. L. R., 4, 37
Johnson, Paul Christopher, 7
Josephs, Kelly Baker, 154

Kant, Immanuel, 176
Kline, David, 201
Kripal, Jeffrey J., 113

Lamming, George, 4
Latin Christendom, 177, 179
Latour, Bruno, 9
Legesse, Asmaron, 46
Le Goff, Jacques, 9
Lennox, Miriam, 221
liminality, 24, 51, 114–15, 211–30. See also hybridity
Linnaeus, Carl, 118–19
Long, Charles, 7, 21
Luhmann, Niklas, 26

Mackey, Nathaniel, 207
Mallet, Ronald, 15, 236
Man: imperial Man, 197–203; overrepresentation of Man as human, 46, 73, 106, 144, 153, 164, 176, 183, 198
Man1: as the rational-political subject, 36, 48, 57, 101, 110, 135, 199, 214; as religio-sacred hybrid, 200; and *studia humanitatis*, 142, 213
Man2: and biocentricism, 10, 48, 70, 73, 79, 133, 136, 182, 184, 214; and the secular, 22, 35–36
Marx, Karl, 51, 177
Marxism, 161–62, 169, 184
material production, 175
Mattis, James, 14, 194–95
Maturana, Humberto, 5, 9, 11, 12, 24–26, 174. See also autopoiesis; Varela, Francisco
Maxwell's demon, 100
McKittrick, Katherine, 2, 21, 31, 97, 106, 115, 153, 198, 204

Middle Ages, 179; Christian imagination during, 35–36, 48–49, 179–80, 199, 213; discrimination during, 34, 108
Mignolo, Walter, 9, 10, 103
minority discourse, 98–99, 107, 115
modernity: capitalist, 173; colonial, 8, 197, 203; racialized, 98; secular, 131, 167; Western, 1, 46, 153, 156, 181, 240
Moraes Farias, Paulo Fernando de, 113
Mudimbe, V.Y., 9, 57

Nagel, Thomas, 37
natural history, 118
natural law, 181
natural necessity, 182–83
natural science, 34, 38, 40, 112, 130, 133, 134, 137–40, 144–46, 175
neo-Augustinianism, 181
new science of the word, 5, 7, 9, 11, 13, 38, 49–51, 106, 111–14, 140–42, 175, 238, 241
nominalism, 179

oceanic feeling, 114
oikonomia, 172
Òrìṣà, 45, 60, 64–65, 72
Ọ̀rúnmìlà, 63

Pagden, Anthony, 9
Pandian, Jacob, 46, 198
parareligion, 98, 114–19
pastoral power, 173
philosophical anthropology, 172, 174, 184
philosophy of history, 172, 184
poetics, 39, 162, 180, 207
polis, 177
political economy, 173, 182
political theology, 171, 173
politics of being, 177, 185
Portuguese slave trade, 180
post-Gregorian church, 179
postreligious, 153, 155, 157, 158, 160, 161, 164, 167, 168
postsecular, 154, 155, 157, 158, 160, 162, 163, 164, 166, 167, 168, 169
Pratt, Mary Louise, 118
praxis, 13, 24, 34, 38, 40, 62, 77, 103, 113, 131, 140–42, 146, 154–60, 178, 221
Ptolemaic astronomy, 179

quantum mechanics, 236
quantum physics, 101
Quijano, Aníbal, 9

race: and chain of being, 110; as measure of humanity, 182; and natural determination, 182; and religion, 6–7, 36, 108, 199; and slavery, 172–73
racism, 36; and accumulation of capital, 214; antiblack, 108, 193; epistemic, 224
Rastafari, 4, 8, 15, 39, 113, 211–12, 215, 219–30
redemption, 172, 178, 181, 182
re-enchantment, 160, 169, 170
religious studies: discipline of, 9–10, 107, 212, 214–15, 230; and race, 214
reoccupation, 173
representation, 183
reproduction, 172, 174–75, 182, 184
Rivera, Mayra, 2, 200
Robinson, Benjamin, 2
Rorty, Richard, 23

Scott, David, 71, 74, 112, 211, 218,
Seck, Amadou, 59
secular, 154, 155, 157, 158, 159, 160–67, 169, 173, 180
secularization, 154, 167, 170; as degodding, 35, 47, 49, 59, 61, 66, 133, 160, 161, 199, 201
self-determination, 182
Seshadri, Keplani, 118
Shakespeare, William, 114, 203
Shaykh Ahmad al-Tijānī, 69
sin, 172
slavery: and abolition, 183; and genesis of the modern world, 172; and labor, 161; post-emancipation culture of, 183; racial, 171–72, 181, 214; and rationality, 181; and sin, 109, 179, 181; spiritual, 181
slave trade, 60, 139, 180–81
Smith, Jonathan Z., 7, 108
Snow, C. P., 12, 129–31, 136–37, 145–46
sociogeny, 172, 174–75, 179, 180–82
Sorentino, Sara-Maria, 1
soteriology, 178

sovereignty, 181
space-time relativity, 236
spirit over flesh, 179
spiritual slavery, 181
Stanford University, 241
storytelling, 5, 23, 28, 30–31, 33, 35, 39, 106, 114, 164, 222. See also *homo narrans studia*, 241
Sufism, 45, 61, 64, 66, 68, 70–74, 78
supralunar and sublunar, 180

Taylor, Mark Lewis, 158
Thomas, Greg, 38
time machine, 235
Todorov, Tzetvan, 197
Toscano, Alberto, 172, 184
trinitarian theology, 173
Trump, Donald, 14, 193–95
two cultures, 12–13, 112, 129–31, 137, 139, 144, 146, 146

University of the West Indies, Mona, 239

Varela, Francisco, 5, 9, 11, 12, 24–26. *See also* Maturana, Humberto
vertical integration, 12, 141
Vial, Theodore, 7

Weheliye, Alexander, 101, 153
Wells, H. G., 235
Wilson, E. O., 12, 130–32, 136, 140–41, 145–46
Wolfe, Cary, 26
Wynter, Sylvia: biography of, 3–4; "Black Metamorphosis," 5, 52, 79, 183; and fiction writing, 239–30; and genres of being human, 28, 33; *Hills of Hebron*, 4, 13, 239; and the study of African religions, 51–55

Yaganisako, Sylvia, 36
Yorùbá, 60, 63–66, 75, 77

www.ingramcontent.com/pod-product-compliance
Lightning Source LLC
Chambersburg PA
CBHW020400080526
44584CB00014B/1103